Pro Express.js

Azat Mardan

Apress®

Pro Express.js

ISBN-13 (pbk): 978-1-4842-0038-4

ISBN-13 (electronic): 978-1-4842-0037-7

Managing Director: Welmoed Spahr
Lead Editor: Ben Renow-Clarke
Technical Reviewers: Peter Elst and Francois-Denis Gonthier
Editorial Board: Steve Anglin, Mark Beckner, Ewan Buckingham, Gary Cornell, Louise Corrigan, Jim DeWolf, Jonathan Gennick, Robert Hutchinson, Michelle Lowman, James Markham, Matthew Moodie, Jeff Olson, Jeffrey Pepper, Douglas Pundick, Ben Renow-Clarke, Dominic Shakeshaft, Gwenan Spearing, Matt Wade, Steve Weiss
Coordinating Editor: Christine Ricketts
Copy Editor: William McManus
Compositor: SPi Global
Indexer: SPi Global
Artist: SPi Global
Cover Designer: Anna Ishchenko

Distributed to the book trade worldwide by Springer Science+Business Media New York, 233 Spring Street, 6th Floor, New York, NY 10013. Phone 1-800-SPRINGER, fax (201) 348-4505, e-mail orders-ny@springer-sbm.com, or visit www.springeronline.com. Apress Media, LLC is a California LLC and the sole member (owner) is Springer Science + Business Media Finance Inc (SSBM Finance Inc). SSBM Finance Inc is a Delaware corporation.

For information on translations, please e-mail rights@apress.com, or visit www.apress.com.

Apress and friends of ED books may be purchased in bulk for academic, corporate, or promotional use. eBook versions and licenses are also available for most titles. For more information, reference our Special Bulk Sales–eBook Licensing web page at www.apress.com/bulk-sales.

Any source code or other supplementary material referenced by the author in this text is available to readers at www.apress.com/9781484200384 and https://github.com/azat-co/proexpressjs. For detailed information about how to locate your book's source code, go to www.apress.com/source-code/. The book's website is at http://proexpressjs.com.

Please submit any errors or bugs to Apress (http://www.apress.com/9781484200384) or GitHub Issues (https://github.com/azat-co/proexpressjs/issues).

Contents at a Glance

Contents

About the Author

Azat Mardan has over a dozen years of experience in web, mobile, and software engineering. With a Bachelor of Science in Informatics and a Master of Science in Information Systems Technology, Azat possesses deep academic knowledge as well as extensive practical experience. He is the author of eight other books on JavaScript and Node.js, including *Practical Node.js* (Apress, 2014), and *Rapid Prototyping with JS*, an Amazon.com #1 Best Seller in its category.

Currently, Azat teaches the Node Program (`http://nodeprogram.com`) and creates online courses, while also working as a Team Lead at `DocuSign.com`. His team rebuilds a 50 million user product (DocuSign web app) using the cutting-edge tech stack of Node.js, Express.js, Backbone.js, CoffeeScript, Jade, Stylus, and Redis.

Recently, Azat worked as an engineer at the curated social media news aggregator web site Storify.com (acquired by `LiveFyre.com` in 2013), which is used by BBC, NBC, CNN, The White House, and others. Storify is a partner of `Joyent.com` (Node.js maintainer) and runs completely on Node.js, (whereas most companies that use Node.js use it only for certain tasks). Storify.com is the company behind the open source library `jade-browser`.

Prior to his stint at `Storify.com`, Azat developed mission-critical applications for government agencies in Washington, DC, including the National Institutes of Health, the National Center for Biotechnology Information, and the Federal Deposit Insurance Corporation, as well as for Lockheed Martin.

Azat has received acclaim for teaching programming classes at Marakana (acquired by Twitter in 2013), pariSOMA, General Assembly San Francisco, and Hack Reactor. In his spare time, Azat writes about technology on his blog `http://webapplog.com`.

Azat is the creator of several open source Node.js projects, including ExpressWorks, mongoui, HackHall.com, and NodeFramework.com, and is a contributor to express, oauth, jade-browser, and other NPM modules.

About the Technical Reviewers

Peter Elst is a web standards enthusiast, coming from a multimedia and application development background. He works as a Web Solutions Engineer in Creative Innovation at Google.

With well over a decade of experience, Peter is a regular technical reviewer, has co-authored a number of books, including *HTML5 Solutions: Essential Techniques for HTML5 Developers* (Apress, 2011), and is a well-respected speaker at many industry events. You can find out more about his latest interests and ongoing projects on his personal blog, `http://peterelst.com`.

Francois-Denis Gonthier is a graduate of the Université de Sherbrooke computer science program. He began his career with a startup company, delivering cryptographic software using open source technologies. From that point, he has never strayed far from the Linux and open source world as a big-picture generalist. He went from programming front ends in JavaScript and HTML 5.0 to coding web site backends using Java, J2EE, JSF, or plain old Unix daemons. The cool Web 2.0 kids would call this being a "full stack developer."

Foreword

Dear reader,

You are reading a book that will lead you to the understanding and fluent use of the Express.js framework—the de facto standard in web application programming on Node.js. I would especially recommend this book because it was written by a practicing engineer who has comprehensive knowledge of the full stack of web application development, and Express.js in particular.

Azat and I worked on the same Node.js/Express.js code base at Storify.com—the social media curation tool that The Washington Post, CNN, BBC, The White House press corps, and other news corps use. It was recently acquired by LiveFyre.com. Azat asked me to write this foreword because he thought it would be objective, sincere, and unbiased coming from the creator of another Node.js framework: CompoundJS (`http://compoundjs.com`).

However, hardly anyone reads the foreword. So, instead of a traditional foreword, I'll share my story. Actually, I never thought it was worth sharing, and there's definitely nothing exciting about it. But from another point of view—that of thousands of young programmers living similar ordinary lives—it could be inspiring: it's a common story, but a rather successful one.

My path to web development started when I was a student. I'd joined a team as a junior PHP programmer. I was working there for about five years, and the main lesson that I learned was that education is nothing compared to real work experience. The next page of my professional life was my work in outsourcing (PHP and Ruby on Rails). And then I found Node.js. It offered something that I had always wanted: processes that do not have to wait for DB/IO operations, which are keeping all the resources, but doing something useful instead. That's why I started using Node.js—it's more efficient compared to synchronous programming environments. By "efficient," I don't mean speed of processing, but rather more flexibility in programming style.

As a good example of its flexibility, I can share a solution I recently programmed for a Redis adapter for the JugglingDB ORM (`https://github.com/1602/jugglingdb`). The problem: during peaks in web site usage, we were running a lot of DB queries to serve pages, and most of the queries were the same. The obvious solution is to cache results of the queries, but this solution requires additional coding and some logic for cache invalidation. We came up with a better solution: cache queries and not results. When a query comes, we don't execute it immediately; instead, we wait for some time, collect identical queries, then execute the query once and run multiple callbacks to serve all clients. This solution is simple and requires no additional logic. As a result, we have flat DB usage, even during peaks. This solution is natural in Node.js, and that's why Node.js rocks!

Life after discovering Node.js was great, full of interesting challenges and work, but one thing was annoying: each time I started a new project, I had to repeat almost the same work to organize code. For me, as a Rails developer, it's really great to be able to create well-structured MVC applications fast, and then generate scaffolding controllers/views and other stuff. But this kind of tool was missing in Node.js, and that's why I spent my Christmas holidays writing it. The project was called express-on-railway at first, then RailwayJS, then CompoundJS.

The main goal of the project was to bring structure to an Express.js application, add the ability to extend applications in a standard way, and generate application code. So, it was not a new framework, but just Express.js with decent MVC structure, which is good for developers because they don't need to learn anything but Express.js to be able to understand what's going on in a CompoundJS application. And I was kind of piggybacking on my Express.js and Rails experience. The idea was to take the best ideas from Rails and bring them to the node platform, and I selected Express.js as the base because it is the most popular framework for Node.js and has a relatively big community, so I wouldn't be alone with my "new framework." It was the start of my open source years, which completely changed my attitude toward programming (and other life matters), but that's another story.

Let me conclude by saying web development in Node.js starts with Express.js. It is a minimalistic and robust framework that gives you all you need to build decent web applications. Even if you decide to move to some more advanced frameworks at some point, Express.js knowledge is still a basic skill you have to learn. This book contains everything you need to know to start using Express.js. It clearly explains all concepts, as well as provides the answers to the most frequent questions that newcomers ask. For these reasons, this book is a must-read!

Anatoliy Chakkaev

Creator of CompoundJS and JugglingDB

Acknowledgments

This book would not be possible without the existence of my parents, the Internet, and JavaScript. Furthermore, I acknowledge the geniuses of Ryan Dahl (creator of Node.js) and TJ Holowaychuk (creator of Express.js).

I express my gratitude to the Apress editors who persuaded me to publish this book as a remake of *Express.js Guide*, and to the following editors who have put a lot of energy into making the book great: Christine Ricketts, Peter Elst, Francois-Denis Gonthier, and William McManus. Also, special thanks to Douglas Wilson and Tom Rutka.

Last but not least, I would like to thank my high school teacher who always had many toy problems for us to solve using Turbo Pascal.

Introduction

If you are considering whether or not to buy this book, this Introduction will help you to make sure it perfectly suits your level of expertise and needs. If you bought this book already, then congratulations! You are now well prepared to dig deeper into the most popular web framework for the fastest-growing platform.

The demand for skills in Node.js and Express.js is on the verge of rapid growth as both startups and big corporations are gradually becoming aware of the benefits of adopting Node.js. There's always a gap between early adopters of new technology and mainstream adoption, and mainstream adoption of Node.js is rapidly approaching. For you, as a developer, that means right now is the best time to become proficient with Node.js. Your skills will be in high demand!

Why This Book Was Written

I started writing about Express.js a few years ago when I wrote *Express.js Guide*. Self-published in 2013, it was one of the first books solely dedicated to Express.js, which is the most popular Node.js web framework yet (as of this writing, December 2014). At the time I wrote *Express.js Guide*, the Express.js official web site (`http://expressjs.com`) offered only bits of insights, and those were intended for advanced Node.js programmers. I had encountered many people—including through the Hack Reactor program and in my Node.js classes at General Assembly and pariSOMA—who were interested in a definitive manual, one that would cover how all the different components of Express.js work together in real life. The goal of *Express.js Guide* was to be that resource.

After *Express.js Guide* became the Amazon.com #1 Best Seller in its category, Apress approached me to write this book to expand upon the material and subject it to formal review by professional technical editors. *Pro Express.js* is much more than a revision or an update of *Express.js Guide*. It's a complete remake, with the addition of comments, descriptions, examples, and extras. *Pro Express.js* has better-reviewed code and text, and up-to-date versions of the libraries (e.g., Express.js v4.8.1).

Many things have changed between writing the two books. Node.js was forked at io.js. TJ Holowaychuk, the creator of Express.js, stopped being actively involved with Node.js, and now StrongLoop (`http:/strongloop.com`) maintains the framework's repository. The development on Express.js is as rapid as ever. It's more stable and more secure. And I see nothing but a brighter future for Express.js and Node.js!

Who Should Own This Book

This book is intended for software engineers and web developers who are already fluent in programming and front-end JavaScript. To get the most benefit from *Pro Express.js*, you should be familiar with basic Node.js concepts, such as process and global, and should also know core modules, including stream, cluster, and buffer.

If you're thinking about starting a Node.js project or rewriting an existing one, and your weapon of choice is Express.js, this guide is for you! It will answer most of your "how" and "why" questions.

What This Book Is

Pro Express.js is an exhaustive book on one particular library. Unlike *Practical Node.js* (Apress, 2014) which covered many libraries, Pro Express.js is focused on the single module Express.js. Of course, where it's necessary to cover other related libraries, such as middleware, the book touches on those as well, but not as extensively as on the framework itself.

Pro Express.js covers middleware, the command-line interface and scaffolding, rendering templates, extracting params from dynamic URLs, parsing payloads and cookies, managing authentication with sessions, error handling, and prepping apps for production.

Pro Express.js is organized into four distinct parts, the individual chapters of which are set forth in the Table of Contents:

1. *Getting Started*: A hands-on, quick-start walkthrough to give you a taste of the framework
2. *Deep API Reference*: Serves as an Express.js v4.8.1 API reference that you can read in full or skim through as you need information about certain methods
3. *Solving Common and Abstract Problems*: The best practices for code organization and patterns—topics that are good to know when working with Express.js
4. *Tutorials and Examples*: Tutorials (meticulously depicted coding exercises) and examples (less detailed explanations of more complex apps) for the real world

What This Book Is Not

This book is not an introduction to Node.js, nor is it a book that covers all aspects of building a modern-day web application in great detail, such as WebSockets, databases, and (of course) front-end development. You won't find aids for learning programming or JavaScript fundamentals here, because this is not a beginners' book.

For an introduction to Node.js, MongoDB, and front-end development with Backbone.js, you might want to take a look at my book *Rapid Prototyping with JS: Agile JavaScript Development* (`http://rapidprototypingwithjs.com`) or consider participating in the Node Program (`http://nodeprogram.com`) either in person or online.

In the real world—and especially in Node.js development, due to its modularized philosophy—we seldom use just a single framework. In this book, however, I have tried to stick to Express.js and leave everything else out as much as possible, without compromising the usefulness of the examples. Therefore, I intentionally left out some important chunks of web development—for example, databases, authentication, and testing. Although these elements are present in tutorials and examples, they're not explained in detail. If you want to learn more about these topics, Appendix A lists some relevant books that you may want to consult.

Examples

Pro Express.js is full of code snippets and run-ready examples. Some of the examples are step-by-step, meticulously explained tutorials, which you are encouraged to reproduce on your own as you read the book. Others are abridged code examples that serve the purpose of illustrating a particular point.

The bulk of the source code is available in the GitHub repository at `https://github.com/azat-co/proexpressjs` under folders `ch1` through `ch18` (corresponding to Chapters 1–18). The examples in Part 4 are more extensive and live in their own repositories. They can be found at these URLs:

- Instagram Gallery: `https://github.com/azat-co/sfy-gallery`
- Todo App: `https://github.com/azat-co/todo-express`
- REST API: `https://github.com/azat-co/rest-api-express`
- HackHall: `https://github.com/azat-co/hackhall`

The provided examples were written and tested only with the given, specific versions of dependencies. Because Node.js and its ecosystem of modules are being developed rapidly, please pay attention to whether new versions have breaking changes. Here is the list of versions that I've used:

- Express.js v4.8.1
- Node.js v0.10.12
- NPM v1.2.32
- MongoDB v2.6.3
- Redis v2.6.7
- Stylus v0.47.3
- Jade v1.5.0
- Foreman v0.75.0
- Google Chrome Version 39.0.2171.7

Errata and Contacts

If you get stuck on an exercise, make sure to check the GitHub repository. It might have more recent code and answers in the GitHub Issues section (`https://github.com/azat-co/proexpressjs/issues`). Also, by submitting your own issues, you can help make the experience better for your fellow programmers.

As for pesky typos, a few of which I'm sure will still remain no matter how many times I review the manuscript, submit them to Apress (via the Errata tab at `www.apress.com/9781484200384`) or to GitHub Issues.

Finally, let's be friends on the Internet! It's lonely to code in isolation. Here are some of the ways to reach me as well as ways to communicate with other developers:

- Write an Amazon.com review: `http://amzn.to/1D6qiqk`
- Join HackHall.com, a community for programmers, hackers, and developers
- Tweet your Node.js questions on Twitter: `@azat_co`
- Follow me on Facebook: `http://facebook.com/1640484994`
- Visit the *Pro Express.js* web site: `http://proexpressjs.com`
- Visit my web site: `http://azat.co`
- Star the Pro Express.js GitHub repository: `https://github.com/azat-co/proexpressjs`
- E-mail me directly: `hi@azat.co`
- Sign up for the blog's newsletter: `http://webapplog.com`

Now that you've reached the end of the Introduction, let everyone on Twitter know that you're about to start learning Express.js via *Pro Express.js*: `http://ctt.ec/91iHS`. And after you've had a chance to read the book, please let others know what you think about it by writing an Amazon.com review: `http://amzn.to/1D6qiqk`.

PART I

Getting Started

CHAPTER 1

Starting with Express.js

Express.js is a web framework based on the core Node.js `http` module[1] and Connect[2] components. Those components are called middleware. They are the cornerstone of the framework's philosophy, which is *configuration over convention*. Some developers familiar with Ruby compare Express.js to Sinatra, which has a very different approach from the Ruby on Rails framework that favors *convention over configuration*. In other words, developers are free to pick whatever libraries they need for a particular project. This approach provides them with flexibility and the capability to highly customize their projects.

If you have written any serious apps using only the core Node.js modules, you most likely found yourself reinventing the wheel by constantly writing the same code for similar tasks, such as:

- Parsing HTTP request bodies
- Parsing cookies
- Managing sessions
- Organizing routes with a chain of `if` conditions based on URL paths and HTTP methods of the requests
- Determining proper response headers based on data types
- Handling errors
- Extracting URL parameter (e.g., `/messages/3233`)

Later, you might have created your own libraries to reuse the code, but your libraries would not be as thoroughly tested as the best community supported libraries. Also, the maintenance would be fully on you and your team. So, my recommendation is to use the community module if it suites your needs. This advice applies to using small libraries and web frameworks as well.

Express.js solves these and many other problems. It provides ways to reuse code elegantly and provides a model-view-controller (MVC)-like structure for your web apps. The model (M) part needs to be supplied by an additional database-driver library (e.g., Mongoose[3]). Those apps could vary from barebones, back-end-only REST APIs to full-blown, full-stack, real-time web apps with additional libraries such as `jade-browser` (`https://npmjs.org/package/jade-browser`) and `socket.io` (`http://socket.io`).

[1]`http://nodejs.org/api/http.html`
[2]`http://www.senchalabs.org/connect`
[3]`http://mongoosejs.com`

To get you started with Express.js quickly and without diving too deep into its API, we'll cover these topics in this chapter:

- How Express.js works
- Express.js installation
- Express.js Generator installation

How Express.js Works

Express.js is a node package manager (NPM or `npm`) module that is a dependency to your application. This means that every project that is built with/on Express.js needs to have the framework's source files in the local `node_modules` folder (not globally!). For this, you install Express.js just like any other NPM module, with `$ npm install`, e.g., `$ npm install express@4.2.0`.

Now, we can overview a typical structure of an Express.js application. Let's say your application is in a `server.js` file and you plan to start your application with `$ node server.js`. In that case, you need to require and configure Express.js in the `server.js` file. This file usually contains statements to accomplish the following:

1. Include third-party dependencies as well as your own modules such as controllers, utilities, helpers, and models
2. Instantiations of the Express.js object and others
3. Connect to databases such as MongoDB[4], Redis[5], or MySQL[6]
4. Configure Express.js app settings such as the template engine and its files' extensions
5. Define middleware such as error handlers, static files folder, cookies, and other parsers
6. Define routes and their request handlers
7. Start the app which will start the server on a particular host and port

Of course, if your application is big, you'll have multiple files to configure your Express.js app, not just a single `server.js` or `app.js` file. The reason for that is better code organization. For example, in one file you will configure sessions, in another authentication, in another routes, and so forth.

■ **Tip** In the advanced stages of your application development (usually leading to deployment into production environment), you might want to use the `forever` (`https://npmjs.org/package/forever`) module and Upstart to accomplish better app uptime. You can also utilize the `cluster` module as outlined in Chapter 13 to spawn multiple workers.

---

[4]`http://www.mongodb.org`
[5]`http://redis.io`
[6]`http://www.mysql.com`

Third-Party Dependencies

Defining third-party dependencies is straightforward:

```
var name = require('name');
```

The dependencies typically include the Express.js library itself, along with necessary middleware such as body-parser. Another way to define multiple dependencies is to follow each definition with a comma:

```
var express = require('express'),
  compression = require('compression'),
  bodyParser = require('body-parser'),
  mongo = require('mongoskin');
```

Instantiations

To use Express.js, you need to instantiate it. At the same time, it's a good practice to instantiate any other objects:

```
var app = express();
var db = mongo.db('mongodb://localhost:27017/integration_tests', {native_parser: true});
```

■ **Tip** You don't have to name the Express.js module express or name the Express.js application app. The variable names can be arbitrary. However, most examples throughout this book use express and app to avoid confusion.

Connecting to Databases

Statements to connect to databases don't have to be in the beginning, as long as they are before step #7 "Starting the app" (from the list earlier in this section)—except in cases in which we use a database as a session store. For example:

```
var session = require('express-session');
var RedisStore = require('connect-redis')(session);
app.use(session({
  store: new RedisStore(options),
  secret: 'Pro Express.js rocks!'
}));
```

Most of the database drivers, such as Mongoskin[7] and Mongoose[8], support buffering of the queries; this way, if the server is running before the connection has been established, the database queries will be buffered for later execution (when the database connection is established).

[7]https://github.com/kissjs/node-mongoskin
[8]http://mongoosejs.com

Configuring Express.js App Settings

Simply put, configuring Express.js app settings consists of setting some values to string keys with `app.set()`. Some of these keys are used by Express.js and augment its behavior, while others are arbitrary. For example, if you are using the Jade template engine and `*.jade` files, use `'view engine'` to let Express.js know that it needs to looks for `*.jade` files:

```
app.set('view engine', 'jade');
```

You'll find a lot more information about configuring settings in the following chapters.

Sometimes we want to store a custom value on the server object for future reference. For example, we can assign `port` to a value from the environment variable `PORT` or, if it's undefined, to `3000` so that we can use the value across all source code:

```
app.set('port', process.env.PORT || 3000);
```

Defining Middleware

Middleware is a special function that allows for better code organization and reuse. Some of the middleware is packaged as third-party (NPM) modules and can be used right out of the box. Other times, we can write our own custom middleware. In both cases the syntax is `app.use()`:

```
app.use(bodyParser.json());
```

Defining Routes

Routes can be either good old web pages or REST API endpoints. In both cases the syntax is similar: we use `app.VERB()`, where `VERB()` is an HTTP method such as GET, POST, DELETE, PUT, OPTIONS, or PATCH. For example, we can define home page (root) routes as

```
app.get('/', renderHomePage);
```

Starting the App

Finally, after everything is configured, we can boot up the server with `server.listen(portNumber)`, where `server` is a core `http server` object created with the app object:

```
var server = http.createServer(app);
var boot = function () {
  server.listen(app.get('port'), function(){
    console.info('Express server listening on port ' + app.get('port'));
  });
};
var shutdown = function() {
  server.close();
};
```

If this file is included by another file (e.g., a test), we might want to export the server object instead of boot it up. The way we perform a check is by using `require.main === module`; if it's true, then this file wasn't included by anything else. The test will boot up the server by itself using the method `boot()` that we export. We also export `shutdown()` and `port`:

```
if (require.main === module) {
  boot();
} else {
  console.info('Running app as a module');
  exports.boot = boot;
  exports.shutdown = shutdown;
  exports.port = app.get('port');
}
```

When an Express.js app is running, it listens to requests. Each incoming request is processed according to a defined chain of middleware and routes, starting from the top and proceeding to the bottom. This aspect is important because it allows you to control the execution flow.

For example, we can have multiple functions handling each request, and some of those functions will be in the middle (hence the name middleware):

1. Parse cookie information and go to the next step when done.
2. Parse parameters from the URL and go to the next step when done.
3. Get the information from the database based on the value of the parameter if the user is authorized (cookie/session), and go to the next step if there is a match.
4. Display the data and end the response.

Express.js Installation

Express.js is a dependency module and should be installed in the local (project) `node_modules` folder: `$ npm install express@4.8.1`.

■ **Tip** NPM looks for either the `node_modules` folder or the `package.json` file. If this is a brand new folder that doesn't include either the folder or the file, you can create `node_modules` with `$ mkdir node_modules`, or create `package.json` with `$ npm init`.

For local Express.js module installation as a dependency, let's create a new folder, `$ mkdir proexpressjs`. This will be our project folder for the book. Now, we can open it with `$ cd proexpressjs`.

■ **Tip** For your convenience, most of the examples are located in the GitHub repository azat-co/proexpressjs (`http://github.com/azat-co/proexpressjs`). However, I strongly encourage you to type the code from the book, and modify it along the way with your text, names, and custom logic. Do not copy/paste code or even worse—just blanty run our GitHub examples. Use the full source code provided in the book and GitHub only as a reference when you're stuck or when you need to use some reciepe for your project after you've read the book. This suggestion is based on numerous studies which show that people who write or type remember and learn more effectively than those who only consume content. Also take notes!

Once we are inside the project folder, we can create `package.json` manually in a text editor or with the `$ npm init` terminal command. When you use this command, you'll be asked to provide details such as project name, description, and so forth, as you can see in Figure 1-1.

```
Azats-Air:ch1 azat$ ls -lah
total 0
drwxr-xr-x+ 2 azat  admin   68B Aug  7 08:21 .
drwxr-xr-x+ 7 azat  admin  238B Aug  7 08:21 ..
Azats-Air:ch1 azat$ npm init
This utility will walk you through creating a package.json file.
It only covers the most common items, and tries to guess sane defaults.

See `npm help json` for definitive documentation on these fields
and exactly what they do.

Use `npm install <pkg> --save` afterwards to install a package and
save it as a dependency in the package.json file.

Press ^C at any time to quit.
name: (ch1)
version: (0.0.0)
description:
entry point: (index.js)
test command:
git repository:
keywords:
author:
license: (ISC)
About to write to /Users/azat/Documents/Code/proexpress/ch1/package.json:

{
  "name": "ch1",
  "version": "0.0.0",
  "description": "",
  "main": "index.js",
  "scripts": {
    "test": "echo \"Error: no test specified\" && exit 1"
  },
  "author": "",
  "license": "ISC"
}


Is this ok? (yes) yes
Azats-Air:ch1 azat$
```

Figure 1-1. *The result of running $ npm init*

This is an example of the package.json file with vanilla `$ npm init` options from Figure 1-1:

```
{
  "name": "ch1",
  "version": "0.0.1",
  "description": "",
  "main": "index.js",
  "scripts": {
    "test": "echo \"Error: no test specified\" && exit 1"
  },
  "author": "",
  "license": "ISC"
}
```

Finally, to install the module utilizing NPM:

```
$ npm install express
```

The preceding command will pull the latest version of Express.js. However, it's recommended for this book that you use the version specified, so run this command instead:

```
$ npm install express@4.8.1 --save
```

The `--save` flag is optional. It creates an entry for this module in `package.json`.

If you want to install Express.js for an existing project and save the dependency into the `package.json` file (smart thing to do!)—which is already present in that project's folder—run:

```
 $ npm install express --save.
```

■ **Note** If you attempt to run the aforementioned `$ npm install express` command without the `package.json` file or `node_modules` folder, the *smart* NPM will traverse up the directory tree to the folder that has either of those two things. This behavior somewhat mimics Git's logic. For more information on the NPM installation algorithm, refer to the official documentation at `https://npmjs.org/doc/folders.html`.

The approach of using `$ npm init` and then `$ npm install express@4.8.1 --save` is good if your project is blank. As a result, the command will download express and its dependencies, and list them (shown in Figure 1-2):

```
...
express@4.8.1 node_modules/express
├── merge-descriptors@0.0.2
├── utils-merge@1.0.0
├── cookie@0.1.2
├── escape-html@1.0.1
...
```

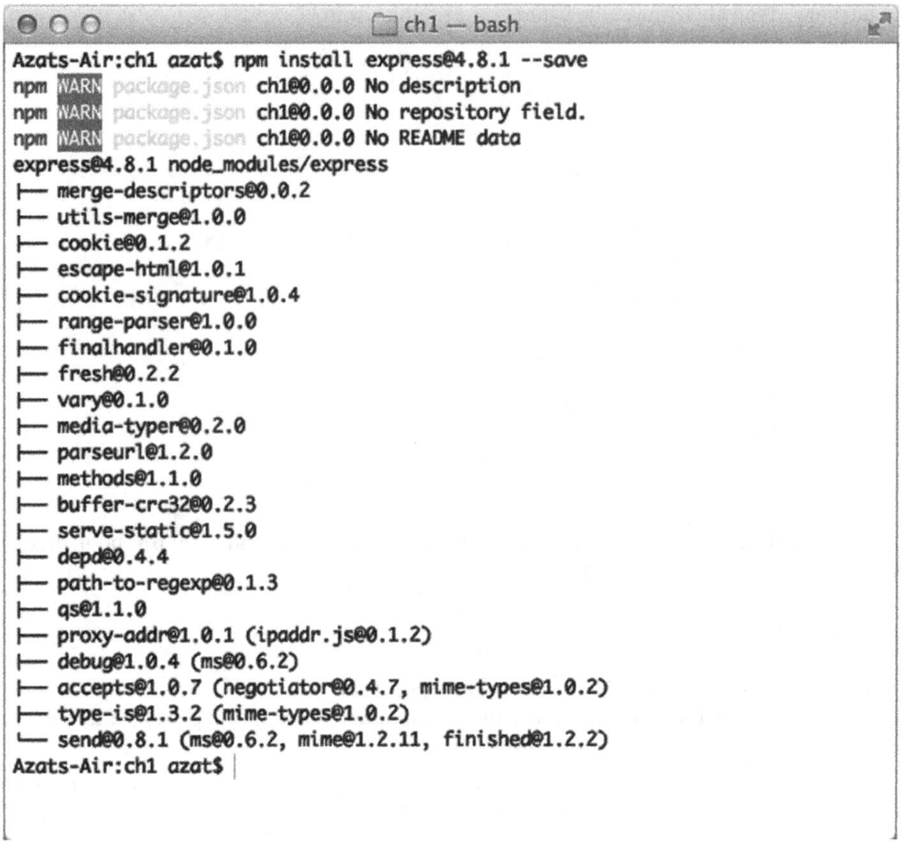

Figure 1-2. *The result of running npm install express@4.8.1 --save*

The information `express@4.8.1 node_modules/express` is important because it tells us where `the express` was placed (in `node_modules`).

Alternatively, if the project is not blank and `package.json` already exists full of useful information, we can add to the `package.json` file our new dependency with its version number or some combination of serendipity (no recommended for production apps), e.g., `"express": "4.8.x"` or `"express": "4.8.1", or "*"`, and run `$ npm install`.

The package.json file with an added Express.js v4.8.1 dependency looks as follows:

```
{
  "name": "proexpress",
  "version": "0.0.1",
  "description": "",
  "main": "index.js",
  "scripts": {
    "test": "echo \"Error: no test specified\" && exit 1"
  },
  "dependencies": {
    "express": "4.8.1"
  },
  "author": "",
  "license": "BSD"
}

$ npm install
```

To double-check the installation of Express.js and its dependencies, we can run a `$ npm ls` command (see Figure 1-3), which lists all the modules in this local project:

```
ch1@0.0.0 /Users/azat/Documents/Code/proexpress/ch1
└─┬ express@4.8.1
  ├─┬ accepts@1.0.7
  │ ├── mime-types@1.0.2
  │ └── negotiator@0.4.7
  ├── buffer-crc32@0.2.3
  ├── cookie@0.1.2
  ├── cookie-signature@1.0.4
...
```

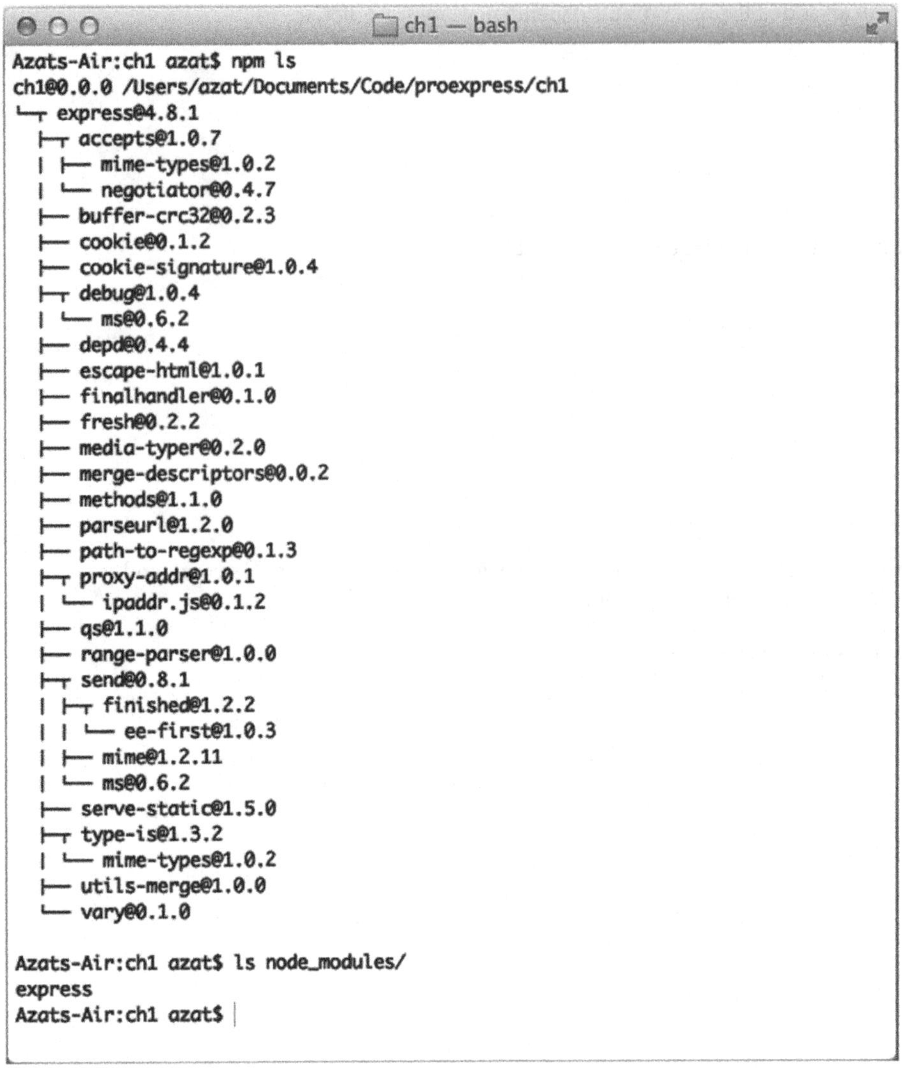

ch1 — bash
Azats-Air:ch1 azat$ npm ls
ch1@0.0.0 /Users/azat/Documents/Code/proexpress/ch1
└─┬ express@4.8.1
├─┬ accepts@1.0.7
│ ├── mime-types@1.0.2
│ └── negotiator@0.4.7
├── buffer-crc32@0.2.3
├── cookie@0.1.2
├── cookie-signature@1.0.4
├─┬ debug@1.0.4
│ └── ms@0.6.2
├── depd@0.4.4
├── escape-html@1.0.1
├── finalhandler@0.1.0
├── fresh@0.2.2
├── media-typer@0.2.0
├── merge-descriptors@0.0.2
├── methods@1.1.0
├── parseurl@1.2.0
├── path-to-regexp@0.1.3
├─┬ proxy-addr@1.0.1
│ └── ipaddr.js@0.1.2
├── qs@1.1.0
├── range-parser@1.0.0
├─┬ send@0.8.1
│ ├─┬ finished@1.2.2
│ │ └── ee-first@1.0.3
│ ├── mime@1.2.11
│ └── ms@0.6.2
├── serve-static@1.5.0
├─┬ type-is@1.3.2
│ └── mime-types@1.0.2
├── utils-merge@1.0.0
└── vary@0.1.0
Azats-Air:ch1 azat$ ls node_modules/
express
Azats-Air:ch1 azat$

Figure 1-3. *The result of running $ npm ls and $ ls node_modules*

The command `$ npm ls` lists the local dependencies for this project (current folder). At this point, we should at least see `express@4.8.1` (as shown in Figure 1-3). Another way to check is to use `$ ls node_modules` (also shown in Figure 1-3), which lists folders in `node_modules`.

Express.js Generator Installation

Express.js Generator (`express-generator`) is a separate module (since Express.js version 4.x, before which they were bundled). It allows for rapid app creation because its scaffolding mechanism takes command-line options and generates Express.js apps based on them.

To install Express.js Generator, a command-line tool for scaffolding, run `$ npm install -g express-generator` from anywhere on your Mac/Linux machine. (For Windows users, the path will be different. Check the `NODE_PATH` environment variable and update it if you want a different global location.) The installation command will download and link the `$ express` terminal command to the proper path so that we can later access its command-line interface (CLI) when creating new apps.

Of course, we can be more specific and tell NPM to install version 4.2.0 using `$ npm install -g express@4.2.0`. Versions of the `express` and `express-generator` modules don't have to (and usually don't) match, because they are separate modules. So you need to know what's compatible with what based on the change log and the GitHub readme documentation.

■ **Tip** When using the `-g` flag with `npm install`, a good rule of thumb is to use it for command-line tools (e.g., `node-dev`, `mocha`, `supervisor`, `grunt`), but not for dependencies of your project. Dependencies in Node.js must be installed locally into the project's `node_modules` folder.

In Figure 1-4, we try the `express` command without success, then install `express-generator`, and get access to the `express` command-line tool.

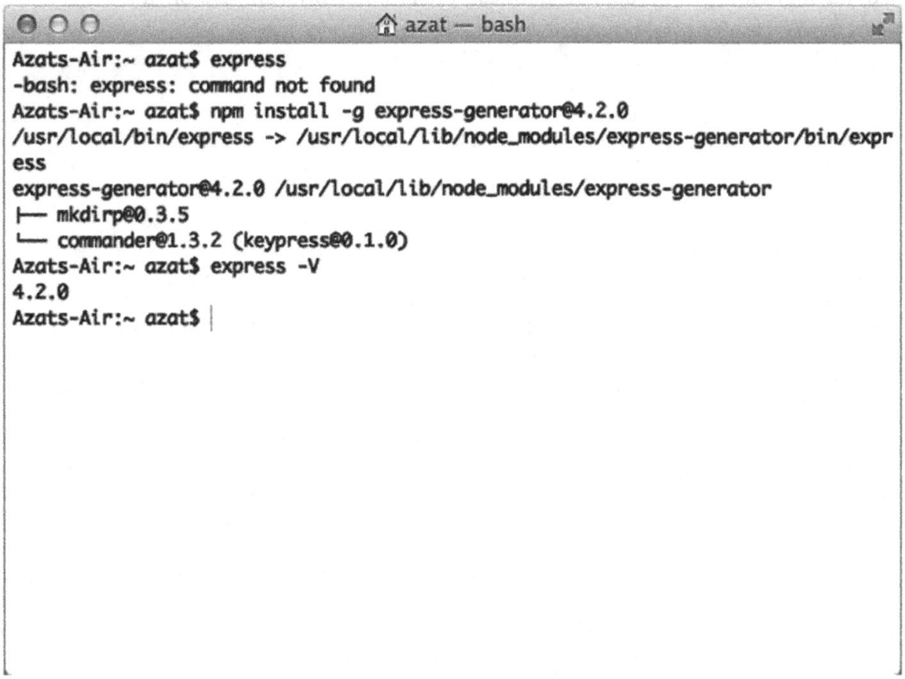

azat — bash
Azats-Air:~ azat$ express
-bash: express: command not found
Azats-Air:~ azat$ npm install -g express-generator@4.2.0
/usr/local/bin/express -> /usr/local/lib/node_modules/express-generator/bin/expr
ess
express-generator@4.2.0 /usr/local/lib/node_modules/express-generator
├── mkdirp@0.3.5
└── commander@1.3.2 (keypress@0.1.0)
Azats-Air:~ azat$ express -V
4.2.0
Azats-Air:~ azat$

Figure 1-4. *The result of running NPM with -g and $ express -V*

■ **Note** Most likely, your system will require a root/administrator right to write to the folder. In this case, you'll need `$ sudo npm install -g express-generator`.

Notice the path `/usr/local/lib/node_modules/express-generator` in Figure 1-4. This is drastically different from the `express` path of the local installation. This is one of the ways to spot an error if you're trying to install something and it's not available—check the location!

Yes, it's might be trivial for some readers who are well versed in Node.js, but I've seen too many times how some people who come from Python, Ruby and Java backgrounds try to install `express` (the dependency) globally so they can use it for all their projects. Please don't do it.

Summary

This chapter laid the foundation for understanding how Express.js works. By covering a typical Express.js app structure, you've been introduced to concepts such as configuration, middleware, and routes that we'll cover in more depth throughout the book. Most importantly, you learned how to install Express.js locally in a blank folder and into existing projects, as well as how to install Express.js Generator.

In the next chapter, we'll build our first Express.js app, the quintessential Hello World, and explore the generator/scaffolding options.

CHAPTER 2

Hello World Example

In this chapter, to help you get your feet wet using Express.js, we'll build the quintessential programming example—the Hello World app. If you've already built some variation of this Express.js app (perhaps by following an online tutorial), feel free to skip to the next chapter and go either to Chapter 3 for the API methods and objects, or to Chapter 19-22 for examples. The topics covered in this chapter are as follow:

- Getting started: creating the minimal Express.js app from scratch
- Generator commands: command-line options of Express.js Generator
- MVC structure and modules: a common way to organize code for Express.js apps
- Watching for file changes: a development tip

Getting Started

I've always liked the bottom-up approach to teaching, starting from the most basic concepts and progressing toward more complex ones. Also, I've noticed that developers gain more confidence when they learn how to create something from scratch instead of just modifying an existing project or using boilerplate.

Note I encourage readers to type in all the code, because this increases learning efficiency. However, for reference and for those who still prefer to copy and paste, the code for this chapter (and others) is in the GitHub repository at `https://github.com/azat-co/proexpressjs`.

To begin, you'll write a web server that runs locally on port 3000. So, when you open the `http://localhost:3000` location in the browser, you should see Hello World. The number 3000 is the de-facto standard port number for Express.js applications.

Tip The browser makes a GET request when you navigate it to some page, so at the very least your server should process GET requests. GET and other types of requests can be performed with CURL (Mac[1] or Windows[2]) or similar tools.

---

[1]`https://developer.apple.com/library/mac/documentation/Darwin/Reference/ManPages/man1/curl.1.html`
[2]`http://www.confusedbycode.com/curl/#downloads` and `http://curl.haxx.se/download.html`

In the folder `proexpressjs/ch2`, create a `hello.js` file. Use your favorite text editor, such as Vim (`www.vim.org`), Emacs (`www.gnu.org/software/emacs/`), Sublime Text 2 (`www.sublimetext.com`), or TextMate (`http://macromates.com`). The file `hello.js` server will utilize Express.js; therefore, let's include this library:

```
var express = require('express');
```

Now we can create an application (i.e., instantiate an Express.js object):

```
var app = express();
```

The web server will run locally on port 3000, so let's define it here:

```
var port = 3000;
```

Next, let's define *a wildcard route* (*) with the `app.get()` function:

```
app.get('*', function(request, response){
  resquest.end('Hello World');
});
```

The `app.get()` function accepts regular expressions[3] of the URL patterns in a string format. In our example, we're processing all URLs by specifying the wildcard * character.

■ **Note** Regular expressions are widely used in, and work similarly across, many programming languages, so if you already use them with Perl, PHP, Java, and so on, then you already know how to use most of them with JavaScript/Node.js.The regular expression, or RegExp for short, uses special symbols to define string patterns for validation, transformation, or parameter extraction. For example, this is one of the e-mail RegExps: `/^(([^<>()[\]\\.,;:\s@\"]+(\.[^<>()[\]\\.,;:\s@\"]+)*)|(\".+\"))@((\[[0-9]{1,3}\.[0-9]{1,3}\.[0-9]{1,3}\.[0-9]{1,3}\])|(([a-zA-Z\-0-9]+\.)+[a-zA-Z]{2,}))$/`

In the case of Express.js, you can use RegExps in routes to define complex URL patterns dynamically. To find out more about regular expressions, check out the documentation at `https://developer.mozilla.org/en-US/docs/Web/JavaScript/Guide/Regular_Expressions`.

[3]`https://developer.apple.com/library/mac/documentation/Darwin/Reference/ManPages/man1/curl.1.html`

Using Request Handlers

The second parameter to the `app.get()` method is a *request handler*. A typical Express.js request handler is similar to the one we pass as a callback to the native/core Node.js `http.createServer()` method. For those unfamiliar with the core `http` module, a request handler is a function that will be executed every time the server receives a particular request, usually defined by an HTTP method (e.g., `GET`) and the URL path (i.e., the URL without the protocol, host, and port). The Express.js request handler needs at least two parameters—`request`, or simply `req`, and `response`, or `res` (more on this later in Chapter 9). Similarly to their core counterparts, we can utilize readable and writable streams interfaces (`http://nodejs.org/api/stream.html`) via `response.pipe()` and/or `response.on('data', function(chunk) {...})`.

Outputting Terminal Messages

Finally, we start the Express.js web server and output a user-friendly terminal message in a callback:

```
app.listen(port, function(){
  console.log('The server is running, ' +
    ' please, open your browser at http://localhost:%s',
    port);
});
```

To run the script, we execute `$ node hello.js` from the project folder. You should see "The server is running, please open your browser at http://localhost:3000" as shown in Figure 2-1.

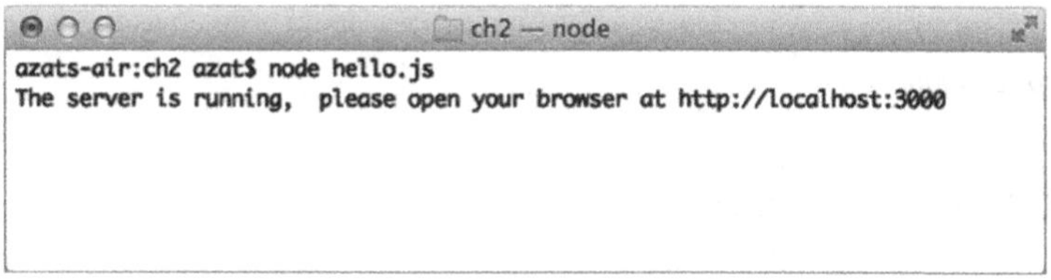

Figure 2-1. *The result of running $ node hello.js*

Now, if you open your browser at `http://localhost:3000` (same as `http://127.0.0.1:3000`, `http://0.0.0.0:3000`, or `http://localhost:3000/`), you should see the Hello World message no matter what the URL path is (see Figure 2-2). The URL path is the string after the domain and port, so for `http://localhost:3000/`, it is / and for `http://localhost:3000/messages/` is it "`/messages/`". When you use "*" in the route definition, this path doesn't matter.

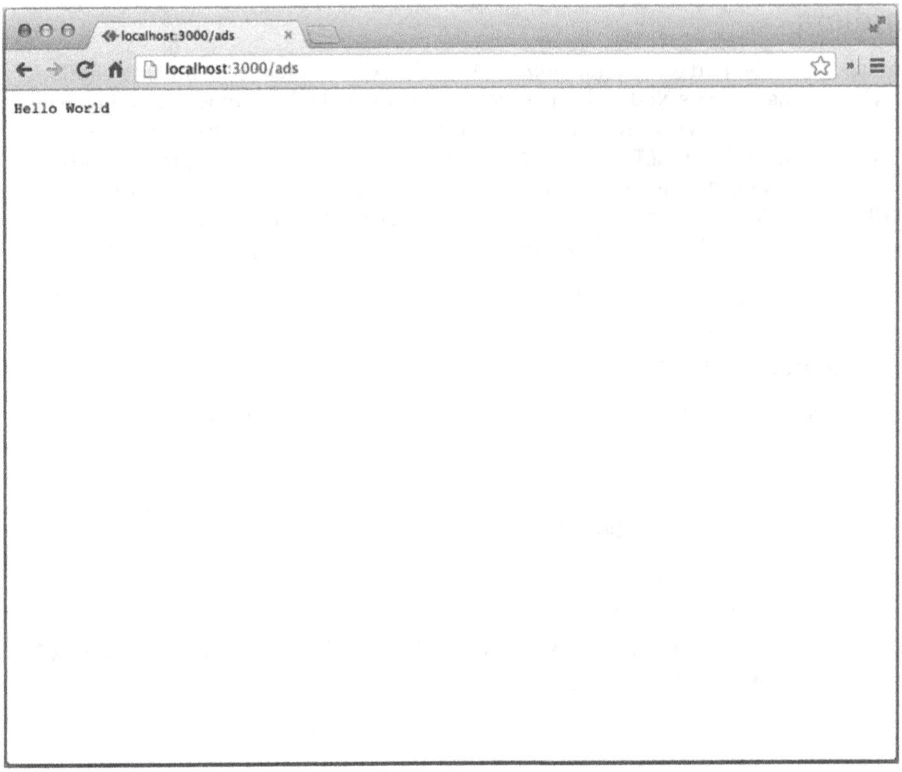

Figure 2-2. *Browser opened at `http://localhost:3000/ads`*

The full code of the `hello.js` file is provided here for your reference:

```
var express = require('express');
var port = 3000;
var app = express();

app.get('*', function(request, response){
  resquest.end('Hello World');
});

app.listen(port, function(){
  console.log('The server is running, ' +
    ' please open your browser at http://localhost:%s',
     port);
});
```

Enhancing the App

We can make our example a bit more interactive by echoing the name that we provide to the server along with the "Hello" phrase. To do so, we can copy the `hello.js` file with `$ cp hello.js hello-name.js` and add the following route right before the all-encompassing route (`all.get('*', ...)`) from the previous example:

```
app.get('/name/:user_name', function(req,res) {
  res.status(200);
  res.set('Content-type', 'text/html');
  res.send('<html><body>' +
    '<h1>Hello ' + req.params.user_name + '</h1>' +
    '</body></html>'
  );
});
```

Inside of the `/name/:name_route` route, we set the proper HTTP status code (200 means OK) and HTTP response headers and wrap our dynamic text in HTML body and `h1` tags.

Note `response.send()` is a special Express.js method that conveniently goes beyond what our old friend from the core http module `response.end()` does. For example, the former automatically adds a `Content-Length` HTTP header for us. It also augments `Content-Type` based on the data provided to it—more details on this are provided in Chapter 8.

The full source code of the `hello-name.js` file is provided next (and is also available in the downloadable source code for this book):

```
var express = require('express');
var port = 3000;
var app = express();

app.get('/name/:user_name', function(request,response) {
  response.status(200);
  response.set('Content-Type', 'text/html');
  response.end('<html><body>' +
    '<h1>Hello ' + req.params.user_name + '</h1>' +
    '</body></html>'
  );
});

app.get('*', function(request, response){
  response.end('Hello World');
});

app.listen(port, function(){
  console.log('The server is running, ' +
    ' please open your browser at http://localhost:%s',
     port);
});
```

After shutting down the previous server and launching the `hello-name.js` script, you'll be able to see the dynamic response; for example, entering `http://localhost:3000/name/azat` in your browser yields the screen shown in Figure 2-3.

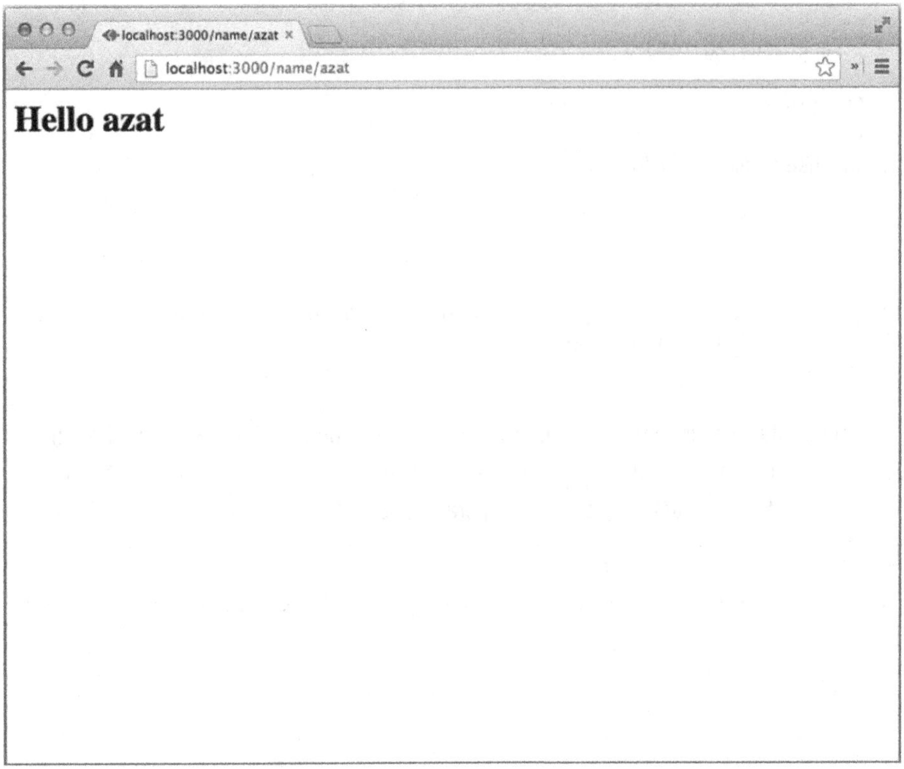

Figure 2-3. *Dynamic Hello User example*

So far we've created two Express.js apps from scratch. Each of them was just a few lines of code. This should give you the confidence, and illustrate how easy it is, to create web servers with Express.js and Node.js! But there's an even faster way—Express.js generator. Let's cover its commands and options.

Generator Commands

Comparable to Ruby on Rails and many other web frameworks, Express.js comes with a command-line interface (CLI) for jump-starting your development process. The CLI generates a basic foundation for the most common cases. Unlike Rails or Sails, Express generator doesn't support the addition of routes/models (as of this writing).

If you followed the global installation instructions in Chapter 1, you should be able to see the version number if you run the `$ express -V` form *anywhere* on your machine. If you type `$ express -h` or `$ express --help`, you get the list of available options and their usage. In this book, we're using the latest (as of this writing) version, 4.2.0, which is compatible with Express.js 4.x (see Figure 2-4).

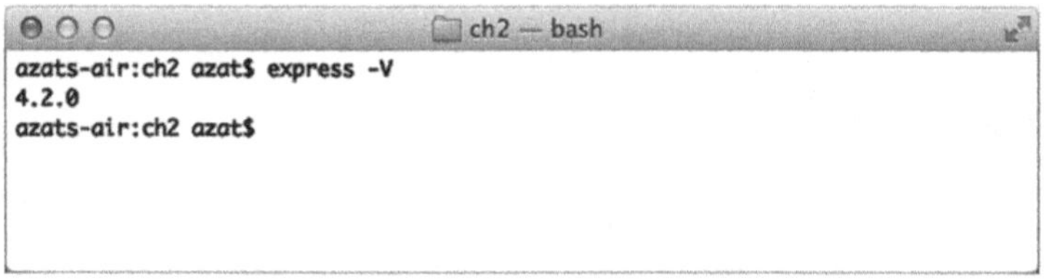
ch2 — bash
azats-air:ch2 azat$ express -V
4.2.0
azats-air:ch2 azat$

Figure 2-4. *Checking the Express.js Generator version*

To generate a skeleton Express.js app, we need to run a terminal command: `express [options] [dir|appname]` (e.g., `express cli-app`), where the options are as follows:

- `-e` or `--ejs` adds EJS engine support (`www.embeddedjs.com`). By default, Jade (`http://jade-lang.com/tutorial/`) is used.
- `-H` or `--hogan` adds hogan.js engine support.
- `-c <engine> or --css <engine>` adds style sheet `<engine>` support for Less (`http://lesscss.org`), Stylus (`http://learnboost.github.io/stylus`), or Compass (`http://compass-style.org`); by default, plain CSS is used.
- `-f` or `--force` forces app generation on a non-empty directory.

These options are optional, of course, so you can just run `express cli-app` and you'll get an app with default settings.

If the `dir/appname` option is omitted, Express.js will create files using the current folder as the base for the project. Otherwise, the application will be under the specified directory.

Generating a Skeleton Express.js app

For the sake of experimenting, let's run this command: `$ express -e -c less -f cli-app`. The generator tool will output created files and suggest commands to run to boot up the server. Figure 2-5 shows the output.

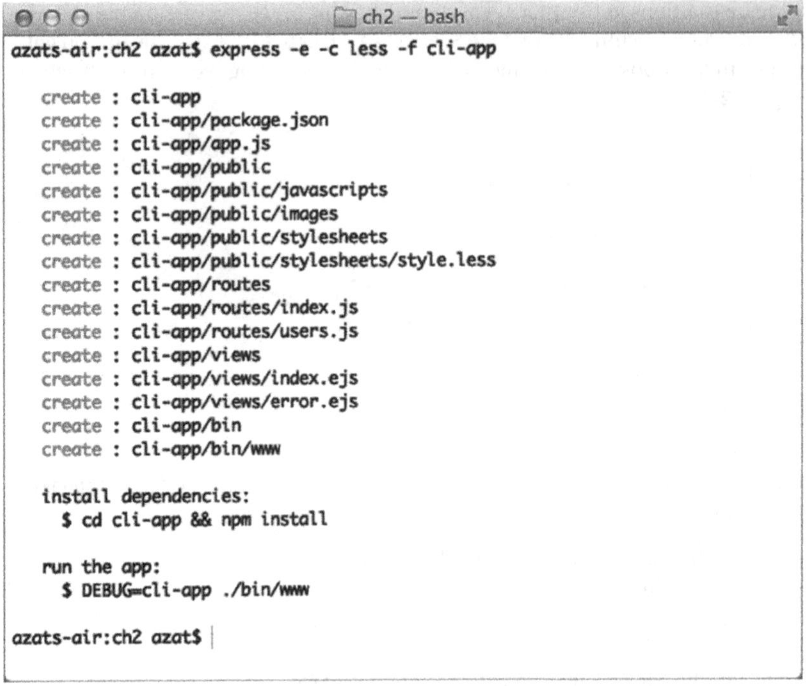

ch2 — bash
azats-air:ch2 azat$ express -e -c less -f cli-app
create : cli-app
create : cli-app/package.json
create : cli-app/app.js
create : cli-app/public
create : cli-app/public/javascripts
create : cli-app/public/images
create : cli-app/public/stylesheets
create : cli-app/public/stylesheets/style.less
create : cli-app/routes
create : cli-app/routes/index.js
create : cli-app/routes/users.js
create : cli-app/views
create : cli-app/views/index.ejs
create : cli-app/views/error.ejs
create : cli-app/bin
create : cli-app/bin/www
install dependencies:
$ cd cli-app && npm install
run the app:
$ DEBUG=cli-app ./bin/www
azats-air:ch2 azat$

Figure 2-5. *The result of running $ express -e -c less -f cli-app*

As you can see, Express.js provides a robust command-line tool for spawning boilerplates rapidly. The downside is that Express.js Generator approach is not very configurable. For example, it's possible to use a Handlebars template engine (and many others not just Hogan, Jade, JSHTML, or EJS provided by CLI) when you create apps manually, but Express.js Generator doesn't have this option (as of this writing). You'll find more info on using different template engines with Express.js in Chapter 5.

Next we'll examine what the generator created—in other words, what app structure the scaffolding uses.

Reviewing the Application's Structure

Let's briefly examine the application structure. The project's root folder includes two very important files, `app.js` and `package.js`, as indicated on these lines shown in Figure 2-5: `create: cli-app/package.json` and `create: cli-app/app.js`. The `app.js` file is the main file (as discussed in the previous chapter) and it connects all the other pieces. The `package.json` file has all the needed dependencies (`express` at the bare minimum). Then, we have three folders:

- `public`: Static assets such as images, browser JavaScript, and CSS files
- `views`: Template file such as `*.jade`, or `*.ejs` as in our example
- `routes`: Request handlers abstracted (a fancy word for copied and pasted) into separate files/ internal modules

The public folder has three folders of its own when project is generated by express-generator:

- images: For storing images
- javascripts: For front-end JavaScript files
- stylesheets: For CSS or, in our example, Less files (the -c less options)

The routes folder has two files: index.js, which handles the home page (root or /), and users.js, which handles the /users route.

The folders in the public folder are not mandatory, and you can create arbitrary folders that will be exposed on the / route of your server by the express.static() middleware. For example, the content of public/img will be available at http://localhost:3000/img. I personally prefer img, js and css instead of images, javascripts and stylesheets. When you rename the folders inside /public, you don't need to make any additional change in the Express.js configuration.

You can also rename the views and public folders themselves, but you'll need to make some additional changes in configuration statements, i.e., change settings. We'll cover these settings later in Chapter 3.

App.js

Open the main web server file app.js in your favorite text editor. We'll briefly go through the auto-generated code and what it does before diving deeper into each one of those configurations later on (Chapter 3).

We include the following module dependencies:

```
var express = require('express');
var path = require('path');
var favicon = require('static-favicon');
var logger = require('morgan');
var cookieParser = require('cookie-parser');
var bodyParser = require('body-parser');

var routes = require('./routes/index');
var users = require('./routes/users');
```

Next, we create the Express.js app object:

```
var app = express();
```

Then, we define configuration settings. For now, you can probably guess their meaning based on their names. That is, where to get template files (views) along with what template engine to use (view engine). More details on these parameters are provided in Chapter 3 so for now let's move along with the app.js file:

```
app.set('views', path.join(__dirname, 'views'));
app.set('view engine', 'ejs');
```

We next define middleware (discussed in detail in Chapter 4) to serve favicon, log events, parse the request body, support old browsers' HTTP methods, parse cookies, and utilize routes:

```
app.use(favicon());
app.use(logger('dev'));
app.use(bodyParser.json());
app.use(bodyParser.urlencoded());
app.use(cookieParser());
```

The following middleware is responsible for compiling Less styles into CSS styled that will be served to the browser:

```
app.use(require('less-middleware')(path.join(__dirname, 'public')));
```

We pass the folder (`public`) as a parameter to make it scan this folder recursively for any `*.less` files. The CSS file name and Less file name need to match, so if we use `/css/style.css(e.g., in HTML or Jade)`, we need to have `/public/css/style.less`. Express.js will compile Less for each request.

This statement takes care of serving static assets from the `public` folder:

```
app.use(express.static(path.join(__dirname, 'public')));
```

The routes are defined as a module in a separate file, so we just pass the functions' expressions instead of defining them right here as anonymous request handlers:

```
app.get('/', routes.index);
app.get('/users', user.list);
```

Express.js gets its environment variable from `process.env.NODE_ENV`, which is passed as `NODE_ENV=production`, for example, either when the server is started or in the machine's configurations. With this condition, we enable a more explicit error handler for the development environment. The generator provides us with a 404 (Not Found) middleware, and two 500 (Internal Server Error) error handlers, one for development (more verbose) and one for production:

```
app.use(function(req, res, next) {
    var err = new Error('Not Found');
    err.status = 404;
    next(err);
});
if (app.get('env') === 'development') {
    app.use(function(err, req, res, next) {
        res.status(err.status || 500);
        res.render('error', {
            message: err.message,
            error: err
        });
    });
}
app.use(function(err, req, res, next) {
    res.status(err.status || 500);
    res.render('error', {
        message: err.message,
        error: {}
    });
});
```

Unlike the Hello World example, this server is not booted right away, but exported:

```
module.exports = app;
```

In /bin/www, the server is imported from the app.js file:

```
#!/usr/bin/env node
var debug = require('debug')('cli-app');
var app = require('../app');
```

This statement sets a custom setting with the name port to use it later for server boot-up:

```
app.set('port', process.env.PORT || 3000);
```

Finally, the server is started with familiar listen():

```
var server = app.listen(app.get('port'), function() {
  debug('Express server listening on port ' + server.address().port);
});
```

For your reference, the following is the full code for app.js:

```
var express = require('express');
var path = require('path');
var favicon = require('static-favicon');
var logger = require('morgan');
var cookieParser = require('cookie-parser');
var bodyParser = require('body-parser');

var routes = require('./routes/index');
var users = require('./routes/users');

var app = express();

// view engine setup
app.set('views', path.join(__dirname, 'views'));
app.set('view engine', 'ejs');

app.use(favicon());
app.use(logger('dev'));
app.use(bodyParser.json());
app.use(bodyParser.urlencoded());
app.use(cookieParser());
app.use(require('less-middleware')(path.join(__dirname, 'public')));
app.use(express.static(path.join(__dirname, 'public')));

app.use('/', routes);
app.use('/users', users);
```

```
/// catch 404 and forward to error handler
app.use(function(req, res, next) {
    var err = new Error('Not Found');
    err.status = 404;
    next(err);
});

/// error handlers

// development error handler
// will print stacktrace
if (app.get('env') === 'development') {
    app.use(function(err, req, res, next) {
        res.status(err.status || 500);
        res.render('error', {
            message: err.message,
            error: err
        });
    });
}

// production error handler
// no stacktraces leaked to user
app.use(function(err, req, res, next) {
    res.status(err.status || 500);
    res.render('error', {
        message: err.message,
        error: {}
    });
});


module.exports = app;
```

If you navigate (`$ cd cli-app`) into the project folder and run `$ npm install`, you should observe the installation of NPM modules based on the `package.json` entry. After the installations are finished, run `npm start` or `$ ./bin/www`. When you navigate to `http://localhost:3000` in your browser, you should see the response shown in Figure 2-6.

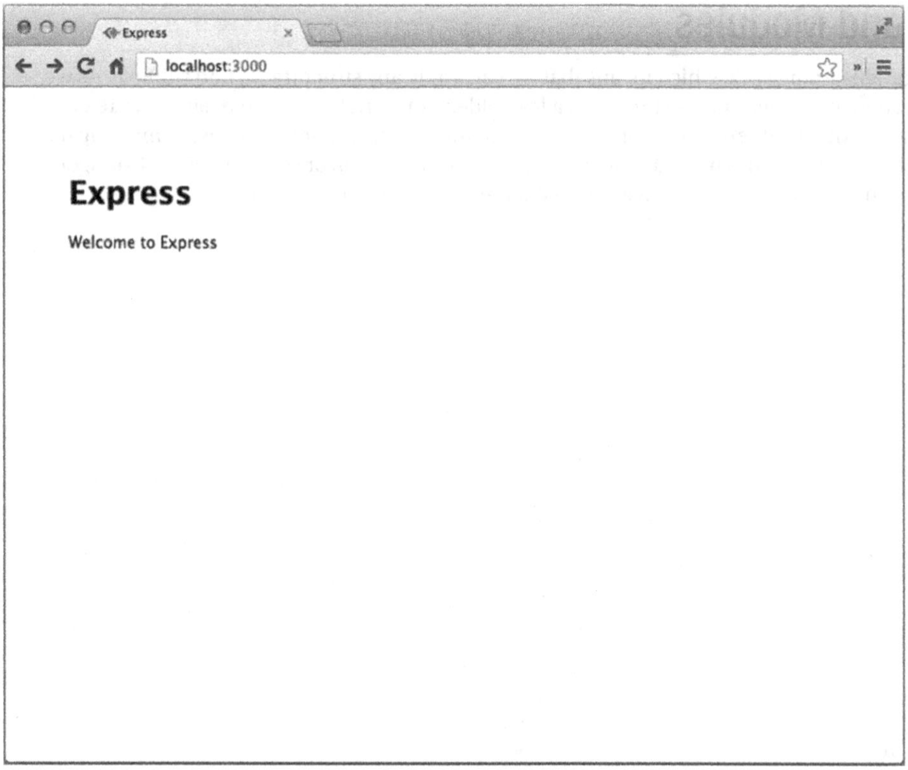

Figure 2-6. *Boilerplate Express.js app created by generator*

Express.js generator is not a very powerful tool, because it doesn't do much after the boilerplate creation. However, it provides developers with boilerplates/skeletons that can be used for rapid prototyping. In addition, beginners can learn about recommended structure and code organization, as well as learn how to include some middleware such as Less and `express.static()`.

The next section summarizes some common patterns and conventions regarding the folder structure of Express.js apps.

MVC Structure and Modules

Express.js is a highly configurable framework, which means that we can apply any structure we find suitable. As we observed in the previous section, the generator tool produces a few folders for us right off the bat: `public`, `views`, and `routes`. What is lacking in order to adhere to the general MVC paradigm is the model. If you use something like Mongoose,[4] you might want to create a folder named `models` and put the models and/or schema objects (Mongoose Schema) there. More advanced applications might have a nested folder structure similar to this:

```
.
├── app.js
├── package.json
├── views
│   └── *.jade
├── routes
│   └── *.js
├── models
│   └── *.js
├── config
│   └── *.js
├── public
│   ├── javascripts
│   │   └── *.js
│   ├── images
│   │   └── *.png, *.jpg
│   └── stylesheets
│       └── *.less, *.styl
├── test
│   └── *.js
├── logs
│   └── *.log
```

The best practice is to have static assets under a special folder. Those assets could also be written in a compilable language such as CoffeeScript or Less.

In case you prefer to rename the folders, just make sure you update the corresponding code in your `app.js` file (or the other main script file, if you're creating an app from scratch with a different file name). For example, if I want to serve my user-related routes from the folder `controllers`, I would update my `app.js` file like this:

```
var user = require('./controllers/user');
```

The patterns for the modules don't have to be complicated. From the main file, we include the object with the `require()` function, and inside of that module file, we apply an `exports` global keyword to attach a method that we want to expose (and use later in the main file):

```
exports.list = function(req, res){
  res.send("respond with a resource");
};
```

[4]`http://mongoosejs.com`

One caveat here—or a feature, depending on how you look at it—is that if we omit the file name and require a folder, such as `var routes = require('./routes');` from our previous example, Node.js will grab the `index.js` file from that folder, if one exists. This might come in handy when declaring some helpers or utility functions that you might want to share across the files of that particular folder.

In Chapter 13 we'll discuss how to make our application a module in itself, so we can spawn multiple processes (i.e., workers) in a production environment.

A similar approach is applicable to a template folder. If we decide that we want to have `templates` instead of `views`, we need to change a settings line to

```
app.set('views', path.join(__dirname, 'views'));
```

In this line, the first parameter to the `app.set()` function is the name of the setting, `views`, and the second is the value that is dynamically prefixed with a global `__dirname` variable.[5] The `__dirname` variable returns the system path to the module being executed.

Watching for File Changes

This topic is bit outside the scope of Express.js, but I believe that it's sufficiently important that it's worth mentioning. Node.js applications are stored in memory, and if we make changes to the source code, we need to restart the process—the running Node.js program. On Mac OS X, this is achieved by the following combination of keys pressed in the terminal: Ctrl+C, Up Arrow, Enter.

The following brilliant file-watching tools can leverage the `watch()` method[6] from the core Node.js `fs` module and restart our servers when we save changes from an editor. For the purpose of this book and its examples, these tools are pretty much the same, so none is given any preference; just pick one of them.

- `forever`: For use on the production server (`https://npmjs.org/package/forever`)
- `node-dev`: *Description* (`https://npmjs.org/package/node-dev`; GitHub: `https://github.com/fgnass/node-dev`)
- `nodemon`: Supports CoffeeScript (`https://npmjs.org/package/nodemon`; GitHub: `https://github.com/remy/nodemon`)
- `supervisor`: Written by the one of the creators of NPM `https://npmjs.org/package/supervisor`; GitHub: `https://github.com/isaacs/node-supervisor`)
- `up`: Written by the team that wrote Express.js (`https://npmjs.org/package/up`; GitHub: `https://github.com/LearnBoost/up`)

■ **Tip** Because Express.js reloads a template file for every new request by default, no server restart is necessary. However, we can cache templates by enabling the `view cache` setting. This and other settings will be covered at length later in the book in Chapter 3.

---

[5]`http://nodejs.org/docs/latest/api/globals.html#globals_dirname`

[6]`http://nodejs.org/docs/latest/api/fs.html#fs_fs_watch_filename_options_listener`

Summary

So far we've created a few apps from scratch, used Express.js Generator and explored its options. Then we looked at one of the ways to structure Express.js apps and organize the code. The Express.js Generator is not a very versatile tool but by using it you can quickly produce some boilerplate code with different CSS libraries, and template engines.

The framework's configurability is one of the primary selling points of Express.js and a contributing factor to its growing popularity. This means that the Express.js way is to provide default settings, so at the bare minimum your server will work just fine without extra configurations (`ch2/hello.js` is just 13 lines). But at the same time, Express.js allows skilled developers to configure settings effortlessly and in a sane manner. Who would object to knowing these settings, right? For this reason, in Chapter 3 we explore the most important configuration settings available in Express.js.

PART II

Deep API Reference

CHAPTER 3

Configuration, Settings, and Environments

This chapter is all about different ways of configuring Express.js settings. As mentioned in Chapter 1, Express.js positions itself as a *configuration over convention* framework. So, when it comes to configurations in Express.js, you can configure pretty much anything! To do so, you use configuration statements and know the settings.

What are the settings? Think of settings as key-value pairs that typically act in a global or application-wide manner. Settings can augment behavior of the server, add information to responses, or be used for references later.

There are two types of settings: Express.js system settings that the framework uses behind the scene, and arbitrary settings that developers use for their own code. The former come with default values so that if you don't configure them—the app will still run okay! Therefore, it's not a big deal if you don't know or don't use some of the Express.js settings. For this reason, don't feel like you must learn all the settings by heart to be able to build Express apps. Just use this chapter as a reference any time you have a question about a specific method or a system setting.

To progress from simple to more complex things, this chapter is organized as follows:

- *Configuration*: Methods to set settings values and to get them
- *Settings*: Names of the settings, their default values, what they affect, and examples of how to augment values
- *Environments*: Determining an environment and putting an application in that mode is an important aspect of any serious application.

The examples for this chapter are available in the `ch3/app.js` project, which is in the GitHub repository at `http://github.com/azat-co/proexpressjs`.

Configuration

Before you can work with settings, you need to learn how to apply them on an Express.js app. The most common and versatile way is to use `app.set` to define a value and use `app.get` to retrieve the value based on the key/name of the setting.

The other configuration methods are less versatile, because they apply only to certain settings based on their type (boolean): `app.enable()` and `app.disable()`.

app.set() and app.get()

The method `app.set(name, value)` accepts two parameters: `name` and `value`. As you might guess, it sets the value for the name. For example, we often want to store the value of the port on which we plan to start our server:

```
app.set('port', 3000);
```

Or, for a more advanced and realistic use case, we can grab the port from system environment variable `PORT` (`process.env.PORT`). If the `PORT` environment variable is undefined, we fall back to the hard-coded value `3000`:

```
app.set('port', process.env.PORT || 3000);
```

The preceding code is a shorter equivalent to using an `if else` statement:

```
if (process.env.PORT) {
  app.set(process.env.PORT);
} else {
  app.set(3000);
}
```

The `name` value could be an Express.js setting or an arbitrary string. To get the value, we can use `app.set(name)` with a single parameter, or we can use the more explicit method `app.get(name)`, as shown in the following example:

```
console.log('Express server listening on port ' + app.get('port'));
```

The `app.set()` method also exposes variables to templates application-wide; for example,

```
app.set('appName', 'HackHall');
```

will be available in *all* templates, meaning this example would be valid in a Jade template layout:

```
doctype 5
html
  head
    title= appName
  body
    block content
```

app.enable() and app.disable()

There are some system Express.js settings that have the type of boolean true and false, instead of the string type, and they can only be set to boolean false or true. For such flags, there are shorthand versions; for example, as an alternative to the `app.set(name, true)` and `app.set(name, false)` functions, you can use the concise `app.enable(name)` and `app.disable(name)` calls accordingly. I recommend using `app.set()` because it keeps the code consistent no matter what is the type of the setting.

For example, the `etag` Express.js setting is a boolean. It turns ETag headers on and off for browser caching (more on `etag` later). To turn this caching off with `app.disable()` write a statement:

```
app.disable('etag');
```

app.enabled() and app.disabled()

To check whether the aforementioned values equal true or false, we can call methods `app.enabled(name)` and `app.disabled(name)`. For example,

```
app.disable('etag');
console.log(app.disabled('etag'));
```

will output `true` in the context of the Express.js app.

Settings

There are two categories of settings:

- *Express.js system settings*: These settings are used by the framework to determine certain configurations. Most of them have default values, so the bare-bones app that omits configuring these settings will work just fine.
- *Custom settings*: You can store any arbitrary name as a setting for reference later. These settings are custom to your application, and you first need to define them to use.

Coverage of system settings is one of the most obscure parts of Express.js documentation, because some of the settings are not documented at all (as of this writing). Express.js is flexible enough so that you don't have to know **all the settings** in order to write apps. But after you've learned about all the setting and have begun to use the ones that you need, you will be more confident in configuring your server. You'll understand the inner workings of the framework better.

In this section, you'll learn about the following settings:

- `env`
- `view cache`
- `view engine`
- `views`
- `trust proxy`
- `jsonp callback name`
- `json replacer` and `json spaces`
- `case sensitive routing`
- `strict routing`
- `x-powered-by`
- `etag`
- `query parser`
- `subdomain offset`

To illustrate settings in action, we wrote a `ch3/app.js` example. To avoid confusion, we'll refrain from showing the whole file now, and instead provide the source code at the end of this section for reference.

env

This variable is used to store the current environment mode for this particular Node.js process. The value is automatically set by Express.js from `process.env.NODE_ENV` (which is fed to Node.js through an environment variable on the executing machine) or, if that is not set, to the `development` value.

The other most common values for env setting are as follows:

- `development`
- `test`
- `stage`
- `preview`
- `production`

The "`production`" and "`development`" values are used by Express.js for certain settings' defaults (`view cache` is one of them). The other values are just convention, meaning you're free to use whatever you want as long as you are consistent. For example, instead of `stage` you can use `qa`.

We can augment the env setting by adding `app.set('env', 'preview');` or `process.env.NODE_ENV=preview` in our code. However, the better way is to start an app with `$ NODE_ENV=preview node app` or to set the `NODE_ENV` variable on the machine.

Knowing in what mode the application runs is very important because logic related to error handling, compilation of style sheets, and rendering of the templates can differ dramatically. Obviously, databases and hostnames are different from environment to environment.

The `app.get('env')` setting is illustrated in the `ch3/app.js` example as

```
console.log(app.get('env'));
```

This line outputs

```
"development"
```

The preceding line is printed if `NODE_ENV` is set to `development` when we launch the process with `$ NODE_ENV=development node app.js` or when `NODE_ENV` is not set. In the latter case, the reason for the "`development`" value is that Express.js defaults the setting to "`development`" when it's undefined.

view cache

This flag, if set to `false`, allows for painless development because templates are read each time the server requests them. On the other hand, if `view cache` is set to `true`, it facilitates template compilation caching, which is a desired behavior in production. If the env setting is `production`, then `view cache` is enabled by default. Otherwise it is set to `false`.

view engine

The `view engine` setting holds the template file extension (e.g., `'ext'` or `'jade'`) to utilize if the file extension is not passed to the `res.render()` function inside of the request handler.

For example, as shown in Figure 3-1, if we comment out this line from the previous chapter's `ch2/cli-app/app.js` example:

```
// app.set('view engine', 'ejs');
```

cli-app — node
> cli-app@0.0.1 start /Users/azat/Documents/Code/proexpressjs/ch2/cli-app
> node ./bin/www
Error: No default engine was specified and no extension was provided.
at new View (/Users/azat/Documents/Code/proexpressjs/ch2/cli-app/node_modules/express/lib/view.js:41:42)
at Function.app.render (/Users/azat/Documents/Code/proexpressjs/ch2/cli-app/node_modules/express/lib/application.js:485:12)
at ServerResponse.res.render (/Users/azat/Documents/Code/proexpressjs/ch2/cli-app/node_modules/express/lib/response.js:802:7)
at Layer.module.exports [as handle] (/Users/azat/Documents/Code/proexpressjs/ch2/cli-app/app.js:53:9)
at trim_prefix (/Users/azat/Documents/Code/proexpressjs/ch2/cli-app/node_modules/express/lib/router/index.js:235:17)
at /Users/azat/Documents/Code/proexpressjs/ch2/cli-app/node_modules/express/lib/router/index.js:208:9
at Function.proto.process_params (/Users/azat/Documents/Code/proexpressjs/ch2/cli-app/node_modules/express/lib/router/index.js:269:12)
at next (/Users/azat/Documents/Code/proexpressjs/ch2/cli-app/node_modules/express/lib/router/index.js:199:19)
at next (/Users/azat/Documents/Code/proexpressjs/ch2/cli-app/node_modules/express/lib/router/index.js:212:7)
at Layer.app.use.res.render.message [as handle] (/Users/azat/Documents/Code/proexpressjs/ch2/cli-app/app.js:32:5)
GET /jsonp?cb=updateView 500 12ms - 1.22kb

Figure 3-1. *The result of not having a proper template extension set*

The server won't be able to locate the file because our instructions in `cli-app/routes/index.js` are too ambiguous:

```
exports.index = function(req, res){
  res.render('index', { title: 'Express' });
};
```

We can fix this by adding an extension to the `cli-app/routes/index.js` file:

```
exports.index = function(req, res){
  res.render('index.ejs', { title: 'Express' });
};
```

For more information on how to apply different template engines, please refer to the chapter 5.

views

The views setting has an absolute path (starts with / on Mac and Unix) to a directory with templates. This setting defaults to the absolute path of the views folder in the project's root (where the main application file, e.g., app.js, is).

As mentioned in the "MVC Structure and Modules" section of Chapter 2, changing the template folder name is trivial. Typically, when we set the custom value for views in app.js, we use path.join() and the __dirname global variable—which gives us the absolute path to the folder where app.js is. For example, if you want to use folder templates use this configuration statement:

```
app.set('views', path.join(__dirname, 'templates'));
```

trust proxy

Set trust proxy to true if your Node.js app is working behind reverse proxy such as Varnish or Nginx. This will permit trusting in the X-Forwarded-* headers, such as X-Forwarded-Proto (req.protocol) or X-Forwarder-For (req.ips). The trust proxy setting is disabled by default.

If you want to turn it on (when you have a proxy server) you can use one of these statements:

```
app.set('trust proxy', true);
app.enable('trust proxy');
```

jsonp callback name

If you're building an application (a REST API server) that serves requests coming from front-end clients hosted on different domains, you might encounter cross-domain limitations when making XHR/AJAX calls. In other words, browser requests are limited to the same domain (and port). The workaround is to use cross-origin resource sharing (CORS) headers on the server.

If you don't want to apply CORS headers to your server, then the JavaScript object literal notation with prefix (JSONP) is the way to go. Express.js has a res.jsonp() method that makes using JSONP a breeze.

■ **Tip** To find out more about CORS, go to http://en.wikipedia.org/wiki/Cross-origin_resource_sharing.

The default callback name, which is a prefix for our JSONP response, is usually provided in the query string of the request with the name callback; for example, ?callback=updateView. However, if you want to use something different, just set the setting jsonp callback name to that value; for example, for the requests with a query string param ?cb=updateView, we can use this setting:

```
app.set('jsonp callback name', 'cb');
```

That way, our responses would be wrapped in updateView JavaScript code (with the proper Content-Type header, of course) as shown in Figure 3-2.

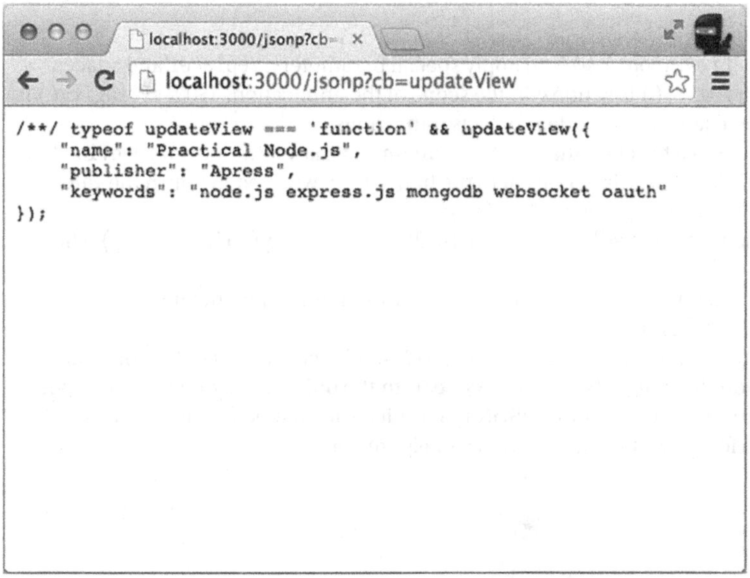

Figure 3-2. *Using cb as the query string name for the callback*

In most cases, we don't want to alter this value because the default `callback` value is somewhat standardized by jQuery `$.ajax` JSONP functions.

If we set `jsonp callback name` to `cb` in the Express.js setting configuration, but make a request with a different property, such as `callback`, then the route won't output JSONP. It will default to JSON format, as shown in Figure 3-3, without the prefix of the function call, which we saw in Figure 3-2.

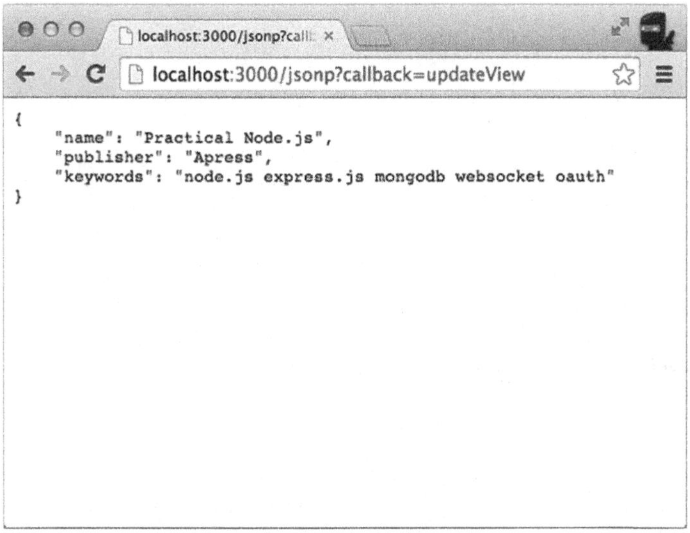

Figure 3-3. *Without the proper callback parameter, JSONP defaults to JSON*

json replacer and json spaces

Likewise, when we use the Express.js method `res.json()`, we can apply special parameters: `replacer` and `spaces`. These parameters are passed to all `JSON.stringify()` functions[1] in the scope of the application. `JSON.stringify()` is a widely used function for transforming native JavaScript/Node.js objects into strings.

The `replacer` parameter acts like a filter. It's a function that takes two arguments: key and value. If `undefined` is returned, then the value is omitted. For the key-value pair to make it to the final string, we need to return the value. You can read more about `replacer` at Mozilla Developer Network (MDN).[2]

Express.js uses `null` as the default value for `json replacer`. I often use `JSON.stringify(obj, null, 2)` when I need to print pretty JSON.

The `spaces` parameter is in essence an indentation size. Its value defaults to `2` in development and to `0` in production. In most cases, we leave these settings alone.

In our example app `ch3/app.js`, we have a `/json` route that sends us back an object with a book's information. We define a `replacer` parameter as a function that omits the discount code from the object (we don't want to expose this info). And the `spaces` parameter is set to `4` so that we can see JSON that is nicely formatted for humans instead of some jumbled code. The resulting response for the `/json` route is shown in Figure 3-4.

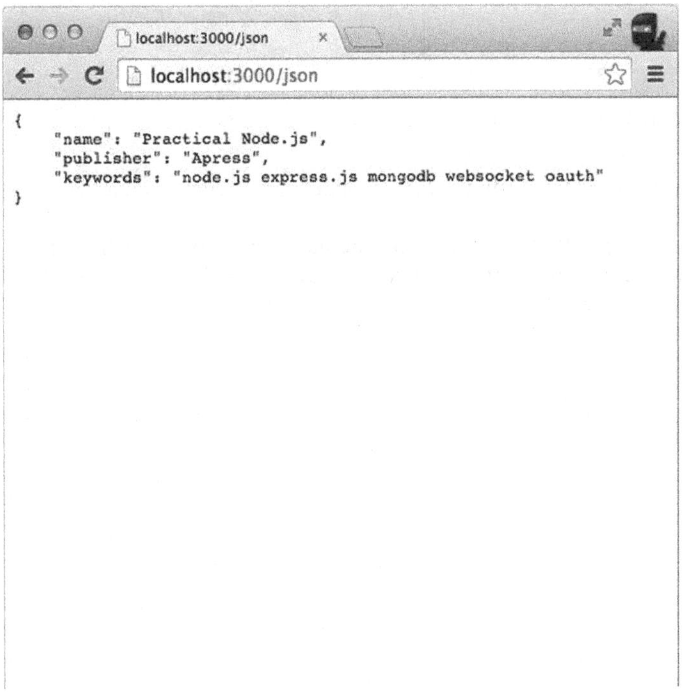

Figure 3-4. *JSON output with replacer and spaces set*

[1] https://developer.mozilla.org/en-US/docs/Web/JavaScript/Reference/Global_Objects/JSON/stringify
[2] https://developer.mozilla.org/en-US/docs/Using_native_JSON#The_replacer_parameter

These are the statements used in the example app:

```
app.set('json replacer', function(key, value){
  if (key === 'discount')
    return undefined;
  else
    return value;
});
app.set('json spaces', 4);
```

If we remove `json spaces`, the app will produce the results shown in Figure 3-5.

Figure 3-5. *JSON output without spaces set*

case sensitive routing

The `case sensitive routing` flag should be self-explanatory. We disregard the case of the URL paths when it's `false`, which is the default value, and do otherwise when the value is set to true. For example, if we have `app.enable('case sensitive routing');`, then `/users` and `/Users` won't be the same. It's best to have this option disabled for the sake of avoiding confusion.

strict routing

The next setting (or a flag because it has the boolean meaning) `strict routing` deals with cases of trailing slashes in URLs. With `strict routing` enabled, such as `app.set('strict routing', true);`, the paths will be treated differently; for example, `/users` and `/users/` will be completely separate routes. In the example `ch3/app.js`, we have two identical routes but one has a trailing slash. They send back different strings:

```
app.get('/users', function(request, response){
  response.send('users');
})
app.get('/users/', function(request, response){
  response.send('users/');
})
```

As a result, the browser will have different messages for `/users` and `/users/`, as shown in Figure 3-6.

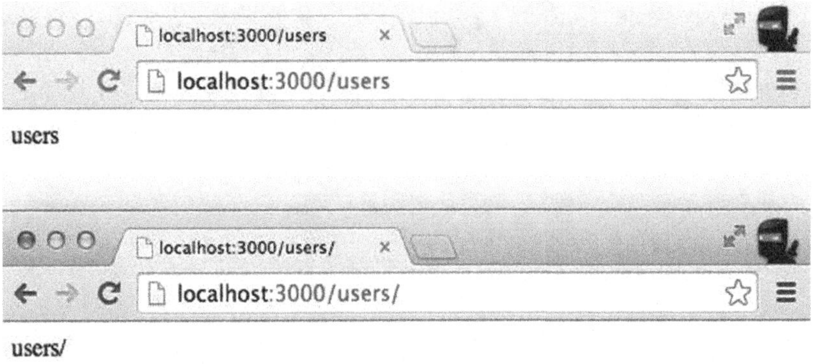

Figure 3-6. *With strict routing enabled, /users and users/ are different routes*

By default, this parameter is set to `false`, which means that the trailing slash is ignored and those routes with a trailing slash will be treated the same as their counterparts without a trailing slash. My recommendation is to leave the default value; that is, treat the routes with slashes the same as the routes without slashes. This recommendation doesn't apply if your API architecture requires them to be treated differently.

x-powered-by

The `x-powered-by` option sets the HTTP response header `X-Powered-By` to the `Express` value. This option is enabled by default, as you can see in Figure 3-7.

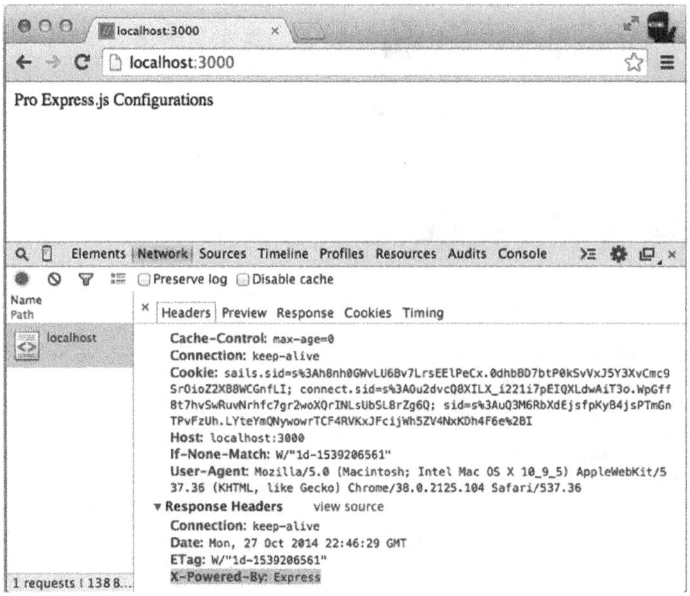

Figure 3-7. *X-Powered-By Express is enabled (by default)*

If you want to disable `x-powered-by` (remove it from the response)—which is recommended for security reasons, because it's harder to find vulnerabilities if your platform is unknown—then apply `app.set('x-powered-by', false)` or `app.disable('x-powered-by')`, which removes the X-Powered-By response header (as in the example `ch3/app.js` and as shown in Figure 3-8).

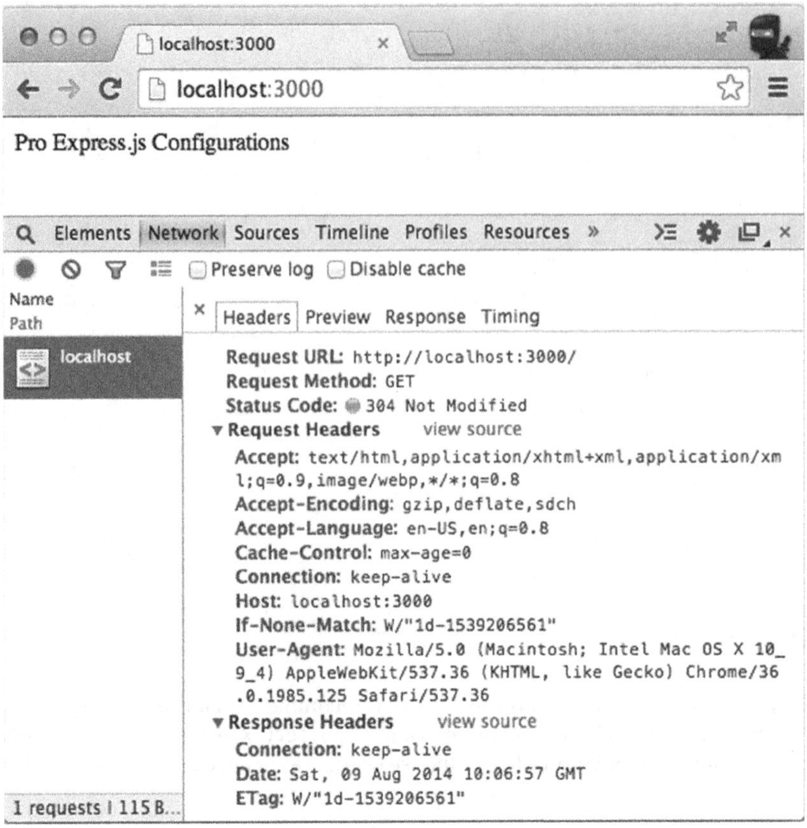

Figure 3-8. *X-Powered-By Express is disabled and there's no response header*

etag

ETag[3] (or entity tag) is a caching tool. The way it works is akin to the unique identifier for the content on a given URL. In other words, if content doesn't change on a specific URL, the ETag will remain the same and the browser will use the cache. Figure 3-7 and Figure 3-8 include an example of the ETag response header. The code for this example is available in `ch3/app.js`.

If someone doesn't know what ETag is or how to use it, then it's better to leave the Express.js default etag setting as it is, which is on (boolean true). Otherwise, to disable ETag, use `app.disable('etag');`, which will eliminate the ETag HTTP response header.

By default, Express.js uses "weak" ETag. Other possible values are `false` (no ETag), `true` (weak ETag), and `strong` (strong ETag). The last option (for advanced developers) that Express.js provides is using your own ETag algorithm:

```
app.set('etag', function (body, encoding) {
  return customEtag(body, encoding); // you define the customEtag function
})
```

---

[3]`http://en.wikipedia.org/wiki/HTTP_ETag`

If you're not familiar with what weak or strong means, here's the short explanation of the differences between these types of ETags: an identical strong ETag guarantees the response is byte-for-byte the same, while an identical weak ETag indicates that the response is semantically the same. So you'll get different levels of caching with weak and strong ETags. Of course, this is a very brief and vague explanation. Please do you own research if this topic is important for your project.

query parser

A *query string* is data sent in the URL after the question mark (for example, `?name=value&name2=value2`). This format needs to be parsed into JavaScript/Node.js object format before we can use it. Express.js automatically includes this query parsing for our convenience. It does so by enabling the `query parser` setting.

The default value for `query parser` is `extended`, which uses the `qs` module's functionality.[4] Other possible values are

- `false`: Disable parsing
- `true`: Uses `qs`
- `simple`: Uses the core `querystring` module's functionality (`http://nodejs.org/api/querystring.html`)

It's possible to pass your own function as an argument, in which case your custom function will be used for parsing instead of parsing libraries. If you pass your own function, your custom parsing function must take a string argument and return a JavaScript/Node.js object similar to the `parse` function's signature from the core `querystring` module.[5]

The following are examples in which we set `query parser` to use `querystring`, no parsing and a custom parsing function:

```
app.set('query parser', 'simple');
app.set('query parser', false);
app.set('query parser', customQueryParsingFunction);
```

subdomain offset

The `subdomain offset` setting controls the value returned by the `req.subdomains` property. This setting is useful when the app is deployed on multiple subdomains, such as `http://ncbi.nlm.nih.gov`.

By default, the last two "subdomains" (the two extreme right parts) in the hostname/URL are dropped and the rest are returned in reverse order in the `req.subdomains`; so for our example of `http://ncbi.nlm.nih.gov`, the resulting `req.subdomains` is `['nlm', 'ncbi']`.

However, if the app has `subdomain offset` set to 3 by `app.set('subdomain offset', 3);`, the result of `req.subdomains` will be just `['ncbi']`, because Express.js will drop the three (3) parts starting from the right (`nlm`, `nih`, and `gov`).

Environments

As many of you know, most applications don't run in a single environment. Those environments usually include at least development, testing and production. Each of the environments puts a different requirement on the app. For example, in development the app error messaging needs to be as verbose as possible, while in production it needs to be user friendly and not compromise any system or user's personally identifiable information (PII[6]) data to hackers.

---

[4]`https://github.com/hapijs/qs`
[5]`http://nodejs.org/api/querystring.html#querystring_querystring_parse_str_sep_eq_options`
[6]`http://en.wikipedia.org/wiki/Personally_identifiable_information`

The code needs to accommodate different environments without us, the developers, having to modify it every time we deploy to a different environment.

Of course, we can write up some `if else` statements based on the `process.env.NODE_ENV` value; for example:

```
if ('development' === process.env.NODE_ENV) {
```

If the line above seems strange to you, keep in mind that it's the exact equivalent of `process.env.NODE_ENV === 'development'`. Alternatively, you can use `process.env.NODE_ENV == 'development'` which will convert the `NODE_ENV` to string for you, before the comparison (if for some reason it's not a string already).

```
  // Connect to development database
} else if ('production' === process.env.NODE_ENV) {
  // Connect to production database
 }; // Continue for staging and preview environments
```

Or using the Express.js env param (refer to the "env" section earlier in the chapter):

```
// Assuming that app is a reference to Express.js instance
if ('development' === app.get('env')) {
  // Connect to development database
} else if ('production' === app.get('env')) {
  // Connect to production database
 }; // Continue for staging and preview environments
```

Another example of `app.get('env')` is one from the skeleton Express.js Generator app. It applies a more verbose error handler (sends the whole stacktrace from the `err` object) for the development environment than one for production or any other environment:

```
if (app.get('env') === 'development') {
    app.use(function(err, req, res, next) {
        res.status(err.status || 500);
        res.render('error', {
            message: err.message,
            error: err
        });
    });
}
```

If the environment is anything but `development`, instead of the error handler above, Express.js will use this one in which no stacktraces are leaked to a user:

```
app.use(function(err, req, res, next) {
    res.status(err.status || 500);
    res.render('error', {
        message: err.message,
        error: {}
    });
});
```

APP.CONFIGURE

The `app.configure()` method, which allows for more elegant environmental configuration, is *deprecated* in Express.js 4.x. However, you should still know how it works, because you might encounter it in older projects.

When the app.configure() method is invoked with one parameter it applies the callback to **all** environments. For example, if you want to set an author email and app name for any environment, then you can write:

```
app.configure(function(){
  app.set('appName', 'Pro Express.js Demo App');
  app.set('authorEmail', 'hi@azat.co');
});
```

However, if we pass two parameters (or more) with the first being an environment and the last one is still a function, the code will be called only when the app is in those environment modes (e.g., development, production).

For example, you can set different `dbUri` values (database connection strings) for development and stage with these callbacks:

```
app.configure('development', function() {
  app.set('dbUri', 'mongodb://localhost:27017/db');
});
app.configure('stage', 'production', function() {
  app.set('dbUri', process.env.MONGOHQ_URL);
});
```

■ **Tip** Express.js often uses the difference in the number of input parameters and their types to direct functions' behavior. Therefore, pay close attention to how you invoke your methods.

Now that you're familiar with the settings, here's the demo kitchen-sink application. In it we gathered all the aforementioned settings to illustrate the examples. As you inspect the code, notice the order of the configuration statements in the file! They must be after the `var app` instantiation, but before middleware and routes. Here's the full source code of the example server `ch3/app.js`:

```
var book = {name: 'Practical Node.js',
  publisher: 'Apress',
  keywords: 'node.js express.js mongodb websocket oauth',
  discount: 'PNJS15'
}
var express = require('express'),
  path = require('path');

var app = express();

console.log(app.get('env'));
```

```
app.set('view cache', true);
app.set('views', path.join(__dirname, 'views'));
app.set('view engine', 'jade');
app.set('port', process.env.PORT || 3000);

app.set('trust proxy', true);
app.set('jsonp callback name', 'cb');
app.set('json replacer', function(key, value){
  if (key === 'discount')
    return undefined;
  else
    return value;
});
app.set('json spaces', 4);

app.set('case sensitive routing', true);
app.set('strict routing', true);
app.set('x-powered-by', false);
app.set('subdomain offset', 3);
// app.disable('etag')

app.get('/jsonp', function(request, response){
  response.jsonp(book);
})
app.get('/json', function(request, response){
  response.send(book);
})
app.get('/users', function(request, response){
  response.send('users');
})
app.get('/users/', function(request, response){
  response.send('users/');
})
app.get('*', function(request, response){
  response.send('Pro Express.js Configurations');
})

if (app.get('env') === 'development') {
    app.use(function(err, req, res, next) {
        res.status(err.status || 500);
        res.render('error', {
            message: err.message,
            error: err
        });
    });
}
var server = app.listen(app.get('port'), function() {
  console.log('Express server listening on port ' + server.address().port);
});
```

Summary

In this chapter, we covered how to configure Express.js system settings using methods such as app.set(), app.disable(), and app.enable(). You learned how to get the settings values with app.get() and app.enabled() and app.disabled(). Then, we covered all the important Express.js settings, their meaning and values. You also saw that settings can be arbitrary and used for storing app-specific custom info (e.g., port number or app name).

If you remember the app structure from Chapter 1, the middleware goes after the configuration section in the main Express.js app file. Both third-party middleware and custom middleware are available to use with Express.js. When you write your own middleware, it's a way to reuse and organize the code.

There is abundance of third-party Express.js middleware modules on NPM. They can do many tasks from parsing to authentication. By using third-party middleware, you are enhancing and customizing the behavior of your application. So middleware can be considered as configuration of its own kind (configuration on steroids!). Read on to master the most commonly used middleware!

CHAPTER 4

Working with Middleware

Middleware is an amazingly useful pattern that allows developers to reuse code within their applications and even share it with others in the form of NPM modules. The essential definition of *middleware* is a function with three arguments: `request` (or `req`), `response` (`res`), and `next`. If you're writing your own middleware, you can use arbitrary names for arguments, but it's better to stick to the common naming convention. Here's an example of how to define your own middleware:

```
var myMiddleware = function (req, res, next) {
  // Do something with req and/or res
  next();
};
```

When writing your own middleware, don't forget to call the `next()` callback function. Otherwise, the request will hang and time out. The request (`req`) and response (`res`) objects are the same for the subsequent middleware, so you can add properties to them (e.g., `req.user = 'Azat'`) to access them later.

In this chapter we'll cover the following topics:

- *Applying middleware*: How to use middleware in Express.js apps
- *Essential middleware*: The most commonly used middleware, Connect.js middleware, and the middleware that was part of Express.js before version 4.x
- *Other middleware*: The most useful and popular third-party middleware

Unlike a traditional technical book chapter that describes how to build a single large project, this chapter extensively describes the most popular and used middleware modules. Similar to Chapter 3, this chapter is something akin to a reference. To demo you the middleware's features, there's a kitchen sink—meaning it has lots of different things—example in the `ch4` folder. As usual, the code will be listed in the book and available in the GitHub repo at `https://github.com/azat-co/proexpressjs`.

Applying Middleware

To set up middleware, we use the `app.use()` method from the Express.js API. This is applicable to both third-party middleware and in-house middleware.

The method `app.use()` has one optional string parameter path and one mandatory function parameter callback. For example, to implement a logger with a date, time, request method, and URL, we use the `console.log()` method:

```
// Instantiate the Express.js app
app.use(function(req, res, next) {
  console.log('%s %s — %s', (new Date).toString(), req.method, req.url);
  return next();
});
// Implement server routes
```

On the other hand, if we want to prefix the middleware, a.k.a. *mounting*, we can use the `path` parameter, which restricts the use of this particular middleware to only the routes that have such a prefix. For example, to limit the logging to only the admin dashboard route `/admin`, we can write

```
// Instantiate the Express.js app
app.use('/admin', function(req, res, next) {
  console.log('%s %s — %s', (new Date).toString(), req.method, req.url);
  return next();
});
// Actually implement the /admin route
```

Writing everything from scratch, even as trivial as logging and serving of the static files, is obviously not much fun. Therefore, instead of implementing our own modules, we can utilize `express.static()` and `morgan` middleware functions. Here's an example of using `express.static()` and `morgan` middleware:

```
var express = require('express');
var logger = require('morgan');
// Instantiate and configure the app
app.use(logger('combined'));
app.use(express.static(__dirname + '/public'));
// Implement server routes
```

■ **Note** In Express.js version 3.x and earlier (i.e., before version 4.x), logger was part of Express.js and could be called with `express.logger()`.

Static is the only middleware that remains bundled with Express.js version 4.x. Its NPM module is `serve-static`. Static middleware enables pass-through requests for static assets. Those assets are typically stored in the `public` folder (please refer to the Chapter 2 for more information on recommended folder structure).

Here's a more advanced static middleware example that restricts assets to their respective folders. This is called mounting and achieved by providing two arguments to `app.use()`: route path and middleware function:

```
app.use('/css', express.static(__dirname + '/public/css'));
app.use('/img', express.static(__dirname + '/public/images'));
app.use('/js', express.static(__dirname + '/public/javascripts'));
```

A global path avoids ambiguity, which is why we use `__dirname`.

The pattern that static middleware is using behind the scenes is another good trick to have in your sleeves when you write your own middleware. This is now how it works: if you look closely, `express.static()` accepts a folder name as a parameter . This enables the middleware to change its behavior or modes dynamically. This pattern is called a monad, although people familiar with functional programming might argue that monad is something different. Anyway, the main idea here is that we have a function that stores data and returns another function.

The way this pattern is implemented in JavaScript/Node.js and modules like `serve-static` is with the `return` keyword. Here's an example where a custom `myMiddleware` function takes a parameter, and returns either different middleware A or the default middleware depending on whether or not the argument deep equals (===) to A :

```
var myMiddleware = function (param) {
  if (param === 'A') {
    return function(req, res, next) { // <---Middleware A
      // Do A stuff
      return next();
    }
  } else {
    return function(req, res, next) { // The default middleware
      // Do default stuff
      return next();
  }
}
```

The `ch4/app.js` example, shown next, demonstrates how to apply (`app.use()`) the middleware `static`, `morgan` and other. The parameters and routes for each middleware used in the example are covered in their respective sections.

The full source code of the `ch4/app.js` to demo how to apply middleware (and to give you something working for the other middleware modules):

```
// Import and instantiate dependencies
var express = require('express'),
  path = require('path'),
  fs = require('fs'),
  compression = require('compression'),
  logger = require('morgan'),
  timeout = require('connect-timeout'),
  methodOverride = require('method-override'),
  responseTime = require('response-time'),
  favicon = require('serve-favicon'),
  serveIndex = require('serve-index'),
  vhost = require('vhost'),
  busboy = require('connect-busboy'),
  errorhandler = require('errorhandler');

var app = express();
// Configure settings
app.set('view cache', true);
app.set('views', path.join(__dirname, 'views'));
app.set('view engine', 'jade');
app.set('port', process.env.PORT || 3000);
app.use(compression({threshold: 1}));
app.use(logger('combined'));
```

```
app.use(methodOverride('_method'));
app.use(responseTime(4));
app.use(favicon(path.join('public', 'favicon.ico')));
// Apply middleware
app.use('/shared', serveIndex(
  path.join('public','shared'),
  {'icons': true}
));
app.use(express.static('public'));
// Define routes
app.use('/upload', busboy({immediate: true}));
app.use('/upload', function(request, response) {
  request.busboy.on('file', function(fieldname, file, filename, encoding, mimetype) {
    file.on('data', function(data){
      fs.writeFile('upload' + fieldname + filename, data);
    });
    file.on('end', function(){
      console.log('File' + filename + 'is ended');
    });

  });
 request.busboy.on('finish', function(){
    console.log('Busboy is finished');
   response.status(201).end();
 })
});

app.get(
  '/slow-request',
  timeout('1s'),
  function(request, response, next) {
    setTimeout(function(){
      if (request.timedout) return false;
      return next();
    }, 999 + Math.round(Math.random()));
  }, function(request, response, next) {
    response.send('ok');
  }
);

app.delete('/purchase-orders', function(request, response){
  console.log('The DELETE route has been triggered');
  response.status(204).end();
});

app.get('/response-time', function(request, response){
  setTimeout(function(){
    response.status(200).end();
  }, 513);
});
```

```
app.get('/', function(request, response){
  response.send('Pro Express.js Middleware');
});
app.get('/compression', function(request, response){
  response.render('index');
})
// Apply error handlers
app.use(errorhandler());
// Boot the server
var server = app.listen(app.get('port'), function() {
  console.log('Express server listening on port' + server.address().port);
});
```

Now that you know how to apply both third-party and in-house middleware, the next step is to identify which third-party middleware is essential. And what is available to developers and allows them to save themselves and teammates from the *"fun"* of implementing, maintaining, and testing the functionality that the NPM modules provide.

Essential Middleware

As you've seen in the previous section, middleware is nothing more than a function that takes `req` and `res` objects. Express.js version 4.x provides only one middleware function out of the box: `express.static()`. Most of the middleware needs to be installed and imported. The essential middleware usually stems from Sencha's Connect library: `http://www.senchalabs.org/connect/` (NPM: `https://npmjs.org/package/connect`; GitHub: `https://github.com/senchalabs/connect`).

The main thing to remember when using middleware is that the order in which middleware functions are applied with the `app.use()` function matters, *because this is the order in which they'll be executed.* In other words, developers need to be cautious about the sequence of the middleware statements (in `app.js`), because this sequence will dictate the order in which each request will go through the corresponding middleware functions.

Are you confused already? Look at this example: a session (`express-session`) must follow a cookie (`cookie-parser`), because any web session depends on the cookies for storing the session ID (and it is provided by `cookie-parser`). If we move them around the sessions won't work! Another example is Cross-Site Request Forgery middleware `csurf` that requires `express-session`.

To make the point completely clear, middleware statements go before routes for the exact same reason. If you put static (`express.static()` or `serve-static`) middleware after a route definition, then the framework will finish the request flow by responding and the static assets (e.g., from `/public`) won't be served to the client.

Let's dig deeper into the following middleware:

- `compression`
- `morgan`
- `body-parser`
- `cookie-parser`
- `express-session`
- `csurf`
- `express.static` or `serve-static`
- `connect-timeout`
- `errorhandler`

- method-override
- response-time
- serve-favicon
- serve-index
- vhost
- connect-busboy

compression

The compression middleware (NPM: http://npmjs.org/compression) gzips transferred data. Gzip or GNU zip is a compression utility. To install compression v1.0.11, run this command in your terminal in the project's root folder:

```
$ npm install compression@1.0.11 --save
```

Do you remember that the order of the middleware statements matters? That's why the compression middleware is usually placed at the very beginning of an Express.js app configuration, so that it precedes the other middleware and routes. The compression is utilized with the compression() method:

```
var compression = require('compression');
// ... Typical Express.js set up...
app.use(compression());
```

■ **Tip** You need to install the compression NPM module in the project (i.e., local) node_modules folder. You can do so with $ npm install compression@1.0.10 --save or by putting the line "compression": "1.0.10" into the package.json file and running $ npm install.

The compression() method is good to go without any extra parameters, but if you are an advanced Node.js programmer, you may want to use the gzip options for compression:

- threshold: The size in kilobits at which to start compression (i.e., the minimum size in kilobits that can go uncompressed)
- filter: Function to filter out what to compress; the default filter is compressible, available at https://github.com/expressjs/compressible.

Gzip uses the core Node.js module zlib (http://nodejs.org/api/zlib.html#zlib_options) and just passes these options to it:

- chunkSize: Size of the chunks to use (default: 16*1024)
- windowBits: Window size
- level: Compression level
- memLevel: How much memory to allocate
- strategy: What gzip compression algorithm to apply
- filter: Function that by default tests for the Content-Type header to be json, text, or javascript

For more information on these options, please see the zlib docs at `http://zlib.net/manual.html#Advanced`.

In the `ch4` project, we create an `index.jade` file with some dummy text, then add the following to the `app.js` file:

```
var compression = require('compression');
// ... Configurations
app.use(compression({threshold: 1}));
```

The `views/index.jade` file will render `h1` and `p` HTML elements with some Lorem Ipsum text, as follows:

```
h1 hi
p Lorem Ipsum is simply dummy text of ...
```

■ **Tip** For a thorough Jade template engine tutorial, consult *Practical Node.js* (Apress, 2014).

As a result of applying `compression`, in the Chrome browser Developer Tools console, you can see the `Content-Encoding: gzip` response header, as shown in Figure 4-1.

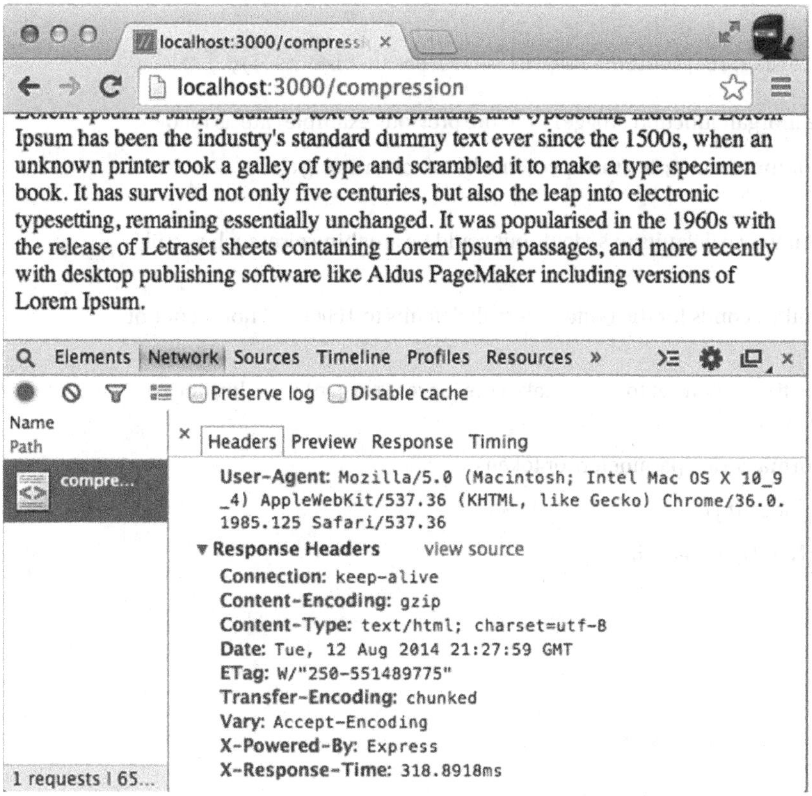

Figure 4-1. *Content-Encoding is gzip with the compression middleware in use*

morgan

The morgan middleware (https://www.npmjs.org/package/morgan) keeps track of all the requests and other important information depending on the output format specified. To install morgan v1.2.2, use

```
$ npm install morgan@1.2.2 --save
```

Morgan takes either an options object or a format string (common, dev, etc.); for example,

```
var logger = require('morgan');
// ... Configurations
app.use(logger('common'));
```

or

```
var logger = require('morgan');
// ... Configurations
app.use(logger('dev'));
```

or

```
var logger = require('morgan');
// ... Configurations
app.use(logger(':method :url :status :res[content-length] - :response-time ms'));
```

Supported options to pass to the morgan function (logger() in the previous example) are as follows:

- format: A string with an output format; see the upcoming list of token string and predefined formats.
- stream: The output stream to use defaults to stdout, but could be anything else, such as a file or another stream.
- buffer: The number of milliseconds for the buffer interval; defaults to 1000ms if not set or not a number.
- immediate: Boolean value that, when set to true, makes the logger (morgan) write log lines on request instead of response.

The following are the available format string parameters or tokens:

- :req[header] (e.g., :req[Accept])
- :res[header] (e.g., :res[Content-Length])
- :http-version
- :response-time
- :remote-addr
- :date
- :method
- :url

- :referrer
- :user-agent
- :status

The following are the predefined formats/tokens that come with Morgan:

- combined: Same as `:remote-addr - :remote-user [:date] ":method :url HTTP/:http-version" :status :res[content-length] ":referrer" ":user-agent"`
- common: Same as `:remote-addr - :remote-user [:date] ":method :url HTTP/:http-version" :status :res[content-length]`
- short: Same as `:remote-addr :remote-user :method :url HTTP/:http-version :status :res[content-length] - :response-time ms`
- tiny: Same as `:method :url :status :res[content-length] - :response-time ms`
- dev: Short and colored development output with response statuses, same as `:method :url :status :response-time ms - :res[content-length]`

You could also define your own formats. For more information, please refer to the morgan documentation at https://www.npmjs.org/package/morgan.

body-parser

The body-parser module (https://www.npmjs.org/package/body-parser) is probably the most essential of all the third-party middleware modules. It allows developers to process incoming data, such as body payload, into usable JavaScript/Node.js objects. To install body-parser v1.6.1, run this command:

```
$ npm install body-parser@1.6.1
```

The body-parser module has the following distinct middleware:

- json(): Processes JSON data; e.g., `{"name": "value", "name2": "value"}`
- urlencoded(): Processes URL-encoded data; e.g., name=value&name2=value2
- raw(): Returns body as a buffer type
- text(): Returns body as string type

If the request has a MIME type of application/json, the json() middleware will try to parse the request payload as JSON. The result will be put in the req.body object and passed to the next middleware and routes.

We can pass the following options as properties:

- strict: Boolean true or false; if it's true (default), then a 400 status error (Bad Request) will be passed to the next() callback when the first character is not [or {.
- reviver: A second parameter to the JSON.parse() function that transforms the output; more info is available at MDN.[1]
- limit: Maximum byte size; disabled by default.

[1]https://developer.mozilla.org/en-US/docs/Web/JavaScript/Reference/Global_Objects/JSON/parse

- `inflate`: Inflates the deflated body; default is `true`.
- `type`: Content-Type to parse; default is `json`.
- `verify`: A function to verify the body.

For example, if you need to skip the private methods/properties (by convention they begin with the underscore symbol, _), apply nonstrict parsing, and have a limit of 5,000 bytes, you could enter the following:

```
var bodyParser = require('body-parser');
// ... Express.js app set up
app.use(bodyParer.json({
  strict: false,
  reviver: function(key, value) {
    if (key.substr(0,1) === '_') {
      return undefined;
    } else {
      return value;
    }
  },
  limit: 5000
}));
// ...Boot-up
```

urlencoded()

This `body-parser` module's `urlencoded()` middleware parses *only* requests with the `x-ww-form-urlencoded` header. It utilizes the qs module's (`https://npmjs.org/package/qs`) `querystring.parse()` function and puts the resulting JS object into `req.body`.

In addition to `limit`, `type`, `verify`, and `inflate`, `urlencoded()` takes an extended boolean option. The extended option is a *mandatory* field. When it is set to `true` (the default value), `body-parser` uses the qs module (`https://www.npmjs.org/package/qs`) to parse query strings.

If you set extended to `false`, body-parser uses the core Node.js module `querystring` for parsing of URL-encoded data. I recommend setting extended to `true` (that is, to use `qs`) because it allows objects and arrays to be parsed from URL-encoded strings.

If you forget what a URL-encoded string looks like, it's a `name=value&name2=value2` string after the question mark (`?`) in the URL.

We can also pass the `limit` parameter to `urlencoded()`. The `limit` option works similarly to the `limit` in the `bodyParser.json()` middleware, which you saw in the previous code snippet. For example, to set the `limit` to 10,000:

```
var bodyParser = require('body-parser');
// ... Express.js set up
app.use(bodyParser.urlencoded({limit: 10000});
```

■ **Caution** In older versions, bodyParser.multipart() middleware is known to be prone to malfunctioning when handling large file uploads. The exact problem is described by Andrew Kelley in the article "Do Not Use bodyParser with Express.js."[2] The current versions of Express.js v 4.x unbundled support for bodyParser.multipart(). Instead, the Express.js team recommends using busboy,[3] formidable,[4] or multiparty.[5]

cookie-parser

The `cookie-parser` middleware (`https://www.npmjs.org/package/cookie-parser`) allows us to access user cookie values from the `req.cookie` object in request handlers. The method takes a string, which is used for signing cookies. Usually, it's some clever pseudo-random sequence (e.g., `very secret string`). To install `cookie-parser` v1.3.2, run this command:

```
$ npm install cookie-parser@1.3.2
```

Use it like this:

```
var cookieParser = require('cookie-parser');
// ... Some Express.js set up
app.use(cookieParser());
```

or with the secret string (arbitrary random string, usually stored in an environment variable):

```
app.use(cookieParser('cats and dogs can learn JavaScript'));
```

■ **Caution** *Avoid* storing any sensitive information in cookies, especially user-related information (personally identifiable information), such as credentials, or their preferences. In most cases, use cookies only to store a unique and hard-to-guess key (session ID) that matches a value on the server. That enables you to retrieve a user session on subsequent requests.

In addition to secret, the cookieParser() also takes these options as a second parameter:

- `path`: A cookie path
- `expires`: Absolute expiration date for the cookie
- `maxAge`: Relative maximum age of the cookie
- `domain`: The web site domain for the cookie
- `secure`: Boolean indicating whether the cookie is secure or not
- `httpOnly`: Boolean indicating whether HTTP only or not

[2]http://andrewkelley.me/post/do-not-use-bodyparser-with-express-js.html
[3]https://www.npmjs.org/package/busboy
[4]https://www.npmjs.org/package/formidable
[5]https://www.npmjs.org/package/multiparty

cookie-parser has some additional methods:

- `JSONCookie(string)`: Parse string into a JSON data format
- `JSONCookies(cookies)`: Same as `JSONCookie(string)` but for objects
- `signedCookie(string, secret)`: Parse a cookie value as a signed cookie
- `signedCookies(cookies, secret)`: Same as `signedCookie(string, secret)` but for objects

express-session

The `express-session` middleware (`https://www.npmjs.org/package/express-session`) allows the server to use web sessions. This middleware *must have* `cookie-parser` enabled before its definition (higher in the `app.js` file). To install `express-session` v1.7.6, run this command:

```
$ npm install express-session@1.7.6 --save
```

The `express-session` v1.7.6 middleware takes these options:

- `key`: Cookie name, defaulting to `connect.sid`
- `store`: Session store instance, usually a Redis object (covered in detail in Chapter 12)
- `secret`: Used to sign the session cookie, to prevent tampering; usually just a random string
- `cookie`: Session cookie settings, defaulting to `{ path: '/', httpOnly: true, maxAge: null }`
- `proxy`: Boolean that indicates whether to trust the reverse proxy when setting secure cookies (via `"X-Forwarded-Proto"`)
- `saveUninitialized`: Boolean that forces the saving of a new session (default is true)
- `unset`: Controls if you want to keep the session in the store after unsetting the session with possible values `keep` and `destroy` (default is `keep`)
- `resave`: Boolean that forces the saving of the unmodified session (default is true)
- `rolling`: Boolean that sets a new cookie on each request which resets the expiration (default is false)
- `genid`: A function that generates session ID (default is `uid2`: `https://www.npmjs.org/package/uid2`, `https://github.com/coreh/uid2`)

By default, sessions are stored in the memory. However, we can use Redis for persistence and for sharing sessions between multiple machines. For more information on Express.js sessions, please refer to Part 3, particularly Chapter 12.

csurf

Cross-site request forgery (CSRF) occurs when a client still has session information from a protected web site, such as a bank's web site, and a malicious script submits data on the client's behalf, which could even be a money transfer. The attack succeeds because the bank's server can't distinguish between the client's valid request from the bank's web site and the malicious request from some compromised or untrustworthy web site. The browser has the right session, but the user wasn't on the bank's website's page!!!

To prevent CSRF, we can enable CSRF protection by using a token with each request and validating that token against our records. This way we know that we served the page or resource from which the subsequent request with submitted data is coming. For more information, please refer to the Wikipedia CSRF entry at `http://en.wikipedia.org/wiki/Cross-site_request_forgery`.

The CSRF protection with the csurf module (https://www.npmjs.org/package/csurf) is handled by Express.js by putting a _csrf token in the session (req.session._csrf) and validating that value against values in req.body, req.query, and the X-CSRF-Token header. If the values don't match, the 403 Forbidden HTTP status code is returned, which means that the resource is forbidden (see, e.g., http://en.wikipedia.org/wiki/HTTP_403). The csurf middleware doesn't check GET, HEAD, or OPTIONS methods by default. To install csurf v1.6.0, run this command:

```
$ npm install csurf@1.6.0 --save
```

The most minimal examples of using csurf v1.6.0 is as follows:

```
var csrf = require('csurf');
// ... Instantiate Express.js application
app.use(csrf());
```

The csurf v1.6.0 takes the following additional parameters:

- value: A function that takes request (req) as an argument, checks for the presense of the token, and returns the value true (found) or false (not found). Look at the example below.
- cookie: Specifies to use the cookie-based store instead of the default session-based one (not recommended)
- ignoreMethods: An array of HTTP methods to ignore when checking for the CSRF token in requests (default value is ['GET', 'HEAD', 'OPTIONS'])

You can override the default function that checks the token value presence by passing a callback function in a value property; for example, to use a different name and check against *only* the request body, you can use

```
var csrf = require('csurf');
// ... Instantiate Express.js application
app.use(express.csrf({
  value: function (req) {
    return (req.body && req.body.cross_site_request_forgery_value);
  }
}));
```

The csrf middleware must be after express-session, cookie-parser, and optionally (meaning if you plan to support tokens in the body of requests) after body-parser middlewares:

```
var bodyParser = require('body-parser');
var cookieParser = require('cookie-parser');
var session = require('express-session');
var csrf = require('csurf');
// ... Instantiate Express.js application
app.use(bodyParser.json());
app.use(cookieParser());
app.use(session());
app.use(csrf());
```

express.static()

The `express.static()` or `serve-static` as a stand-alone module (`https://www.npmjs.org/package/serve-static`) is the only middleware that comes with Express.js version 4.x, so you don't have to install it. In other words, under the hood, `express.static()` is a `serve-static` module: `https://github.com/expressjs/serve-static`. We already covered the `express.static(path, options)` method that serves files from a specified root path to the folder, such as:

```
app.use(express.static(path.join(__dirname, 'public')));
```

or (not recommended because this might not work on Windows):

```
app.use(express.static(__dirname + '/public'));
```

A relative path is also an option:

```
app.use(express.static('public'));
```

The `express.static(path, options)` v1.5.0 (for Express.js v4.8.1) method takes these options:

- `maxAge`: Number of milliseconds to set for browser cache maxAge, which defaults to `0`
- `redirect`: Boolean `true` or `false` (default is `true`) indicating whether to allow a redirect to a trailing slash (/) when the URL pathname is a directory
- `dotfiles`: Indicates how to treat hidden system folders/files (e.g., `.gitignore`); possible values are `ignore` (default), `allow`, and `deny`
- `etag`: Boolean indicating whether or not to use ETag caching (default is `true`)
- `extensions`: Boolean indicating whether or not to use the default file extensions (default is `false`)
- `index`: Identifies the index file; default is `index.html`; an array, a string and `false` (disable) are possible values
- `setHeaders`: A function to set custom response headers

Here's an example of the express.static() advanced usage with some arbitrary values:

```
app.use(express.static(__dirname + '/public', {
  maxAge: 86400000,
  redirect: false,
  hidden: true,
  'index': ['index.html', 'index.htm']
}));
```

connect-timeout

The `connect-timeout` module (`https://www.npmjs.org/package/connect-timeout`) sets a timeout. Use of this middleware is recommended only on specific routes (e.g., `'/slow-route'`) that you suspect might be slower than average ones. To use `connect-timeout` v1.2.2, install it with:

```
$ npm install connect-timeout@1.2.2 --save
```

In your server file, write these statements as shown in example ch4/app.js:

```
var timeout = require('connect-timeout');
// ... Instantiation and configuration
app.get(
  '/slow-request',
  timeout('1s'),
  function(request, response, next) {
    setTimeout(function(){
      if (request.timedout) return false;
      return next();
    }, 999 + Math.round(Math.random()));
  }, function(request, response, next) {
    response.send('ok');
  }
);
// ... Routes and boot-up
```

Run the server with $ node app. Then, from the separate terminal, send a few GET requests with CURL:

```
$ curl http://localhost:3000/slow-request -i
```

The response should time out about half of the time with a 503 Service Unavailable status code. The good response returns status code 200. Both are shown in Figure 4-2. It's possible to customize the message in the error handlers.

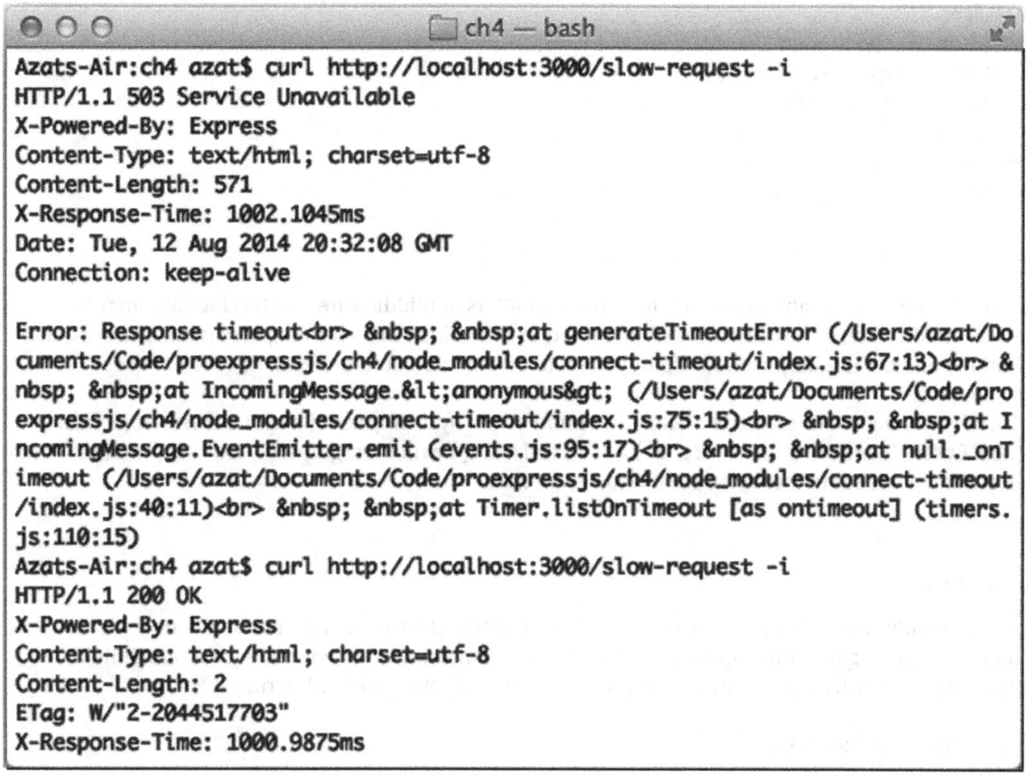

Figure 4-2. *The responses when the timeout middleware is in action and when it's not*

errorhandler

The errorhandler middleware (`https://www.npmjs.org/package/errorhandler`) can be used for basic error handling. This is especially useful in development and for prototyping. This module doesn't do anything that you can't do yourself with custom error-handling middleware. However, it will save you time. For production environments, please consider customizing error handling to your needs.

The `errorhandler` v1.1.1 module installation is done with the following NPM command:

```
$ npm install errorhandler@1.1.1 --save
```

We apply it in the server file like this:

```
var errorHandler = require('errorhandler');
// ... Configurations
app.use(errorHandler());
```

Or, only for development mode:

```
if (app.get('env') === 'development') {
  app.use(errorhandler());
}
```

It's trivial to write your own error handlers. In fact, you've already seen it done in Chapter 2, when we examined code created by the generator, and in Chapter 3. For example, this is a primitive handler that renders an error template with an error message:

```
app.use(function(err, req, res, next) {
    res.status(err.status || 500);
    res.render('error', {
        message: err.message,
        error: {}
    });
});
```

As you can see, the method signature is similar to request handlers or middleware, but has four arguments instead of three, like middleware, or two, like a core Node.js request handler. This is how Express.js determines that this is an error handler and not middleware—four parameters in the function definition: `error` (`err`), `request` (`req`), `response` (`res`), and `next`.

This error handler is triggered from inside of the other middleware by calling `next()` with an error object; for example, `next(new Error('something went wrong'))`. If we call `next()` without arguments, Express.js assumes that there were no errors and proceeds to the next middleware in the chain.

method-override

The method-override middleware (`https://www.npmjs.org/package/method-override`) enables your server to support HTTP methods that might be unsupported by clients—for example, systems where requests are limited to GET and POST (such as an HTML form in the browser). To install `method-override` v2.1.3, run:

```
$ npm install method-override@2.1.3 --save
```

The method-override module can use the X-HTTP-Method-Override=VERB header from the incoming requests:

```
var methodOverride = require('method-override');
// ... Configuratoins
app.use(methodOverride('X-HTTP-Method-Override'));
```

In addition to the header, we can use a query string. For example, to support requests with ?_method=VERB:

```
var methodOverride = require('method-override');
// ... Configuratoins
app.use(methodOverride('_method'));
```

In ch4/app.js, after we install, import, and apply the method-override middleware with the query string approach and _method name, we can define a DELETE route like this:

```
app.delete('/purchase-orders', function(request, response){
  console.log('The DELETE route has been triggered');
  response.status(204).end();
});
```

After we start the app with $ node app, we submit *the POST* request with CURL in a separate terminal window. In the URL, we specify the _method as DELETE:

```
$ curl http://localhost:3000/purchase-orders/?_method=DELETE -X POST
```

This CURL request is treated by Express.js as the DELETE HTTP method request, and we will see the following message on the server:

```
The DELETE route has been triggered
```

For Windows users, CURL can be installed from http://curl.haxx.se/download.html. Or, you can use jQuery's $.ajax() function from the Chrome Developer Tools.

response-time

The response-time middleware (https://www.npmjs.org/package/response-time) adds the X-Response-Time header with the time in milliseconds from the moment the request entered this middleware.

To install response-time v2.0.1, run

```
$ npm install response-time@2.0.1 --save
```

The response-time() method takes a number of digits after the point that need to be included in the result (3 is the default). Let's ask for 4 digits:

```
var responseTime = require('response-time');
// ... Middleware
app.use(responseTime(4));
```

To illustrate this middleware in action, run `ch4/app.js` with $ node app. The server has these statements pertaining to the response-time middleware:

```
app.use(responseTime(4));
// ... Middleware
app.get('/response-time', function(request, response){
  setTimeout(function(){
    response.status(200).end();
  }, 513);
});
```

The idea behind the preceding /response-time route is to delay the response by 513 ms. Then, in a separate terminal window, run the `curl` command with `-i` to make a GET request and output response information:

```
$ curl http://localhost:3000/response-time -i
```

As shown in Figure 4-3, this header appears in the response:

```
X-Response-Time: 514.3193ms
```

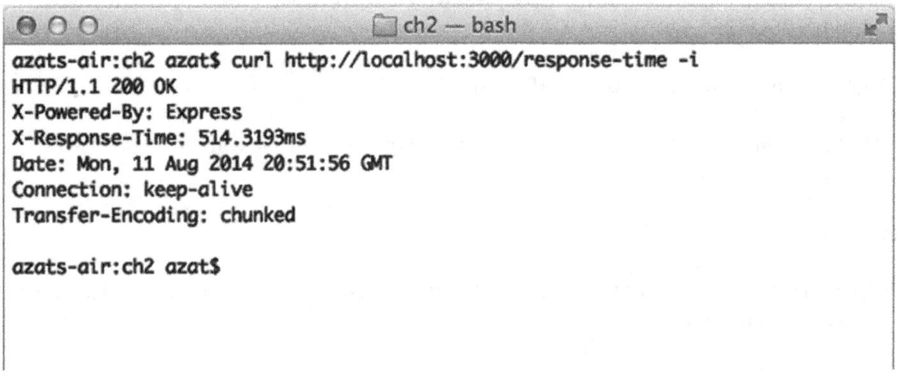
ch2 — bash
azats-air:ch2 azat$ curl http://localhost:3000/response-time -i
HTTP/1.1 200 OK
X-Powered-By: Express
X-Response-Time: 514.3193ms
Date: Mon, 11 Aug 2014 20:51:56 GMT
Connection: keep-alive
Transfer-Encoding: chunked
azats-air:ch2 azat$

Figure 4-3. *HTTP response with the X-Response-Time header that shows response time*

serve-favicon

The serve-favicon middleware (`https://www.npmjs.org/package/serve-favicon`) enables you to change the default favorite icon in the browser into a custom one.

To install the `static-favicon` v2.0.1 module, run:

```
$ npm install serve-favicon@2.0.1 --save
```

To include and apply the middleware, run

```
var favicon = require('serve-favicon');
// ... Instantiations
app.use(favicon(path.join(__dirname, 'public', 'favicon.ico')));
```

The `serve-favicon` v2.0.1 module has two parameters:

- `path`: The path to the favorite icon file, or Buffer with the icon data (Buffer is a Node.js binary type)
- `options`: maxAge in milliseconds—how long to cache the favorite icon; the default is 1 day

When you run `ch4/app.js`, you should see the webapplog.com logo on the tab, as shown in Figure 4-4.

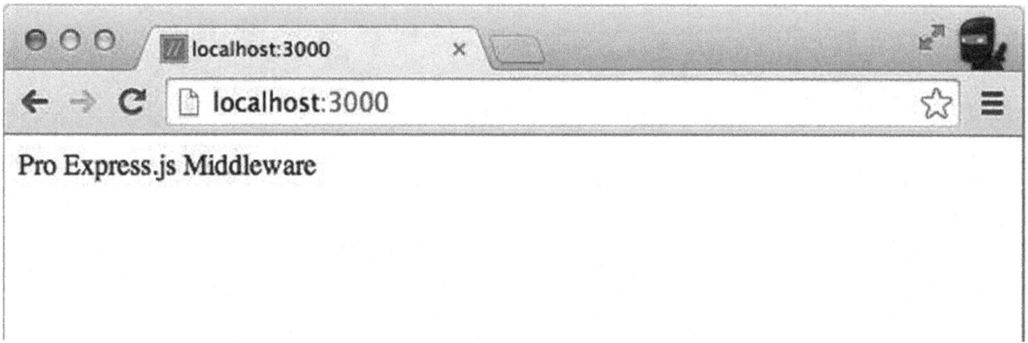

***Figure 4-4.** Favorite icon with the serve-favicon middleware in use*

serve-index

The `serve-index` middleware (`https://www.npmjs.org/package/serve-index`) enables you to create a directory listing based on a particular folder's content. Think about it as a terminal `$ ls` command (or `dir` on Windows). You can even customize the look with your own template and style sheet (the options are discussed later in this section).

To install `serve-index` v1.1.6, run:

```
$ npm install serve-index@1.1.6 --save
```

To apply the middleware, write these lines in your server file:

```
var serveIndex = require('serve-index');
// ... Middleware
app.use('/shared', serveIndex(
  path.join('public','shared'),
  {'icons': true}
));
app.use(express.static('public'));
```

In the `serveIndex` statement, specify the `'/shared'` folder and pass the `path.join('public', 'shared');` path to the `public/shared` folder in the project directory. A value of `true` for icons (`icons: true`) means to display icons. The static middleware is needed to display the actual file.

These lines of code are taken from `ch4/app.js`, and, if you run it and navigate to `http://localhost:3000/shared`, you'll see a web interface with the folder name (`shared`) and file name (`abc.txt`) as shown in Figure 4-5.

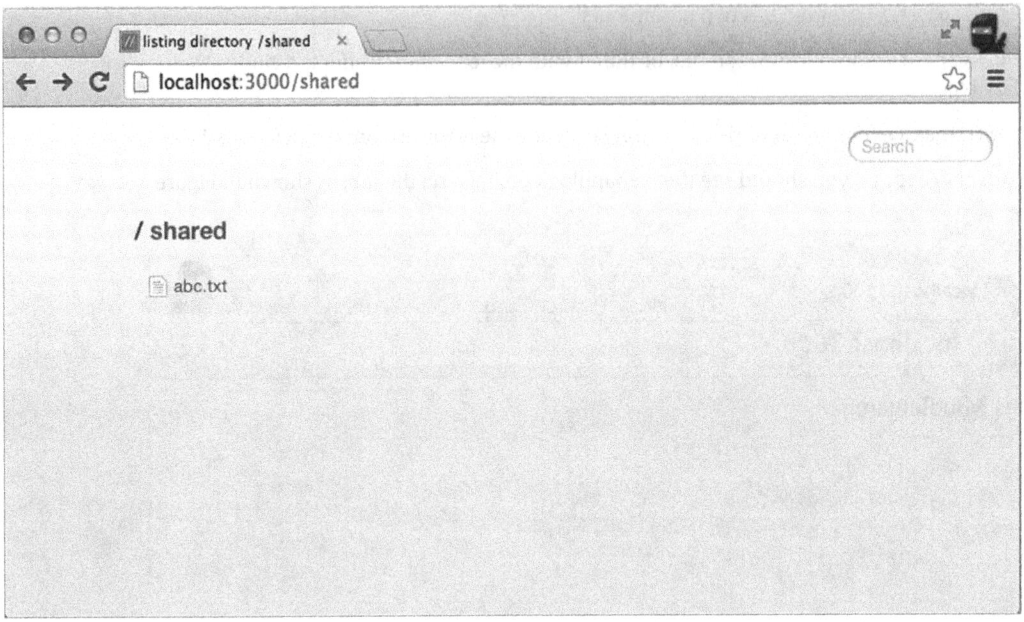

Figure 4-5. *The default serve-index web interface with folder and a file*

If you resize the browser to be narrow enough, the interface should change—responsiveness! Also, there's the search bar, thanks to the default `serve-index` interface.

Clicking the file name `abc.txt` should open the file displaying the message "secret text," as shown in Figure 4-6. This is a a result of using the `expsess.static()` middleware, and not `serve-index`.

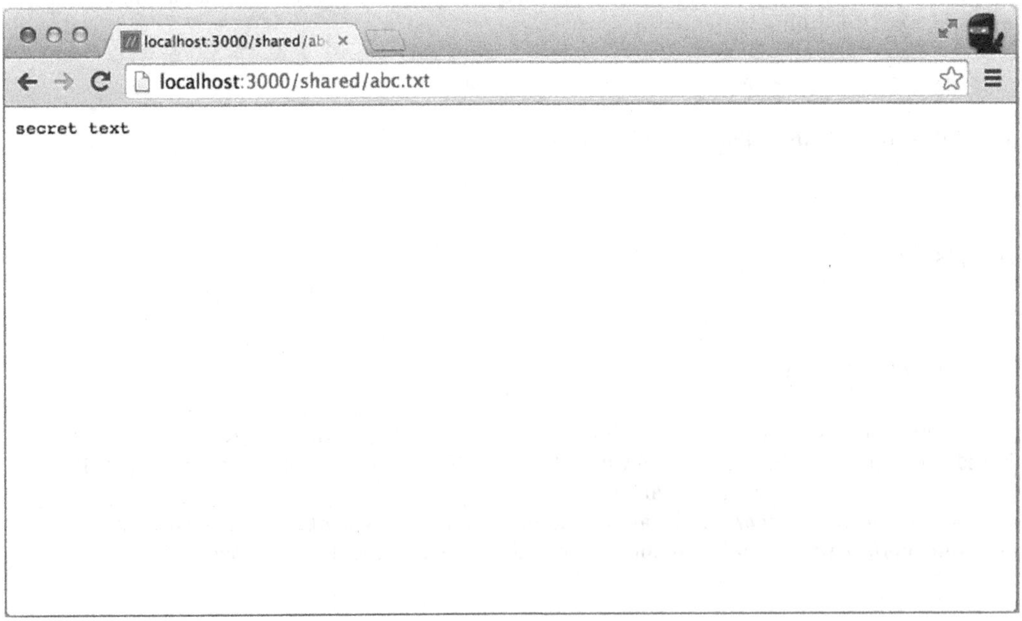

Figure 4-6. *Text file served by the static middleware*

The serve-index middleware takes an options object as a second parameter (the first is the path). The options can have the following properties:

- hidden: Boolean indicating whether or not to display hidden (dot) files; defaults to false
- view: Display mode (tiles or details); defaults to tiles
- icons: Boolean indicating whether or not to show icons next to file names/folder names; defaults to false
- filter: A filter function; defaults to false
- stylesheet: Path to a CSS style sheet (optional); defaults to the built-in style sheet
- template: Path to an HTML template (optional); defaults to the built-in template

In the template, you can use: {directory} for the name of the directory, {files} for the HTML of an unordered list (<ol>) of file links, {linked-path} for the HTML of a link to the directory, and {style} for the specified stylesheet and embedded images.

■ **Caution** Don't use serve-index liberally on system folders and secret files. It's good to keep it constrained to a certain subfolder, such as public.

---

vhost

The vhost middleware (https://www.npmjs.org/package/vhost) enables you to use a different routing logic based on the domain. For example, we can have two Express.js apps, api and web, to organize code for different routes based on the domain, api.hackhall.com or www.hackhall.com, respectively:

```
var app =express()
var api = express()
var web = express()
// ... Configurations, middleware and routes
app.use(vhost('www.hackhall.com', web))
app.use(vhost('api.hackhall.com', api))
app.listen(3000)
```

To install vhost v2.0.0, run:

```
$ npm install vhost@2.0.0 --save
```

The vhost v2.0.0 middleware takes two parameters (as shown in the previous example):

- domain: String or RegExp; for example, *.webapplog.com
- server: Server object (express or connect); for example, api or web

connect-busboy

The connect-busboy module (https://www.npmjs.org/package/connect-busboy) is connect.js/Express.js middleware that is built to be used with busboy the form parser (https://www.npmjs.org/package/busboy). The busboy form parser basically takes the incoming HTTP(S) request multipart body and allows us to use its fields, uploaded files, and so forth. To install the connect-busboy v0.0.1 middleware, which already includes busboy, run

```
$ npm install connect-busboy@0.0.1 --save
```

Then, in your server file (app.js), write something similar to the following to implement a file upload functionality on the /upload route:

```
var busboy = require('connect-busboy');
// ... Configurations
app.use('/upload', busboy({immediate: true }));
app.use('/upload', function(request, response) {
  request.busboy.on('file', function(fieldname, file, filename, encoding, mimetype) {
    file.on('data', function(data){
      fs.writeFile('upload' + fieldname + filename, data);
    });
    file.on('end', function(){
      console.log('File' + filename + 'is ended');
    });

  });
 request.busboy.on('finish', function(){
    console.log('Busboy is finished');
   response.status(201).end();
 })
});
```

The preceding example writes the file to the disk and outputs 201 to the client upon finishing. In the terminal, we should see the file name with the word "ended".

To simulate a file upload without the web page form, we can use our good old friend CURL (one-line command):

```
$ curl -X POST -i -F name=icon -F filedata=@./public/favicon.ico http://localhost:3000/upload
```

The file that we're uploading is in ch4/public/favicon.ico. This is the favorite icon from the earlier serve-favicon example. As a result, there should be a file named uploadfiledatafavicon.ico in the project folder. And in your terminal on the server window, you should see messages:

```
File favicon.ico is ended
Busboy is finished
```

In your terminal on the client (i.e., curl window), you'll see 201 Created.

■ **Note** In addition to the ch4 example, please see the chapters in Part 4 for more advanced examples on middleware.

Other Middleware

There are many other noteworthy modules that are compatible with Connect.js and Express.js. The following is only a brief list of some of the currently popular modules; many more are coming out every month, and some are being discontinued or abandoned, so check NPM for updates regularly. You can find each of these modules at `https://www.npmjs.org/package/package` *name*, where *package name* is the name of the module in the following list.

- `cookies` and `kegrip`: Alternatives to `cookie-parser` (`https://www.npmjs.org/package/cookies`, `https://www.npmjs.org/package/keygrip`, `https://www.npmjs.org/package/cookie-parser`)
- `cookie-session`: Cookie-based session store (`https://www.npmjs.org/package/cookie-session`)
- `raw-body`: For requests as buffers (`https://www.npmjs.org/package/raw-body`)
- `connect-multiparty`: Uses `mutliparty` and acts as an alternative to `connect-busboy` (`https://www.npmjs.org/package/connect-multiparty`, `https://www.npmjs.org/package/multiparty`, `https://www.npmjs.org/package/connect-busboy`)
- `qs`: Alternative to query and querystring (`https://www.npmjs.org/package/qs`, `https://www.nodejs.org/api/querystring.html`)
- `st`, `connect-static`, and `static-cache`: Caching of static assets (`https://www.npmjs.org/package/st`, `https://www.npmjs.org/package/connect-static`, and `https://www.npmjs.org/package/static-cache`)
- `express-validator`: Incoming data validation/sanitation (`https://www.npmjs.org/package/express-validator`)
- `everyauth` and `passport`: Authentication and authorization middleware (`https://www.npmjs.org/package/everyauth` and `https://www.npmjs.org/package/passport`)
- `oauth2-server`: OAuth2 server middleware (`https://www.npmjs.org/package/oauth2-server`)
- `helmet`: Collection of security middleware (`https://www.npmjs.org/package/helmet`)
- `connect-cors`: Cross-origin resource sharing (CORS) support for Express.js servers (`https://www.npmjs.org/package/connect-cors`)
- `connect-redis`: Redis session store for Express.js sessions (`https://www.npmjs.org/package/connect-redis`)

Summary

This chapter covered how to create and apply your own custom middleware and how to install and apply third-party middleware from NPM. You learned how the most essential middleware works, which parameters their functions take, and how they behave. You might have noticed that we used a small template for the error page and for the compression page in the `ch4` example project.

The next chapter is a continuation of the configuration and middleware theme. Those are distinct parts of virtually any Express.js app, as we discussed the high-level `app.js` structure in Chapter 1 (or `server.js` or `index.js`, meaning the main Express.js file). The next topic is all about configuring views that are facilitated by templates. Chapter 4 is a deep dive into how we can use different template engines. We explore how to utilize the most popular options with Express.js, such as Jade and Handlebars, and other libraries.

CHAPTER 5

Template Engines and Consolidate.js

Template engines are libraries that allow us to use different template languages (EJS, Handlebars, Jade, etc.). But what is a template language? Template language is a special set of instructions (syntax and control structures) that instructs the engine how to process data. The language is specific to a particular template engine. The instructions in the template are usually used to present data in a better format suitable for end-users. In the case of web apps such final representation format is HTML. So basically, we have some data (JSON or JavaScript/Node.js objects), and templates (EJS, Handlebars, Jade, etc.). When they are combined, we get the output, which is good old HTML.

The process of combining data with templates is called *rendering*. Some template engines have functionality to *compile* templates as an extra step before rendering. Compilation is similar to caching and is geared towards optimizing for frequent reuse.

"Why the heck use templates?" you might ask if you haven't used them before. There are multiple advantages of using templates over not using them, the most important of which is that you can reuse code—for example, menus, headers, footers, buttons and other form elements, and so forth. This way, if you need to make a change later, you'll have to update code in only one place instead of changing it in every file. Another advantage is that, depending on what library you're using, you can make templates more dynamic. This means that you can add some logic to the template and make it smarter (e.g., a `for` loop to iterate over each row of the table).

Jade allows pretty much any JavaScript/Node.js in its code; that is, the developers can harness the full power of rich JavaScript API in the templates!

This comes as a startling contrast to the approach used by Handlebars, which won't allow you to use JavaScript/Node.js functions in its templates. Although Handlebars' philosophy is to limit standard functions, it allows registering custom functions in the JavaScript/Node.js code (i.e., outside of the template itself).

Embedded JavaScript (EJS) is another popular choice for Node.js apps and it might be a better alternative when performance is important because in benchmark tests EJS performs better than Jade. Most of these template engines are suited for both browser JavaScript and Node.js.

In this chapter we'll cover the following topics:

- How to use template engines: Plugging different template engines into Express.js projects
- Uncommon libraries: Using rare template engines with Express.js
- Template engine choices: Different stand-alone template engine libraries
- Consolidate.js: a one-stop library for seamless integration of virtually all template engines with Express.js

How to Use Template Engines

Some of the examples from the previous chapters used these two configuration statements:

```
app.set('views', path);
app.set('view engine', name);
```

Or, with values:

```
var path = require('path')
// ... Configurations
app.set('views', path.join(__dirname, 'templates'));
app.set('view engine', 'ejs');
```

where `path` is a path to the folder with the templates, and `name` is a template filename extension and an NPM library name (e.g., `jade is both an extension and an NMP name`).

These two lines were enough to make Express.js render EJS or Jade templates. We didn't even have to import Jade in the `app.js` files. (But we still need to install the modules locally!) This is because, under the hood, the Express.js library imports the libraries based on the extension (the exact way it works is described in the next section of this chapter):

```
require('jade');
```

or

```
require('ejs');
```

There are two approaches to specifying a template engine extension:

- With the `render()` function
- With the `view engine` setting

Usually the file extension is the NPM module name for that template engine. Here's an example of the first approach where the extension can simply be put after the file name in the render function's argument:

```
response.render('index.jade');
```

The response.render is called inside of the route request handler. More details on render and other response object methods are provided later in the chapter.

If we use this approach (i.e., full file names with the extension), we can omit this line:

```
app.set('view engine', 'jade');
```

You can mix and match different template engines in one Express.js application.

Of course, the libraries that Express.js calls need to be installed in the local `node_modules` folder. For example, to install `jade` v1.5.0, we have to define it in the `package.json` and then run:

```
$ npm install
```

Here's the line from `ch4/package.json`:

```
"jade": "1.5.0",
```

To use any other template engine, make sure that you install that module with NPM, preferably by adding it to `package.json` as well, either manually or with `npm install` *name* `--save`.

Interestingly enough, Express.js uses `views` as the default value. Therefore, if you have templates in the `views` folder, you can omit this line:

```
app.set('views', path.join(__dirname, 'views'));
```

You know how to use `app.set()` for EJS and Jade templates, so now let's cover how to use alternative template engines with the configuration method: `app.engine()`.

app.engine()

The `app.engine()` method is a lower-level method for setting up template engines. Express.js uses this method under the hood.

By default, Express.js will try to require a template engine based on the extension provided (the template engine NPM module name—that's why we use this name as the extension!). For example, when we call `res.render('index.jade');` (more on this method later) in the request handler of the route or in middleware with the `index.jade` file name as an argument, the framework is calling `require('jade')` internally.

The full statement in the Express.js code (you don't need to implement it yourself just yet) is something like this: `app.engine('jade', require('jade').__express);`, where `__express` is a convention that template libraries should implement.

Let's say you prefer `*.html` or `*.template` instead of `*.jade` for your Jade files. In this case you can use `app.set()` and `app.engine()` to overwrite the default extension. For example, to use `*.html`, write these statements:

```
app.set('view engine', 'html');
app.engine('html', require('jade').__express);
```

and then, in each route, write something like this to render `index.html`:

```
response.render('index');
```

Or, for the `'*.template'` example, you can use an alternative approach without the view engine and with the full file name in the request handler (basically copying the internal Express.js code):

```
app.engine('template', require('jade').__express);
```

The following is the request handler call:

```
response.render('index.template');
```

This overwriting is especially cool for Handlebars and other template engines that take plain HTML, because you can reuse your legacy HTML files without much of a hassle.

Uncommon Libraries

Now let's cover the use of uncommon template engines. You can safely skip the rest of this section, if you plan to use only common libraries such as Jade or EJS.

Less common Node.js choices of libraries need to expose the _express method, which is the common convention to indicate that a template library supports this Express.js format. So check if the template engine has __express() on the source file that you import with require(). If the __express() method is present, then the contributors made this library compatible with Express.js. Again, most of the libraries are already outfitted to work with Express.js and they have __express().

What if the library of your choice doesn't have __express? If the template module has a method with a signature similar to the __express method signature, you can easily define your template engine's method with app.engine; for example, in swig (https://github.com/paularmstrong/swig), it's the renderFile() method. So, considering that renderFile in a template engine library of your choice supports a function signature with these arguments:

- path: Path to a template file
- locals: Data to use for rendering HTML
- callback: The callback function

you can write code like this to apply this library as Express.js middleware:

```
// ... Declare dependencies
// ... Instantiate the app
// ... Configure the app
app.engine('swig', require('swig').renderFile);
// ... Define the routes
```

The example in the ch5 folder shows how you can use multiple template engines and various extensions. This is the scoop of the app.js statements:

```
// ... Declare dependencies
// ... Instantiate the app
// ... Configure the app
var jade = require('jade');
var consolidate = require('consolidate');

app.engine('html', jade.__express);
app.engine('template', jade.__express);
app.engine('swig', consolidate.swig);
// ... Define the routes
app.get('/', function(request, response){
  response.render('index.html');
});

app.get('/template', function(request, response){
  response.render('index.template');
});

app.get('/swig', function(request, response){
  response.render('index.swig');
})
```

The consolidate library will be explained later in this chapter.

The package.json file has the following dependencies (install them with npm install):

```
{
  "name": "template-app",
  "version": "0.0.1",
  "private": true,
  "scripts": {
    "start": "node app"
  },
  "dependencies": {
    "consolidate": "^0.10.0",
    "errorhandler": "1.1.1",
    "express": "4.8.1",
    "jade": "1.5.0",
    "morgan": "1.2.2",
    "swig": "^1.4.2",
    "serve-favicon": "2.0.1"
  }
}
```

Starting the application with $ node app should start the server that will render "Hi, I'm Jade from index.html" when you go to the home page (see Figure 5-1).

Figure 5-1. *Jade template rendered from the index.html file*

Also, the server should render "Hi, I'm Swig from index.swig" when you go to the `/swig` (see Figure 5-2).

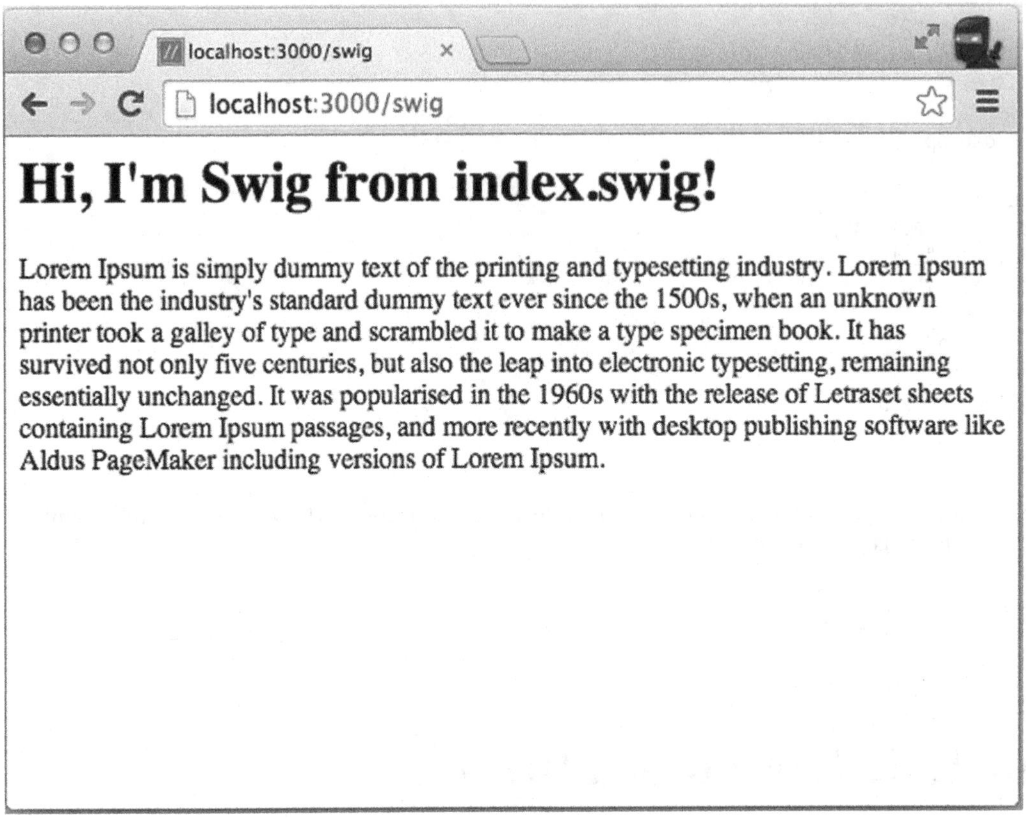

Figure 5-2. *Swig template rendered from the index.swig file*

And lastly, it should render "hi, I'm Jade in index.template file" when you go to the `/template` (see Figure 5-3).

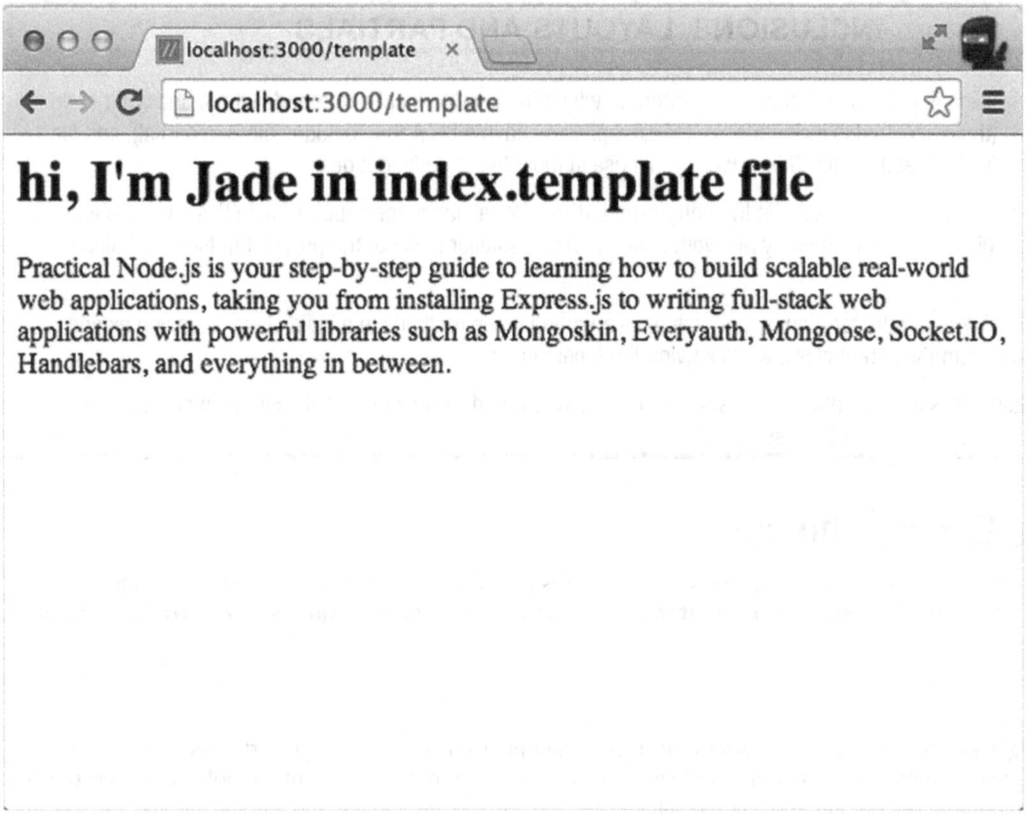

Figure 5-3. *Jade template rendered from the index.jade file*

This is probably an over-the-top example, because you will rarely use more than one template engine in a single Express.js app. However, it's good to know that the framework is flexible enough to allow you to implement it with just a few configuration statements.

It's worth noting, in our `proexpressjs/ch5` example, both Jade files `index.html` and `index.template` use the so-called top-down inclusion via `include filename` (without quotes). This allows us to reuse the Lorem Ipsum text of the paragraph in the `lorem-ipsum.html` file.

The file in our example is just a plain text file, but it can have Jade template content in it. The `index.html` looks like this:

```
h1 Hi, I'm Jade from index.html file
p
  include lorem-ipsum.html
```

And the index.temlate is similar:

```
h1 hi, I'm Jade in index.template file
p
  include lorem-ipsum.html
```

INCLUSIONS, LAYOUTS AND PARTIALS

Top-down inclusion is a standard inheritance pattern in which the parent object commands where and what to do with the child (the object that is included). So, for example, you have a file A that includes file B (a partial), and file A will do with file B what it wants. This is what you'll use in most template languages.

The alternative to top-down inclusion is the bottom-up pattern. Not all languages support it. In this case, file A is a larger and higher-up-the-chain entity (a layout), and file B is a smaller piece of the puzzle, but file B will dictate what it wants.

You can also think about the top-down approach as overwriting some methods in a child class when you extend those methods from the parent class, while leaving the others intact.

In Jade, bottom-up is implemented with a set of `extend`, `layout`, and `block` statements. For deep coverage on Jade, refer to *Practical Node.js* (Apress, 2014).

Template Engine Choices

This section briefly introduces the libraries that support Express.js without any modifications. This list of choices is derived from the list at the Express.js wiki page: `https://github.com/strongloop/express/wiki#template-engines`.

Jade

Jade (`https://github.com/jadejs/jade`) is a Haml-inspired template engine. It's very powerful because it has two types of inheritances, supports all JavaScript/Node.js, and requires a minimum number of symbols/characters due to treating whitespace and indentation as part of the language.

Haml.js

Haml.js (`https://github.com/tj/haml.js`) is a Haml implementation. Haml is a standard choice for Rails developers. This language treats whitespace and indentation as part of the language, which makes code more compact and less prone to typos, thus making it more pleasurable to write.

EJS

EJS (`https://github.com/tj/ejs`) is an embedded JavaScript template engine. According to some benchmark performance tests, EJS is faster than Jade or Haml (see, for example, `http://paularmstrong.github.io/node-templates/benchmarks.html`).

Handlebars.js

Hbs (`https://github.com/donpark/hbs`) is an adapter for Handlebars.js, which is an extension of the Mustache.js template engine. By design, Handlebars prohibits putting complex logic in the templates. Instead, developers need to write functions outside of templates and register them. This is the easiest template engine to learn. It's often used in reactive templates. If you're familiar with (or plan to use) Angular.js, Meteor, or DerbyJS, this choice might be better for you because it is similar to what they use.

Alternative adapter is express-hbs (https://github.com/barc/express-hbs) which is the Handlebars with layouts, partials and blocks for Express 3 from Barc (http://barc.com).

Another adapter is express-handlebars (https://github.com/ericf/express-handlebars).

Hogan.js Adapters

h4e (https://github.com/tldrio/h4e) is an adapter for Hogan.js, with support for partials and layouts. Hulk-hogan (https://github.com/quangv/hulk-hogan) is an adapter for Twitter's Hogan.js (Mustache syntax), with support for partials.

Combyne.js

The Combyne.js (https://github.com/tbranyen/combyne.js) is a template engine that, hopefully, works the way you'd expect. And combynexpress (https://github.com/tbranyen/combynexpress) is an Express library for Combyne.js.

Swig

Swig (https://github.com/paularmstrong/swig) is a fast, Django-like template engine.

Whiskers

Whiskers (https://github.com/gsf/whiskers.js) is small, fast, and mustachioed (looks like Handlebars or Mustache). It is faster than Jade (per http://paularmstrong.github.io/node-templates/benchmarks.html).

Blade

Blade (https://github.com/bminer/node-blade) is an HTML template compiler, inspired by Jade and Haml that treats whitespace as part of the language.

Haml-Coffee

Haml-Coffee (https://github.com/netzpirat/haml-coffee) provides Haml templates in which you can write inline CoffeeScript. It is perfect if you're using CoffeeScript for your Node.js code (the benefits of CoffeeScript are highlighted in this presentation: http://www.infoq.com/presentations/coffeescript-lessons).

Webfiller

Webfiller (https://github.com/haraldrudell/webfiller) is a plain HTML5 dual-side rendering engine with self-configuring routes, organized source tree. Webfiller is 100% JS.

Consolidate.js

In case the template engine of your choice does not provide an __express() method, or you're not sure and don't want to bother finding out, consider the consolidate library (https://npmjs.org/package/consolidate; GitHub: https://github.com/tj/consolidate.js).

The consolidate library streamlines and generalizes a few dozen template engine modules so that they "play nicely" with Express.js. This means there's no need to look up the source code to search for the presence of the __express() method. All you need to do is require consolidate and then map the engine of your choice to the extension.

Here is a Consolidate.js example:

```
var express = require('express');
var consolidate = require('consolidate');

var app = express();

// ... Configure template engine
app.engine('html', consolidate.handlebars);
app.set('view engine', 'html');
app.set('views', __dirname + '/views');
```

That's it; res.render() is ready to use Handlebars!

The template engines that Consolidate.js supports, as of this writing, are shown in Table 5-1 (compiled from the Consolidate.js GitHub page: https://github.com/tj/consolidate.js/blob/master/Readme.md).

Table 5-1. *Template Engines Supported by Consolidate.js*

Template Engine	GitHub	Web Site (if applicable)
atpl	https://github.com/soywiz/atpl.js	
dust	https://github.com/akdubya/dustjs	http://akdubya.github.io/dustjs/
eco	https://github.com/sstephenson/eco	
ect	https://github.com/baryshev/ect	http://ectjs.com
ejs	https://github.com/tj/ejs	http://www.embeddedjs.com
haml	https://github.com/tj/haml.js	http://haml.info
haml-coffee	https://github.com/9elements/haml-coffee	http://haml.info
handlebars.js	https://github.com/wycats/handlebars.js/	http://handlebarsjs.com
Hogan.js	https://github.com/twitter/hogan.js	http://twitter.github.io/hogan.js
Jade	https://github.com/jadejs/jade	http://jade-lang.com
jazz	https://github.com/shinetech/jazz	
jqtpl	https://github.com/kof/jqtpl	
JUST	https://github.com/baryshev/just	
liquor	https://github.com/chjj/liquor	
lodash	https://github.com/lodash/lodash	https://lodash.com
mustache	https://github.com/janl/mustache.js	http://mustache.github.io
nunjunks	http://mozilla.github.io/nunjucks/	
QEJS	https://github.com/jepso/QEJS	
ractive	https://github.com/ractivejs/ractive	

(*continued*)

Table 5-1. *(continued)*

Template Engine	GitHub	Web Site (if applicable)
swig	`https://github.com/paularmstrong/swig`	`http://paularmstrong.github.com/swig/`
templayed	`http://archan937.github.io/templayed.js/`	
toffee	`https://github.com/malgorithms/toffee`	
underscore	`https://github.com/jashkenas/underscore`	`http://documentcloud.github.io/underscore/`
walrus	`https://github.com/jeremyruppel/walrus`	`http://documentup.com/jeremyruppel/walrus/`
whiskers	`https://github.com/gsf/whiskers.js/`	

Jade template language is quite extensive in itself and is beyond the scope of this book. To learn about every feature and the differences between extend and include (top-down and bottom-up), refer to *Practical Node.js* (Apress, 2014), which has a whole chapter dedicated to Jade and Handlebars.

Summary

Templates are a staple of modern web development. Without them, developers would have to write way more code and the maintenance would be painful. When it comes to Node.js, Jade—a close relative to Ruby on Rails' Haml—is a powerful choice. This is due to its rich set of features and elegance of style (whitespaces and indentations are part of the language). But don't attempt to write Jade without learning it first. It might be painful.

Express.js supports different approaches to configuring the location of templates and file extensions. Also, Express.js shines when it comes to configuring different pieces of the puzzle; changing a template engine is a matter of a few lines of code.

The NPM userland provides tons of template engine choices—there are dozens of other template libraries that are easily compatible with Express.js, as you saw in the "Consolidate.js" section. They have different styles, design, and performances. For example, Swig, EJS, and some other libraries often outperform Jade in benchmark tests. And if you get used to the `{{...}}}` style of Handlebar and Mustache (e.g., from Angular.js)—or you don't have the time to learn Jade properly—then you can use those libraries right away!

This chapter concludes the configuration section of the `app.js` file. We move on to the routes. We'll start with the definition of routes and the extraction of parameters from URLs.

CHAPTER 6

Parameters and Routing

To review, the typical structure of an Express.js app (which is usually a `server.js` or `app.js` file) roughly consists of these parts, in the order shown:

1. *Dependencies*: A set of statements to import dependencies
2. *Instantiations*: A set of statements to create objects
3. *Configurations*: A set of statements to configure system and custom settings
4. *Middleware*: A set of statements that is executed for every incoming request
5. *Routes*: A set of statements that defines server routes, endpoints, and pages
6. *Bootup*: A set of statements that starts the server and makes it listen on a specific port for incoming requests

This chapter covers the fifth category, routes and the URL parameters that we define in routes. These parameters, along with the app.param() middleware, are essential because they allow the application to access information passed from the client in the URLs (e.g., books/proexpressjs). This is the most common convention for REST APIs. For example, the `http://hackhall.com/api/posts/521eb002d00c970200000003` route will use the value of 521eb002d00c970200000003 as the post ID.

Parameters are values passed in a query string of a URL of the request. If we didn't have Express.js or a similar library, and had to use just the core Node.js modules, we'd have to extract parameters from an `HTTP.request` (`http://nodejs.org/api/http.html#http_http_request_options_callback`) object via some `require('querystring').parse(url)` or `require('url').parse(url, true)` function "trickery."

Let's look closer at how to define a certain rule or logic for a particular URL parameter.

Parameters

The first approach to extracting parameters from the URLs is to write some code in the request handler (route). In case you need to repeat this snippet in other routes, you can abstract the code and manually apply the same logic to many routes. (To *abstract* code means to refactor the code so that it can be reused in other places and/or be organized better. This improves maintainability and readability of the code.)

For example, imagine that we need user information on a user profile page (/v1/users/azat defined as /v1/users/:username) and on an admin page (/v1/admin/azat defined as /v1/admin/:username). One way to do this is to define a function that looks up the user information (findUserByUsername) and call this function twice inside of each of the routes. This is how we can implement it (example ch6/app.js):

```
var users = {
  'azat': {
    email: 'hi@azat.co',
    website: 'http://azat.co',
    blog: 'http://webapplog.com'
  }
};

var findUserByUsername = function (username, callback) {
  // Perform database query that calls callback when it's done
  // This is our fake database
  if (!users[username])
    return callback(new Error(
      'No user matching '
       + username
      )
    );
  return callback(null, users[username]);
};

app.get('/v1/users/:username', function(request, response, next) {
  var username = request.params.username;
  findUserByUsername(username, function(error, user) {
    if (error) return next(error);
    return response.render('user', user);
  });
});

app.get('/v1/admin/:username', function(request, response, next) {
  var username = request.params.username;
  findUserByUsername(username, function(error, user) {
    if (error) return next(error);
    return response.render('admin', user);
  });
});
```

You can run the app from the ch6 folder with $ node app command. Then, open a new terminal tab/window, and CURL a GET request with:

```
$ curl http://localhost:3000/v1/users/azat
```

To see this:

```
user profile</h2><p>http://azat.co</p><p>http://webapplog.com</p>
```

And with

```
$ curl http://localhost:3000/v1/admin/azat
```

To see this:

```
admin: user profile</h2><p>hi@azat.co</p><p>http://azat.co</p><p>http://webapplog.com</
p><div><Practical>Node.js is your step-by-step guide to learning how to build scalable real-world
web applications, taking you from installing Express.js to writing full-stack web applications with
powerful libraries such as Mongoskin, Everyauth, Mongoose, Socket.IO, Handlebars, and everything in
between.</Practical></div>
```

■ **Note** Windows users can download CURL from `http://curl.haxx.se/download.html`.

Alternatively, you can use the Postman Chrome extension at `http://bit.ly/JGSQwr`.

Or, for GET requests only, you can use your browser—just go to the URL. The browser won't make PUT or DELETE requests, and it will make POST requests only if you submit a form.

The last approach is to use jQuery to make AJAX/XHR requests, but be mindful about the cross-origin limitations, which means using the same domain, or CORS headers on the server. Or you could simply go to `http://localhost:3000/v1/users/azat` (see Figure 6-1) and `http://localhost:3000/v1/admin/azat` (see Figure 6-2) in your browser.

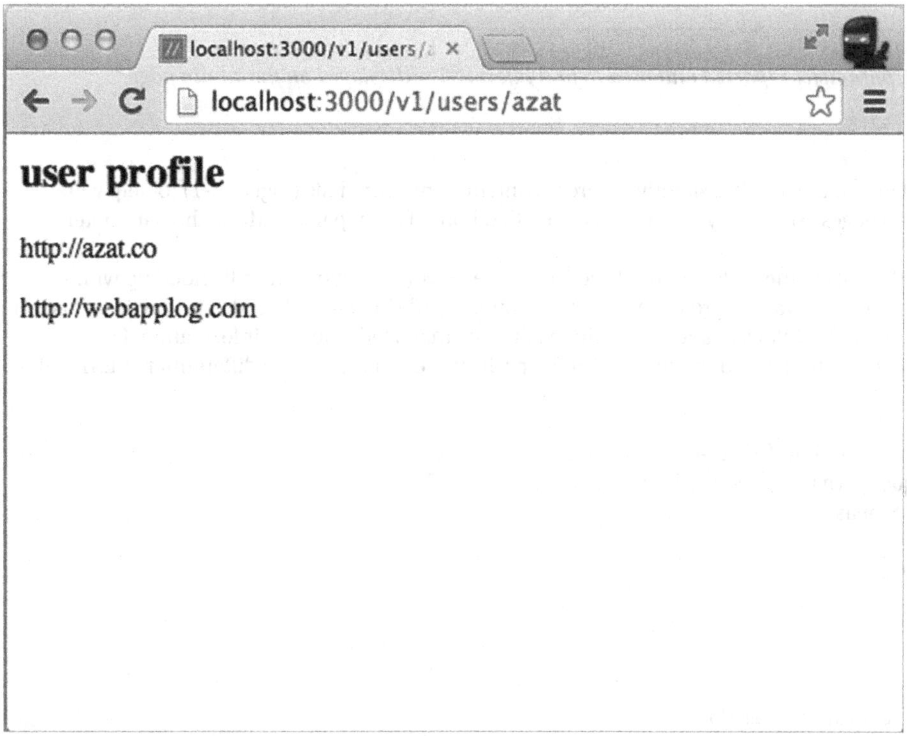

Figure 6-1. *Username URL parameter is parsed and used to find information displayed on the user page (example ch6)*

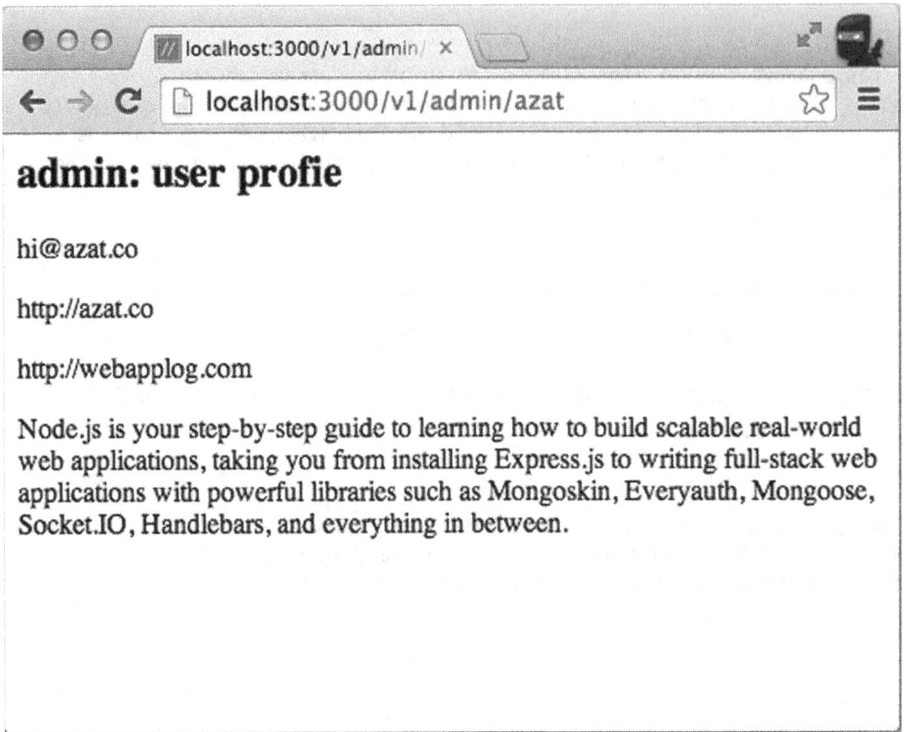

Figure 6-2. *Username URL parameter is parsed and used to find information displayed on the admin page (example ch6)*

The `admin.jade` template (Figure 6-2) has slightly different content from `user.jade` (Figure 6-1) to help you differentiate between the two pages/routes so you can be assured that both of them parse and use the parameters correctly.

Even after abstracting the bulk of the code into the `findUserByUsername()` function, we still ended up with ineloquent code. If we use the middleware approach, the code becomes a little bit better. The idea is to write a custom middleware findUserByUsernameMiddleware and use it with each route that needs the user information. Here's how you can refactor the same two routes and use the `/v2` prefix (prefixes are usually used to differentiate REST API versions):

```
var findUserByUsername = function (username, callback) {
  // Perform database query that calls callback when it's done
  // This is our fake database!
  if (!users[username])
    return callback(new Error(
      'No user matching '
       + username
      )
    );
  return callback(null, users[username]);
};
```

```
var findUserByUsernameMiddleware = function(request, response, next){
  if (request.params.username) {
    console.log('Username param was detected: ', request.params.username)
    findUserByUsername(request.params.username, function(error, user){
      if (error) return next(error);
      request.user = user;
      return next();
    })
  } else {
    return next();
  }
}
// The v2 routes that use the custom middleware
app.get('/v2/users/:username',
  findUserByUsernameMiddleware,
  function(request, response, next){
  return response.render('user', request.user);
});
app.get('/v2/admin/:username',
  findUserByUsernameMiddleware,
  function(request, response, next){
  return response.render('admin', request.user);
});
```

The middleware findUserByUsernameMiddleware checks for the presence of the parameter (`request.params.username`) and then, if it's present, proceeds to fetch the information. This is a better pattern because it keeps routes lean and abstracts logic. However, Express.js has an even better solution. It's similar to the middleware method, but it makes our lives a bit easier by automatically performing the parameter presence checks (i.e., a check to see if the parameter is in the request). Meet the `app.param()` method!

app.param()

Anytime the given string (e.g., `username`) is present in the URL pattern of the route, and server receives a request that matches that route, the callback to the `app.param()` will be triggered. For example, with `app.param('username', function(req, res, next, username){...})` and `app.get('/users/:username', findUser)` every time we have a request `/username/azat` or `/username/tjholowaychuk`, the closure in `app.param()` will be executed (before `findUser`).

The `app.param()` method is very similar to `app.use()` but it provides the value (`username` in our example) as the fourth, last parameter, to the function. In this snippet, the username will have the value from the URL (e.g., `'azat'` for `/users/azat`):

```
app.param('username', function (request, response, next, username) {
  // ... Perform database query and
  // ... Store the user object from the database in the req object
  req.user = user;
  return next();
});
```

No need of extra lines of code since we have `req.user` object populated by the `app.param()`:

```
app.get('/users/:username', function(request, response, next) {
  //... Do something with req.user
  return res.render(req.user);
});
```

No need for extra code in this route either. We get `req.user` for free because of the `app.param()` defined earlier:

```
app.get('/admin/:username', function(request, response, next) {
  //... Same thing, req.user is available!
  return res.render(user);
});
```

Here is another example of how we can plug param middleware into our app:

```
app.param('id', function(request, response, next, id){
  // Do something with id
  // Store id or other info in req object
  // Call next when done
  next();
});

app.get('/api/v1/stories/:id', function(request, response){
  // Param middleware will be executed before and
  // We expect req objects to already have needed info
  // Output something
  res.send(data);
});
```

■ **Tip** If you have a large application with many versions of API and routes (v1, v2, etc.), then it's better to use the `Router` class/object to organize the code of these routes. You create a `Router` object and mount it on a path, such as `/api` or `/api/v1`. Router is just a stripped-down version of the `var app = express()` object. More details about the `Router` class are provided later in the chapter.

The following is an example of plugging param middleware into an app that has a Mongoskin/Monk-like database connection in `req.db`:

```
app.param('id', function(request, response, next, id){
  req.db.get('stories').findOne({_id: id}, function (error, story){
    if (error) return next(error);
    if (!story) return next(new Error('Nothing is found'));
    req.story = story;
    next();
  });
});
```

```
app.get('/api/v1/stories/:id', function(request, response){
  res.send(req.story);
});
```

Or we can use multiple request handlers, but the concept remains the same: we can expect to have a `req.story` object or an error thrown prior to the execution of this code, so we abstract the common code/logic of getting parameters and their respective objects. Here is an example:

```
app.get('/api/v1/stories/:id', function(request, response, next) {
  //do authorization
  },
  //we have an object in req.story so no work is needed here
  function(request, response) {
    //output the result of the database search
    res.send(story);
});
```

■ **Note** Authorization and input sanitation are good candidates for residing in the middleware. For extensive examples of OAuth and Express.js, refer to *Practical Node.js*[1] (Apress, 2014).

The `param()` function is especially cool, because we can combine different variables in the routes; for example:

```
app.param('storyId', function(request, response, next, storyId) {
  // Fetch the story by its ID (storyId) from a database
  // Save the found story object into request object
  request.story = story;

});
app.param('elementId', function(request, response, next, elementId) {
  // Fetch the element by its ID (elementId) from a database
  // Narrow down the search when request.story is provided
  // Save the found element object into request object
  request.element = element;
});
app.get('/api/v1/stories/:storyId/elements/:elementId', function(request, response){
  // Now we automatically get the story and element in the request object
  res.send({ story: request.story, element: request.element});
});
app.post('/api/v1/stories/:storyId/elements', function(request, response){
  // Now we automatically get the story in the request object
  // We use story ID to create a new element for that story
  res.send({ story: request.story, element: newElement});
});
```

[1]http://practicalnodebook.com

To summarize, by defining app.param once, its logic will be triggered for every route that has the matching URL parameter name. You might be wondering, "How is it different from writing your own function and calling it, or from writing your own custom middleware?" They will both execute the code properly, but param is a more elegant approach. We can refactor our earlier example to show the difference.

Let's go back to the ch6 project. If we refactor our previous example from `ch6/app.js` and use `v3` as a new route prefix, we might end up with elegant code like this:

```
app.param('v3Username', function(request, response, next, username){
  console.log(
    'Username param was is detected: ',
    username
  )
  findUserByUsername(
    username,
    function(error, user){
      if (error) return next(error);
      request.user = user;
      return next();
    }
  );
});

app.get('/v3/users/:v3Username',
  function(request, response, next){
    return response.render('user', request.user);
  }
);
app.get('/v3/admin/:v3Username',
  function(request, response, next){
    return response.render('admin', request.user);
  }
);
```

So, extracting parameters is important, but defining routes is more important. Defining routes is also an alternative to using `app.param()` to extract values from URL parameters—this method is recommended when a parameter is used only once. If it's used more than once, param is a better pattern.

A lot of routes have already been defined in the five previous chapters. In the next section, we'll explore in more detail how to define various HTTP methods, chain middleware, abstract middleware code, and define all-method routes.

Routing

Express.js is a Node.js framework that, among other things, provides a way to organize routes into smaller subsections (Routers—instances of `Router` class/object). In Express.js 3.x and earlier, the only way to define routes is to use the `app.VERB()` pattern, which we'll cover next. However, starting with Express.js v4.x, using the new `Router` class is the *recommended* way to define routes, via `router.route(path)`. We'll cover the traditional approach first.

app.VERB()

Each route is defined via a method call on an application object with a URL pattern as the first parameter (regular expressions[2] are also supported); that is, `app.METHOD(path, [callback...], callback)`.

For example, to define a GET `/api/v1/stories` endpoint:

```
app.get('/api/v1/stories/', function(request, response){
  // ...
})
```

Or, to define an endpoint for the POST HTTP method and the same route:

```
app.post('/api/v1/stories', function(request, response){
  // ...
})
```

DELETE, PUT, and other methods are supported as well. For more information, see `http://expressjs.com/api.html#app.VERB`.

The callbacks that we pass to `get()` or `post()` methods are called *request handlers* (covered in detail in Chapter 7), because they take requests (`req`), process them, and write to the response (`res`) objects. For example:

```
app.get('/about', function(request, response){
  res.send('About Us: ...');
});
```

We can have multiple request handlers in one route. All of them except the first and the last will be in the middle of the flow (order in which they are executed), hence the name *middleware*. They accept a third parameter/function, `next`, which when called (`next()`), switches the execution flow to the next handler. For example, we have three functions that perform authorization, database search and output:

```
app.get('/api/v1/stories/:id', function(request, response, next) {
  // Do authorization
  // If not authorized or there is an error
  // Return next(error);
  // If authorized and no errors
  return next();
}), function(request, response, next) {
  // Extract id and fetch the object from the database
  // Assuming no errors, save story in the request object
  request.story = story;
  return next();
}), function(request, response) {
  // Output the result of the database search
  res.send(response.story);
});
```

[2]`http://en.wikipedia.org/wiki/Regular_expression`

The name `next()` is an arbitrary convention, which means you can use anything else you like instead of `next()`. The Express.js uses the order of the arguments in the function to determine their meaning. The ID of a story is the URL parameter, which we need for finding matching items in the database.

Now, what if we have another route `/admin`. We can define multiple request handlers, which perform authentication, validation, and loading of resources:

```
app.get('/admin',
  function(request, response, next) {
    // Check active session, i.e.,
    // Make sure the request has cookies associated with a valid user session
    // Check if the user has administrator privileges
    return next();
  },  function(request, response, next){
    // Load the information required for admin dashboard
    // Such as user list, preferences, sensitive info
    return next();
  }, function(request, response) {
    // Render the information with proper templates
    // Finish response with a proper status
    res.end();
   })
```

But what if some of the code for `/admin`, such as authorization/authentication, is duplicated from the `/stories`? The following accomplishes the same thing, but is much *cleaner* with the use of named functions:

```
var auth = function (request, response, next) {
  // ... Authorization and authentication
  return next();
}
var getStory = function (request, response, next) {
  // ... Database request for story
  return next();
}
var getUsers = function (request, response, next) {
  // ... Database request for users
  return next();
}
var renderPage = function (request, response) {
  if (req.story) res.render('story', story);
  else if (req.users) res.render('users', users);
  else res.end();
}

app.get('/api/v1/stories/:id', auth, getStory, renderPage);
app.get('/admin', auth,  getUsers, renderPage);
```

Another useful technique is to pass callbacks as items of an array, made possible thanks to the inner workings of the arguments JavaScript mechanism:[3]

```
var authAdmin = function (request, response, next) {
  // ...
  return next();
}
var getUsers = function (request, response, next) {
  // ...
  return next();
}
var renderUsers = function (request, response) {
  // ...
  res.end();
}
var admin = [authAdmin, getUsers, renderUsers];
app.get('/admin', admin);
```

One distinct difference between request handlers in routes and middleware is that we can bypass the rest of the callbacks in the chain by calling `next('route');`. This might come in handy if, in the previous example with the `/admin` route, a request fails authentication in the first callback, in which case there's no need to proceed. You can also use `next()` to jump to the next route if you have multiple routes matching the same URL.

Please note that, if the first parameter we pass to `app.VERB()` contains query strings (e.g., `/?debug=true`), that information is disregarded by Express.js. For example, `app.get('/?debug=true', routes.index);` will be treated exactly as `app.get('/', routes.index);`.

The following are the most commonly used Representational State Transfer (REST) server architecture HTTP methods and their counterpart methods in Express.js along with the brief meaning:

- GET: `app.get()`—Retrieves an entity or a list of entities
- HEAD: `app.head()`—Same as GET, only without the body
- POST: `app.post()`—Submits a new entity
- PUT: `app.put()`—Updates an entity by complete replacement
- PATCH: `app.patch()`—Updates an entity partially
- DELETE: `app.delete()` and `app.del()`—Deletes an existing entity
- OPTIONS: `app.options()`—Retrieves the capabilities of the server

[3]See `https://developer.mozilla.org/en-US/docs/Web/JavaScript/Reference/Functions_and_function_scope/arguments`

■ **Tip** An HTTP method is a special property of every HTTP(S) request, similar to its headers or body. Opening a URL in your browser is a GET request, and submitting a form is a POST request. Other types of requests, such as PUT, DELETE, PATCH, and OPTIONS, are only available via special clients such as CURL, Postman, or custom-built applications (both front-end and back-end).

For more information on HTTP methods, please refer to RFC 2616 (`http://tools.ietf.org/html/rfc2616`) and its "Method Definitions" section (section 9).

app.all()

The `app.all()` method allows the execution of specified request handlers on a particular path regardless of what the HTTP method of the request is. This procedure might be a lifesaver when defining *global* or namespace logic, as in this example:

```
app.all('*', userAuth);
...
app.all('/api/*', apiAuth);
```

Trailing Slashes

Paths with trailing slashes at the end are treated the same as their normal counterparts by default. To turn off this feature, use `app.enable('strict routing');` or `app.set('strict routing', true);`. You can learn more about setting options in Chapter 3.

Router Class

The `Router` class is a mini Express.js application that has only middleware and routes. This is useful for abstracting certain modules based on the business logic that they perform. For example, all `/users/*` routes can be defined in one router, and all `/posts/*` routes can be defined in another. The benefit is that, after we define a portion of the URL in the router with `router.path()` (see the next section), we don't need to repeat it over and over again, such as is the case with using the `app.VERB()` approach.

The following is an example of creating a router instance:

```
var express = require('express');
var router = express.Router(options);
// ... Define routes
app.use('/blog', router);
```

where `options` is an object that can have following properties:

- `caseSensitive`: Boolean indicating whether to treat routes with the same name but different letter case as different, `false` by default; e.g., if it's set to `false`, then `/Users` is the same as `/users`.
- `strict`: Boolean indicating whether to treat routes with the same name but with or without a trailing slash as different, `false` by default; e.g., if it's set to `false`, then `/users` is the same as `/users/`.

router.route(path)

The `router.route(path)` method is used to chain HTTP verb methods. For example, in a create, read, update, and delete (CRUD) server that has POST, GET, PUT, and DELETE endpoints for the `/posts/:id` URL (e.g., `/posts/53fb401dc96c1caa7b78bbdb`), we can use the `Router` class as follows:

```
var express = require('express');
var router = express.Router();
// ... Importations and configurations
router.param('postId', function(request, response, next) {
  // Find post by ID
  // Save post to request
  request.post = {
    name: 'PHP vs. Node.js',
    url: 'http://webapplog.com/php-vs-node-js'
  };
  return next();
});

router
  .route('/posts/:postId')
  .all(function(request, response, next){
    // This will be called for request with any HTTP method
  })
  .post(function(request, response, next){
  })
  .get(function(request, response, next){
    response.json(request.post);
  })
  .put(function(request, response, next){
    // ... Update the post
    response.json(request.post);
  })
  .delete(function(request, response, next){
    // ... Delete the post
    response.json({'message': 'ok'});
  })
```

The `Router.route(path)` method provides the convenience of chaining methods, which is a more appealing way to structure, your code than re-typing router for each route.

Alternatively, we can use `router.VERB(path, [callback...], callback)` to define the routes just as we would use `app.VERB()`. Similarly, the `router.use()` and `router.param()` methods work the same as `app.use()` and `app.param()`.

Going back to our example project (in the ch6 folder), we can implement v4/users/:username and v4/admin/:username with Router:

```
router.param('username', function(request, response, next, username){
  console.log(
    'Username param was detected: ',
    username
  )
  findUserByUsername(
    username,
    function(error, user){
      if (error) return next(error);
      request.user = user;
      return next();
    }
  );
})
router.get('/users/:username',
  function(request, response, next){
    return response.render('user', request.user);
  }
);
router.get('/admin/:username',
  function(request, response, next){
    return response.render('admin', request.user);
  }
);
app.use('/v4', router);
```

As you can see, `router.get()` methods include no mention of v4. Typically, the `router.get()` and `router.param()` methods are abstracted into a separate file. This way, the main file (`app.js` in our example) stays lean and easy to read and maintain—a nice principle to follow!

Request Handlers

Request handlers in Express.js are strikingly similar to callbacks in the core Node.js `http.createServer()` method, because they're just functions (anonymous, named, or methods) with req and res parameters:

```
var ping = function(req, res) {
  console.log('ping');
  res.end(200);
};

app.get('/', ping);
```

In addition, we can utilize the third parameter, next(), for control flow. It's closely related to the topic of error handling, which is covered in Chapter 9. Here is a simple example of two request handlers, ping and pong where the former just skips to the latter after printing a word ping:

```
var ping = function(req, res, next) {
  console.log('ping');
  return next();
};
var pong = function(req, res) {
  console.log('pong');
  res.end(200);
};
app.get('/', ping, pong);
```

When a request comes on the / route, Express.js calls ping(), which acts as middleware in this case (because it's in the middle!). Ping, in turn, when it's done, calls pong with that finished response with res.end().

The return keyword is also very important. For example, we don't want to continue processing the request if the authentication has failed in the first middleware:

```
// Instantiate app and configure error handling

// Authentication middleware
var checkUserIsAdmin = function (req, res, next) {
  if (req.session && req.session._admin !== true) {
    return next (401);
  }
  return next();
};

// Admin route that fetches users and calls render function
var admin = {
  main: function (req, res, next) {
    req.db.get('users').find({}, function(e, users) {
      if (e) return next(e);
      if (!users) return next(new Error('No users to display.'));
      res.render('admin/index.html', users);
    });
  }
};

// Display list of users for admin dashboard
app.get('/admin', checkUserIsAdmin, admin.main);
```

The return keyword is essential, because if we don't use it for the next(e) call, the application will try to render (res.render()) even when there is an error and/or we don't have any users. For example, the following is probably a *bad idea* because after we call next(), which will trigger the appropriate error in the error handler, the flow goes on and tries to render the page:

```
var admin = {
  main: function (req, res, next) {
    req.db.get('users').find({}, function(e, users) {
      if (e) next(e);
      if (!users) next(new Error('No users to display.'));
      res.render('admin/index.html', users);
   });
  }
};
```

We should be using something like this:

```
if (!users) return next(new Error('No users to display.'));
res.render('admin/index.html', users);
```

or something like this:

```
if (!users)
  return next(new Error('No users to display.'));
else
  res.render('admin/index.html', users);
```

Summary

In this chapter we covered two major aspects of the typical structure of an Express.js app: defining routes and extracting URL parameters. We explored three different ways of how to get them out of the URL and use them in request handlers (req.params, custom middleware and app.param()). You learned how to define routes for various HTTP methods. Finally, we delved deep into the Router class, which acts as a mini Express.js application, and implemented yet another set of routes for the example project using the Router class.

Every time we defined a router (or a middleware), we used either an anonymous function definition or a named function in callbacks to define the request handler. The request handler usually has three parameters: request (or req), response (or res), and next. In the next chapter, you'll learn more about these objects, and how, in Express.js, they are different from the core Node.js http module's request and response. Knowing these differences will give you more features and functionality!

CHAPTER 7

Express.js Request Object

The Express.js request object (`req` for short) is a wrapper for a core Node.js `http.request` object, which is the Node.js representation of the incoming HTTP(S) request. In web, the request has these parts:

- Method: GET, POST or others
- URI: the location for example `http://hackhall.com/api/posts/`
- Headers: host: `www.hackhall.com`
- Body: content in the urlencoded, JSON or other formats

The Express.js request object has some additional neat functionality, but essentially it supports everything that the native `http.request` object can do.

For example, Express.js automatically adds support for query parsing, which is essential when the system needs to access data in the URL in the following format (after the question mark): `http://webapplog.com/?name1=value&name2=value`.

Here the list of methods and objects of the Express.js request object that we'll cover in this chapter:

- `request.query`: query string parameters
- `request.params`: URL parameters
- `request.body`: request body data
- `request.route`: the route path
- `request.cookies`: cookie data
- `request.signedCookies`: signed cookie data
- `request.header()` and `request.get()`: request headers

Tip When you see `request.`*`doSomething`* in the code, don't confuse the Express.js request object with Mikeal Roger's `request` module (`https://github.com/mikeal/request`) or with the core Node.js http module's request (`http://nodejs.org/api/http.html#http_event_request`).

To better understand the request object, let's create a brand new Express.js app with Express.js version 4.8.1. This is the `package.json` file of the project (`ch7/package.json`):

```
{
  "name": "request",
  "version": "0.0.1",
  "private": true,
  "scripts": {
    "start": "node app.js"
  },
  "dependencies": {
    "express": "4.8.1",
    "errorhandler": "1.1.1",
    "jade": "1.5.0",
    "morgan": "1.2.2",
    "serve-favicon": "2.0.1",
    "cookie-parser": "1.3.2",
    "body-parser": "1.6.5",
    "debug": "~0.7.4",
    "serve-favicon": "2.0.1"
  }
}
```

Next we install the modules with NPM into our local project `node_modules` folder:

```
$ npm install
```

Now start the app with `$ node app`. It should display a standard Express.js Generator page with the text "Welcome to Express" (on `http://localhost:3000`). The full source code of `app.js` is provided for reference at the end of this chapter. You can download it from GitHub at `https://github.com/azat-co/proexpressjs`.

request.query

The query string is everything to the right of the question mark in a given URL; for example, in the URL `https://twitter.com/search?q=js&src=typd`, the query string is `q=js&src=typd`. After the query string is parsed by `Express.js`, the resulting JS object would be `{q:'js', src:'typd'}`. This object is assigned to `req.query` or `request.query` in your request handler, depending on what variable name you used in the function signature.

By default, the parsing is done by the `qs` module (`http://npmjs.org/qs`), which is used by Express.js behind the scenes via the `express/lib/middleware/query.js` internal module. This setting can be changed by the `query parser` setting, about which you learned in Chapter 3 (hopefully).

The way `request.query` works resembles `body-parser`'s `json()` and `cookie-parser` middleware in that it puts a property (`query` in this case) on a request object `req` that is passed to the next middleware and routes. So, without query parsing of some sort we can't access the `request.query` object. Again, Express.js uses `qs` parser by default—no extra code is needed on our part.

To illustrate `request.query` in an example, we can add a search route that will print the incoming search term in a query data format. The data in this example is `q=js`, `q=nodejs`, and `q=nodejs&lang=fr`. The server sends back JSON with the same query string data that we sent to it. We can add this route to any Express.js server, such as the one we've created with the CLI (i.e., `ch7/request`):

```
app.get('/search', function(req, res) {
  console.log(req.query)
  res.end(JSON.stringify(req.query)+'\r\n');
})
```

■ **Tip** The `\n` and `\r` are line feed and carriage return symbols, respectively, in ASCII and Unicode. They allow the text to start on a new line. For more information, please refer to `http://en.wikipedia.org/wiki/Newline` and `http://en.wikipedia.org/wiki/Carriage_return`.

Keep the server running (`$ node app` to start it) and, in another terminal window, make the following GET requests with CURL:

```
$ curl -i "http://localhost:3000/search?q=js"
$ curl -i "http://localhost:3000/search?q=nodejs"
$ curl -i "http://localhost:3000/search?q=nodejs&lang=fr"
```

The result of CURL GET requests is shown in Figure 7-1, and the result of the server output is shown in Figure 7-2.

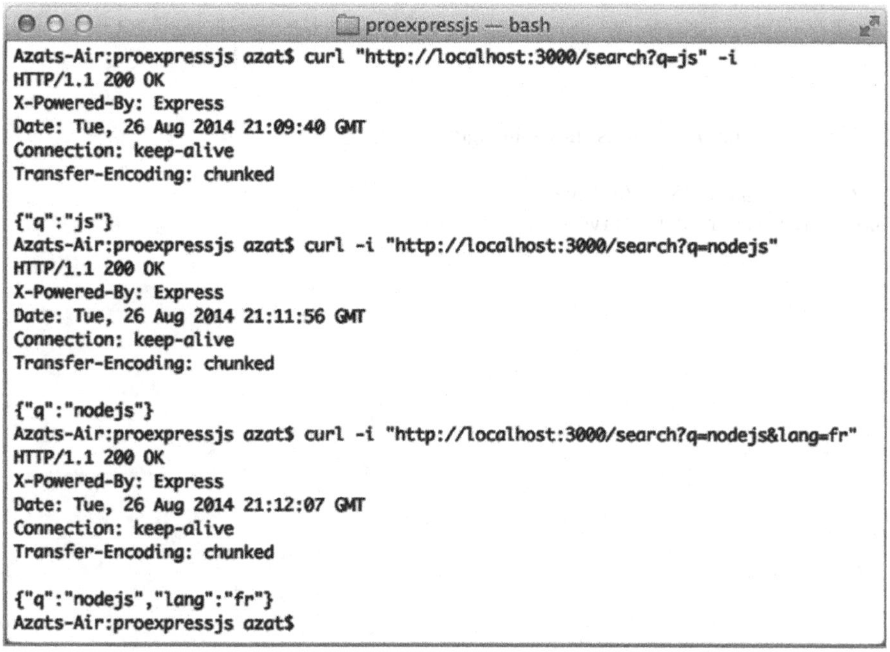
proexpressjs — bash
Azats-Air:proexpressjs azat$ curl "http://localhost:3000/search?q=js" -i
HTTP/1.1 200 OK
X-Powered-By: Express
Date: Tue, 26 Aug 2014 21:09:40 GMT
Connection: keep-alive
Transfer-Encoding: chunked
{"q":"js"}
Azats-Air:proexpressjs azat$ curl -i "http://localhost:3000/search?q=nodejs"
HTTP/1.1 200 OK
X-Powered-By: Express
Date: Tue, 26 Aug 2014 21:11:56 GMT
Connection: keep-alive
Transfer-Encoding: chunked
{"q":"nodejs"}
Azats-Air:proexpressjs azat$ curl -i "http://localhost:3000/search?q=nodejs&lang=fr"
HTTP/1.1 200 OK
X-Powered-By: Express
Date: Tue, 26 Aug 2014 21:12:07 GMT
Connection: keep-alive
Transfer-Encoding: chunked
{"q":"nodejs","lang":"fr"}
Azats-Air:proexpressjs azat$

Figure 7-1. *Client-side results of running CURL commands with the query string parameters*

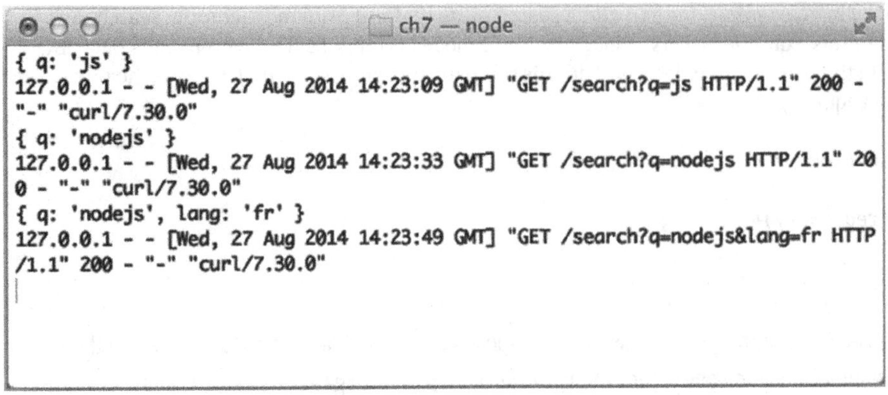

ch7 — node
{ q: 'js' }
127.0.0.1 - - [Wed, 27 Aug 2014 14:23:09 GMT] "GET /search?q=js HTTP/1.1" 200 -
"-" "curl/7.30.0"
{ q: 'nodejs' }
127.0.0.1 - - [Wed, 27 Aug 2014 14:23:33 GMT] "GET /search?q=nodejs HTTP/1.1" 20
0 - "-" "curl/7.30.0"
{ q: 'nodejs', lang: 'fr' }
127.0.0.1 - - [Wed, 27 Aug 2014 14:23:49 GMT] "GET /search?q=nodejs&lang=fr HTTP
/1.1" 200 - "-" "curl/7.30.0"

Figure 7-2. *Server-side results of running CURL commands with the query string parameters*

request.params

Chapter 6 covered how to set up middleware to process data taken from the URLs of the requests. However, sometimes it's more convenient just to get such values from within a specific request handler directly. For this, there's a `request.params` object, which is an array with key/value pairs.

To experiment with the `request.params` object, we can add a new route to our `ch7/request` application. This route will define URL parameters and print them in the console. Add the following route to `request/app.js`:

```
app.get('/params/:role/:name/:status', function(req, res) {
  console.log(req.params);
  res.end();
});
```

Next, run the following CURL terminal commands, as shown in Figure 7-3:

```
$ curl http://localhost:3000/params/admin/azat/active
$ curl http://localhost:3000/params/user/bob/active
```

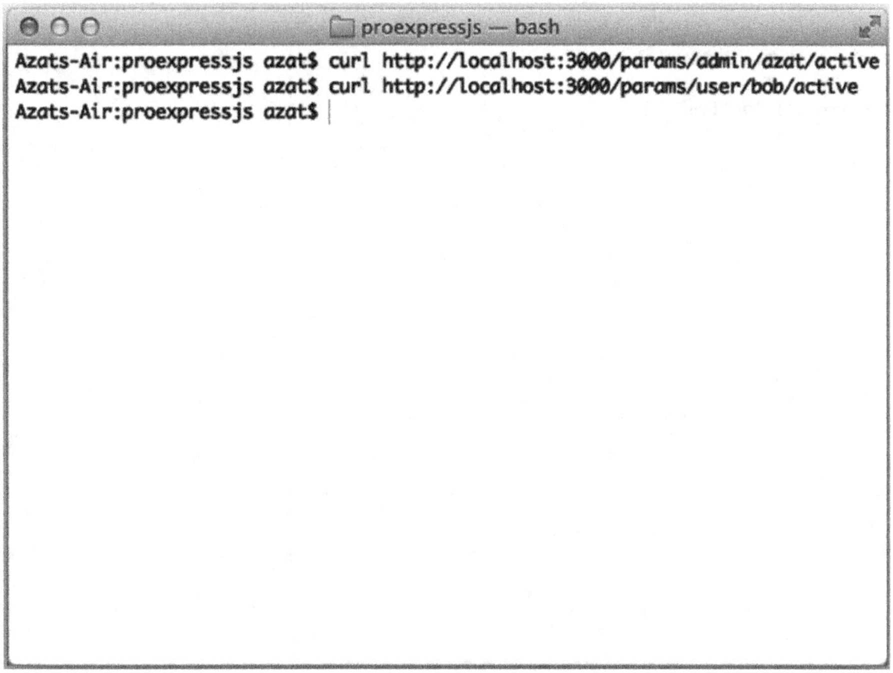

Figure 7-3. *Sending GET requests with CURL (client window)*

As shown in Figure 7-4, we see these server logs of the `request.params` object:

```
[ role: 'admin', name: 'azat', status: 'active' ]
[ role: 'user', name: 'bob', status: 'active' ]
```

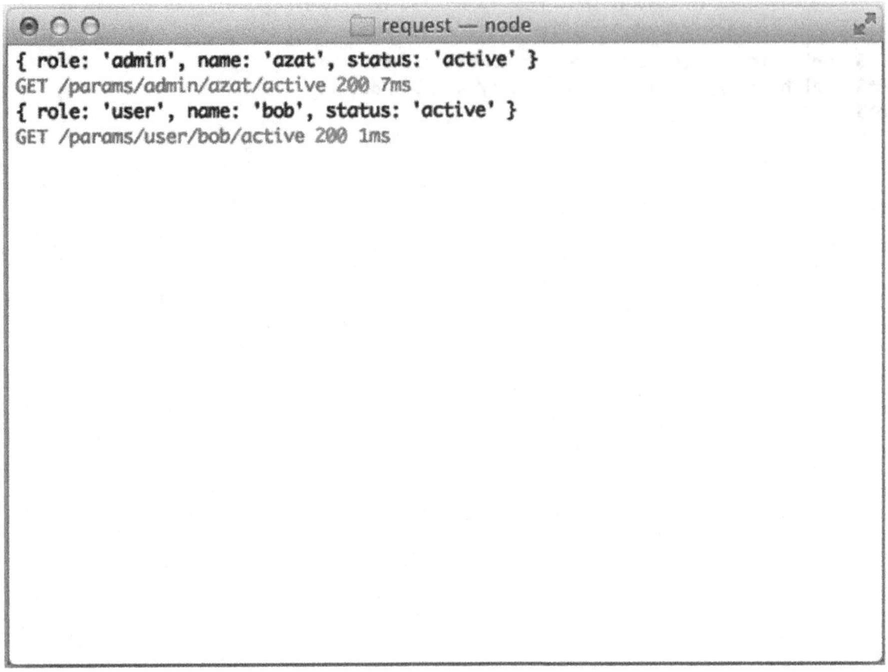

Figure 7-4. *Server result of processing request.params*

request.body

The `request.body` object is another magicical object that's provided to us by Express.js. It's populated by applying the `body-parser` (`express.bodyParser()` in Express.js 3.x) middleware functions. The body-parser module has two functions/middleware:

- `json()`: For parsing HTTP(S) payload into JavaScript/Node.js objects
- `urlencoded()`: For parsing URL-encoded HTTP(S) requests' data into JavaScript/Node.js objects

In both cases the resulting objects and data are put into the `request.body` object—extremely convenient!

To use `request.body`, we need to install body-parser separately (if you're using `ch7`, you can skip this step, because the generator put it in `package.json` for us):

```
$ npm install body-parser@1.0.0
```

Then we need to import and apply it:

```
var bodyParser = require('body-parser');
// ...
app.use(bodyParser.json());
app.use(bodyParser.urlencoded());
```

You don't have to use both the `json()` and `urlencoded()` methods. Use only the one that is needed, if that is sufficient.

To illustrate `request.body` in action, let's reuse our previous project and add the following route to see how the `request.body` object works, remembering that both `bodyParser()` middleware functions have been applied to the Express.js app already and are in the code:

```
app.post('/body', function(req, res){
  console.log(req.body);
  res.end(JSON.stringify(req.body)+'\r\n');
});
```

Again, submit a couple of HTTP POST requests with CURL or a similar tool:

```
$ curl http://localhost:3000/body -d 'name=azat'
$ curl -i http://localhost:3000/body -d 'name=azat&role=admin'
$ curl -i -H "Content-Type: application/json" -d '{"username":"azat","password":"p@ss1"}'
http://localhost:3000/body
```

■ **Tip** A brief CURL tip: The `-H` option sets headers, `-d` passes data, and `-i` enables verbose logging.

The preceding commands yield `request.body` objects, as you can see in the client terminal in Figure 7-5 and in the server terminal in Figure 7-6:

```
{ name: 'azat' }
{ name: 'azat', role: 'admin' }
{ username: 'azat', password: 'p@ss1' }
```

proexpressjs — bash
Azats-Air:proexpressjs azat$ curl http://localhost:3000/body -d 'name=azat'
{"name":"azat"}
Azats-Air:proexpressjs azat$ curl -i http://localhost:3000/body -d 'name=azat&role=admin'
HTTP/1.1 200 OK
X-Powered-By: Express
Date: Tue, 26 Aug 2014 21:40:59 GMT
Connection: keep-alive
Transfer-Encoding: chunked
{"name":"azat","role":"admin"}
Azats-Air:proexpressjs azat$ curl -i -H "Content-Type: application/json" -d '{"username":"azat","password":"p@ss1"}' http://localhost:3000/body
HTTP/1.1 200 OK
X-Powered-By: Express
Date: Tue, 26 Aug 2014 21:41:03 GMT
Connection: keep-alive
Transfer-Encoding: chunked
{"username":"azat","password":"p@ss1"}
Azats-Air:proexpressjs azat$

Figure 7-5. *Sending POST requests with CURL (client logs)*

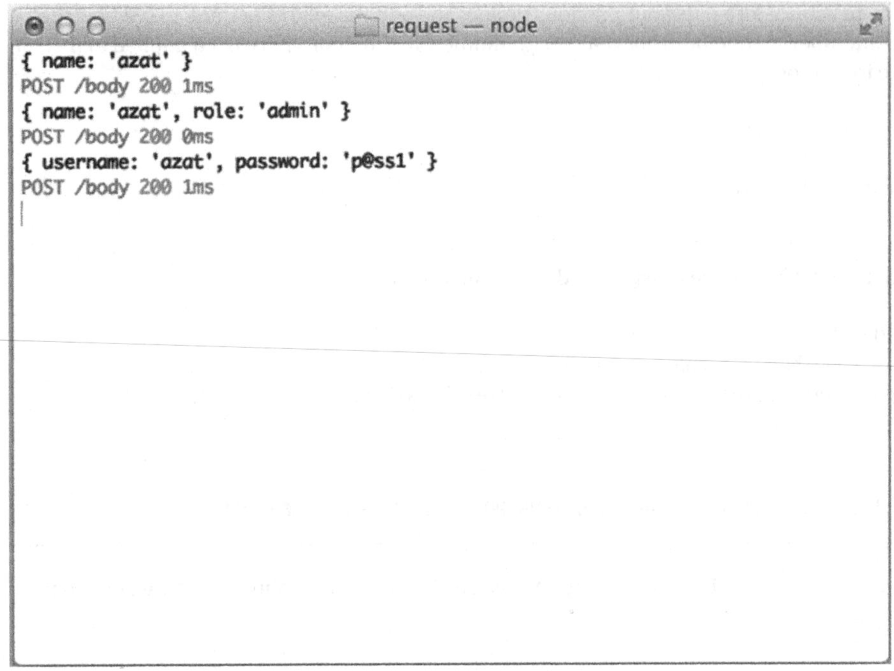
request — node
{ name: 'azat' }
POST /body 200 1ms
{ name: 'azat', role: 'admin' }
POST /body 200 0ms
{ username: 'azat', password: 'p@ss1' }
POST /body 200 1ms

Figure 7-6. *Result of processing request.body (server logs)*

request.route

The `request.route` object simply has the current route's information, such as:

- `path`: Original URL pattern of the request
- `method`: HTTP method of the request
- `keys`: List of parameters in the URL pattern (i.e., values prefixed with `:`)
- `regexp`: Express.js-generated pattern for the path
- `params`: `request.params` object

We can add the `console.log(request.route);` statement to our `request.params` route from the example in the previous section like this:

```
app.get('/params/:role/:name/:status', function(req, res) {
  console.log(req.params);
  console.log(req.route);
  res.end();
});
```

Then, if we send the HTTP GET request

```
$ curl http://localhost:3000/params/admin/azat/active
```

we should get the server logs of the `request.route` object, which has `path`, `stack`, and `methods` properties:

```
{ path: '/params/:role/:name/:status',
  stack: [ { method: 'get', handle: [Function] } ],
  methods: { get: true } }
```

The `request.route` object might be useful when used from within middleware (i.e., that is used on multiple routes) to find out which route is currently used.

request.cookies

The cookie-parser (formerly `express.cookieParser()` in Express.js 3.x and earlier) middleware (`https://www.npmjs.org/package/cookie-parser`, `https://github.com/expressjs/cookie-parser`) allows us to access requests' cookies in a JavaScript/Node.js format. The `cookie-parser` is required for express-session middleware, because web sessions work by storing their session ID in the browser cookies.

With `cookie-parser` installed (with NPM), imported (with `require()`), and applied (with `app.use()`), we get access to the HTTP(S) request cookies (user-agent cookies) via the `request.cookies` object. Cookies are automatically presented as a JavaScript object; for example, you can extract the session ID with:

```
request.cookies['connect.sid']
```

■ **Caution** Storing sensitive information in browser cookies is discouraged because of security concerns. Also, some browsers impose a limitation on the size of a cookie, which might lead to bugs (Internet Explorer!). I usually use `request.cookie` only for the `request.session` support.

■ **Note** Refer to Chapter 4 for more information on how to install and apply middleware.

The cookie info can be stored using `response.cookie()` or `res.cookie()`. The Express.js response object is covered in Chapter 8. To illustrate `request.cookies`, we can implement a `/cookies` route that will increment a counter, change the value of a cookie, and display the result on a page. This is the code that you can add to `ch7/request`:

```
app.get('/cookies', function(req, res){
  if (!req.cookies.counter)
    res.cookie('counter', 0);
  else
    res.cookie('counter', parseInt(req.cookies.counter,10) + 1);
  res.status(200).send('cookies are: ', req.cookies);
})
```

■ **Tip** The `parseInt()` method is needed to prevent JavaScript/Node.js from treating the number value as a string, which would result in 0, 01, 011, 0111, etc. instead of 0, 1, 2, 3, etc. Using `parseInt()` with the radix/base (second argument) is recommended to prevent numbers from being converted incorrectly.

As a result of going to `http://localhost:3000/cookies` and refreshing it a few times, you should see the counter increment from 0 up, as shown in Figure 7-7.

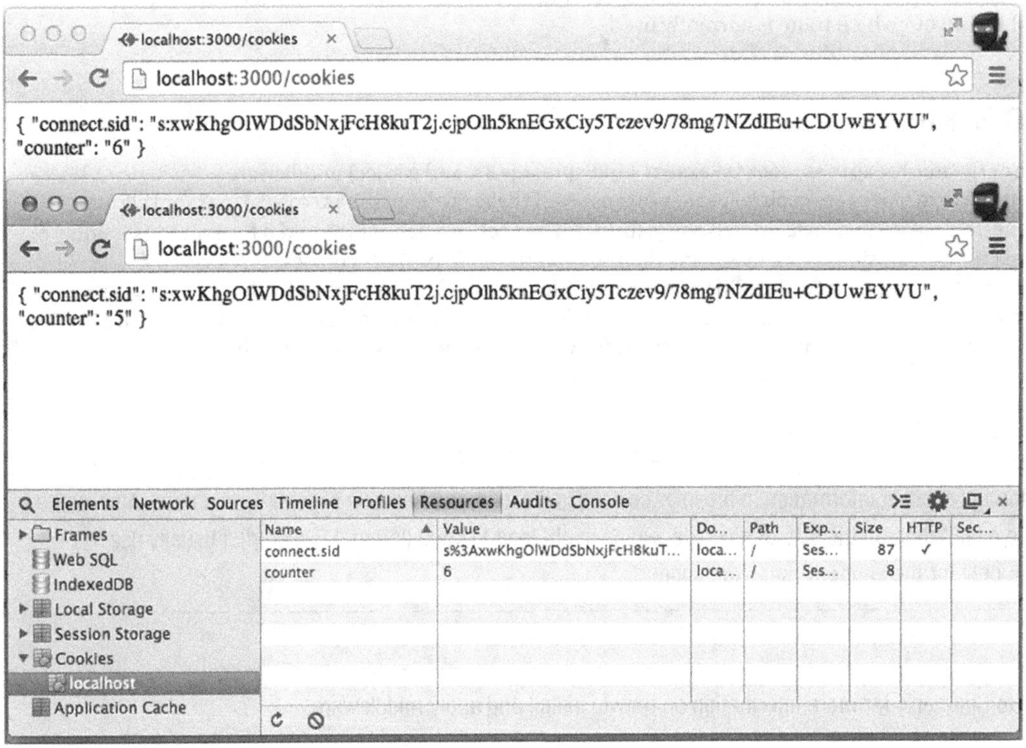

Figure 7-7. *Cookie value is saved in the browser and incremented by the server on each request*

Inspection of the Network or Resource tab in Chrome Developer Tools will reveal the presence of a cookie with the name `connect.sid` (see Figure 7-7). The cookies are shared between browser windows, so even if we open a new window, the counter will increment by 1 from the value in the original window.

request.signedCookies

`request.signedCookies` is akin to `request.cookies`, but it's used when the secret string is passed to the `express.cookieParser('some secret string');` method. To populate `request.signedCookies`, you can use `response.cookie` with the flag `signed: true`. Here's how we can modify our previous route to switch to signed cookies:

```
app.use(cookieParser('abc'));
// ... Other middleware
app.get('/signed-cookies', function(req, res){
  if (!req.signedCookies.counter)
    res.cookie('counter', 0, {signed: true});
  else
    res.cookie('counter', parseInt(req.signedCookies.counter,10) + 1, {signed: true});
  res.status(200).send('cookies are: ', req.signedCookies);
});
// ... Server boot-up
```

So, all we did was change `request.cookies` to `request.signedCookies` and add `signed: true` when assigning cookie values on response. The parsing of the signed cookies is done automatically, and they are placed in plain JavaScript/Node.js objects. Note that `'abc'` is an arbitrary string. You can use `$ uuidgen` on Mac OS X to generate a random key to sign your cookies or web-based services like Random.org (`http://bit.ly/1F1fbL8`).

■ **Caution** Signing a cookie *does not* hide or encrypt the cookie. It's a simple way to prevent tampering by applying a private value. Signing (or hashing) is not the same as encryption. The former is for identification and tampering prevention. The latter is for hiding the content from unauthorized recipients (see, e.g., `http://danielmiessler.com/study/encoding_encryption_hashing`). You can encrypt your cookie data on the server (and decrypt it when reading), but, hypothetically, this is still vulnerable to brute-force attacks. The level of vulnerability depends on the encryption algorithm that you use.

---

request.header() and request.get()

The `request.header()` and `request.get()` methods are identical and allow for retrieval of the HTTP(S) requests' headers by their names. Fortunately, the header naming is case insensitive:

```
request.get('Content-Type');
request.get('content-type');
request.header('content-type');
```

Other Attributes and Methods

We've covered the most commonly used and most important methods and objects of the Express.js request object. They should suffice in the majority of cases. But the list doesn't stop there. For convenience, there are plenty of *sugar-coating* objects in the Express.js request (see Table 7-1). Sugar-coating means that most of the functions of these objects can be implemented with the foundational methods, but they are more eloquent than the foundational methods. For example, the `request.accepts` can be replaced with `if/else` and `request.get()`, which gives us request headers. Of course, if you understand these methods, you can use them to make your code more elegant and easier to read.

Table 7-1. Other Attributes and Methods in the Express.js Request

Attribute/Method	Conditions/Definition	API
request.accepts()	true if a passed string (single or comma-separated values) or an array of MIME types (or extensions) matches the request Accept header; false if there's no match	http://expressjs.com/api.html#req.accepts
request.accepted	An array of accepted MIME types	http://expressjs.com/api.html#req.accepted
request.is()	true if a passed MIME type string matches the Content-Type header types; false if there's no match	http://expressjs.com/api.html#req.is
request.ip	The IP address of the request; see trust proxy configuration in Chapter 3	http://expressjs.com/api.html#req.ip
request.ips	An array of IPs when trust proxy configuration is enabled	http://expressjs.com/api.html#req.ips
request.path	String with a URL path of the request	http://expressjs.com/api.html#req.path
request.host	Value from the Host header of the request	http://expressjs.com/api.html#req.host
request.fresh	true if request is *fresh* based on Last-Modified and ETag headers; false otherwise	http://expressjs.com/api.html#req.fresh
request.stale	Opposite of req.fresh	http://expressjs.com/api.html#req.stale
request.xhr	true if the request is an AJAX call via X-Requested-With header and its XMLHttpRequest value	http://expressjs.com/api.html#req.xhr
request.protocol	Request protocol value (e.g., http or https)	http://expressjs.com/api.html#req.protocol
request.secure	true if the request protocol is https	http://expressjs.com/api.html#req.secure
request.subdomains	Array of subdomains from the Host header	http://expressjs.com/api.html#req.subdomains
request.originalUrl	Unchangeable value of the request URL	http://expressjs.com/api.html#req.originalUrl
request.acceptedLanguages	Array of language code (e.g., en-us, en) from the request's Accept-Language header	http://expressjs.com/api.html#req.acceptedLanguages
request.acceptsLanguage()	true if a passed language code is in the request header	http://expressjs.com/api.html#req.acceptsLanguage
request.acceptedCharsets	Array of charsets (e.g., iso-8859-5) from the request's Accept-Charset header	http://expressjs.com/api.html#req.acceptedCharsets
request.acceptsCharset()	true if a passed charset is in the request header	http://expressjs.com/api.html#req.acceptsCharset

We've been making small adjustments to the ch7 project throughout this chapter, so now it's time to see the whole picture. Therefore, here's the full source code of the final request server from the ch7/app.js file (available at https://github.com/azat-co/proexpressjs):

```
var express = require('express');
var path = require('path');
var favicon = require('serve-favicon');
var logger = require('morgan');
var cookieParser = require('cookie-parser');
var bodyParser = require('body-parser');

var routes = require('./routes/index');

var app = express();

// View engine setup
app.set('views', path.join(__dirname, 'views'));
app.set('view engine', 'jade');
app.use(logger('combined'));
app.use(favicon(path.join(__dirname, 'public', 'favicon.ico')));
app.use(bodyParser.json());
app.use(bodyParser.urlencoded({extended: true}));
app.use(cookieParser('abc'));
app.use(express.static(path.join(__dirname, 'public')));

app.use('/', routes);

app.get('/search', function(req, res) {
  console.log(req.query);
  res.end(JSON.stringify(req.query)+'\r\n');
});

app.get('/params/:role/:name/:status', function(req, res) {
  console.log(req.params);
  console.log(req.route);
  res.end();
});

app.post('/body', function(req, res){
  console.log(req.body);
  res.end(JSON.stringify(req.body)+'\r\n');
});

app.get('/cookies', function(req, res){
  if (!req.cookies.counter)
    res.cookie('counter', 0);
  else
    res.cookie('counter', parseInt(req.cookies.counter,10) + 1);
  res.status(200).send('cookies are: ', req.cookies);
});
```

```
app.get('/signed-cookies', function(req, res){
  if (!req.signedCookies.counter)
    res.cookie('counter', 0, {signed: true});
  else
    res.cookie('counter', parseInt(req.signedCookies.counter,10) + 1, {signed: true});
  res.status(200).send('cookies are: ', req.signedCookies);
});

/// Catch 404 and forward to error handler
app.use(function(req, res, next) {
    var err = new Error('Not Found');
    err.status = 404;
    next(err);
});

/// Error handlers

// Development error handler
// Will print stacktrace
if (app.get('env') === 'development') {
    app.use(function(err, req, res, next) {
        res.status(err.status || 500);
        res.render('error', {
            message: err.message,
            error: err
        });
    });
}

// Production error handler
// No stacktraces leaked to user
app.use(function(err, req, res, next) {
    res.status(err.status || 500);
    res.render('error', {
        message: err.message,
        error: {}
    });
});

module.exports = app;

var debug = require('debug')('request');

app.set('port', process.env.PORT || 3000);

var server = app.listen(app.get('port'), function() {
  debug('Express server listening on port ' + server.address().port);
});
```

Summary

Understanding and working with HTTP requests is at the foundation of web development. The way in which Express.js approaches requests is by adding objects and properties. Developers use them inside of the request handlers. Express.js provides many objects and methods in the request and, in areas where it does not, there are plenty of third-party options.

In the next chapter we'll cover the Express.js response. The response object is the counterpart of the request object. Response is the stuff that we actually send back to the client. Similar to request, the Express.js response object has special methods and objects as its properties. We'll cover the most important and then list the rest of the built-in properties.

CHAPTER 8

Express.js Response Object

The Express.js response object (`res` for short)—which is an argument in the request handler callbacks—is the same good old Node.js `http.response` object[1] on steroids. This is because the Express.js response object has new methods. In other words, the Express.js response object is the extension of the `http.response` class.

Why would some use these additional methods? Indeed, you can use the `response.end()` method[2] and other core methods, but then you'll have to write more code. For example, you would have to add Content-Type header manually. But with the Express.js response object, which contains convenient wrappers, such as `response.json()` and `response.send()`, appropriate Content-Type is added automatically.

In this chapter, we'll cover the following methods and attributes of the Express.js response object in great detail:

- `response.render()`
- `response.locals`
- `response.set()`
- `response.status()`
- `response.send()`
- `response.json()`
- `response.jsonp()`
- `response.redirect()`

To demonstrate these methods in action, they are used in the kitchen-sink app `ch8/app.js`. Other methods and properties, along with their meanings, will be listed in the Table 8-1. At the end of the chapter, we'll cover how to work with streams and Express.js response.

To start with the example app, create a brand new Express.js app with `express-generator` and the `$ express response` terminal command. Obviously, now you need to run `$ cd response && npm install` to download the dependencies. The initial `ch8/app.js` app will be identical to the initial app from Chapter 7.

response.render()

The `response.render()` method is the staple of Express.js. From our previous examples and from the function's name, you could guess that it has something to do with generating HTML out of templates (such as Jade, Handlebars, or EJS) and data.

---

[1]`http://nodejs.org/api/http.html#http_class_http_serverresponse`
[2]`http://nodejs.org/api/http.html#http_response_end_data_encoding`

The `response.render(name, [data,] [callback])` method takes three parameters, but only one is mandatory, and it's the first parameter: `name`, which is the template name in a string format. The other parameters are `data` and `callback`. If you omit `data`, but have `callback`, then `callback` becomes the number two argument.

The template name can be identified with or without an extension. For more information on template engine extensions, please refer to Chapter 5.

To illustrate the most straightforward use case for `response.render()`, we'll create a page that shows a heading and a paragraph from a Jade template.

First, add a route. Here is an example of a simple setup for the home page route in the `response/app.js` file:

```
app.get('/render', function(req, res) {
  res.render('render');
});
```

Then, add a new `views/render.jade` file that looks static for now (i.e., it has no variables or logic):

```
extends layout

block content
  h1= 'Pro Express.js'
  p Welcome to the Pro Express.js Response example!
```

Finally, start the response application with `$ node app` and go to `http://localhost:3000` in a browser. You should see the welcome message shown in Figure 8-1.

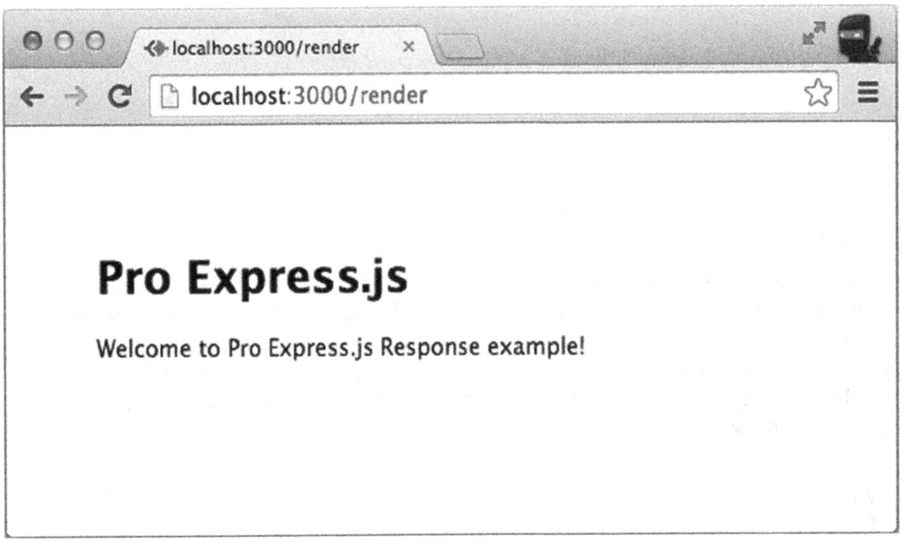

Figure 8-1. *The result of plain response.render() call without parameters*

■ **Note** Jade uses Python/Haml-like syntax, which takes into account whitespace and tabs. Be careful with the markup. We can use = as a *print* command (h1 tag) or nothing (p tag). For more information, please visit the official documentation (http://jade-lang.com/) or check out *Practical Node.js* (Apress, 2014).[3]

In addition to the mandatory name parameter, response.render(), has two optional parameters: data and callback. The data parameter makes templates more dynamic than static HTML files and allows us to update the output. For example, we can pass "title" to overwrite the value in the default value:

```
app.get('/render-title', function(req, res) {
  res.render('index', {title: 'Pro Express.js'});
});
```

The index.jade file remains the same. It prints the title value, and looks like this:

```
extends layout

block content
  h1= title
  p Welcome to #{title}
```

The result of the /render-title route is shown in Figure 8-2. The h1 title text has changed to Pro Express.js.

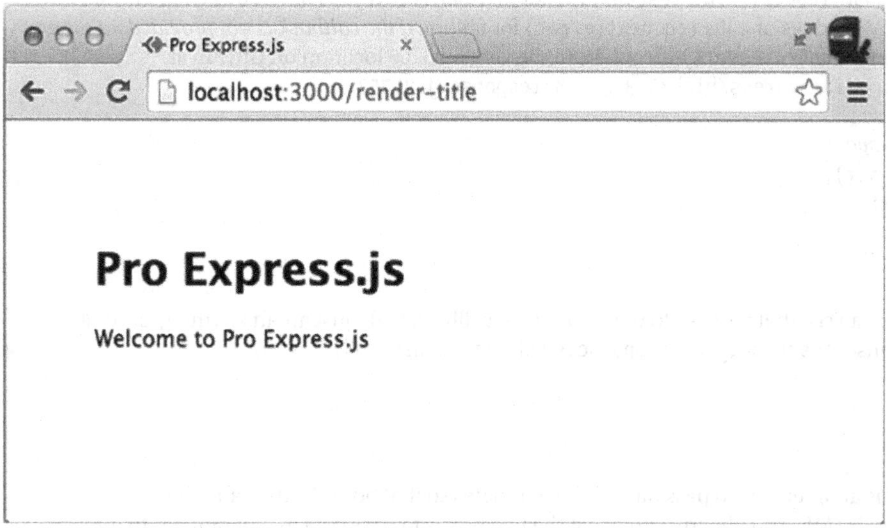

Figure 8-2. *The response.render() example with the data parameter that has a title property*

[3]http://practicalnodebook.com

The `response.render()` callback parameter accepts two parameters itself: `error` and `html` (an HTML string that is the output). This example is not in the `res/app.js` project, but shows how to pass callbacks to `response.render()`:

```
app.get('/render-title', function(req, res) {
  res.render('index', {title: 'Pro Express.js'}, function (error, html) {
    // Do something
  });
});
```

■ **Caution** The properties of the `data` parameter are your locals in the template. In other words, if you want to access a value of a title inside of your template, the data object must contain a key/value pair. Nested objects are supported by most of the template engines.

The `callback` can take the place of the `data` because Express.js is able to determine the type of the parameter. This example is not within `response/app.js`, but shows how to pass callbacks with our data:

```
app.get('/render-title', function(req, res) {
  res.render('index', function (error, html) {
    // Do something
  });
});
```

Behind the scenes, `response.render()` calls `response.send()` (which is covered later in this chapter) for successful compilation of HTML strings or calls `req.next(error)` for failure, *if the callback is not provided.* In other words, the default callback to `response.render()` is code from the version 3.3.5 location on GitHub at `https://github.com/visionmedia/express/blob/3.3.5/lib/response.js#L753`:

```
// Default callback to respond
fn = fn || function(err, str){
  if (err) return req.next(err);
  self.send(str);
};
```

Looking at this code, you can see that it's easy to write your own callback to do just about anything, as long as there's an ending to the response (`response.json`, `response.send`, or `response.end`).

response.locals

The `response.locals` object is another way to pass data to the templates so that both the data and the template can be compiled into HTML. You already know that the first way is to pass data as a parameter to the `response.render()` method, as previously outlined:

```
app.get('/render-title', function(req, res) {
  res.render('index', {title: Pro Express.js'});
});
```

However, with `response.locals`, we can achieve the same thing. Our object will be available inside of the template:

```
app.get('/locals', function(req, res){
  res.locals = { title: 'Pro Express.js' };
  res.render('index');
});
```

Again, the `index.jade` Jade template remains the same:

```
extends layout

block content
  h1= title
  p Welcome to #{title}
```

You can see the web page that has the Pro Express.js title in Figure 8-3. But, if nothing has changed, then what is the benefit of `response.locals`? The advantage is that we can expose (i.e., pass to templates) info in one middleware, but render the actual template later in another request handler. For example, you can perform authentication without rendering (this code is not in the `ch8/app.js`):

```
app.get('/locals',
  function(req, res){
    res.locals = { user: {admin: true}};
    next();
  }, function(req, res){
    res.render('index');
});
```

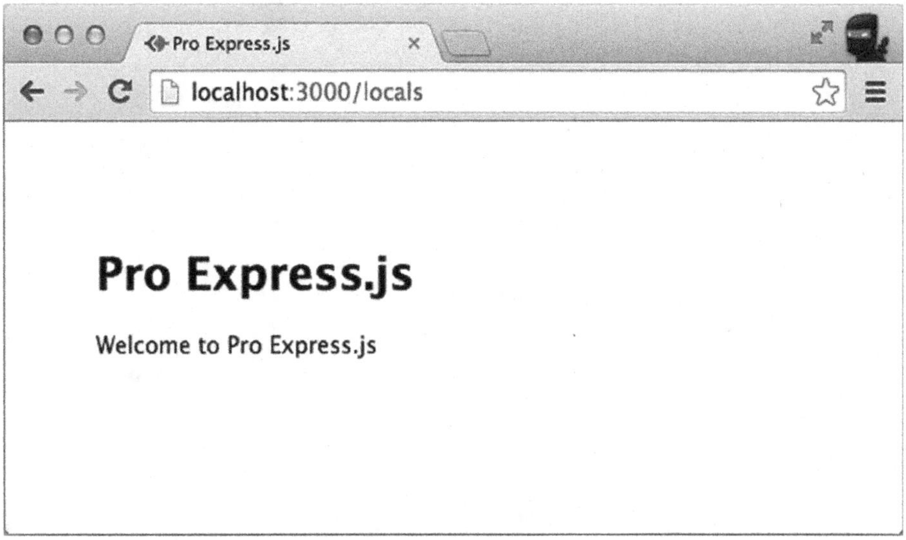

Figure 8-3. *The response.locals example renders the same page as the response.render() example*

■ **Tip** Sometimes, for debugging, it's useful to see a list of all the variables available in a particular Jade template. To do so, simply insert this log statement: `- console.log(locals);`. For more information on Jade, please refer to *Practical Node.js* (Apress, 2014).[4]

response.set()

The `response.set(field, [value])` method is an alias of `response.header()` (or the other way around) and serves as a wrapper for the Node.js http core module's `response.setHeader()` function.[5] The main difference is that Express.js' `response.set()` is smart enough to call itself recursively when we pass multiple header-value pairs to it in the form of an object. See the CSV example later in this section if the previous sentence didn't make much sense to you.

Here is an example from `ch8/app.js` of setting a single `Content-Type` response header to `text/html` and then sending some simple HTML to the client:

```
app.get('/set-html', function(req, res) {
  // Some code
  res.set('Content-Type', 'text/html');
  res.end('<html><body>' +
    '<h1>Express.js Guide</h1>' +
    '</body></html>');
});
```

You can see the results in the Network tab of Chrome Developer Tools, under the Headers subtab, which says `Content-Type: text/html` (see Figure 8-4). If we didn't have `response.set()` with `text/html`, then the response would still have the HTML, but *without the header*. Feel free to comment the `response.set()` and see it for yourself.

[4]http://practicalnodebook.com

[5]http://nodejs.org/api/http.html#http_response_setheader_name_value

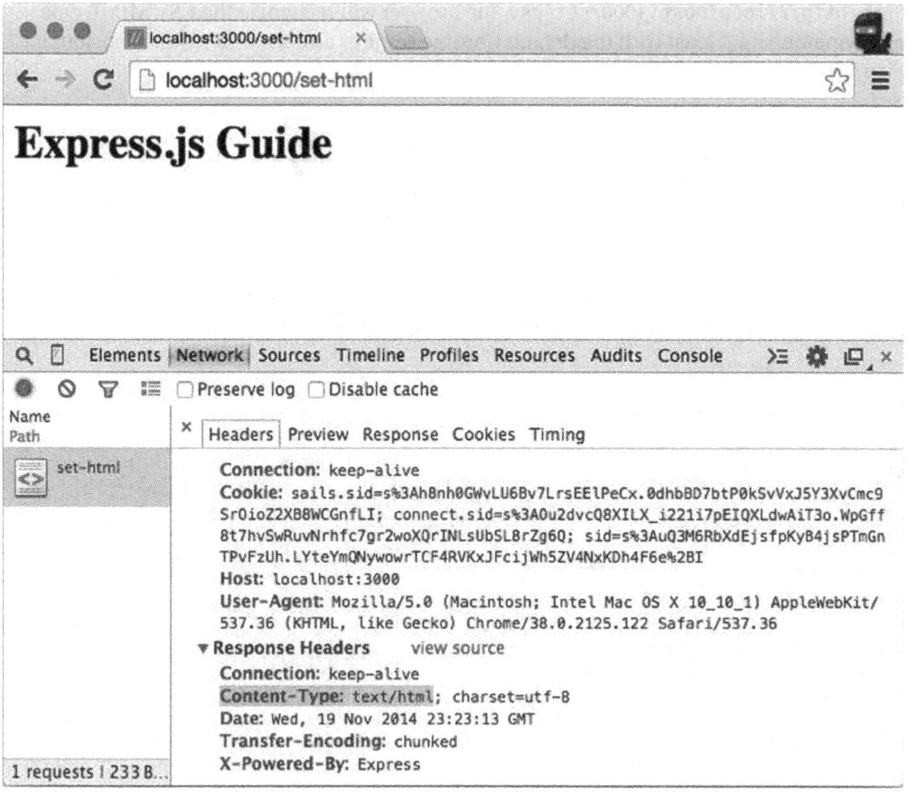

Figure 8-4. *The response.set() example rendering HTML with the Content-Type: text/html header*

The Content-Type disappears when we don't set it explicitly with `response.set()`, because Express.js' `response.send()` automatically adds `Content-Type` and other headers, but core `response.end()` does not. More on `response.send()` later in this chapter.

Often though, our servers need to provide more than one header so that all the different browsers and other HTTP clients process it properly. Let's explore an example of passing multiple values to the `response.set()` method.

Imagine that the service we are building sends out comma-separated value (CVS) files with books' titles and their tags. This is how we can implement this route in the `ch8/app.js` file:

```
app.get('/set-csv', function(req, res) {
  var body = 'title, tags\n' +
    'Practical Node.js, node.js express.js\n' +
    'Rapid Prototyping with JS, backbone.js node.js mongodb\n' +
    'JavaScript: The Good Parts, javascript\n';
  res.set({'Content-Type': 'text/csv',
    'Content-Length': body.length,
    'Set-Cookie': ['type=reader', 'language=javascript']});
  res.end(body);
});
```

Now, if you steer Chrome to `http://localhost:3000/set-csv`, the browser will recognize the CSV MIME type and download the file instead of opening it (at least with the default Chrome settings and without extra extensions). You can see the headers in Figure 8-5.

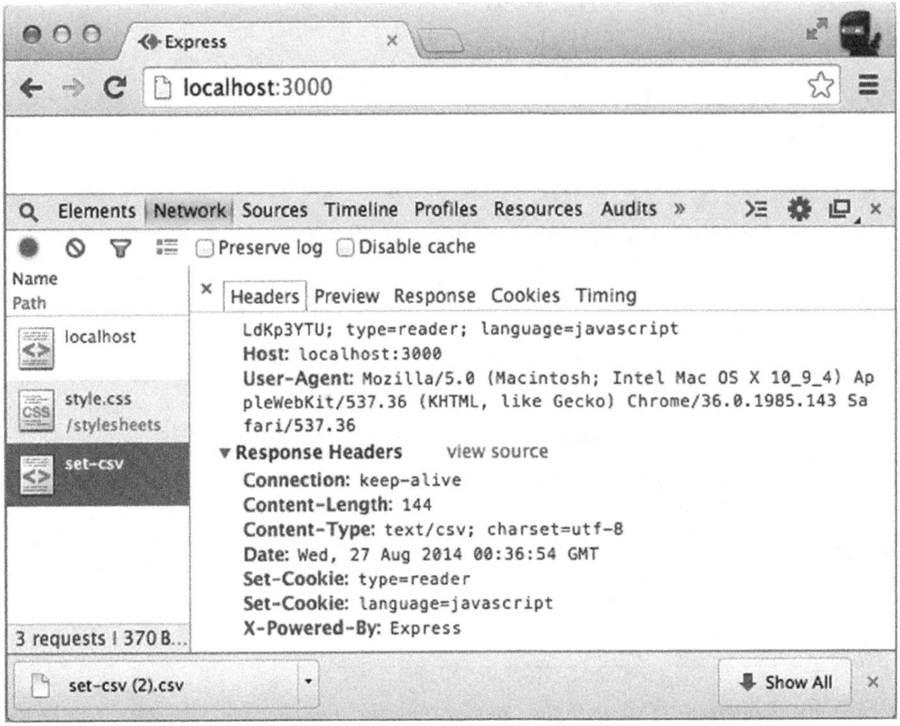

Figure 8-5. *The response.set() example rendering Content-Length, Content-Type, and Set-Cookie headers with CSV data*

response.status()

The `response.status()` method accepts an HTTP status code[6] number and sends it in response. The most common HTTP status codes are:

200: OK

201: Created

301: Moved Permanently

401: Unauthorized

404: Not Found

500: Internal Server Error

[6]`http://www.w3.org/Protocols/rfc2616/rfc2616-sec10.html`

You can find a lengthier list of HTTP statuses in Chapter 9. The only difference between its core counterpart[7] is that `response.status()` is chainable. Status codes are important for building REST APIs because they enable you to standardize the outcome of the request.

Let's demo how `response.status()` works on the pulse route, which returns 200 (OK) if the server is still up and running. This route won't send back any text or HTML on purpose. We use `response.end()` because `response.send()` will automatically add the proper status code 200:

```
app.get('/status', function(req, res) {
  res.status(200).end();
});
```

If you go to `http://localhost:3000/status`, you'll see a green circle and the number 200, as shown in Figure 8-6.

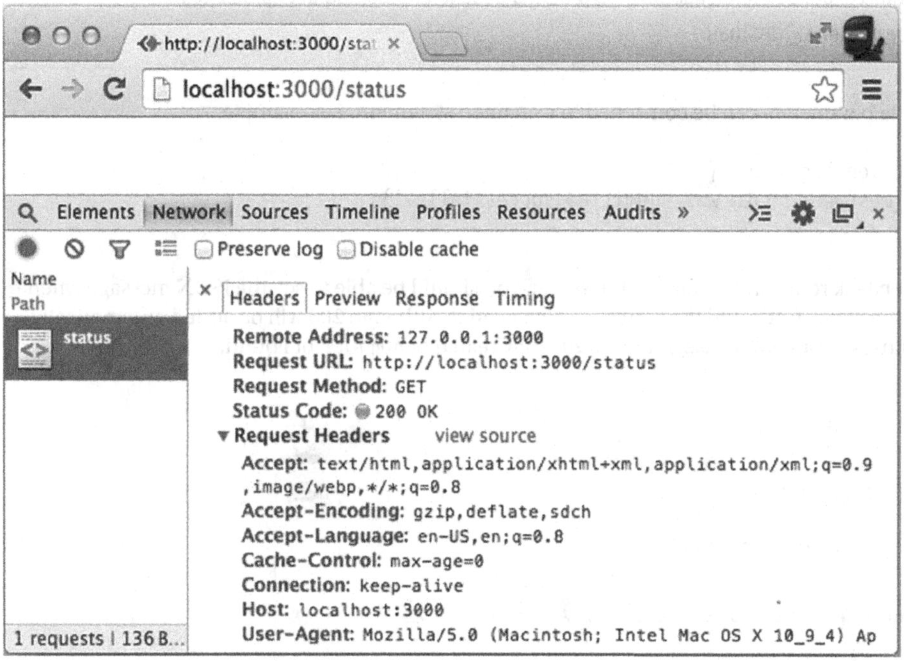

Figure 8-6. *The response.status() example response*

response.send()

The `response.send()` method lies somewhere between high-level `response.render()` and low-level `response.end()`. The `response.send()` method conveniently outputs any data application thrown at it (such as strings, JavaScript objects, and even Buffers) with automatically generated *proper* HTTP headers (e.g., Content-Length, ETag, or Cache-Control).

[7]`http://nodejs.org/api/http.html#http_response_statuscode`

Due to its omnivorous (consumes any input) behavior (caused by `arguments.length`), `response.send()` can be used in countless ways with these input parameters:

- *String*: `response.send('success');` with text/html
- *Object*: `response.send({message: 'success'});` or `response.send({message: 'error'});` with JSON representation
- *Array*: `response.send([{title: 'Practical Node.js'}, {title: 'Rapid Prototyping with JS'}]);` with JSON representation
- *Buffer*: `response.send(new Buffer('Express.js Guide'));` with `application/octet-stream`

■ **Tip** Sending numbers with `response.send(number)` as a status code is deprecated in Express.js 4.x. Use `response.status(number).send()` instead.

The status code and data parameters can be combined in a chained statement. For example:

```
app.get('/send-ok', function(req, res) {
  res.status(200).send({message: 'Data was submitted successfully.'});
});
```

After adding the new `send-ok` route and restarting the server, you should be able to see the JSON message when you go to `/send-ok`. Notice the Status Code and the `Content-Type` header. Although 200 will be added automatically, it's recommended to set statuses for all other cases, such as `201` for Created or `404` for Not Found.

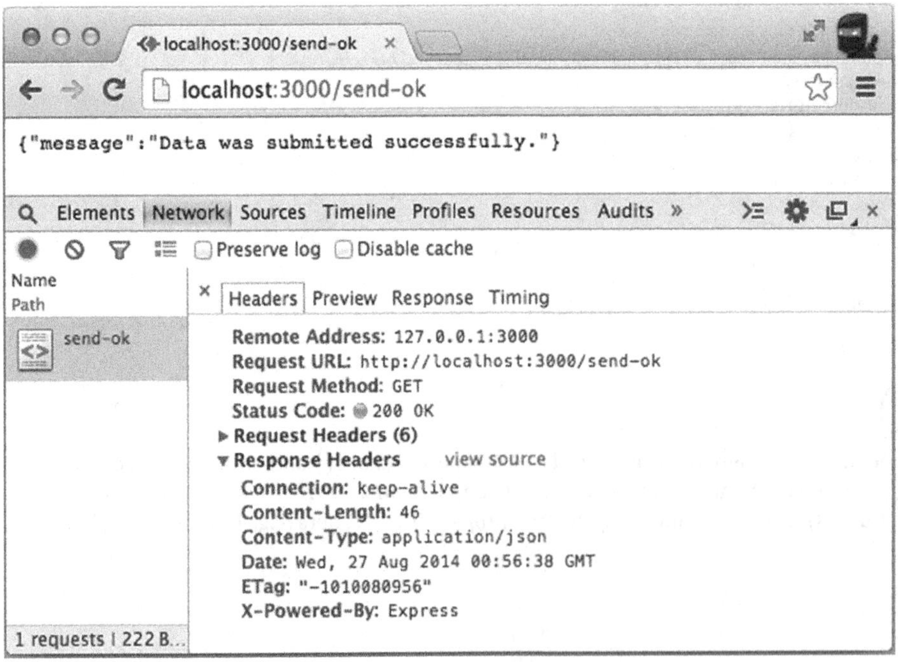

Figure 8-7. *The response.send() 200 status code example response*

The following is an example of sending the 500 Internal Server Error status code along with the error message (used for server errors):

```
app.get('/send-err', function(req, res) {
  res.status(500).send({message: 'Oops, the server is down.'});
});
```

Again, when you check this route in the browser, there's a JSON content type, but now you see a red circle and the number 500.

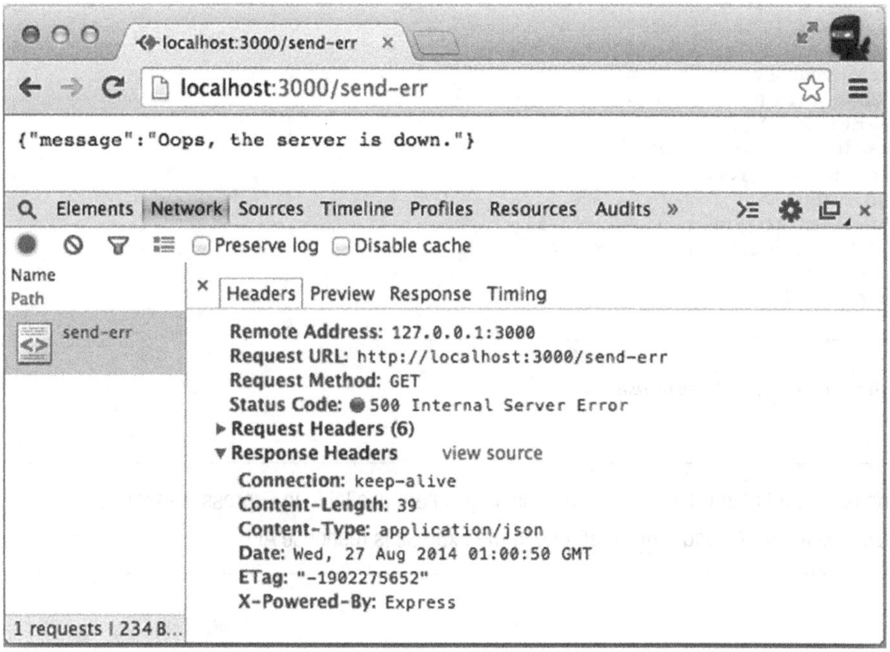

Figure 8-8. *The response.status(500).send() 500 status code example response*

The headers generated by `response.send()` might be overwritten if specified explicitly before. For example, the Buffer type will have `Content-Type` as `application/octet-stream`, but we can change it to `text/plain` with

```
app.get('/send-buf', function(req, res) {
  res.set('Content-Type', 'text/plain');
  res.send(new Buffer('text data that will be converted into Buffer'));
});
```

The resulting content type and text are shown in Figure 8-9.

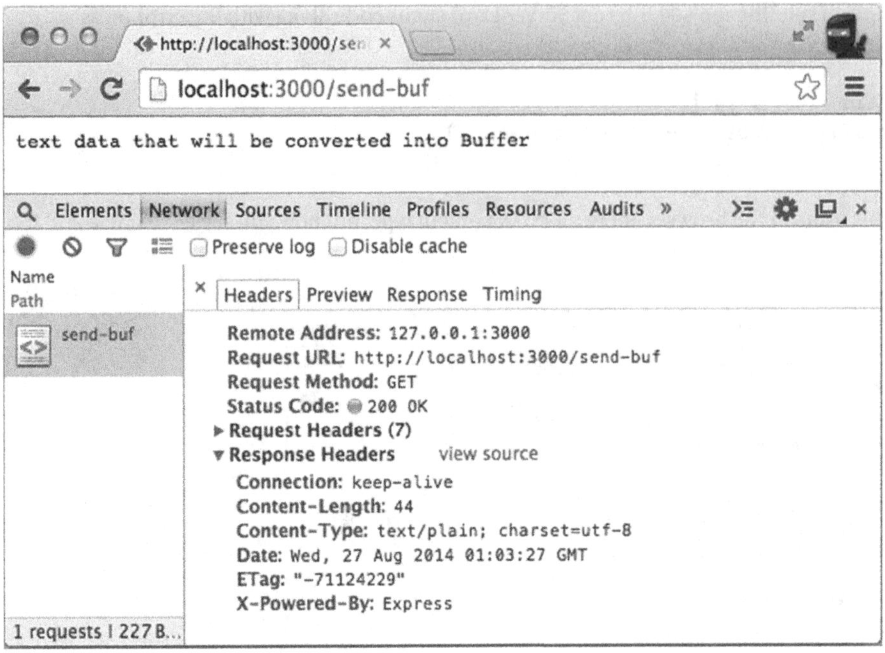

Figure 8-9. *The response.send() Buffer example response*

■ **Note** Virtually all core Node.js methods (and Connect.js methods as well) are available in Express.js objects. Therefore, we have access to `response.end()` and other methods in the Express.js response API.

---

response.json()

The `response.json()` method is a convenient way of sending JSON data. It's equivalent to `response.send()` when data passed is Array or Object type. In other cases, `response.json()` forces data conversion with `JSON.stringify()`. By default, the header `Content-Type` is set to `application/json`, but can be overwritten prior to `response.json()` with `response.set()`.

If you remember our old friends from Chapter 3, `json replacer` and `json spaces`, that's where these settings are taken into account.

The most common use of `response.json()` is with appropriate status codes:

```
app.get('/json', function(req, res) {
  res.status(200).json([{title: 'Practical Node.js', tags: 'node.js express.js'},
    {title: 'Rapid Prototyping with JS', tags: 'backbone.js node.js mongodb'},
    {title: 'JavaScript: The Good Parts', tags: 'javascript'}
  ]);
});
```

Please note the JSON Content-Type and Content-Length headers produced by `response.json()` in Figure 8-10.

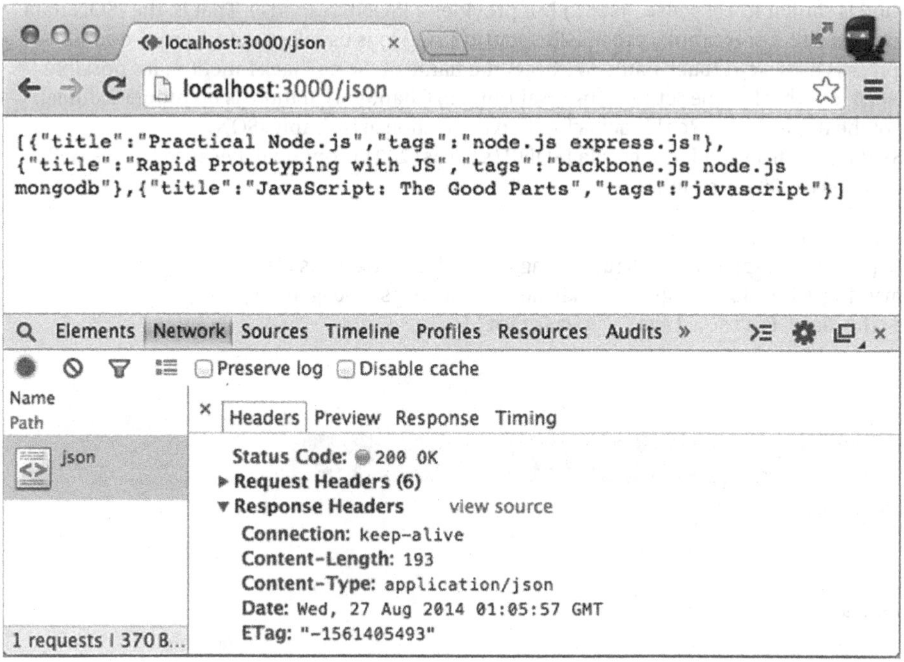

Figure 8-10. *The result of using response.json(): automatically generated headers*

■ **Note** The screenshot of the `response.json()` example in Figure 8-10 was taken after adding the route to the `ch8/app.js` file of the `ch8/app.js` project. You are encouraged to try doing this on your own.

Other uses of `response.json()` are possible as well— for example, with no status code:

```
app.get('/api/v1/stories/:id', function(req,res){
  res.json(req.story);
});
```

Assuming `req.story` is an array or an object, the following code would produce similar results as the preceding snippet (no need to set the header to `application/json` in either case):

```
app.get('/api/v1/stories/:id', function(req,res){
  res.send(req.story);
});
```

response.jsonp()

The `response.jsonp()` method is similar to `response.json()` but provides a JSONP response. That is, the JSON data is wrapped in a JavaScript function call. For example, `processResponse({...});` is usually used for cross-domain calls support. By default, Express.js uses a `callback` name to extract the name of the callback function. It's possible to override this value with `jsonp callback` name settings (more about it in Chapter 3). If there is no proper callback specified in the query string of the request (e.g., `?callback=cb`), then the response is simply JSON.

Assume that serving CSV data to a front-end request via JSONP (`status(200)` is optional, because Express will automatically add the proper status of 200 by default):

```
app.get('/', function (req, res) {
  res.status(200).jsonp([{title: 'Express.js Guide', tags: 'node.js express.js'},
    {title: 'Rapid Prototyping with JS', tags: 'backbone.js, node.js, mongodb'},
    {title: 'JavaScript: The Good Parts', tags: 'javascript'}
  ]);
});
```

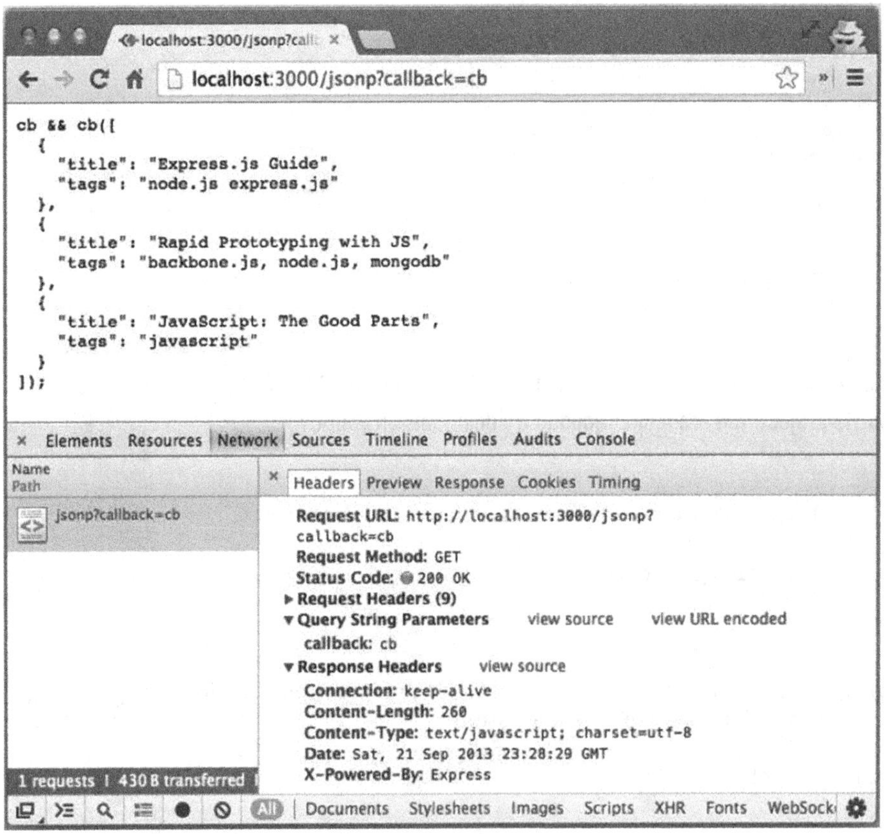

Figure 8-11. *The result of response.jsonp() and ?callback=cb is a text/javascript header and JavaScript function prefix*

■ **Note** The screenshot of the `response.json()` example in Figure 8-11 was taken after adding the route to the `index.js` file of the ch2/`cli-app/app.js` project. You are encouraged to try doing this on your own.

---

response.redirect()

Sometimes we simply need to redirect users/requests to another route. We can use absolute, relative, or full paths:

```
res.redirect('/admin');
res.redirect('../users');
res.redirect('http://rapidprototypingwithjs.com');
```

By default, `response.redirect()` sends the 302 (Found/Temporarily Moved) status code.[8] Of course, we can configure it to our liking in the same manner as `response.send()`; that is, pass the first status code number as the first parameter (301 is Moved Permanently):

```
res.redirect(301, 'http://rpjs.co');
```

Other Response Methods and Properties

Most of the methods and properties outlined in Table 8-1 are convenient alternatives to the methods covered already in the book. In other words, we can accomplish most of the logic with the main methods, but knowing the following shortcuts can save developers a few keystrokes and improve readability. For example, `response.type()` is a niche case of `response.header()` for a `Content-Type` only header.

Table 8-1. *Method and property alternatives*

Method/Property	Description/Conditions	API
`response.get()`	String value of response header for a passed header type	`http://expressjs.com/api.html#res.get`
`response.cookie()`	Takes cookie key/value pair and sets it on response	`http://expressjs.com/api.html#res.cookie`
`response.clearCookie()`	Takes cookie key/name and optional path parameter to clear the cookies	`http://expressjs.com/api.html#res.clearCookie`
`response.location()`	Takes a relative, absolute, or full path as a string and sets that value to `Location` response header	`http://expressjs.com/api.html#res.location`
`response.charset`	The charset value of the response	`http://expressjs.com/api.html#res.charset`
`response.type()`	Takes a string and sets it as a value of `Content-Type` header	`http://expressjs.com/api.html#res.type`
`response.format()`	Takes an object as a mapping of types and responses and executes them according to `Accepted` request header	`http://expressjs.com/api.html#res.format`

(continued)

[8]`http://www.w3.org/Protocols/rfc2616/rfc2616-sec10.html`

Table 8-1. (*continued*)

Method/Property	Description/Conditions	API
response.attachment()	Takes optional file name as a string and sets Content-Disposition (and if file name provided, Content-Type) header(s) to attachment and file type accordingly	http://expressjs.com/api.html#res.attachment
response.sendfile()	Takes path to a file on the server and various options and callback parameters, and sends the file to the requester	http://expressjs.com/api.html#res.sendfile
response.download()	Takes same parameters as response.sendfile(), and sets Content-Disposition and calls response.sendfile()	http://expressjs.com/api.html#res.download
response.links()	Takes an object of URLs to populate Links response header	http://expressjs.com/api.html#res.links

You can find the full source code for this chapter's example in the ch8 folder and on GitHub (https://github.com/azat-co/proexpressjs). Listing 8-1 shows what the ch8/app.js file looks like (including other examples).

Listing 8-1. ch8/app.js File

```
var express = require('express');
var fs = require('fs');
var path = require('path');
var favicon = require('serve-favicon');
var logger = require('morgan');
var cookieParser = require('cookie-parser');
var bodyParser = require('body-parser');

var routes = require('./routes/index');

var largeImagePath = path.join(__dirname, 'files', 'large-image.jpg');

var app = express();

// View engine setup
app.set('views', path.join(__dirname, 'views'));
app.set('view engine', 'jade');
app.use(logger('combined'));
app.use(favicon(path.join(__dirname, 'public', 'favicon.ico')));
app.use(bodyParser.json());
app.use(bodyParser.urlencoded({extended: true}));
app.use(cookieParser('abc'));
app.use(express.static(path.join(__dirname, 'public')));

app.use('/', routes);
```

```
app.get('/render', function(req, res) {
  res.render('render');
});

app.get('/render-title', function(req, res) {
  res.render('index', {title: 'Pro Express.js'});
});

app.get('/locals', function(req, res){
  res.locals = { title: 'Pro Express.js' };
  res.render('index');
});

app.get('/set-html', function(req, res) {
  // Some code
  res.set('Content-Type', 'text/html');
  res.end('<html><body>' +
    '<h1>Express.js Guide</h1>' +
    '</body></html>');
});

app.get('/set-csv', function(req, res) {
  var body = 'title, tags\n' +
    'Practical Node.js, node.js express.js\n' +
    'Rapid Prototyping with JS, backbone.js node.js mongodb\n' +
    'JavaScript: The Good Parts, javascript\n';
  res.set({'Content-Type': 'text/csv',
    'Content-Length': body.length,
    'Set-Cookie': ['type=reader', 'language=javascript']});
  res.end(body);
});

app.get('/status', function(req, res) {
  res.status(200).end();
});

app.get('/send-ok', function(req, res) {
  res.status(200).send({message: 'Data was submitted successfully.'});
});

app.get('/send-err', function(req, res) {
  res.status(500).send({message: 'Oops, the server is down.'});
});

app.get('/send-buf', function(req, res) {
  res.set('Content-Type', 'text/plain');
  res.status(200).send(new Buffer('text data that will be converted into Buffer'));
});
```

```
app.get('/json', function(req, res) {
  res.status(200).json([{title: 'Practical Node.js', tags: 'node.js express.js'},
    {title: 'Rapid Prototyping with JS', tags: 'backbone.js node.js mongodb'},
    {title: 'JavaScript: The Good Parts', tags: 'javascript'}
  ]);
});

app.get('/non-stream', function(req, res) {
  var file = fs.readFileSync(largeImagePath);
  res.end(file);
});

app.get('/non-stream2', function(req, res) {
  var file = fs.readFile(largeImagePath, function(error, data){
    res.end(data);
  });
});

app.get('/stream1', function(req, res) {
  var stream = fs.createReadStream(largeImagePath);
  stream.pipe(res);
});

app.get('/stream2', function(req, res) {
  var stream = fs.createReadStream(largeImagePath);
  stream.on('data', function(data) {
    res.write(data);
  });
  stream.on('end', function() {
    res.end();
  });
});

/// Catch 404 and forward to error handler
app.use(function(req, res, next) {
    var err = new Error('Not Found');
    err.status = 404;
    next(err);
});

/// Error handlers

// Development error handler
// Will print stacktrace
if (app.get('env') === 'development') {
    app.use(function(err, req, res, next) {
        res.status(err.status || 500);
        res.render('error', {
```

```
                message: err.message,
                error: err
            });
        });
}

// Production error handler
// No stacktraces leaked to user
app.use(function(err, req, res, next) {
    res.status(err.status || 500);
    res.render('error', {
        message: err.message,
        error: {}
    });
});

module.exports = app;

var debug = require('debug')('request');

app.set('port', process.env.PORT || 3000);

var server = app.listen(app.get('port'), function() {
  debug('Express server listening on port ' + server.address().port);
});
```

Streams

As far as sending nonstreaming responses between `response.send()` and `response.end()`, you should be well covered from the previous discussion. However, for streaming data back, `response.send()` is not going to work; instead, you should use the response object (which is a writable stream and inherited from `http.ServerResponse`):

```
app.get('/stream1', function(req, res) {
  var stream = fs.createReadStream(largeImagePath);
  stream.pipe(res);
});
```

Alternatively, use event handlers with `data` and `end` events:

```
app.get('/stream2', function(req, res) {
  var stream = fs.createReadStream(largeImagePath);
  stream.on('data', function(data) {
    res.write(data);
  });
  stream.on('end', function() {
    res.end();
  });
});
```

The nonstreaming equivalent might look like this:

```
app.get('/non-stream', function(req, res) {
  var file = fs.readFileSync(largeImagePath);
  res.end(file);
});
```

For this demo we're using a relatively large image of 5.1MB, which is located at `ch8/files/large-image.jpg`. Notice the drastic difference in waiting time between streaming, shown in Figure 8-12, and nonstreaming, shown in Figure 8-13. The nonstreaming route waited for the whole file to load and then sent the whole file back (~49ms), while the streaming route waited much less (only ~7ms). The fact that we use a synchronous function in the nonstreaming example shouldn't matter because we load pages serially (one by one).

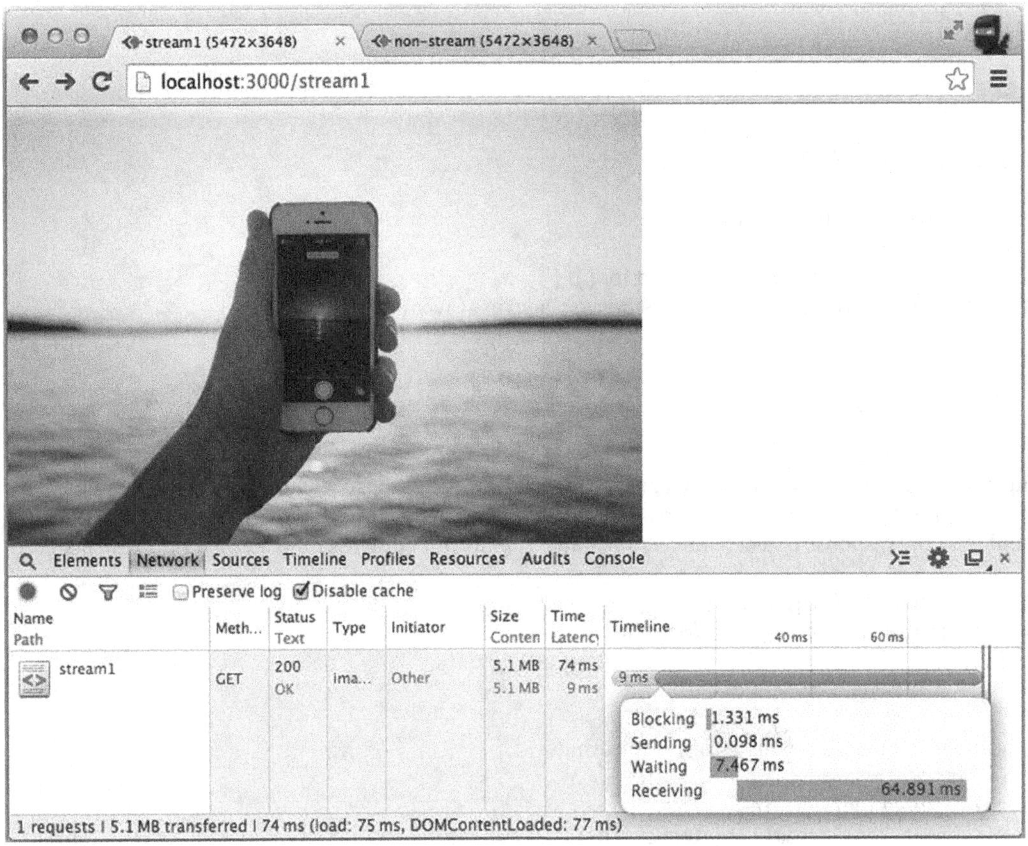

Figure 8-12. *Streaming an image shows a faster waiting time than nonstreaming*

Figure 8-13. *Nonstreaming an image shows a slower waiting time than streaming*

■ **Tip** In addition to using streams for response, they can be used for requests as well. Streaming is useful when dealing with large amounts of data (video, binary data, audio, etc.) because the streams allow processing to start without finishing transfers. For more information about streams, check out `https://github.com/substack/stream-handbook` and `https://github.com/substack/stream-adventure`.

Summary

If you've made it thus far through each of the properties of the response, you probably know more than the average Express.js developer. Congratulations! Understanding request and response is the bread and butter (or meat and veggies for paleo lifestyle people) of the Express.js development.

We're almost done with the Express.js interface (a.k.a. API). The remaining pieces are error handling and actually starting the app.

CHAPTER 9

Error Handling and Running an App

Good web applications must have informative error messages to notify clients exactly why their request has failed. Errors might be caused either by the client (e.g., wrong input data) or by the server (e.g., a bug in the code).

The client might be a browser, in which case the application should display an HTML page. For example, a 404 page should display when the requested resource is not found. Or the client might be another application consuming our resources via the REST API. In this case, the application should send the appropriate HTTP status code and the message in the JSON format (or XML or another format that is supported). For these reasons, it's always the best practice to customize error-handling code when developing a serious application.

In a typical Express.js application, error handlers follow the routes. Error handling deserves its own section of the book because it's different from other middleware. After the error handlers, we'll cover the Express.js application methods and ways to start the Express.js app. Therefore, the major topics of this chapter are as follows:

- Error handling
- Running an app

Error Handling

Because of the asynchronous nature of Node.js and callback patterns, it's not a trivial task to catch and log for future analysis the state in which errors happen. In the Chapter 17, we cover the use of domains with Express.js apps. The use of domains for error handling in Express.js is a more advanced technique and, for most implementations right out of the box, framework's built-in error handling might prove sufficient (along with custom error handling middleware).

We can start with the basic development error handler from our `ch2/cli-app` example. The error handler spits out the error status (`500`, Internal Server Error), stack trace, and error message. It is enabled by this code *only* when the app is in development mode:

```
if (app.get('env') === 'development') {
    app.use(function(err, req, res, next) {
        res.status(err.status || 500);
        res.render('error', {
            message: err.message,
            error: err
        });
    });
}
```

■ **Tip** `app.get('env')` is a convenient method for `process.env.NODE_ENV`; in other words, the preceding line can be rewritten with `process.env.NODE_ENV === 'development'`.

This makes sense because error handling is typically used across the whole application. Therefore, it's best to implement it as middleware.

For custom error-handler implementations, the middleware is the same as any other except that it has one more parameter, `error` (or `err` for short):

```
// Main middleware
app.use(function(err, req, res, next) {
  // Do logging and user-friendly error message display
  console.error(err);
  res.status(500).send();
});
// Routes
```

We can use `res.status(500).end()` to achieve a similar result, because we're not sending any data (e.g., an error message). It's recommended to send at least a brief error message, because it will help the debugging process when problems occur. In fact, the response can be anything: JSON, text, a redirect to a static page, or something else.

For most front-end and other JSON clients, the preferred format is, of course, JSON:

```
app.use(function(err, req, res, next) {
  // Do logging and user-friendly error message display
  console.error(err);
  res.status(500).send({status:500, message: 'internal error', type:'internal'});
})
```

■ **Note** Developers can use the `req.xhr` property or check if the `Accept` request header has the `application/json` value.

The most straightforward way is to just send a text:

```
app.use(function(err, req, res, next) {
  // Do logging and user-friendly error message display
  console.error(err);
  res.status(500).send('internal server error');
})
```

Or, if we know that it's secure to output the error message, we could use the following:

```
app.use(function(err, req, res, next) {
  // Do logging and user-friendly error message display
  console.error(err);
  res.status(500).send('internal server error: ' + err);
})
```

To simply render a static error page with the name 500 (template is the file `500.jade`, the engine is Jade) and the default extension, we could use

```
app.use(function(err, req, res, next) {
  // Do logging and user-friendly error message display
  console.error(err);
  // Assuming that template engine is plugged in
  res.render('500');
})
```

Or we could use the following, if we want to overwrite the file extension, for a full filename of `500.html`:

```
app.use(function(err, req, res, next) {
  // Do logging and user-friendly error message display
  console.error(err);
  // Assuming that template engine is plugged in
  res.render('500.html');
})
```

We can also use `res.redirect()`:

```
app.use(function(err, req, res, next) {
  // Do logging and user-friendly error message display
  res.redirect('/public/500.html');
})
```

Always using proper HTTP response statuses such as 401, 400, 500, and so on, is recommended. Refer to Table 9-1 for a quick reference.

Table 9-1. *Main HTTP Status Codes*

Code	Name	Meaning
200	OK	Standard response for successful HTTP requests
201	Created	Request has been fulfilled. New resource created
204	No Content	Request processed. No content returned
301	Moved Permanently	This and all future requests directed to the given URI
304	Not Modified	Resource has not been modified since last requested
400	Bad Request	Request cannot be fulfilled due to bad syntax
401	Unauthorized	Authentication is possible, but has failed
403	Forbidden	Server refuses to respond to request
404	Not Found	Requested resource could not be found
500	Internal Server Error	Generic error message when server fails
501	Not Implemented	Server does not recognize method or lacks ability to fulfill
503	Service Unavailable	Server is currently unavailable

■ **Tip** For the complete list of available HTTP methods, please refer to RFC 2616 at `www.w3.org/Protocols/rfc2616/rfc2616-sec10.html`.

This is how we can send the status 500 (Internal Server Error) without sending back any data:

```
app.use(function(err, req, res, next) {
  // Do logging and user-friendly error message display
  res.end(500);
})
```

To trigger an error from within our request handlers and middleware, we can just call

```
app.get('/', function(req, res, next){
  next(error);
});
```

Or, if we want to pass a specific error message, then we create an Error object and pass it to `next()`:

```
app.get('/', function(req,res,next){
  next(new Error('Something went wrong :-('));
});
```

It would be a good idea to use the `return` keyword for processing multiple error-prone cases and combine both of the previous approaches. For example, we pass the database error to `next()`, but an empty query result will not cause a database error (i.e., `error` will be `null`), so we check for this condition with `!users`:

```
// A GET route for the user entity
app.get('/users', function(req, res, next) {
  // A database query that will get us any users from the collection
  db.get('users').find({}, function(error, users) {
    if (error) return next(error);
    if (!users) return next(new Error('No users found.'));
    // Do something, if fail the return next(error);
    res.send(users);
});
```

For complex apps, it's best to use multiple error handlers. For example, use one for XHR/AJAX requests, one for normal requests, and one for generic catch-everything-else. It's also a good idea to use named functions (and organize them in modules) instead of anonymous ones.

For an example of this type of advanced error handling, refer to Chapter 22.

■ **Tip** There's an easy way out in regards to managing error handling that is especially good for development purposes. It's called `errorhandler` (`https://www.npmjs.org/package/errorhandler`) and it has the default error handlers for Express.js/Connect.js. For more information on `errorhandler`, refer to the Chapter 4.

Running an App

The Express.js class provides a few *app-wide* objects and methods on its object, which is app in our examples. These objects and methods are recommended because they can improve code reuse and maintenance. For example, instead of hard-coding the number 3000 everywhere, we can just assign it once with `app.set('PORT', 3000);`. Then, if we need to update it later, we have only one place where it needs to be changed. Therefore, we'll cover the following properties and methods in this section:

- `app.locals`
- `app.render()`
- `app.mountpath`
- `app.on('mount', callback)`
- `app.path()`
- `app.listen()`

app.locals

The `app.locals` object is similar to the `res.locals` object (discussed in Chapter 8) in the sense that it exposes data to templates. However, there's a main difference: `app.locals` makes its properties available in *all* templates rendered by app, while `res.locals` restricts them *only* to that request. Therefore, developers need to be careful not to reveal any sensitive information via `app.locals`. The best use case for this is app-wide settings such as locations, URLs, contact info, and so forth. For example:

```
app.locals.lang = 'en';
app.locals.appName = 'HackHall';
```

The `app.locals` object can also be invoked like a function:

```
app.locals([
  author: 'Azat Mardan',
  email: 'hi@azat.co',
  website: 'http://proexpressjs.com'
]);
```

app.render()

The `app.render()` method is invoked either with a view name and a callback or with a view name, data, and a callback. For example, the system might have an e-mail template for a "Thank you for signing up" message and another for "Reset your password":

```
var sendgrid  = require('sendgrid')(api_user, api_key);

var sendThankYouEmail = function(userEmail) {
  app.render('emails/thank-you', function(err, html){
    if (err) return console.error(err);
    sendgrid.send({
      to:      userEmail,
      from:     app.get('appEmail'),
```

```
      subject:  'Thank you for signing up',
      html:  html // The html value is returned by the app.render
    }, function(err, json) {
      if (err) { return console.error(err); }
      console.log(json);
    });
  });
};

var resetPasswordEmail = function(userEmail) {
  app.render('emails/reset-password', {token: generateResetToken()}, function(err, html){
    if (err) return console.error(err);
    sendgrid.send({
      to:      userEmail,
      from:     app.get('appEmail'),
      subject:  'Reset your password',
      html:  html
    }, function(err, json) {
      if (err) { return console.error(err); }
      console.log(json);
    });
  });
};
```

■ **Note** The `sendgrid` module used in the example is available at NPM[1] and GitHub.[2]

app.mountpath

The `app.mountpath` property is used in the mounted/sub apps. Mounted apps are sub-apps that can be used for better code reuse and organization. The `app.mountpath` property returns the path on which app is mounted.

For example, in `ch9/app-mountpath.js` there are two sub applications: `post` and `comment`. The post is mounted on the `/post` path of app, while comment is mounted on `/comment` of post. As a result of logs, mountpath returns values `/post` and `/comment`:

```
var express= require('express'),
  app = express(),
  post = express(),
  comment = express();

app.use('/post', post);
post.use('/comment', comment);

console.log(app.mountpath); // ''
console.log(post.mountpath); // '/post'
console.log(comment.mountpath); // '/comment'
```

[1] https://www.npmjs.org/package/sendgrid
[2] https://github.com/sendgrid/sendgrid-nodejs

app.on('mount', function(parent){...})

The mount is triggered when the sub app is mounted on a specific path of a parent/main app. For example, in ch9/app-on-mount.js, we have two sub apps with on mount event listeners that print parents' mountpaths. The values of the paths are / for post's parent (app) and /post for comment's parent (post):

```
var express= require('express'),
  app = express(),
  post = express(),
  comment = express();

post.on('mount', function(parent){
  console.log(parent.mountpath); // '/'
})
comment.on('mount', function(parent){
  console.log(parent.mountpath); // '/post'
})

app.use('/post', post);
post.use('/comment', comment);
```

app.path()

The app.path() method will return the canonical path for the Express.js application. This is useful if you are using multiple Express.js apps mounted to different routes (for better code organization).

For example, you have comments resource (routes related to comments) for posts by the way of mounting the comment app on the /comment path of the post app. But you can still get the "full" path with comment.path() (from ch9/app-path.js):

```
var express= require('express'),
  app = express(),
  post = express(),
  comment = express();

app.use('/post', post);
post.use('/comment', comment);

console.log(app.path()); // ''
console.log(post.path()); // '/post'
console.log(comment.path()); // '/post/comment'
```

app.listen()

The Express.js app.listen(port, [hostname,] [backlog,] [callback]) method is akin to server.listen()[3] from the core Node.js http module. This method is one of the ways to start an Express.js app. The port is a port number on which the server should accept incoming requests. The hostname is the name of the domain. You might need to set it when you deploy your apps to the cloud. The backlog is the maximum number of queued pending connections. The default is 511. And the callback is an asynchronous function that is called when the server is booted.

[3]http://nodejs.org/api/http.html#http_server_listen_port_hostname_backlog_callback

To spin up the Express.js app directly on a particular port (3000):

```
var express = require('express');
var app = express();
// ... Configuration
// ... Routes
app.listen(3000);
```

This approach was created by Express.js Generator in the `ch2/hello.js` and `ch2/hell-name.js` examples in the Chapter 2 Hello World example. In it, the `app.js` file doesn't start a server, but it exports the object with

```
module.exports = app;
```

We don't run the `app.js` file with `$ node app.js` either. Instead, we launch a shell script `www` with `$ ./bin/www`. The shell script has this special string on its first line:

```
#!/usr/bin/env node
```

The line above turns the shell script into a Node.js program. This program imports the app object from the `app.js` file, sets the port, and starts the app serverwith `listen()` and a callback:

```
var debug = require('debug')('cli-app');
var app = require('../app');

app.set('port', process.env.PORT || 3000);

var server = app.listen(app.get('port'), function() {
  debug('Express server listening on port ' + server.address().port);
});
```

Having your server object exported as a module is necessary when another process requires the object, e.g., a testing framework. In the previous example, the main server file (`ch2/cli-app/app.js`) exported the object and there is was no way of starting the server with `$ node app`. If you don't want to have a separate shell file for launching the server, but still want to export the server when you need to, you can use the following trick. The gist of this approach is to check whether the module is a dependency with `require.main === module` condition. If it's true, then we start the application. If it's not, then we expose the methods and the app object.

```
var server = http.createServer(app);
var boot = function () {
  server.listen(app.get('port'), function(){
    console.info('Express server listening on port ' + app.get('port'));
  });
}
var shutdown = function() {
  server.close();
}
```

```
if (require.main === module) {
  boot();
} else {
  console.info('Running app as a module');
  exports.boot = boot;
  exports.shutdown = shutdown;
  exports.port = app.get('port');
}
```

Another way to start a server besides `app.listen()` is to apply the Express.js app to the core Node.js server function. This is useful for spawning an HTTP server and an HTTPS server with the same code base:

```
var express = require('express');
var https = require('https');
var http = require('http');
var app = express();
var ops = require('conf/ops');
//... Configuration
//... Routes
http.createServer(app).listen(80);
https.createServer(ops, app).listen(443);
```

You can create a self-signed SSL certificate (for example, the `server.crt` file) to test your HTTPS server locally for development purposes with `OpenSSL` by running these commands:

```
$ sudo ssh-keygen -f host.key
$ sudo openssl req -new -key host.key -out request.csr
$ sudo openssl x509 -req -days 365 -in request.csr -signkey host.key -out server.crt
```

The OpenSSL is an open-source implementation of Secure Socket Layer (SSL) protocol and a toolkit. You can find more about it at `https://www.openssl.org`. When you use OpenSSL, Chrome and many other browsers will complain with a warning about self-signed certificates—you can ignore it by clicking Proceed anyway (see Figure 9-1).

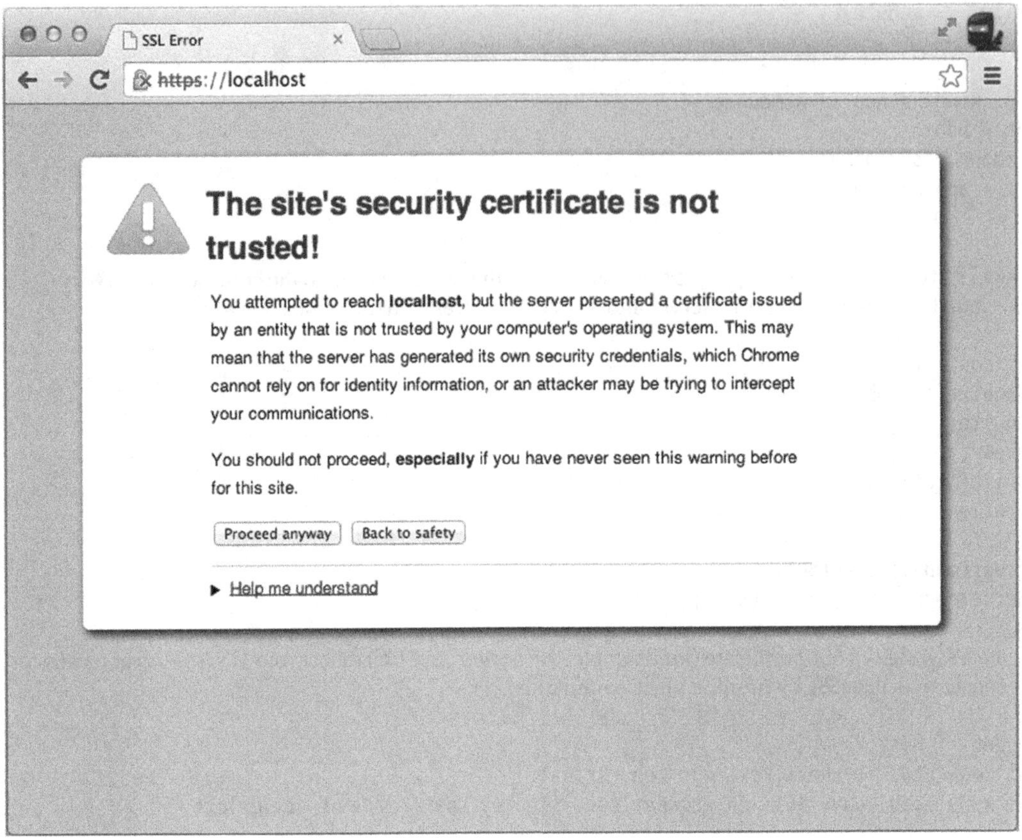

Figure 9-1. *You can ignore this warning cause by a self-signed SSL certificate*

■ **Tip** To install `OpenSSL` on Mac OS X, run `$ brew install OpenSSL`. On Windows, download the installer from `http://gnuwin32.sourceforge.net/packages/openssl.htm`. On Ubuntu, run `apt-get install OpenSSL`.

After `server.crt` is ready, feed it to the `https.createServer()` methods like this (the `ch9/app.js` file):

```
var express = require('express');
var https = require('https');
var http = require('http');
var app = express();
var fs = require('fs');

var ops = {
    key: fs.readFileSync('host.key'),
    cert: fs.readFileSync('server.crt') ,
    passphrase: 'your_secret_passphrase'
};
```

```
app.get('/', function(request, response){
  response.send('ok');
});
http.createServer(app).listen(80);
https.createServer(ops, app).listen(443);
```

The passphrase is the one you used during the certificate creation with `OpenSSL`. Leave it out if you didn't put in any passphrase. To start the process, you might have to use sudo, such as `$ sudo node app`.

If everything worked well, you should see an okay message as shown in Figure 9-2.

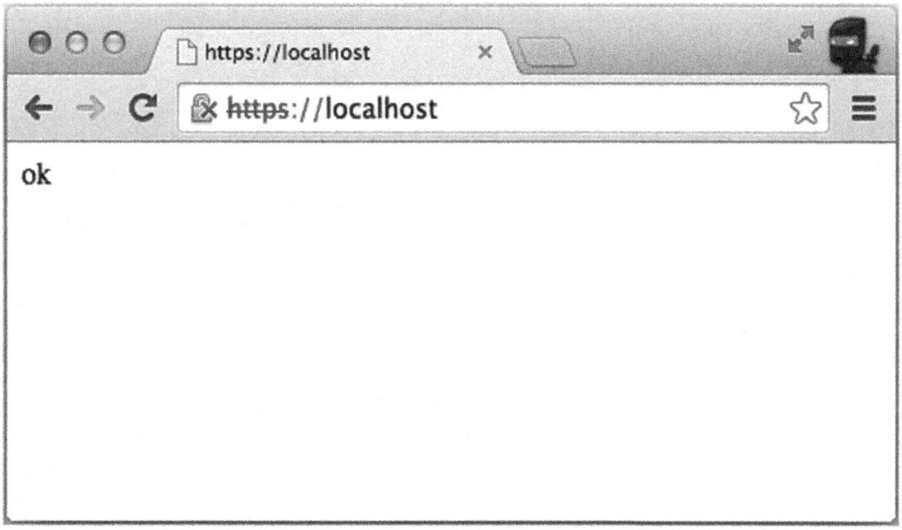

Figure 9-2. *Using self-signed SSL certificate for local development*

Finally, if your application performs a lot of blocking work, you might want to start multiple processes with `cluster` module. This topic is covered in Chapter 13.

Summary

This chapter covered multiple ways to implement error handlers, the app object interface, and ways to start the Express.js server. This concludes Part 2, "Deep API Reference." Hopefully, you've learned many new properties and methods of the Express.js framework's objects, such as response, request, and the app itself. If you had any doubts about middleware, then Chapter 4 cleared any concerns. Last but not least, we covered routing, error handling and template utilization topics. All these topics built your foundation so you can apply this knowledge to creating amazing and exciting new apps with Express.js.

As the reference part of the book is over, we are moving into more practical and complex topics, which include "how to use X" or "how to do Y" examples. Onward to Part 3, "Solving Common and Abstract Problems."

PART III

Solving Common and Abstract Problems

CHAPTER 10

Abstraction

This chapter deals with code organization. *Abstraction* usually means breaking monolithic logic into a few pieces. Most of the techniques presented in this chapter can be applied to any Node.js code, not just Express.js code.

An Express.js app usually has a main file (`app.js` or `server.js`). You should try to keep this file as small as possible, because as it grows larger, it becomes harder to maintain. The most suitable types of code to use instead of a large main file are middleware and routes. Configuration statements can also be abstracted, but they are typically less numerous than routes, which might exceed 200 to 300.

Middleware

As described in Chapter 4, the middleware concept provides flexibility. Software engineers can use anonymous functions or named functions as middleware. The approach of using anonymous functions looks something like this:

```
app.use(function(request, response) {
// ...
});
app.get(function(request, response) {
//...
}, function(request, response) {
// ...
});
```

The named functions approach looks as follows:

```
var middleware = function(request, response){
};
var middleware2 = function(request, response){
//...
};
var middleware3= function(request, response){
//...
};
app.use(middleware);
app.get(middleware2, middleware3);
```

For purposes of code reuse, the named functions approach is more appealing. That is, if you name a function, you can use it in multiple routes by passing the name. On the contrary, the approach of using anonymous functions allows you to use that middleware only once, in the place where you defined the function.

When using named functions, as the application grows larger, the best practice is to abstract the named functions into external modules based on their functionality, e.g., authentication or database tasks.

Routes

Let's say we have a REST API with the following resources: stories, elements, and users. We can separate request handlers into files accordingly, so that `routes/stories.js` has

```
module.exports.findStories = function(req, res, next) {
// ... Query to find stories from the database
};
module.exports.createStory = function(req, res, next) {
// ... Query to create a story in the database
};
// ....
```

The `routes/users.js` file holds the logic for user entities:

```
module.exports.findUser = function(req, res, next){
// ...
};
module.exports.updateUser = function(req, res, next){
// ...
};
module.exports.removeUser = function(req, res, next){
// ...
};
```

The main server file (`app.js` or `server.js`) can use the preceding modules in this manner:

```
// ...
var stories = require('./routes/stories');
var users = require('./routes/users');
// ...
app.get('/stories', stories.findStories);
app.post('/stories', stories.createStory);
app.get('/users/:user_id', users.findUser);
app.put('/users/:user_id', users.updateUser);
app.del('/users/:user_id', users.removeUser);
// ...
```

In the example with `var stories = require('./routes/stories');`, `stories` is file `stories.js` with an omitted (optional) `.js` extension.

■ **Tip** The period (.) in `'./routes/stories'` means the path starts with the current folder. On Windows, the path uses \ rather than /, so a better way would be to write `require(path.join('routes', 'stories'));`, because it's more cross-platform friendly.

Please notice that the code repeats itself over and over with each line/module; that is, developers have to duplicate code by importing the same modules (e.g., `users`). Imagine that we need to include these three modules in each file! To avoid this repetition, there's a clever way to include multiple files: put the `index.js` file inside the `stories` folder and let that file include all the routes. This is a good practice because, if you want to add more files to the `routes` folder later or change names of the existing files, you don't need to require a new file from `app.js`. You simply need to modify the `routes/index.js` code.

For example, in `app.js` we import `index.js` by passing only the folder name (`require` looks for `index.js` if we pass the folder name):

```
app.get('/stories', require('./routes').stories.findStories);
```

Or, we can use routes multiple times:

```
var routes = ('./routes');
app.get('/stories', routes.stories.findStories);
app.post('/stories', routes.stories. createStory);
```

This code will access `index.js`, which should expose the `stories` object (and others), which in turn is imported from the `stories.js` file in the `routes` folder:

```
module.exports.stories = require('./stories');
module.exports.users = require('./users);
```

The preceding code can be rewritten as follows:

```
exports.stories = require('./stories');
exports.users = require('./users);
```

Or as follows, which is my personal favorite, due to its eloquence:

```
module.exports = {
  stories: require('./stories'),
  users: require('./users)
};
```

Finally, the `stories.js` file that is read by the `./routes/index.js` code has

```
exports.findStories = function(req, res, next) {
// ...
};
exports.createStory = function(req, res, next) {
// ...
};
// ...
```

■ **Tip** To organize routes even better, you can use the `Router` class, covered in Chapter 6.

Each bit of functionality can be split into a separate file. For example, the `findStories` method goes into `ch10/routes-exports/find-stories.js` with the following content:

```
exports.findStories = function(ops){
  ops=ops || '';
  console.log ('findStories module logic ' + ops);
};
```

In the `index.js` we simply import the `find-stories.js`:

```
exports.stories = require('./find-stories.js');
```

For a working example, you can run `node -e "require('./routes-exports').stories.findStories();"` from the `expressjsguide` folder to see a string output by `console.log` from the module, as shown in Figure 10-1.

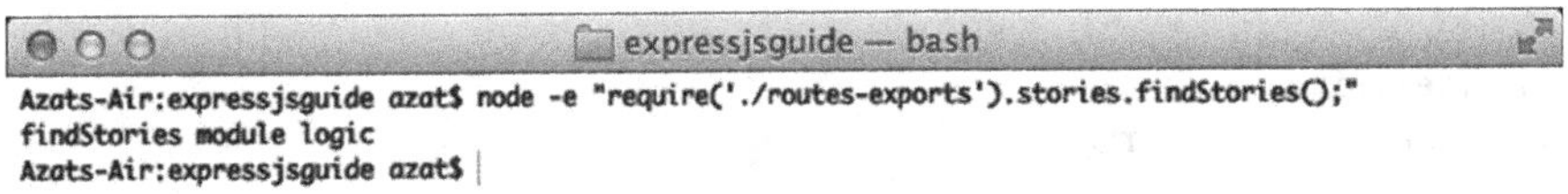
expressjsguide — bash
Azats-Air:expressjsguide azat$ node -e "require('./routes-exports').stories.findStories();"
findStories module logic
Azats-Air:expressjsguide azat$

***Figure 10-1.** Importing modules via a folder and index.js file*

Combining Middleware and Routes

To illustrate another approach of code reuse, assume that there's an app with the routes `/admin` and `/api/stories`:

```
app.get('/admin', function(req, res, next) {
  if (!req.query._token) return next(new Error('No token was provided.'));
  }, function(req, res, next) {
  res.render('admin');
});
// Middleware that applied to all /api/* calls
app.use('/api/*', function(req, res, next) {
  if (!req.query.api_key) return next(new Error('No API key was provided.'));
});
app.get('/api/stories', findStory, function(req, res){
  res.json(req.story):
});
```

In both of them, we check for a query string parameter, with the following lines:

```
  if (!req.query._token) return next(new Error('no token provided'));
```

and

```
  if (!req.query.api_key) return next(new Error('No API key was provided.'));
```

However, the parameters are different, so we cannot abstract both statements into one function. Wouldn't it be slick to not have to repeat ourselves?

To avoid repetition, we can implement a function that returns a function instead, as follows:

```
var requiredParam = function (param) {
  // Do something with the param, e.g.,
  // Create a private attribute paramName based on the value of param variable
  var paramName = '';
  if (param === '_token')
    paramName = 'token';
  else if (param === 'api_key')
    paramName = 'API key'
  return function (req,res, next) {
    // Use paramName, e.g.,
    // If query has no such parameter, proceed next() with error using paramName
    if (!req.query[param]) return next(new Error('No ' + paramName +' was provided.'));
    next();
  });
}

app.get('/admin', requiredParam('_token'), function(req, res, next) {
  res.render('admin');
});
    // Middleware that applied to all /api/* calls
app.use('/api/*', requiredParam('api_key'));
```

In a sense, this "function that returns a function" pattern is a switch that changes modes based on the argument passed.

■ **Tip** The aforementioned "function that returns a function" pattern resembles a state monad (`http://en.wikipedia.org/wiki/Monad_(functional_programming)#State_monads`). This can serve as a great topic for discussion during an interview.

The preceding example is very basic and, in most cases, developers don't worry about mapping for proper error text messages. Nevertheless, you can use this pattern for many purposes, such as restricting output, managing permissions, and switching between different blocks.

■ **Note** The `__dirname` global variable provides an absolute path to the file that uses it, while `./` returns the current working directory, which might be different depending on where we execute the Node.js script (e.g., `$ node ~/code/app/index.js` vs. `$ node index.js`). One exception to the `./` rule is when it's used in the `require()` function, such as `conf = require('./config.json');`, in which case it acts as `__dirname`.

As you can see, middleware/request handler use is a powerful concept for keeping code organized. The best practice is to keep the router lean and thin by moving all of the logic into corresponding external modules/files. This way, important server configuration parameters will all be neatly in one place when you need them.

The globals `module.exports` and `exports` are not quite the same when it comes to assigning new values to each of them. In the previous example, `module.exports = function(){...}` works fine and makes total sense, but `exports = function() {...}` or even `exports = someObject;` will fail miserably. The reason is JavaScript fundamentals: the properties of the object can be replaced without losing the reference to that object, but when we replace the whole object (i.e., `exports = ...,`), we lose the link to *the outside world* that exposes our functions.

This behavior is also referred to as *objects being mutable and primitive* (strings, numbers, and booleans are immutable in JavaScript). Therefore, `exports` only works by creating and assigning properties to it, such as `exports.method = function() {...};`. For example, we can run the following code in the `ch10` folder:

```
$ node -e "require('./routes-module-exports').FindStories('databases');"
```

As a result, you can see in Figure 10-2 that our nested structure is reduced by one level.

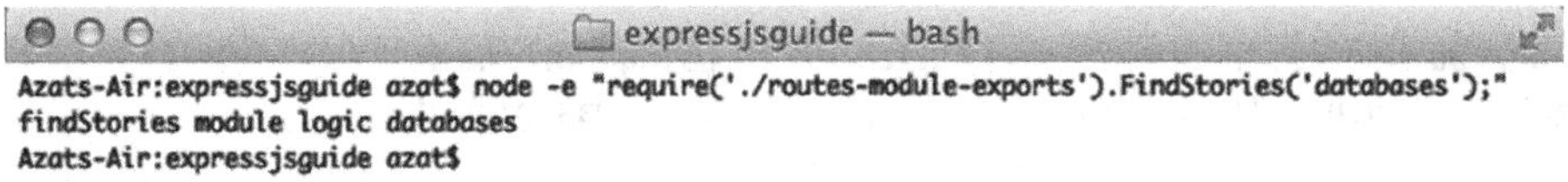

expressjsguide — bash
Azats-Air:expressjsguide azat$ node -e "require('./routes-module-exports').FindStories('databases');"
findStories module logic databases
Azats-Air:expressjsguide azat$

Figure 10-2. *The result of using module.exports*

For more examples, refer to the article "Node.js, Require and Exports" by Karl Sequin (`http://openmymind.net/2012/2/3/Node-Require-and-Exports`). For a working example in this book, check out the HackHall example in Chapter 22.

Summary

It is extremely important to develop good habits and practices of code organization. Without them, projects will be hard to maintain. This applies even more so in large projects.

In the next chapter, we'll continue with this topic, but apply it to databases. We'll also explore how to handle keys (and other sensitive information that you don't want to have hacked), and work with streams as they apply to Express.js applications.

CHAPTER 11

Database, Keys and Stream Tips

This chapter continues the previous chapter's theme of better code organization in Express.js apps. The chapter provides tips on how to connect to a database from another module, access keys and passwords that ought to remain secret, and stream data.

Using Databases in Modules

This section deals with code organizing patterns. It is not a detailed tutorial on databases and Express.js. For such coverage, refer to Chapters 20 to 22.

Before I show you how to approach accessing a database connection from another module, which might be needed if you abstracted routes into separate `app.js/server.js` files, let's brush up on some basics first.

With the native Node.js MongoDB driver, the Express.js server needs to wait for the connection to be created before it can use the database:

```
// ... Modules importing
var routes = require('routes');
var mongodb = require('mongodb');
var Db = mongodb.Db;
var db = new Db('test', new Server(dbHost, dbPort, {}));
// ... Instantiation
db.open(function(error, dbConnection){
  var app = express();
  app.get('/', routes.home);
  // ... Other routes
  app.listen(3000);
});
```

We can make it a bit better by moving routes and configuration outside of the database callback:

```
// ... Modules importing
var routes = require('routes');
var mongodb = require('mongodb');
var Db = mongodb.Db;
var db = new Db('test', new Server(dbHost, dbPort, {}));
```

```
// ... Instantiation
var app = express();
app.get('/', routes.home);
// ... Other routes

db.open(function(error, dbConnection){
app.listen(3000);
});
```

However, the app.listen() call still needs to be called after the database connection has been established.

Thanks to more advanced libraries such as Mongoskin, Monk, and Mongoose that have buffering of the db requests, we don't need to put the app.listen() call inside of the db callback. The developers' tasks can be as easy as this:

```
var express = require('express'),
  mongoskin = require('mongoskin'),
  bodyParser = require('body-parser');

var app = express();
app.use(bodyParser.json());
// ... Configurations and middleware

var db = mongoskin.db('localhost:27017/test', {safe:true});
app.get('/', function(req, res) {
  res.send('please select a collection, e.g., /collections/messages')
});
// ... Routes
app.listen(3000);
```

In a case in which routes need to access to database objects, such as connections, models, and so forth, but those routes aren't in the main server file, all we need to do is attach the required object to the request (i.e., req) using custom middleware:

```
app.use(function(req, res, next) {
  req.db = db;
  next();
});
```

This way, all the middleware and routes declared after the custom middleware just shown will have the req.db object; the req object is the same instance of the Request object.

Alternatively, we could pass or accept the needed variables into the constructor when we import or export the module. In JavaScript/Node.js, objects are passed by their references, so we'll be dealing with the original object in the module. The example of the routes.js module is as follows:

```
module.exports = function(app){
  console.log(app.get('db')); // app has everything we need!
  // ... Initialize other objects as needed
  return {
    findUsers: function(req, res) {
    // ...
    },
```

```
    createUser: function(req, res) {
    // ...
    }
  } // for "return"
}
```

And here's the main file:

```
var app = express();
// ... Configuration
app.set('db', db);
routes = require('./routes.js')(app);
// ... Middleware
app.get('/users', routes.findUser);
// ... Routes
```

Or, we can refactor in a variable:

```
var app = express();
// ... Configuration
app.set('db', db);
Routes = require('./routes.js');
routes = Routes(app);
// ... Middleware
app.get('/users', routes.findUser);
// ... Routes
```

You can try to pass data to modules themselves with the example in the `proexpressjs/ch11` folder. For that, simply run the following command:

```
$ node -e "require('./routes-module-exports').FindStories('databases');"
```

Run it from the `proexpressjs/ch11` folder. The command simply imports the module and calls a method from it. As a result, you'll see the word "databases" (or any other string that you pass to `FindStories`) printed in the terminal.

For a real-life example of passing a Mongoose database object to routes via a `req` object, take a look at Chapter 22.

Keys and Passwords

A typical web service likely requires connections to other services via usernames and passwords in the case of databases, and API keys and secrets/tokens in the case of third-party APIs. As you might guess, it's not a good idea to store this sensitive data in the source code! The two most widespread approaches to solving this issue are

- JSON file
- Environment variables

■ **Note** We are talking about Node.js, not browser JavaScript, in this section. Typically, you don't want to expose your passwords and API keys on the front end.

JSON File

The JSON file approach is as easy as it sounds. All we need is a JSON file. For example, suppose we have a local database and two external services, such as HackHall and Twitter, in `conf/keys.json`:

```
{
  "db": {
    "host": "http://localhost",
    "port": 27017,
    "username": "azat",
    "password": "CE0E08FE-E486-4AE0-8441-2193DF8D5ED0"
  },
  "hackhall": {
    "api_key": "C7C211A6-D8A7-4E41-99E6-DA0EB95CD864"
  },
  "twitter": {
    "consumer_key": "668C68E1-B947-492E-90C7-F69F5D32B42E",
    "consumer_secret": "4B5EE783-E6BB-4F4E-8B05-2A746056BEE1"
  }
}
```

The latest versions of Node.js allow developers to import JSON files with the `require()` function. Hurray for not messing around with the `fs` module! Therefore, the main application file might use these statements:

```
var configurations = require('/conf/keys.json');
var twitterConsumerKey = configurations.twitter.consumer_key;
```

Alternatively, we can just read the file manually with the `fs` module and parse the stream into a JavaScript object. Try this on your own.

As far as access to `configurations` goes, it's even better if we can share this configuration object globally, using `app.set(name, value)`:

```
app.set('configurations', configurations);
```

Or, using middleware, propagate to every request that comes after:

```
app.use(function(req, res, next) {
  req.configurations = configurations;
});
```

Adding `conf/keys.json` to .gitignore prevents tracking and exposing the file. To add it, simply create a new system file `.gitignore` and add this line:

```
conf/keys.json
```

If you committed your keys to Git once, they will stay in the history even if you delete the file. The solution to remove the sensitive data from the Git history is tricky. It's best to regenerate the keys to avoid an exposure.

The problem is still present with the delivery of the JSON configuration file to the server. This can be done via SSH and the scp (secure copy) command:

```
$ scp [options] username1@source_host:directory1/filename1 username2@destination_host:directory2/
filename2
```

For example, `$ scp ./keys.json azat@webapplog:/var/www/conf/keys.json`.

Alternatively, you can use rsync, because it transfers only the delta. For example:

```
$ rsync -avz ./keys.json azat@webapplog:var/www/conf
```

Environment Variables

The second approach involves the use of environment variables (env vars). The easiest way to illustrate env vars is to start a script with a key=value prefix, for example `$ NODE_ENV=test node app`. This will populate process.env.NODE_ENV. Try this script that prints NODE_ENV right back to you:

```
$ NODE_ENV=test node -e 'console.log(process.env.NODE_ENV)'
```

To deliver/deploy these vars into a remote server, we can use Ubuntu's /etc/init/nodeprogram.conf. More details are available in this neat tutorial by Kevin van Zonneveld: "Run Node.js as a Service on Ubuntu."[1]

Furthermore, there is a Nodejitsu tool (http://www.nodejitsu.com) to daemonize node processes forever (http://npmjs.org/forever; GitHub: https://github.com/nodejitsu/forever).

For Heroku, the process of synching env vars with the cloud is even simpler: locally, we put vars into an .env file in the project folder for Foreman[2] (comes with the Heroku toolbelt) and then push them to the cloud with heroku-config (https://github.com/ddollar/heroku-config). More information is at the Heroku Dev Center.[3]

For a working example (obviously sans sensitive info), take a look at Chapter 22.

Streams

The Express.js request and response objects are readable and writable Node.js streams, respectively. Streams are powerful tools for processing chunks of data before a particular process (reading, receiving, writing, sending) actually ends. This makes streams useful when dealing with huge data such as audio or video. Another case for streams is when performing big database migrations.

■ **Tip** For more information on how to use streams, substack's James Halliday (http://substack.net/) offers some amazing resources: stream-handbook (https://github.com/substack/stream-handbook) and stream-adventure (https://npmjs.org/package/stream-adventure).

---

[1]http://kvz.io/blog/2009/12/15/run-nodejs-as-a-service-on-ubuntu-karmic/

[2]https://devcenter.heroku.com/articles/procfile#developing-locally-with-foreman

[3]https://devcenter.heroku.com/articles/config-vars

Here is an example of piping a stream to a normal response from `proexpressjs/ch11/streams-http-res.js`:

```
var http = require('http');
var fs = require('fs');
var server = http.createServer(function (req, res) {
    fs.createReadStream('users.csv').pipe(res);
});
server.listen(3000);
```

The GET request with CURL from the terminal looks like this:

```
$ curl http://localhost:3000
```

The preceding line will cause the server to output the content of the file `users.csv`; for example:

```
...
Stanton Botsford,Raina@clinton.name,619
Dolly Feeney,Aiden_Schaefer@carmel.tv,670
Oma Beahan,Mariano@paula.tv,250
Darrion Johnson,Miracle@liliana.com,255
Garth Huels V,Patience@leda.co.uk,835
Chet Hills II,Donna.Lesch@daniela.co.uk,951
Margarette Littel,Brenda.Prosacco@heber.biz,781
Alexandrine Schiller,Brown.Kling@jason.name,779
Concepcion Emmerich,Leda.Hudson@cara.biz,518
Mrs. Johnpaul Brown,Conrad.Cremin@tavares.tv,315
Aniyah Barrows,Alexane@daniela.tv,193
Okey Kohler PhD,Cordell@toy.biz,831
Bill Murray,Tamia_Reichert@zella.com,962
Allen O'Reilly,Jesus@joey.name,448
Ms. Bud Hoeger,Ila@freda.us,997
Kathryn Hettinger,Colleen@vincenza.name,566
...
```

The result is also shown in Figure 11-1.

res — bash
Eugenia Heidenreich,Helene@astrid.biz,997
Kolby Ferry IV,Erin@liliane.biz,13
Cecile Reinger,Chelsie.Lind@lysanne.ca,816
Aurelia Gleason,Dulce@simone.info,870
Mrs. Odessa Konopelski,Reinhold.Grant@barrett.name,951
Ken Muller,Alexandrine@darien.co.uk,276
Pearline Murphy,Darwin@serenity.biz,347
Erin Kihn,Lowell@francesca.ca,165
Miss Frances Ankunding,Ulices@trisha.tv,963
Marisa Gleichner,Cruz_Kuhn@joy.io,142
Norbert Champlin III,Jordy@rubye.me,237
Justyn Upton,Euna_Davis@barbara.io,559
Mr. Maggie Labadie,Earlene_Smitham@thelma.com,274
Elbert Glover,Bernadette@martina.biz,37
Isabel Langworth PhD,Damian.Abshire@kiley.name,245
Isabelle VonRueden Jr.,Keagan@dedrick.name,322
Dr. Emile Rosenbaum,Marcella@julie.info,481
Stanton Botsford,Raina@clinton.name,619
Dolly Feeney,Aiden_Schaefer@carmel.tv,670
Oma Beahan,Mariano@paula.tv,250
Darrion Johnson,Miracle@liliana.com,255
Garth Huels V,Patience@leda.co.uk,835
Chet Hills II,Donna.Lesch@daniela.co.uk,951
Margarette Littel,Brenda.Prosacco@heber.biz,781
Alexandrine Schiller,Brown.Kling@jason.name,779
Concepcion Emmerich,Leda.Hudson@cara.biz,518
Mrs. Johnpaul Brown,Conrad.Cremin@tavares.tv,315
Aniyah Barrows,Alexane@daniela.tv,193
Okey Kohler PhD,Cordell@toy.biz,831
Bill Murray,Tamia_Reichert@zella.com,962
Allen O'Reilly,Jesus@joey.name,448
Ms. Bud Hoeger,Ila@freda.us,997
Kathryn Hettinger,Colleen@vincenza.name,566
Wilburn Johns DDS,Hank.Mraz@winfield.tv,31
Mrs. Al Herman,Alfredo@nya.ca,927
Hugh Stamm,Athena_Stehr@brenda.net,27
Junius Stark,Virginie_Parisian@antonio.biz,114
Ms. Marilou Goyette,Desiree@gilda.org,401
Jerad Sawayn,Ramiro_Hoeger@katlyn.tv,977
Geo Leannon,Ubaldo@duncan.me,986
Ms. Alisa Ledner,Carroll_VonRueden@susanna.org,491
Tamara Harris,Dino@jany.org,838
Sydni Hickle,Justyn@stefanie.us,696
Lester Volkman,Kade_Lang@mohammed.com,412
Melyssa Shanahan,Uriah_Schmidt@yasmeen.ca,927
Emmet Bayer Sr.,Blair_Lynch@daphnee.us,681
Mr. Eldridge Wisozk,Abbie@natalia.me,267
Fletcher Pfeffer,Deion.Koch@delta.biz,129
Quincy Effertz,Nikita_Blanda@jettie.tv,542
Azats-Air:res azat$

Figure 11-1. *The result of running the stream response from the users.csv file*

If you want to create your own test file such as `users.csv`, you can install Faker.js (`https://npmjs.org/package/Faker`; GitHub: `https://github.com/marak/Faker.js/`) and rerun the `seed-users.js` file:

```
$ npm install Faker@0.7.2
$ node seed-users.js
```

The Express.js implementation is strikingly similar in `proexpressjs/ch11/stream-express-res.js`:

```
var fs = require('fs');
var express = require('express');

var app = express();
```

```
app.get('*', function (req, res) {
    fs.createReadStream('users.csv').pipe(res);
});

app.listen(3000);
```

Keeping in mind that the request is a readable stream, and the response is a writable one, we can implement a server that saves POST requests into a file. Here is the content of `proexpressjs/ch11/stream-http-req.js`:

```
var http = require('http');
var fs = require('fs');
var server = http.createServer(function (req, res) {
    if (req.method === 'POST') {
        req.pipe(fs.createWriteStream('ips.txt'));
    }
    res.end('\n');
});
server.listen(3000);
```

We call Faker.js to generate test data consisting of names, domains, IP addresses, latitudes, and longitudes. This time, we won't save the data to a file, but instead will pipe it to CURL.

Here is the bit of Faker.js script that outputs a JSON object of 1000 records to the stdout from `proexpressjs/ch11/seed-ips.js`:

```
var Faker = require('Faker');
var body = [];

for (var i = 0; i < 1000; i++) {
  body.push({
    'name': Faker.Name.findName(),
    'domain': Faker.Internet.domainName(),
    'ip': Faker.Internet.ip(),
    'latitude': Faker.Address.latitude(),
    'longitude': Faker.Address.longitude()
  });
}
process.stdout.write(JSON.stringify(body));
```

To test our `stream-http-req.js`, let's run

```
$ node seed-ips.js | curl -d@- http://localhost:3000.
```

The result is an array of IPs, as shown in Figure 11-2.

expressjsguide — bash
Azats-Air:expressjsguide azat$ node seed-ips.js | curl -d@- http://localhost:3000
Azats-Air:expressjsguide azat$ cat ips.txt
[{"name":"Isaias Weimann","domain":"jettie.name","ip":"37.155.164.45","latitude":"-67.5678","longitude":"152.5048"},{"name":
"Christopher Bayer PhD","domain":"jakob.org","ip":"240.38.163.149","latitude":"-51.7992","longitude":"45.3832"},{"name":"Jav
onte Schultz","domain":"berry.tv","ip":"58.27.234.54","latitude":"28.4039","longitude":"139.6028"},{"name":"Uriel Trantow V"
,"domain":"ines.me","ip":"88.239.48.23","latitude":"-15.9482","longitude":"81.2255"},{"name":"Chance Deckow","domain":"annab
el.biz","ip":"55.236.206.112","latitude":"86.5181","longitude":"91.2605"},{"name":"Ike Hand","domain":"gus.co.uk","ip":"204.
4.45.194","latitude":"-83.7226","longitude":"121.2440"},{"name":"Mercedes Eichmann","domain":"renee.biz","ip":"108.193.151.2
14","latitude":"-61.4857","longitude":"23.4696"},{"name":"Annetta Kihn","domain":"sienna.us","ip":"120.216.151.34","latitude
":"87.8300","longitude":"85.2472"},{"name":"Retta Cole","domain":"stewart.name","ip":"73.156.126.60","latitude":"55.2242","l
ongitude":"-75.8730"},{"name":"Kaylin Rutherford I","domain":"keyon.net","ip":"12.213.30.22","latitude":"16.1348","longitude
":"-30.2185"},{"name":"Audra Stoltenberg","domain":"green.name","ip":"9.10.123.128","latitude":"8.5137","longitude":"-152.77
60"},{"name":"Jordane Anderson","domain":"katelyn.io","ip":"206.165.254.110","latitude":"21.3815","longitude":"44.6550"},{"n
ame":"Ms. Delmer Ferry","domain":"emelie.co.uk","ip":"205.143.234.232","latitude":"56.7577","longitude":"-132.4979"},{"name"
:"Gage Stiedemann","domain":"rickey.biz","ip":"227.203.65.208","latitude":"47.5024","longitude":"-111.5114"},{"name":"Jaylen
Ziemann","domain":"brad.org","ip":"238.51.107.144","latitude":"25.7064","longitude":"170.0055"},{"name":"Laila Davis","doma
in":"danielle.com","ip":"53.78.10.226","latitude":"71.2072","longitude":"-123.5552"},{"name":"Vaughn Auer PhD","domain":"jon
athan.co.uk","ip":"116.174.114.57","latitude":"-52.9560","longitude":"46.2061"},{"name":"River Pacocha","domain":"lilla.org"
,"ip":"153.123.156.225","latitude":"-56.2901","longitude":"19.5602"},{"name":"Alvah Roberts","domain":"maxie.info","ip":"211
.97.65.133","latitude":"-34.9807","longitude":"-115.3701"},{"name":"Lauryn Gleichner","domain":"sydni.us","ip":"234.218.226.
77","latitude":"-82.5250","longitude":"128.4832"},{"name":"Jackie Koepp","domain":"melvina.me","ip":"72.230.77.60","latitude
":"-1.3331","longitude":"-165.6801"},{"name":"Lucio Labadie","domain":"jamison.net","ip":"232.247.35.250","latitude":"-72.76
64","longitude":"-134.4110"},{"name":"Brooke Schamberger","domain":"elva.biz","ip":"88.5.138.60","latitude":"51.8362","longi
tude":"-175.6648"},{"name":"Keaton Grant II","domain":"kylee.io","ip":"18.139.48.96","latitude":"-3.3140","longitude":"-137.
9866"},{"name":"Malika Langosh","domain":"hunter.tv","ip":"22.72.139.221","latitude":"-2.4666","longitude":"102.1456"},{"nam
e":"Mr. Sylvester Kozey","domain":"darby.ca","ip":"33.100.59.230","latitude":"-3.7564","longitude":"-45.4578"},{"name":"Jack
y Raynor","domain":"leonora.ca","ip":"190.111.69.31","latitude":"21.4536","longitude":"-147.6291"},{"name":"Pansy Quitzon IV
","domain":"lurline.com","ip":"184.214.165.87","latitude":"-31.2855","longitude":"-102.0654"},{"name":"Mr. Shane Auer","doma
in":"felicity.us","ip":"20.244.61.218","latitude":"30.2989","longitude":"168.5343"},{"name":"Lindsay Turner","domain":"lolit
a.me","ip":"253.141.74.55","latitude":"-13.2037","longitude":"55.7290"},{"name":"Joshuah Bode","domain":"krystel.me","ip":"6
9.194.212.98","latitude":"-26.4837","longitude":"-93.6033"},{"name":"Thad Haley","domain":"helga.info","ip":"82.117.129.110"
,"latitude":"22.3714","longitude":"-70.7244"},{"name":"Freeman Streich","domain":"hailee.co.uk","ip":"239.161.124.24","latit
ude":"-35.5401","longitude":"-149.3609"},{"name":"Sterling Kuhic","domain":"hassie.biz","ip":"60.16.81.27","latitude":"66.07
43","longitude":"139.1632"},{"name":"Sister Rolfson","domain":"loraine.info","ip":"99.34.115.107","latitude":"-87.6446","lon
gitude":"-96.5152"},{"name":"Dr. Arne Ziemann","domain":"fay.tv","ip":"87.103.76.3","latitude":"80.9848","longitude":"-16.20
04"},{"name":"Mr. Kamryn Kshlerin","domain":"greg.info","ip":"134.173.27.241","latitude":"74.6978","longitude":"-79.3544"},{
"name":"Kenyon Emmerich","domain":"bernardo.org","ip":"186.125.47.39","latitude":"-7.8301","longitude":"85.3581"},{"name":"M
ayra Rogahn","domain":"modesta.co.uk","ip":"73.9.205.162","latitude":"-86.0358","longitude":"-168.4751"},{"name":"Finn Aufde
rhar","domain":"lane.tv","ip":"87.26.88.120","latitude":"-64.7770","longitude":"-150.3316"},{"name":"Hilario Reilly","domain
":"gianni.net","ip":"65.154.40.90","latitude":"36.7354","longitude":"111.2826"},{"name":"Ava O'Hara","domain":"deion.org","i
p":"152.72.11.191","latitude":"-75.9839","longitude":"-28.9916"},{"name":"Aurelia Schuster","domain":"dulce.biz","ip":"234.1
79.219.56","latitude":"22.7885","longitude":"45.1911"},{"name":"Susan Bernhard","domain":"shannon.me","ip":"60.30.44.152","l
atitude":"-66.1458","longitude":"-10.1975"},{"name":"Genesis Dickens","domain":"adalberto.tv","ip":"88.24.46.75","latitude":
"66.8723","longitude":"82.1799"},{"name":"Adolphus Prohaska","domain":"eileen.biz","ip":"193.26.237.214","latitude":"64.5686
","longitude":"-123.5918"},{"name":"Fausto Fahey","domain":"elenora.us","ip":"102.17.142.66","latitude":"73.1700","longitude
":"17.7238"},{"name":"Dr. Amelia McKenzie","domain":"brendan.us","ip":"230.90.177.157","latitude":"-29.3075","longitude":"-1
13.1779"},{"name":"Dolly Flatley","domain":"rachael.tv","ip":"19.52.176.12","latitude":"77.0003","longitude":"140.9243"},{"n
ame":"Theresia Thiel","domain":"garrett.biz","ip":"38.62.54.226","latitude":"-72.5508","longitude":"75.1925"},{"name":"Evera
rdo Turner","domain":"haskell.biz","ip":"175.154.220.171","latitude":"-14.3528","longitude":"-12.1423"},{"name":"Marta Nolan

Figure 11-2. *Beginning of the file written by the Node.js server*

Once more, let's convert this example into an Express.js app in `proexpressjs/ch11/stream-express-req.js`:

```
var http = require('http');
var express = require('express');
var app = express();

app.post('*', function (req, res) {
   req.pipe(fs.createWriteStream('ips.txt'));
   res.end('\n');
});
app.listen(3000);
```

■ **Tip** In some cases, it's good to have pass-through logic that doesn't consume too many resources. For that, check out the module through (`https://npmjs.org/package/through`; GitHub: `https://github.com/dominictarr/through`). Another useful module is concat-stream (`https://npmjs.org/package/concat-stream`; GitHub: `https://github.com/maxogden/node-concat-stream`). It allows concatenation of streams.

Summary

So far, we've covered ways to implement a database connection from other, non-`app.js`/`server.js` files. We also worked with hiding sensitive information from our source base, and streaming the data. These concepts and approaches will come in handy when working on the examples in Chapters 19 through 22.

The next chapter will give you some Express.js tips on working with Redis and implementing an Authentication pattern.

CHAPTER 12

Redis and Authentication Patterns

This chapter deals with two Express.js topics: Redis and authentication patterns. Redis is a fast database that is often used for storing Express.js sessions.

Redis

Redis (`http://redis.io`) is often used in Express.js applications for session persistence, because storing sessions in a physical storage keeps apps from losing users' data when a system is restarted or redeployed. It also enables the use of multiple RESTful servers because they can connect to the same Redis server. In addition, Redis can be used for queues and scheduling tasks (e.g., e-mail jobs).

Redis itself is a stand-alone service. Therefore, to use Redis with Express.js, we need two things:

- *Redis server*: A database server that can listen on a particular port and be accessed via the Redis console or applications
- *Connect-redis*: An NPM module (`https://www.npmjs.org/package/connect-redis`; GitHub: `https://github.com/tj/connect-redis`) that enables Express.js to use the Redis store and includes the redis module (`https://www.npmjs.org/package/redis`; GitHub: `https://github.com/mranney/node_redis`)

To download Redis 2.6.7, enter these simple commands:

```
$ wget http://download.redis.io/releases/redis-2.6.7.tar.gz
$ tar xzf redis-2.6.7.tar.gz
$ cd redis-2.6.7
$ make
```

For more Redis instructions, you can visit `http://redis.io/download`.

To start Redis, enter

```
$ src/redis-server
```

To stop Redis, just press Ctrl+C.

To access the Redis command-line interface, enter

```
$ src/redis-cli
```

Following is an uncomplicated example of how to use Redis to manage Express.js sessions.

First, to access Redis, utilize the `connect-redis` driver. You can do so with the familiar dependency key/value pair in `ch12/package.json`:

```
{
  "name": "redis-example",
  "dependencies": {
    "express": "4.8.1",
    "connect-redis": "2.1.0",
    "cookie-parser": "1.3.2",
    "express-session": "1.7.6"
  }
}
```

To use Redis as a session store in an Express.js server (`ch12/app.js`), enter the following:

```
var express = require('express');
var app = express();
var cookieParser = require('cookie-parser');
var session = require('express-session');
var RedisStore = require('connect-redis')(session);

app.use(cookieParser());
app.use(session({
  resave: true,
  saveUninitialized: true,
  store: new RedisStore({
    host: 'localhost',
    port: 6379
  }),
  secret: '0FFD9D8D-78F1-4A30-9A4E-0940ADE81645',
  cookie: { path: '/', maxAge: 3600000 }
}));
```

Next, define the "/" route that will increment the counter for each unique session. In other words, if we close the browser, stop the Express.js server, wait awhile, restart the server, and reopen the browser, the value will be saved and incremented, as long as the cookie with the session ID is not expired or deleted. Also, output the counter and the session ID:

```
app.get('/', function(request, response){
  console.log('Session ID: ', request.sessionID);
  if (request.session.counter) {
    request.session.counter = request.session.counter +1;
  } else {
    request.session.counter = 1;
  }
  response.send('Counter: ' + request.session.counter);
});

app.listen(3000);
```

Now, when you start the server, it should show you `Counter: 1` and the `connect.sid` cookie should have a value similar to the following (see Figure 12-1):

```
s%3AA3l_jSr25tbWWjRHot9sEUM5OApCn21R.qxxe7TLSaZBwuCGKmSfvI9jpVcnLyUrKMEkXxXMvAzM
```

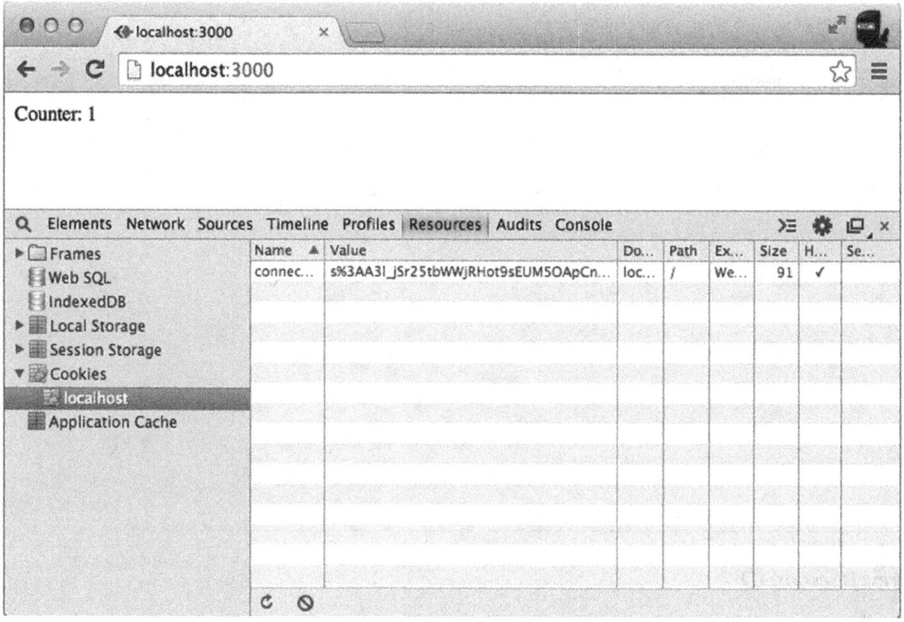

Figure 12-1. *Output of the Redis store Express.js session example*

Your session ID will be different, but the format and the length will be the same. Let's decode this value with the `decodeURIComponent()` method, either in the browser or the Node.js console (see Figure 12-2):

```
decodeURIComponent('s%3AA3l_jSr25tbWWjRHot9sEUM5OApCn21R.qxxe7TLSaZBwuCGKmSfvI9jpVcnLyUrKMEkXxXMvAzM')
```

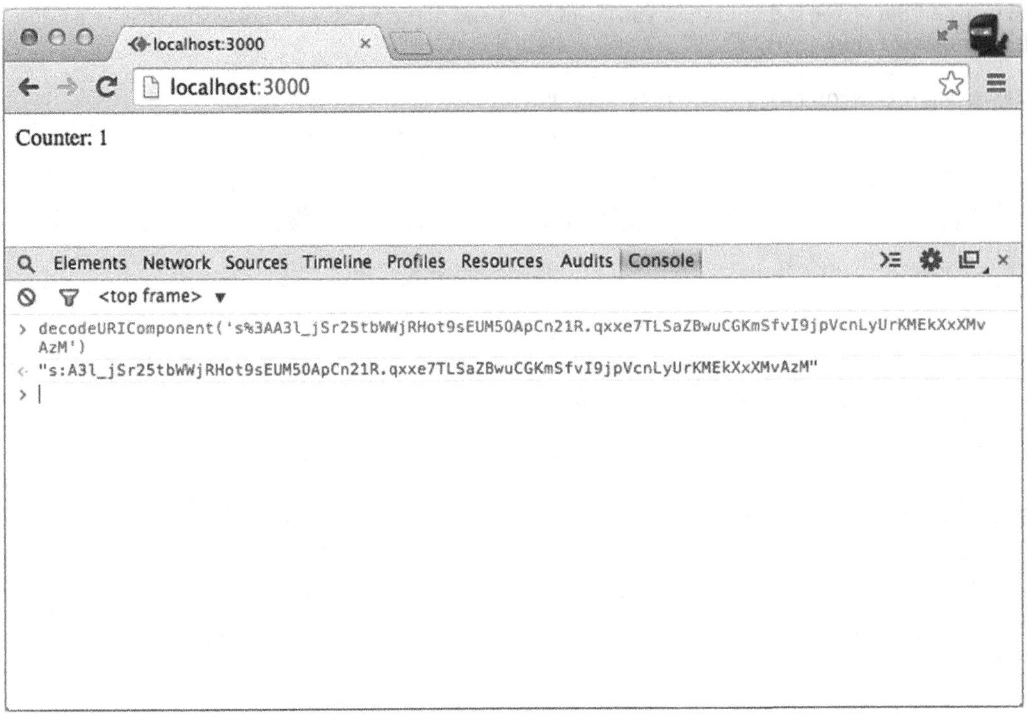

Figure 12-2. *Decoding Express.js session ID*

The value between `s:` and `.` is the session ID. Compare it with the value that was printed in the server logs. They should match.

To double-check that the counter value is actually stored in Redis and not somewhere else, copy the session ID and open the Redis console in a new terminal window with

```
$ redis-cli
```

Then, type this command to get the session values: `get sess:SESSION_ID`, where `SESSION_ID` is your session ID; for example:

```
> get sess:A3l_jSr25tbWWjRHot9sEUM50ApCn21R
```

You should see the string of the JSON object with your session value counter, along with some options. For example, my output is

```
"{\"cookie\":{\"originalMaxAge\":3600000,\"expires\":\"2014-09-03T19:03:55.007Z\",
\"httpOnly\":true,\"path\":\"/\"},\"counter\":1}"
```

You can also use the `>` keys command to get the list of stored session keys (the prefix is `sess`):

```
> keys sess*
```

As mentioned at the beginning of the chapter, the connect-redis module is backed by the redis module. With this module, Redis can be used as a flat, stand-alone database. Interestingly, Redis supports four types of data: strings, lists, sets, and hashes.

■ **Tip** For a deeper study of Redis, you can find an interactive tutorial available at `http://try.redis.io`.

Authentication Patterns

The most common type of authentication is to require a username and password combination. We can check for the match against our database and then store an `authenticated=true` flag in the session. The session data is automatically stored by Express.js for *every* other request by that agent:

```
app.use(function(req, res, next) {
  if (req.session && req.session.authenticated)
     return next();
  else {
    return res.redirect('/login');
  }
}
```

In case we need additional user information, it also can be stored in the session:

```
app.post('/login', function(req, res) {
  // Check the database for the username and password combination
  // In a real-world scenario you would salt the password
db.findOne({username: req.body.username,
    password: req.body.password},
    function(error, user) {
      if (error) return next();
      if (!user) return next(new Error('Bad username/password');
      req.session.user = user;
      res.redirect ('/protected_area');
    }
  );
});
```

For a tool to salt passwords, take a look at bcryptjs (`https://www.npmjs.org/package/bcryptjs`), which is compatible with bcrypt, but doesn't need compilation, because it fully runs on JavaScript/Node.js. Another cool thing about `bcryptjs` (and bcrypt), compared to other libraries or your own implementation of hashing/salting, is that the salt is a part of the password, so you don't need to store an additional field for salt for each user in the database. For example:

```
var bcrypt = require('bcryptjs');
bcrypt.hash('pr0expressr0cks!, 8, function(err, hash) {
// ... Store the hash, which is a password and salt together
});
```

Use asynchronous bcryptjs methods, because they will be really slow (the slower the better for protection!).

Authentication with third parties is often done via OAuth. For a working example of the `oauth` module (`https://www.npmjs.org/package/oauth`; GitHub: `https://github.com/ciaranj/node-oauth`)—to which this author contributed some docs—check out the HackHall example in Chapter 22.

OAuth 1.0/2.0 requires callback routes for the user redirect back to our sites. This is effortless with Express.js. In addition, there are fully automated solutions that take care of everything (database, signing, routing, etc.): Everyauth (`https://npmjs.org/package/everyauth`) and Passport (`https://npmjs.org/package/passport`).

■ **Tip** For a quick introduction to OAuth that is applicable to Node.js, consider reading my book, *Introduction to OAuth with Node.js: Twitter API OAuth 1.0, OAuth 2.0, OAuth Echo, Everyauth and OAuth2.0 Server Examples* (webapplog.com, 2014).

Summary

In this chapter we installed and used Redis so that session information can be persistent, meaning it won't be lost if the server is down. Redis (or any other persistent store) allows us to share sessions between multiple servers. Then we covered the implementation of authentication with middleware.

In the next chapter, we'll cover multithreading with clusters, continuing with the theme of getting your Express.js app production-ready.

CHAPTER 13

Multithreading with Clusters

There are a lot of detractors out there arguing against the use of Node.js, many of whose arguments are rooted in the myth that Node.js-based systems *have* to be single-threaded. Nothing could be further from the truth—and with the `cluster` module, we can effortlessly fork a Node.js process to create multiple processes. Yes, each process will still be single-threaded and be blocked by inapt synchronous code or some laborious processes (such as hashing of passwords). However, the whole system, now consisting of a few processes, won't be blocked.

In the case of web apps, the processes can listen on the same port, thus ensuring that, if the first process is busy, the request will be handled by the second (or third or fourth) process. Typically, we spawn as many processes as we have CPUs on that machine so that we can utilize all the machine's CPUs.

A Multithreading Example

Here is a working example of an Express.js app that runs on four processes. One of them is the so-called *master* process and the other three are *worker* processes. The master is responsible for managing and monitoring workers, while a worker is a separate Express.js app itself. The code for master and worker is contained in the same file.

At the beginning of the file, we import dependencies:

```
var cluster = require('cluster');
var http = require('http');
var numCPUs = require('os').cpus().length;
var express = require('express');
```

The `cluster` module has a property that tells us if the process is master or child. We use that property to spawn four workers (the default workers will use the same file, but this can be overwritten with the `setupMaster()` method).[1] In addition to that, we can attach event listeners and receive messages from workers (e.g., `'kill'`).

```
if (cluster.isMaster) {
  console.log('Fork %s worker(s) from master', numCPUs)
  for (var i = 0; i < numCPUs; i++) {
    cluster.fork();
  };
  cluster.on('online', function(worker) {
    console.log('Worker is running on %s pid', worker.process.pid)
  });
  cluster.on('exit', function(worker, code, signal) {
    console.log('Worker with %s is closed', worker.process.pid );
  });
```

[1]http://nodejs.org/docs/v0.9.0/api/cluster.html#cluster_cluster_setupmaster_settings

The worker code is just an Express.js app with a twist. We're getting the process ID, or PID (the following code continues from the previous snippet):

```
} else if (cluster.isWorker) {
```

Now we write the good old Express.js server code with a port of 3000:

```
  var port = 3000;
  console.log('Worker (%s) is now listening to http://localhost:%s',
    cluster.worker.process.pid, port);
  var app = express();
```

The server has a catchall route that will print the PID:

```
  app.get('*', function(req, res) {
    res.send(200, 'cluster '
      + cluster.worker.process.pid
      + ' responded \n');
  })
  app.listen(port);
}
```

Feel free to use the full source code of `ch13/cluster.js` in your projects:

```
var cluster = require('cluster');
var numCPUs = require('os').cpus().length;
var express = require('express');

if (cluster.isMaster) {
  console.log('Fork %s worker(s) from master', numCPUs);
  for (var i = 0; i < numCPUs; i++) {
    cluster.fork();
  }
  cluster.on('online', function(worker) {
    console.log('Worker is running on %s pid', worker.process.pid);
  });
  cluster.on('exit', function(worker, code, signal) {
    console.log('Worker with %s is closed', worker.process.pid );
  });
} else if (cluster.isWorker) {
  var port = 3000;
  console.log('Worker (%s) is now listening to http://localhost:%s',
    cluster.worker.process.pid, port);
  var app = express();
  app.get('*', function(req, res) {
    res.send(200, 'cluster ' + cluster.worker.process.pid + ' responded \n');
  });
  app.listen(port);
}
```

As usual, to start an app, run `$ node cluster`. There should be four (or two, depending on your machine's architecture) processes, and the logs might look like this (see Figure 13-1):

```
worker is running on 15279 pid
worker is running on 15277 pid
...
```

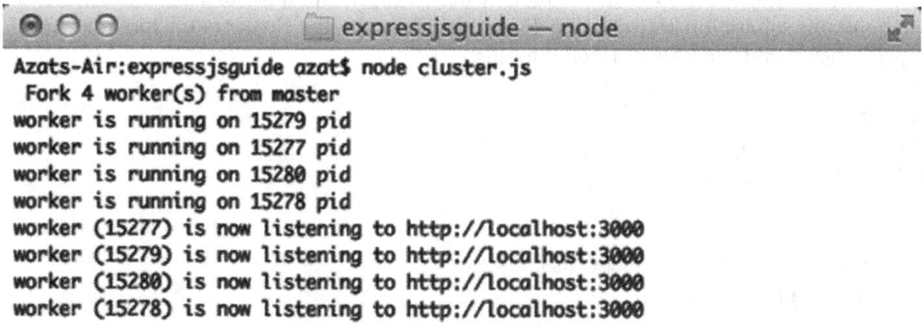

expressjsguide — node
Azats-Air:expressjsguide azat$ node cluster.js
Fork 4 worker(s) from master
worker is running on 15279 pid
worker is running on 15277 pid
worker is running on 15280 pid
worker is running on 15278 pid
worker (15277) is now listening to http://localhost:3000
worker (15279) is now listening to http://localhost:3000
worker (15280) is now listening to http://localhost:3000
worker (15278) is now listening to http://localhost:3000

Figure 13-1. *Starting of four processes with cluster*

There are different processes that listen to the *same* port and respond to us. For example, the responses could be as follows (see Figure 13-2):

```
cluster 15278 responded
cluster 15280 responded
```

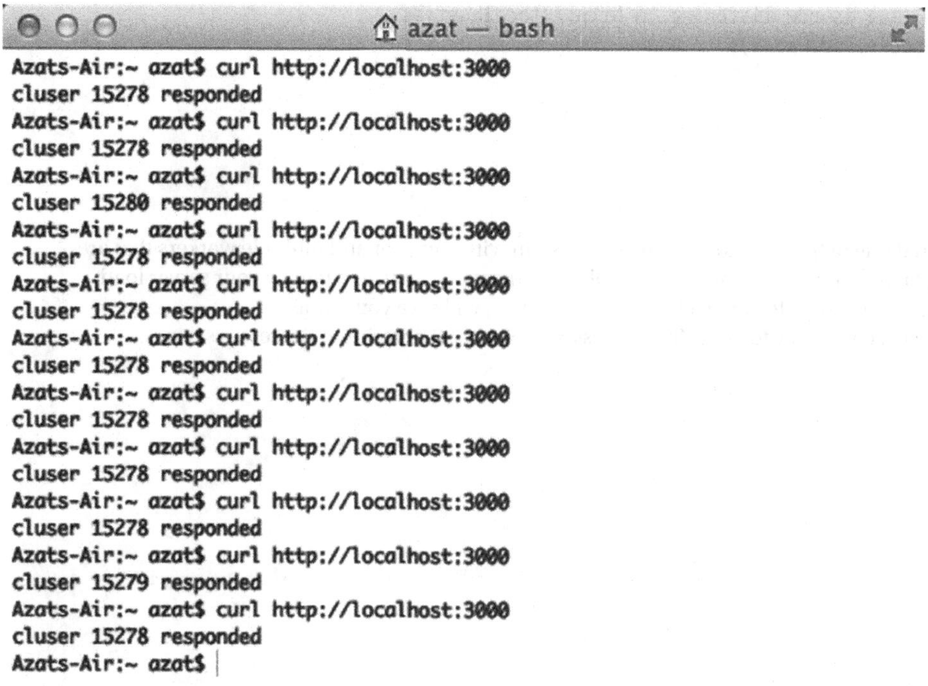

Figure 13-2. *Server response is rendered by different processes*

■ **Tip** If you prefer ready-made solutions to low-level libraries (such as `cluster`), check out the real-world production library created and used by eBay: `cluster2` (`https://www.npmjs.org/package/cluster2`; GitHub: `https://github.com/ql-io/cluster2`).

Looking again at `ch13/cluster.js`, notice that we can abstract the actual Express.js app into a separate file. This a good thing to do because it maintains separation between two distinct logical units, the cluster and Express.js app. For example, the cluster file previously listed can be refactored into this:

```
var cluster = require('cluster');
var numCPUs = require('os').cpus().length;
var app = require('./app'); // <- THIS FILE!

if (cluster.isMaster) {
  console.log('Fork %s worker(s) from master', numCPUs);
  for (var i = 0; i < numCPUs; i++) {
    cluster.fork();
  }
  cluster.on('online', function(worker) {
    console.log('Worker is running on %s pid', worker.process.pid);
  });
  cluster.on('exit', function(worker, code, signal) {
    console.log('Worker with %s is closed', worker.process.pid );
  });
} else if (cluster.isWorker) {
  var port = 3000;
  console.log('Worker (%s) is now listening to http://localhost:%s',
    cluster.worker.process.pid, port);
  app.listen(port);
}
```

Summary

In this chapter, we explored one of the ways to implement a system with a master and multiple workers that are Express.js apps listening on the same port. This is a valuable trick that you can use to reduce your server load, enabling you to serve more traffic with fewer machines, which in turn will save you money.

In the next chapter, we'll cover how to apply Stylus, Less, and Sass CSS libraries to Express.js servers.

CHAPTER 14

Applying Stylus, Less, and Sass

Using Cascading Style Sheets (CCS) is a must for any web project, but CSS style sheets are tedious to write and manage in complex projects. This is mainly due to the fact that CSS is not a real programming language. CSS has no inheritance, variables, or functions. Code reuse and maintainability is a pain in the neck for plain CSS resources. This is especially true for large projects or CSS libraries that are intended to be shared among various projects.

The solution to the pain of using plain CSS is to use another, better language that is compiled into CSS at the time of the build (for production) or on-the-fly (for development). For the latter, Express.js uses middleware, so each time a web page requests a CSS asset, the framework converts the better-CSS code into plain CSS. Some of the better-CSS libraries include Stylus (my favorite), Less (favorite of the Twitter Bootstrap team), and Sass.

So, Stylus, Less, and Sass bring the much needed sanity of reusability (mixins, extensions, variables, etc.) to style sheets so that we as developers can be more productive and reuse CSS code more easily. Let's see how we can tap into this pool of awesomeness when we work with Express.js.

Coverage of the libraries and their features in detail is beyond the scope of this chapter, because the features are numerous and prone to future changes (so it's better to refer to the official documentation, links to which are provided at the end of the chapter). This chapter teaches you how to plug in the libraries to Express.js apps. The libraries themselves are backward compatible (for the most part) with plain CSS; therefore, they have a forgiving, flat learning curve.

Tip Express Generator v4.2.0 supports the Less and Stylus libraries, but not Sass.

Stylus

Stylus is a sibling of Express.js and is the most-often used CSS framework.[1] It's my favorite for the same reason that I favor Jade: it achieves eloquence by minimizing the number of characters needed for it to work. The fewer characters that I have to type, the less chance that I will make mistakes and the more time that I have to solve real problems.

To install Stylus, type and run

```
$ npm install stylus@0.42.3 --save.
```

Apply Stylus with `app.use` and the folder name. Then, to apply `static` middleware, include this in your server file:

```
//... Import dependencies and instantiate app
app.use(require('stylus').middleware(__dirname + '/public'));
app.use(express.static(path.join(__dirname, 'public')));
//... Routes and app.listen()
```

[1]https://www.npmjs.org/package/stylus

Put `*.styl` files inside the folder that we exposed (e.g., `public` or `public/css`) and include them in Jade (or any other) templates using the `*.css` extension. Yes, that's right! The file is `*.styl` but in the Jade or HTML code we ask for the `*.css` file. Express.js will do the magic! For example, we have `style.styl`, in `public/stylesheets/`, so we use `/stylesheets/style.css` in the template/HTML:

```
//...
  head
    link(rel='stylesheet', href='/stylesheets/style.css')
//...
```

Or, in any other templates of your choice, or in plain HTML file(s), enter the following:

```
<link rel="stylesheet" href="/stylesheets/style.css"/>
```

For a project created from scratch, you can use the generator command:

```
$ express -c stylus express-app-name command
```

You'll find the Stylus-enabled project in the `ch14/stylus` folder as well as on GitHub (`https://github.com/azat-co/proexpressjs`).

Less

To use Less with Express.js, we need `less-middleware`, which is an external NPM module (`https://www.npmjs.org/package/less-middleware`):

```
$ npm install less-middleware@1.0.0 --save
```

Then, we need to add `less-middleware` *before* the `static` and router ones (`ch14/less/app.js`):

```
//... Import dependencies and instantiate app
app.use(require('less-middleware')(path.join(__dirname, 'public')));
app.use(express.static(path.join(__dirname, 'public')));
//... Routes and app.listen()
```

Assuming the Less file(s) are in `public/css`, we can link the `*.css` file(s), and the rest will be handled automatically; for example, a Jade template might use this:

```
//...
  head
    link(rel='stylesheet', href='/stylesheets/style.css')
//...
```

Or, in any other template of your choice, or in plain HTML file(s), use the following:

```
<link rel="stylesheet" href="/stylesheets/style.css"/>
```

For a project created from scratch, you can use the `$ express -c less express-app-name` command.

You'll find the Less-enabled project in the `ch14/less` folder as well as on GitHub (`https://github.com/azat-co/proexpressjs`).

Sass

To use Sass with Express.js, we need node-sass, which is an external NPM module (https://npmjs.org/package/node-sass; GitHub: https://github.com/sass/node-sass):

```
$ npm install node-sass@0.6.7 --save
```

This is our Express.js plug-in for Sass (ch14/sass/app.js):

```
// ... Import dependencies and instantiate app
app.use(require('node-sass').middleware({
  src: __dirname + '/public',
  dest: __dirname + '/public',
  debug: true,
  outputStyle: 'compressed'
}));
app.use(express.static(path.join(__dirname, 'public')));
// ... Routes and app.listen()
```

The Jade template also imports the *.css file:

```
link(rel='stylesheet', href='/stylesheets/style.css')
```

The Sass-enabled project is in the ch14/sass folder, as well as on GitHub (https://github.com/azat-co/proexpressjs).

Summary

Most code of the CSS frameworks we touched upon in this chapter is compatible with plain CSS. In other words, plain CSS code will work just fine inside of Stylus, Sass, or Less. Therefore, there is no harm in including such a CSS framework into your project.

The benefits of using such a framework are numerous, including the availability of mixins, variables, inheritance, and so forth. These features are quite extensive, which is why they are not included in this book. For complete information, please refer to the official online documentation for Stylus (http://learnboost.github.io/stylus), Sass (http://sass-lang.com), and Less (http://lesscss.org).

The next chapter provides some important tips regarding Express.js and security.

CHAPTER 15

Security Tips

The set of tips in this chapter deals with security in Express.js applications. Security is often a neglected topic that is deferred until the last minute before the release. Obviously, this approach of treating security as an afterthought is prone to leaving holes for attackers. A better approach is to consider and implement security matters from the ground up.

Browser JavaScript has earned a bad reputation for security vulnerabilities, so we need to keep our Node.js apps as secure as possible! With the simple modifications and middleware covered in this chapter, you can effortlessly address some basic security concerns.

This chapter covers the following topics:

- Cross-site request forgery (CSRF)
- Process permissions
- HTTP security headers
- Input validation

Cross-Site Request Forgery

CSRF and the `csurf` middleware were briefly covered in Chapter 4. Please refer to that chapter for the CSRF definition and explanation.

The `csurf` middleware does most of the job of matching incoming values from requests. However, we still need to expose the values in responses and pass them back to the server in templates (or JavaScript XHRs). First, we install the `csurf` module like any other dependency with

```
$ npm install csurf@1.6.0
```

Then, we apply `csurf` with `var csrf = require('csurf'); app.use()`, as covered in Chapter 4:

```
app.use(csrf());
```

The `csrf` *must be preceded* by `cookie-parser` and `express-session` because it depends on these middleware (i.e., to install, import, and apply the necessary modules).

One of the ways to implement the validation is to use custom middleware to pass the CSRF token to all the templates using `response.local`. This custom middleware must precede the routes (as is the case for most middleware statements):

```
app.use(function (request, response, next) {
  response.locals.csrftoken = request.csrfToken();
  next();
});
```

In other words, we manually facilitate the presence of the token in the body (shown in this example), query, or header. (Depending on your preference or a contract between the client, you can use the query or header.)

So, to render the value in the template as a hidden form value, we can use

```
input(type="hidden", name="_csrf", value="#{csrftoken}")
```

This hidden input field will add the token value to the submitted form data, facilitating the sending of the CSRF token to the /login route along with other fields such as email and password.

Here's the full Jade language content in file ch15/index.jade:

```
doctype html
html
  head
    title= title
    link(rel='stylesheet', href='/css/style.css')
  body
    if errors
      each error in errors
        p.error= error.msg
    form(method="post", action="/login")
      input(type="hidden", name="_csrf", value="#{csrftoken}")
      input(type="text", name="email", placeholder="hi@webapplog.com")
      input(type="password", name="password", placeholder="Password")
      button(type="submit") Login
    p
      include lorem-ipsum
```

To see the demo of CSRF in ch15/app.js, start the server as you typically do with $ node app. Then navigate to the home page located at http://localhost:3000. You should see the token in the hidden field of the form, as shown in Figure 15-1. Keep in mind that your token value will be different, but its format will be the same.

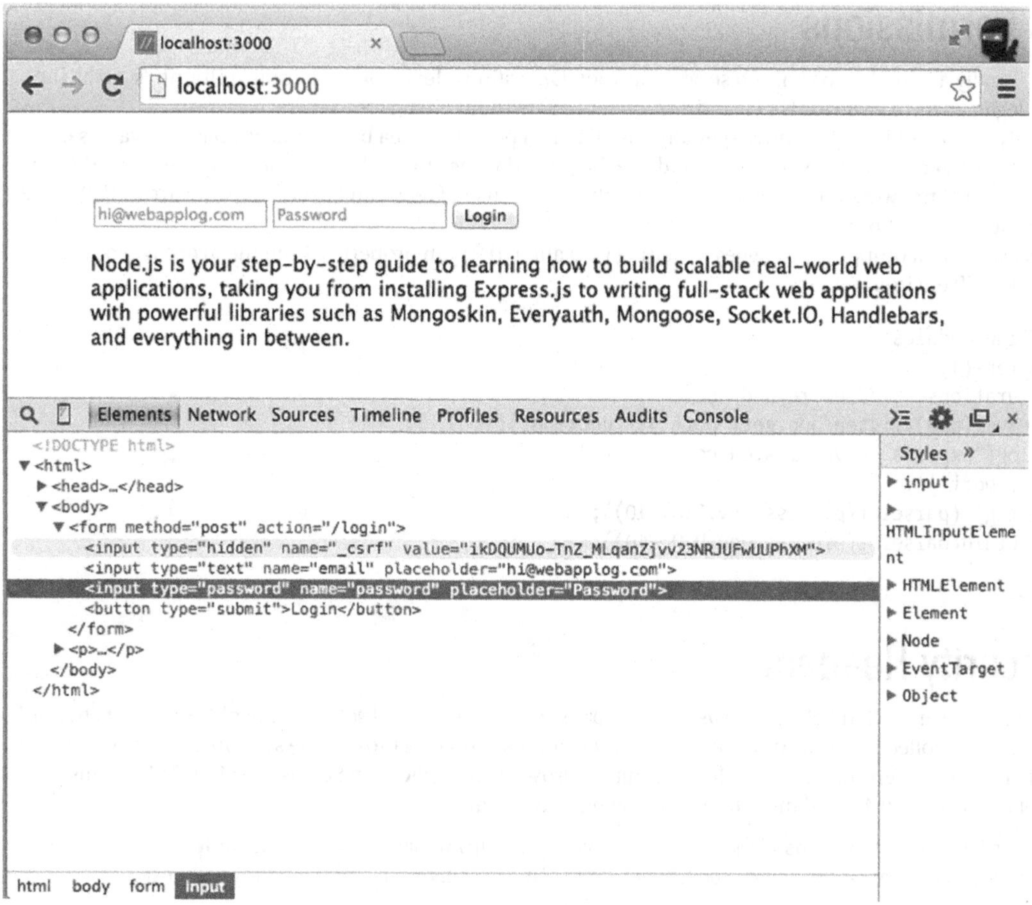

Figure 15-1. *CSRF token from the* `csurf` *module inserted into the form to be sent later to the /login route*

For each request to the home page (/) or refresh of the page, you'll get a new token. But, if you augment the token to simulate the attack (you can do it right there in the Chrome Developer Tools), you'll get this error:

```
403 Error: invalid csrf token
  at verifytoken...
```

Process Permissions

Obviously, it's usually a bad idea to run web services as root. Operations developers can utilize Ubuntu's authbind[1] to bind to privileged ports (e.g., 80 for HTTP and 443 for HTTPS) without giving root access.

Alternatively, it's possible to drop privileges after binding to a port. The idea here is that we pass the values of GID (group ID) and UID (user ID) to the Node.js app and use the parsed values to set the group identity and user identity of the process. This will not work on Windows, so you might want to use if/else and process.platform or NODE_ENV to make your code cross-platform.

Here is an example of dropping privileges by setting GID and UID[2] with properties from the process.env.GID and process.evn.UID environmental vars:

```
// ... Importing modules
var app = express();
// ... Configurations, middleware and routes
http.createServer(app).listen(app.get('port'), function(){
    console.log("Express server listening on port "
    + app.get('port'));
    process.setgid(parseInt(process.env.GID, 10));
    process.setuid(parseInt(process.env.UID, 10));
});
```

HTTP Security Headers

The Express.js middleware called helmet (https://www.npmjs.org/package/helmet; GitHub: https://github.com/helmetjs/helmet) is a collection of security-related middleware that provides most of the security headers described in the Recx article "Seven Web Server HTTP Headers that Improve Web Application Security for Free."[3] As of this writing, helmet is at version 0.4.1 and includes the following middleware:

- crossdomain: Serves /crossdomain.xml to prevent Flash from loading certain unwanted content (see http://www.adobe.com/devnet/articles/crossdomain_policy_file_spec.html)
- csp: Adds Content Security Policy that allows for whitelisting of content to load (see http://content-security-policy.com and http://www.html5rocks.com/en/tutorials/security/content-security-policy)
- hidePoweredBy: Removes X-Powered-By to prevent revealing that you are using Node.js and Express.js
- hsts: Adds HTTP Strict Transport Security to prevent your web site from being viewed on HTTP (instead of HTTPS)
- ienoopen: Sets the X-Download-Options header for Internet Explorer 8+ to prevent the loading of untrusted HTML in IE browsers (see http://blogs.msdn.com/b/ie/archive/2008/07/02/ie8-security-part-v-comprehensive-protection.aspx)
- nocache: Cache-Control and Pragma headers to stop caching (helpful to flush old bugs from users' browsers)
- nosniff: Sets the proper X-Content-Type-Options header to mitigate MIME type sniffing (see http://msdn.microsoft.com/en-us/library/gg622941%28v=vs.85%29.aspx)

---

[1]http://manpages.ubuntu.com/manpages/hardy/man1/authbind.1.html
[2]http://www.gnu.org/software/coreutils/manual/html_node/Directory-Setuid-and-Setgid.html
[3]http://recxltd.blogspot.com/2012/03/seven-web-server-http-headers-that.html

- `xframe`: Sets the `X-Frame-Options` heading to `DENY` to prevent your resource from being put into a frame for clickjacking attacks (see `https://en.wikipedia.org/wiki/Clickjacking`)
- `xssFilter`: Sets the `X-XSS-Protection` header for IE8+ and Chrome to protect from XSS attacks (see `http://blogs.msdn.com/b/ieinternals/archive/2011/01/31/controlling-the-internet-explorer-xss-filter-with-the-x-xss-protection-http-header.aspx`)

To install `helmet`, simply run

```
$ npm install helmet@0.4.1
```

Import the module as you always do:

```
var helmet = require('helmet');
```

Then apply the middleware *before the routes*. The default usage is as follows (`ch15/app.js`):

```
app.use(helmet());
```

Figure 15-2 shows how the `helmet` v0.4.1 HTTP response will look when used with the default options:

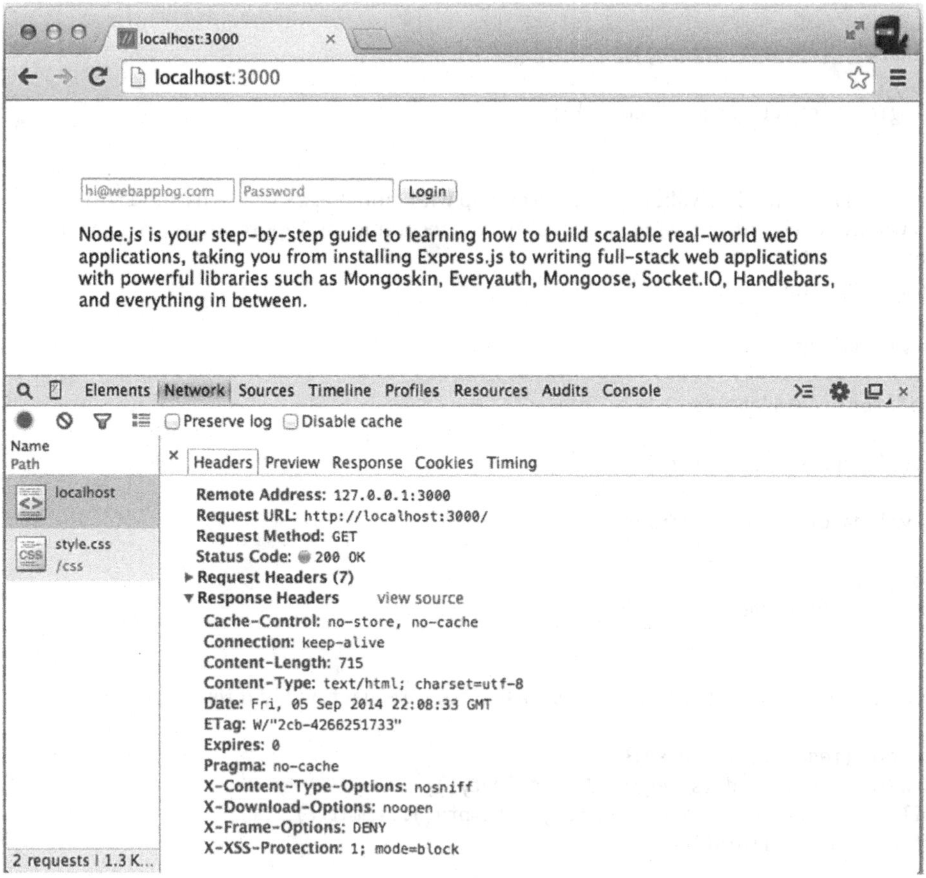

***Figure 15-2.** helmet v0.4.1 HTTP response when used with default options*

Input Validation

Express.js doesn't perform any user/client input sanitation or validation when you use body-parser or query as input data. And, as we all know, we should never trust the input. Malicious code can be inserted (XSS or SQL injections) into your system. For example, browser JavaScript code that you treat as a benign string can turn into an attack when you print that string on your page (especially if your template engine doesn't escape special characters automatically!).

The first line of defense is to check data manually with regular expressions on the routes that accept external data. The additional "defense" can be added on the object-relational mapping layer, such as the Mongoose Schema (see Chapter 22). Remember that front-end/browser validation is performed *only* for usability purposes (i.e., it is more user-friendly)—it *does not* protect your web site from anything.

For example, in `ch15/app.js` we can implement the validation that uses a RegExp pattern on the `email` field, `if-else` statements, and the `test()` method to append an error message to the `errors` array like this:

```
app.post('/login-custom', function(request, response){
  var errors = [];
  var emailRegExp = /^(([^<>()[\]\\.,;:\s@\"]+(\.[^<>()[\]\\.,;:\s@\"]+)*)|(\".+\"))@((\[[0-9]
{1,3}\.[0-9]{1,3}\.[0-9]{1,3}\.[0-9]{1,3}\])|(([a-zA-Z\-0-9]+\.)+[a-zA-Z]{2,}))$/;
  if (!request.body.password) errors.push({msg: 'Password is required'});
  if (!request.body.email || !emailRegExp.test(request.body.email) ) errors.push({msg: 'A valid
email is required'});
  if (errors)
    response.render('index', {errors: errors});
  else
    response.render('login', {email: request.email});
});
```

As you add more routes and input fields to validate, you will end up with more RegExp patterns and `if/else` statements. Although that will work better than having *no validation*, the recommended approach is to write your own module or use `express-validator`.

To install `express-validator`, run:

```
$ npm install express-validator@2.4.0
```

Import `express-validator` in `ch15/app.js`:

```
var  validator = require('express-validator');
```

Then apply `express-validator` *after* `body-parser`:

```
app.use(bodyParser.json());
app.use(bodyParser.urlencoded({extended: true}));
app.use(validator());
```

Now, within the request handlers, we get to access `request.assert` and `request.validationErrors()`:

```
app.post('/login', function(request, response){
  request.assert('password', 'Password is required').notEmpty();
  request.assert('email', 'A valid email is required').notEmpty().isEmail();
  var errors = request.validationErrors();
  if (errors)
    response.render('index', {errors: errors});
```

```
  else
    response.render('login', {email: request.email});
});
```

The index.jade file simply prints errors from the array, if there are any:

```
if errors
  each error in errors
    p.error= error.msg
```

And the login.jade template prints the e-mail. This template is rendered only if the validation went successfully.

```
p= email
```

To demonstrate, go to the home page and try to enter some data. If there are errors, you'll be shown the home page with errors as shown in Figure 15-3. The double "A valid email is required" message comes from the fact that we have two assertions for the email field (notEmpty and isEmail) and *both of them fail* when the email field is empty.

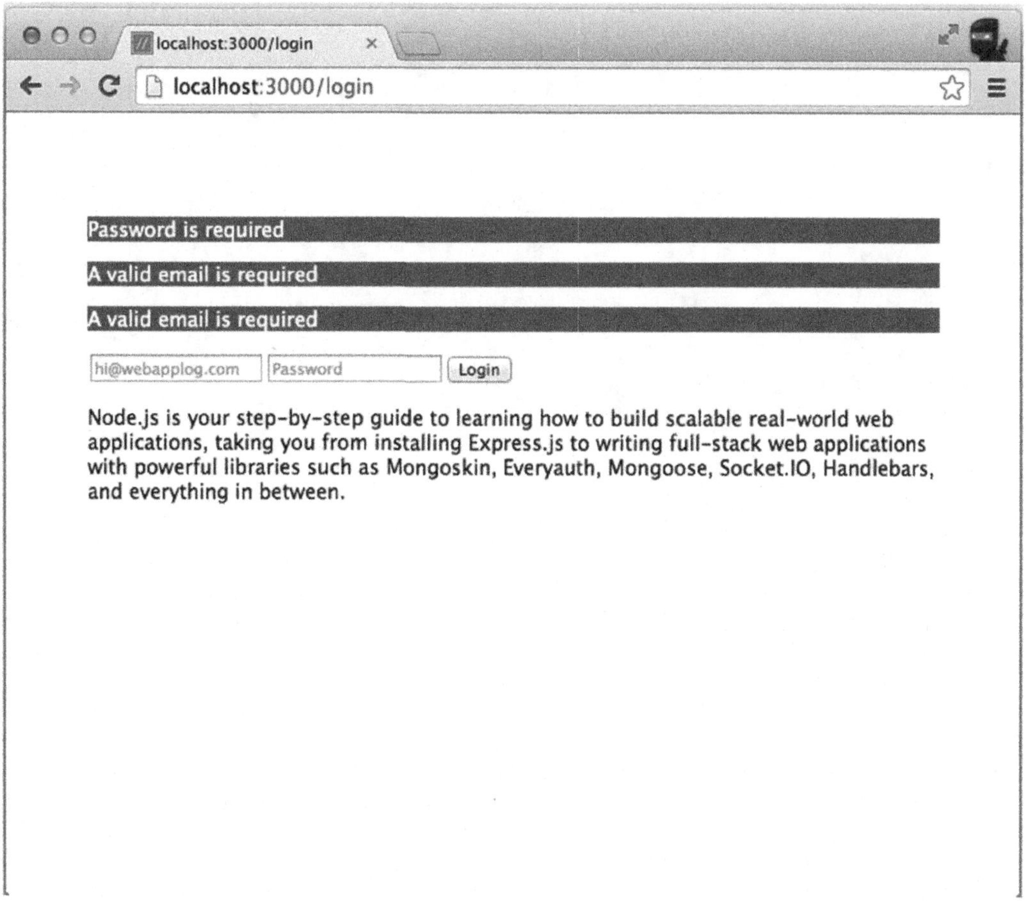

Figure 15-3. *Error messages from using express-validator to assert form values*

Summary

Security is paramount, but often neglected. This is especially true during early stages of development. The typical thought process goes like this: let's focus on delivering more features, then we'll take care of security later when we are about to release. This decision is usually well-intended, but rarely plays out as planned. As the result, the security of the systems suffers.

With middleware libraries, such as `csurf`, `helmet`, and `express-validator`, we can get a good amount of basic security without adding too many development cycles.

In the next chapter, we'll shift gears and cover some approaches to using Express.js with the Socket.IO library for reactive (i.e., updated in real time) views.

CHAPTER 16

Socket.IO and Express.js

Socket.IO (`http://socket.io`) is a library that provides the capability to establish two-way communication between a client and the server in real time. This two-way communication is driven by the WebSocket technology.

The WebSocket technology is available in most modern browsers, and the easiest way to conceptualize it is to imagine a constant connection between a browser and the server, as opposed to the traditional sporadic HTTP requests. Another difference between WebSocket and traditional HTTP requests is that the former is a two-way channel, meaning that the server can initiate the data transfer. This is great for updating the page in real time.

WebSocket is not the only option for real-time-like systems. You can implement close-to-real-time systems with *polling*, which is when browser code makes a lot of HTTP requests within a short interval (e.g., 100 milliseconds). And Socket.IO is not the only library that you can use to implement WebSocket. In *Practical Node.js* (Apress, 2014), I present an example that uses `ws` as the server library and a native (no library at all) browser API. However, the advantage of using Socket.IO is that it has broad, cross-platform and cross-browser support; falls back to polling when WebSocket is unavailable; and uses events as its main implementation pattern.

Full coverage of the Socket.IO library deserves its own book. However, it's so cool and easy to start using with Express.js that I included this chapter to show you a basic example.

Using Socket.IO

The example will echo (browser to server and back) our input in reverse in real time. This means we'll build an Express.js server with a web page that includes a form input field. The web page will also have some front-end JavaScript code that transfers the input field characters to the server in real time as we type. The server will reverse the string and send it back to the browser, where our front-end JavaScript code will print the final string to the browser console. We'll be using the Socket.IO methods and event listeners for all that functionality.

In the final product, if you type "!stekcoS," the app will convert it to "Sockets!" as shown in Figure 16-1. And the browser console output will display

```
!
sending ! to server
received !
!
sending !
received !
!s
sending !s to server
received s!
...
```

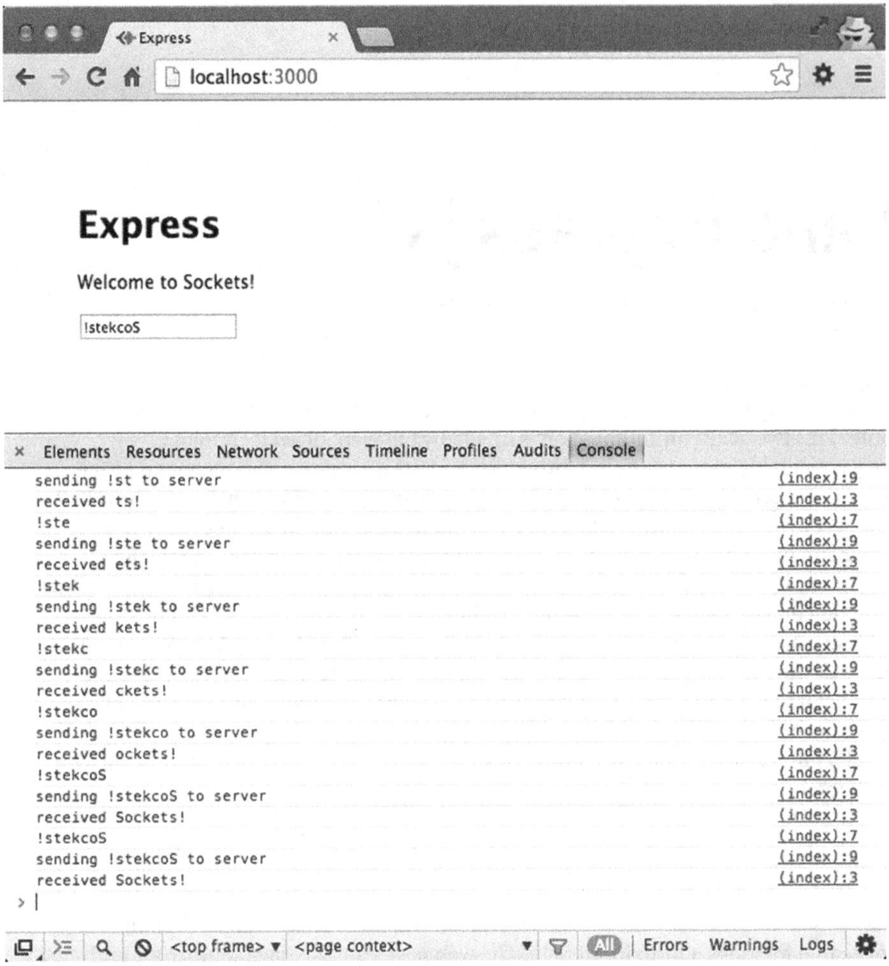

***Figure 16-1.** The input of !stekcoS yields Sockets!*

You can start with a fresh Express.js app created by `$ express socket`, or download the source code from the `ch16/socket` folder. Then, install dependencies with `$ cd socket && npm install`.

■ **Tip** If you need an Express.js 3.x example, you can refer to the version of this app written for Express.js 3.3.5. The source code is in the GitHub repo: `https://github.com/azat-co/proexpressjs/tree/master/ch16/socket-express3`.

To include Socket.io, we can use:

```
$ npm install socket.io@1.1.0 --save
```

Alternatively, we can use `package.json`:

```
{
  "name": "socket-app",
  "version": "0.0.1",
  "private": true,
  "scripts": {
    "start": "node app.js"
  },
  "dependencies": {
    "errorhandler": "1.1.1",
    "express": "4.8.1",
    "jade": "1.5.0",
    "morgan": "1.2.2",
    "serve-favicon": "2.0.1",
    "socket.io": "1.1.0"
  }
}
```

Socket.IO, in some sense, might be considered another server. We can refactor auto-generated Express.js code by passing the Express.js app object to the `createServer()` method and then calling the Socket.IO `listen()` method on the server object:

```
var server = http.createServer(app);
var io = require('socket.io').listen(server);

//...
server.listen(app.get('port'), function(){
  console.log('Express server listening on port '
  + app.get('port'));
});
```

After the `io` object is instantiated, the following code can be used to establish a connection:

```
io.sockets.on('connection', function (socket) {
```

Once the connection is established—and we know that it is because we're inside the callback—we attach the `messageChange` event listener, which will be triggered by the user actions on the browser:

```
socket.on('messageChange', function (data) {
  console.log(data);
```

Once the message has been changed (i.e., the user has typed something), we can reverse the string and send it back in the form of the `receive` event with `socket.emit()`:

```
    socket.emit('receive',
    data.message.split('').reverse().join('') );
  })
});
```

Here's the full content of `ch16/socket/app.js`:

```
var http = require('http'),
  express = require('express'),
  path = require('path'),
  logger = require('morgan'),
  favicon = require('serve-favicon'),
  errorhandler = require('errorhandler'),
  bodyParser = require('body-parser');

var app = express();

app.set('view engine', 'jade');
app.set('port', process.env.PORT || 3000);
app.use(logger('combined'));
app.use(favicon(path.join(__dirname, 'public', 'favicon.ico')));
app.use(express.static('public'));

app.use(bodyParser.json());
app.use(bodyParser.urlencoded({extended: true}));

app.get('/', function(request, response){
  response.render('index');
});

app.use(errorhandler());

var server = http.createServer(app);
var io = require('socket.io').listen(server);

io.sockets.on('connection', function (socket) {
  socket.on('messageChange', function (data) {
    console.log(data);
    socket.emit('receive', data.message.split('').reverse().join('') );
  });
});

server.listen(app.get('port'), function(){
  console.log('Express server listening on port ' + app.get('port'));
});
```

Lastly, our app needs some front-end love in `index.jade` in the form of an input box and JavaScript code to send and receive user input. The input box might be implemented like this:

```
input(type='text', class='message', placeholder='what is on your mind?', onkeyup='send(this)')
```

On every key up event, it calls the `send()` function, but before we write this function, let's include the Socket.IO library:

```
script(src="/socket.io/socket.io.js")
```

The socket.io.js file is not a real file that you need to download, like, for example, a jQuery file. The Node.js Socket.IO server will provide this file "automagically."

Now we can connect to the socket server and attach the receive event listener:

```
var socket = io.connect('http://localhost');
socket.on('receive', function (message) {
  console.log('received %s', message);
  document.querySelector('.received-message').innerText = message;
});
```

document.querySelector is just a modern browsers' analog to the jQuery selector. It simply gives us an HTML element so that we don't need to depend on jQuery. We use the innerText property to show the new text on the page.

The send function emits the event messageChange that passes the message to the server. This happens on each keystroke, and for this reason changes appear in real time.

```
var send = function(input) {
  console.log(input.value)
  var value = input.value;
  console.log('sending %s to server', value);
  socket.emit('messageChange', {message: value});
    }
```

Following is the full source code of ch16/socket/index.jade:

```
extends layout

block content
  h1= title
  p Welcome to
    span.received-message #{title}
  input(type='text', class='message', placeholder='what is on your mind?', onkeyup='send(this)')
  script(src="/socket.io/socket.io.js")
  script.
    var socket = io.connect('http://localhost');
    socket.on('receive', function (message) {
      console.log('received %s', message);
      document.querySelector('.received-message').innerText = message;
    });
    var send = function(input) {
      console.log(input.value)
      var value = input.value;
      console.log('sending %s to server', value);
      socket.emit('messageChange', {message: value});
    }
```

Running the App

Now everything should be ready for you to start the app ($ node app). Go to the home page (http://localhost:3000) and type "!stekcoS" and the app will convert it to "Sockets!" as previously shown in Figure 16-1.

As you view the browser output, you might think the code is just transformed on the client side without the server's involvement. That's not the case, and the proof is in the server logs, where you'll see that the conversion actually happened on the server (see Figure 16-2).

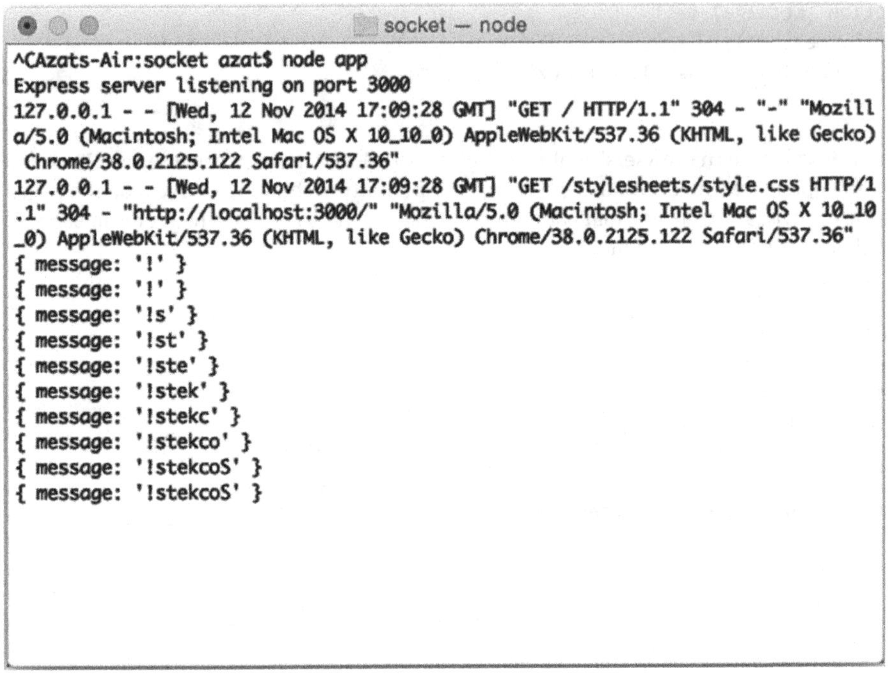

socket — node
^CAzats-Air:socket azat$ node app
Express server listening on port 3000
127.0.0.1 - - [Wed, 12 Nov 2014 17:09:28 GMT] "GET / HTTP/1.1" 304 - "-" "Mozilla/5.0 (Macintosh; Intel Mac OS X 10_10_0) AppleWebKit/537.36 (KHTML, like Gecko) Chrome/38.0.2125.122 Safari/537.36"
127.0.0.1 - - [Wed, 12 Nov 2014 17:09:28 GMT] "GET /stylesheets/style.css HTTP/1.1" 304 - "http://localhost:3000/" "Mozilla/5.0 (Macintosh; Intel Mac OS X 10_10_0) AppleWebKit/537.36 (KHTML, like Gecko) Chrome/38.0.2125.122 Safari/537.36"
{ message: '!' }
{ message: '!' }
{ message: '!s' }
{ message: '!st' }
{ message: '!ste' }
{ message: '!stek' }
{ message: '!stekc' }
{ message: '!stekco' }
{ message: '!stekcoS' }
{ message: '!stekcoS' }

Figure 16-2. *Express.js server catching and processing input in real time*

For more Socket.IO examples, go to `http://socket.io/#how-to-use`.

Summary

Again, you have seen Express.js seamlessly integrate with another library. In this short example of dual-channel communication, we used event listeners from the Socket.IO library. The library is compatible with both Node.js and browser JavaScript, which makes it even easier to use. Socket.IO provides good cross-browser support for real-time applications. It seamlessly integrates with the Express.js stack, and has many advantages over using native browser API for WebSocket.

In the next chapter, we'll cover the usage of domains for better asynchronous error handling.

CHAPTER 17

Domain and Express.js

The domain module is a core Node.js module (`http://nodejs.org/api/domain.html`) that aids developers in tracking and isolating errors, often a daunting task, through the use of *domains*. Think of domains as a smarter version of `try/catch` statements[1].

Defining the Problem

To illustrate the hurdle that asynchronous code might introduce to error handling and debugging, look at this synchronous code that prints "Custom Error: Fail!" as we would expect:

```
try {
  throw new Error('Fail!');
} catch (e) {
  console.log('Custom Error: ' + e.message);
}
```

Now, let's add asynchronous code in the form of the `setTimeout()` function, which will delay the execution for a random number of milliseconds from 10 to 100 (from the file `ch17/async-errors.js`):

```
try {
setTimeout(function () {
    throw new Error('Fail!');
  }, Math.round(Math.random()*100));
} catch (e) {
  console.log('Custom Error: ' + e.message);
}
```

Instead of a "Custom Error: Fail!" message, we see a standard, unhandled error ("Error: Fail!") that might look like this:

```
/Users/azat/Documents/Code/proexpressjs/ch17/async-errors.js:4
      throw new Error("Fail!");
            ^
Error: Fail!
    at null._onTimeout (/Users/azat/Documents/Code/proexpressjs/ch17/async-errors.js:4:13)
    at Timer.listOnTimeout [as ontimeout] (timers.js:110:15)
```

[1]https://developer.mozilla.org/en-US/docs/Web/JavaScript/Reference/Statements/try...catch

Therefore, try/catch fails at asynchronous errors. A good rule of thumb is to use try/catch only for synchronous JavaScript/Node.js code.

■ **Tip** try/catch might also be slower, especially when you define functions inside, because the JavaScript engine cannot optimize that code ahead of time. For more about try/catch implications, refer to https://github.com/joyent/node/wiki/Best-practices-and-gotchas-with-v8 and http://jsperf.com/try-catch-performance-overhead.

Exploring a Basic Domain Example

Before we dive deep into domain and Express.js, let's explore the basic domain example (ch17/basic.js). In it, we instantiate the domain object:

```
var domain = require('domain').create();
```

Then, we attach an event listener, that tells what to do with the error:

```
domain.on('error', function(error){
  console.log(error);
});
```

The main bulk of the code and the error-prone code go in the callback to domain.run():

```
domain.run(function(){
  throw new Error('Failed!');
});
```

Now, let's modify the setTimeout() example by replacing try/catch with domain (ch17/basic-timeout.js):

```
var domain = require('domain');
var d = domain.create();
d.on('error', function(e) {
   console.log('Custom Error: ' + e);
});
d.run(function() {
  setTimeout(function () {
    throw new Error('Failed!');
  }, Math.round(Math.random()*100));
});
```

When we run it with $ node basic-timeout.js, the output is

```
Custom Error: Error: Failed!
```

Writing a Domain App

Having covered the basics of domain, let's explore the app in ch17/domain. It has two routes, /error-domain and /error-no-domain. From the names of the routes, you can guess that they both will crash. The domain route (/error-domain) will send back some JSON, while the non-domain route (/error-no-domain) will use the standard error handling middleware from the errorhandler module.

This is the domain-powered error-prone route:

```
app.get('/error-domain', function (req, res, next) {
  var d = domain.create();
  d.on('error', function (error) {
    console.error(error.stack);
    d.exit()
    res.status(500).send({'Custom Error': error.message});
  });
  d.run(function () {
    // Error prone code goes here
    throw new Error('Database is down.');
  });
});
```

We don't have to use domain in every route; for example, `/error-no-domain` is using the standard Express.js approach with the `errorhandler` module's middleware:

```
app.get('/error-no-domain', function (req, res, next) {
  // Error prone code goes here
  next(new Error('Database is down.'));
});
```

We add some custom logic to differentiate domain and non-domain cases (routes) by using `domain.active` (`http://nodejs.org/api/domain.html#domain_domain_enter`):

```
app.use(function (error, req, res, next) {
  console.log(domain)
  if (domain.active) {
    console.info('Caught with domain', domain.active);
    domain.active.emit('error', error);
  } else {
    console.info('No domain');
    defaultHandler(error, req, res, next);
  }
});
```

When you run the application with `$ node app.js` and go to `http://localhost:3000/error-domain` and `http://localhost:3000/error-no-domain`, you'll see the JSON page and HTML page, respectively. On the server logs, you'll see "Caught with domain" for `/error-domain` and "No domain" for `/error-no-domain`.

Notice that in both cases the Express.js app handled errors graciously and *didn't crash*. By now you might be wondering why you should go through all this trouble with domain if the standard Express.js stuff works. The routes in the previous example had the errors thrown at the "surface" level—that is, synchronous errors. However, most stuff happens in the asynchronous code. Remember the `setTimeout` example from earlier in the chapter? It can simulate a database call, so let's make our example more realistic by adding async errors to both routes:

```
app.get('/error-domain', function (req, res, next) {
  var d = domain.create();
  d.on('error', function (error) {
    console.error(error.stack);
    d.exit()
    res.status(500).send({'Custom Error': error.message});
```

```
  });
  d.run(function () {
    // Error-prone code goes here
    // throw new Error('Database is down.');
    setTimeout(function () {
      throw new Error('Database is down.');
    }, Math.round(Math.random()*100));
  });
});

app.get('/error-no-domain', function (req, res, next) {
  // Error-prone code goes here
  // throw new Error('Database is down.');
  setTimeout(function () {
    throw new Error('Database is down.');
  }, Math.round(Math.random()*100));
});
```

Now, check the routes in your browser. The non-domain route will fail miserably and stop the server! The message might look like this:

```
/Users/azat/Documents/Code/proexpressjs/ch17/domain/app.js:41
    throw new Error('Database is down.');
          ^
Error: Database is down.
    at null._onTimeout (/Users/azat/Documents/Code/proexpressjs/ch17/domain/app.js:41:11)
    at Timer.listOnTimeout [as ontimeout] (timers.js:110:15)
```

Unlike the non-domain route, the domain-enabled route didn't crash the server. Instead, it sent back our custom error JSON. Hence, the benefit of using domain!

The working (or perhaps "crashing" is more precise) example is in the ch17/domain folder and on GitHub.[2]

The following is the full content of ch17/domain/app.js:

```
var http = require('http'),
  express = require('express'),
  path = require('path'),
  logger = require('morgan'),
  favicon = require('serve-favicon'),
  errorHandler = require('errorhandler');

var app = express();

app.set('port', process.env.PORT || 3000);
app.set('views', __dirname + '/views');
app.set('view engine', 'jade');
app.use(logger('combined'));
app.use(favicon(path.join(__dirname, 'public', 'favicon.ico')));
app.use(express.static(path.join(__dirname, 'public')));
```

[2]https://github.com/azat-co/expressjsguide/tree/master/domains

```
var domain = require('domain');
var defaultHandler = errorHandler();

app.get('/error-domain', function (req, res, next) {
  var d = domain.create();
  d.on('error', function (error) {
    console.error(error.stack);
    d.exit()
    res.status(500).send({'Custom Error': error.message});
  });
  d.run(function () {
    // Error prone code goes here
    // throw new Error('Database is down.');
    setTimeout(function () {
      throw new Error('Database is down.');
    }, Math.round(Math.random()*100));
  });
});

app.get('/error-no-domain', function (req, res, next) {
  // Error prone code goes here
  // throw new Error('Database is down.');
  setTimeout(function () {
    throw new Error('Database is down.');
  }, Math.round(Math.random()*100));
});

app.use(function (error, req, res, next) {
  console.log(domain)
  if (domain.active) {
    console.info('Caught with domain', domain.active);
    domain.active.emit('error', error);
  } else {
    console.info('No domain');
    defaultHandler(error, req, res, next);
  }
});

var server = app.listen(app.get('port'), function() {
  console.log('Express server listening on port ' + server.address().port);
});
```

You can apply the domain approach to every route with minimal code repetition by implementing domain in the middleware. Make sure to put this middleware before the routes.

And as usual with Express.js, there's a third-party module that wraps each route in domain: `express-domain-middleware` (`https://www.npmjs.org/package/express-domain-middleware`).

You can install `express-domain-middleware` v0.1.0 with:

```
$ npm install express-domain-middleware@0.1.0
```

Then, import the module into your project with `require()`:

```
var expressDomain = require('express-domain-middleware');
```

Apply this middleware to your Express.js application with `app.use()` *before* other middleware and routes:

```
app.use(expressDomain);
```

Enjoy!

Another good module to use with domain and Express.js for error handling is okay (https://www.npmjs.org/package/ok). The idea here that okay is a more eloquent replacement of manual error checks such as:

```
if (error) return next(error);
```

Instead of the preceding line, which is repeated in each nested callback (if you wrote it correctly, you should handle the error in each callback), all you need to do is call okay with two arguments: a callback for errors (e.g., `next`) and a callback for no errors (e.g., regular closure). In a way, okay is an extra layer between the function and your regular callback.

With okay the code becomes cleaner, as you can see in this Express.js route:

```
var okay = require('okay');
app.get('/', function(req, res, next) {
   fs.readFile('file.txt', 'utf8', okay(next, function(contents) {
      res.send(contents);
   });
});
```

■ **Caution** The domain module is in an *Unstable* stage as of this writing (2014). This means that its methods and behavior likely will change. Therefore, stay updated and use exact versions in the `package.json` file.

Summary

Using domains might be a hard concept to grasp for most programmers. If you are one of them, don't despair! This happens because we have to deal with asynchronous code problems. We need to shift our whole mindset. For this reason, this chapter started with some very basic examples of asynchronous code to illustrate the challenges. Then, we progressed into domain and Express.js usage. When it comes to Express.js, one of the brilliant things about its popularity and Node.js' NPM is that they are middleware for almost anything. So, if understanding domain isn't a priority Node.js topic to you, you can just apply the middleware and forget about it.

Using the domain module was the last of the Express.js tips and tricks for working with the framework. In the next chapter, we'll return into "Hello World" mode to find out why it's important to start learning the Node.js stack with Express.js, even if you plan to use a different framework (Spoiler Alert: it's because a lot of Node.js frameworks borrow some concepts from or depend on Express.js).

CHAPTER 18

Sails.js, DerbyJS, LoopBack, and Other Frameworks

If you want to accomplish more comprehensive tasks than a standard Express.js app can accomplish out of the box, then you might want to consider exploring other true MVC frameworks. The good news is that some of the most popular alternative Node.js frameworks use Express.js. Therefore, by understanding Express.js, you can understand the inner workings of the other frameworks faster and better.

This chapter introduces the following, more *advanced* frameworks that depend on Express.js:

- Sails.js
- DerbyJS
- LoopBack

The purpose of introducing these other frameworks is to demonstrate that, even if you're using frameworks other than Express.js, your knowledge of Express.js will be handy.

Sails.js

Sails.js is a *convention over configuration* type of framework. This means that it's similar in philosophy to Ruby on Rails. Sails.js is a *true MVC* framework, unlike Express.js, which relies on developers for adding ORMs like Mongoose. Sails.js uses the Waterline ORM (`https://github.com/balderdashy/waterline`).

To get started with Sails.js:

```
$ npm -g install sails@0.10.5
```

This will give you the `sails` command, which you can use as follows to see the list of available options:

```
$ sails -h
```

Let's use the `new` command to generate an app with the name `sails` (`ch18/sails`):

```
$ sails new sails
```

After the app has been generated, start it with `sails lift`:

```
$ cd sails
$ sails lift
```

Now, if you go to `http://localhost:1337`, you will see a Sails.js page with some instructions and links, as shown in Figure 18-1.

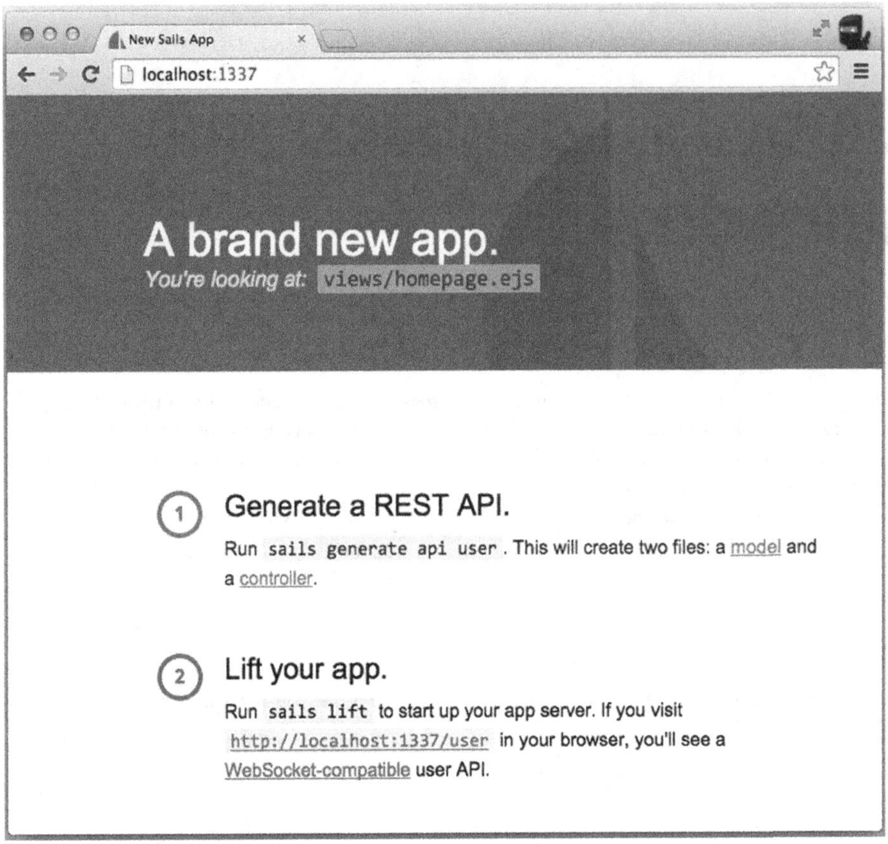

Figure 18-1. *The default Sails.js page with some instructions and links*

Sails.js has a rich scaffolding. To generate resources, you can use the following commands (substitute values with your own names) as specified.

Build a new model and controller, `api/models/NAME.js` and `api/controllers/NAMEController.js`:

```
$ sails generate api NAME
```

Build a new model, `api/models/NAME.js`, with attributes (optional):

```
$ sails generate model NAME [attribute1:type1, attribute2:type2 ... ]
```

Build a new controller, `api/controllers/NAMEController.js`, with actions (optional):

```
$ sails generate controller NAME [action1, action2, ...]:
```

Build a new adapter, `api/adapters/NAME`:

```
$ sails generate adapter NAME:
```

Build a new generator with the name NAME:

```
$ sails generate generator NAME
```

Each controller is structured as a module with methods. These methods are actions, such as /controller/action. Each action has a request and a response. Their arguments are inherited from their Express.js counterparts. To illustrate this point, let's create a controller and add some custom code to it using Express.js methods response.json() and response.redirect().

First, run this command:

```
$ sails generate api user
```

Open the newly created file, ch18/sails/api/controllers/UserController.js, and add two actions to it, json, which will output the current time, and buy-oauth, which will use the redirect:

```
module.exports = {
  json: function (request, response) {
    response.json({time: new Date()})
  },
  'buy-oauth': function (request, response) {
    return res.redirect('https://gum.co/oauthnode');
  }
};
```

If you go to http://localhost:1337/user/json, you'll see

```
{   "time": "2014-09-09T14:59:28.377Z" }
```

And if you go to http://localhost:1337/user/buy-oauth, you'll be redirected to the web page for *Introduction to OAuth with Node.js* (webapplog.com, 2014).

This brief introduction has demonstrated that writing controllers in Sails.js will be easy for you because you are already familiar with Express.js. Controllers are intermediaries between views and models, and typically contain the bulk of the code and logic. For more information on Sails.js concepts and its documentation, go to http://sailsjs.org/#/documentation/concepts and http://irlnathan.github.io/sailscasts.

DerbyJS

DerbyJS is a full-stack framework, which means that it handles both client and server code. It also provides a database connection and abstraction layer (model): http://derbyjs.com. DerbyJS is similar to Meteor (https://www.meteor.com) in its reactive full-stack approach, but DerbyJS is less opinionated and not pushy in the usage of its packages (vs. NPM modules).

First, create a package.json file with these versions (ch18/derby/package.json):

```
{
  "name": "derby-app",
  "description": "",
  "version": "0.0.1",
  "main": "./server.js",
  "dependencies": {
    "derby": "0.6.0-alpha24",
    "derby-less": "0.1.0",
```

```
    "derby-starter": "0.2.3"
  }
}
```

To install the dependencies, run

```
$ npm install
```

Obviously, derby is the framework's module. Less obvious is derby-starter, which is a set of files that takes the derby application (derby-app.js) and runs it through setup. The setup involves connecting to Redis and MongoDB and mounting the DerbyJS app to an Express.js server.

To launch a DerbyJS application with derby-starter, use server.js. You can copy and customize derby-starter to suit your needs, or write your own mini-module. The derby-starter/lib/server.js file uses familiar Express.js statements:

```
//...
  expressApp
    // Creates an express middleware from the app's routes
    .use(app.router())
    .use(expressApp.router)
    .use(errorMiddleware)
//...
```

To utilize derby-starter, let's create a server.js file that will launch the server:

```
require('derby-starter').run(__dirname+'/derby-app.js');
```

The main DerbyJS logic will be in the derby-app.js file, and its content starts with instantiations:

```
var path = require('path'),
  derby = require('derby'),
  app = derby.createApp('derby-app', __filename);
```

The next assignment is needed to access the DerbyJS app from derby-starter:

```
module.exports = app;
```

Just for the sake of variety, we're using the Less CSS library here, but Derby supports Stylus and others:

```
app.serverUse(module, 'derby-less');
```

Here's how we can load the styles:

```
app.loadStyles(path.join(__dirname, 'styles', 'derby-app'));
```

Similarly, we load the template (ch18/derby/views/derby-app.html), which is similar in syntax to Handlebars:

```
app.loadViews (path.join(__dirname, 'views', 'derby-app'));
```

The routes we'll define are akin to Express.js routes. The main difference is in the request handlers: page, model, and params. The page handler is the page that is rendered with page.render(), the model handler is a database abstraction layer that is passed to and from the browser, and the params handler is the object that has the URL parameters (e.g., /:id):

```
app.get('/', function(page, model, params) {
  model.subscribe('d.message', function() {
    page.render();
  });
});
```

The next method, app.proto.create, is used when the page is loaded on both the server and the client. Notice that this is Node.js code and not browser code. Hence the full-stack nature of the framework:

```
app.proto.create = function(model) {
  model.on('set', 'd.message', function(path, object) {
    console.log('message has been changed: ' + object);
  });
};
```

The content of ch18/derby/views/derby-app.html uses a special DerbyJS tag, <Body:>:

```
<Body:>
  <input value="{{d.message}}"><h1>{{d.message}}</h1>
```

The Less file derby-app.less has this style:

```
h1 {
  color: blue;
}
```

derby-starter also connects to Redis and MongoDB. Therefore, let's start Redis and MongoDB in two separate terminal windows/tabs:

```
$ redis-server
$ mongod
```

Then start the server with either one of these two commands:

```
$ node server
$ node .
```

Then, go to http://localhost:3000 and type something. The text will be automatically updated on the page in the <h1> tags (see Figure 18-2), and also saved to the MongoDB database. All in real time! This means that, if you restart the server and refresh the page, you'll see the same message again.

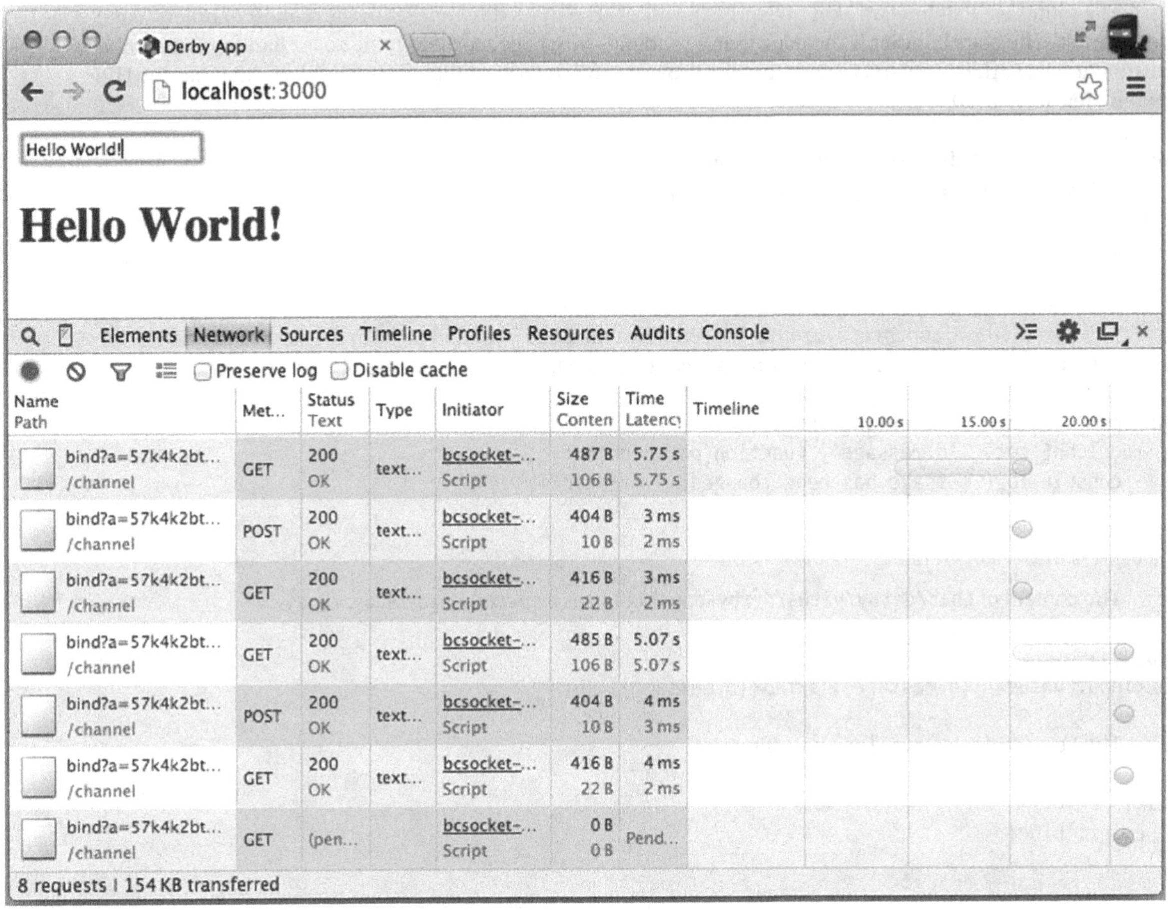

Figure 18-2. *Real-time communication in a DerbyJS app*

LoopBack

LoopBack is a comprehensive framework with command-line scaffolding and a web API explorer: `http://strongloop.com/node-js/loopback`.

To install the command-line tool, run:

```
$ npm install -g strongloop@2.9.1
```

To create the boilerplate app, run this command and answer the subsequent questions:

```
$ slc loopback
```

At the end, the command-line tool will show you some of the available options:

> Change directory to your app:
>
> `$ cd loopback`
>
> Create a model in your app:
>
> `$ slc loopback:model`
>
> Optional: Enable StrongOps monitoring:
>
> `$ slc strongops`
>
> Run the app:
>
> `$ slc run .`

Let's create a model Book with property `name` of type string, plural `Books`, a memory store, and REST API (`slc` will ask for inputs):

```
$ cd loopback
$ slc loopback:model
```

After you're finished with the model, run:

```
$ slc run
```

Then go to `http://localhost:3000/explorer` in your browser (see Figure 18-3) and click Books to explore the API.

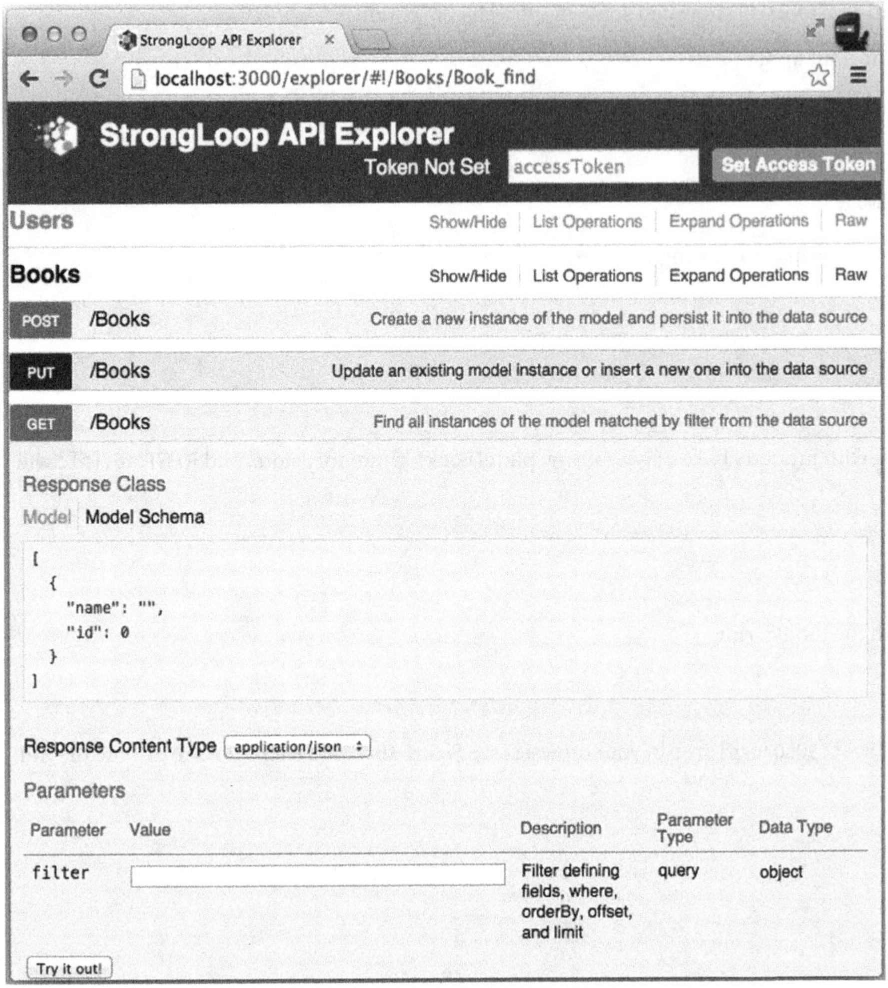

Figure 18-3. *LoopBack's explorer is a web interface for APIs*

To demonstrate that LoopBack is built on top of Express.js, edit `ch18/loopback/common/models/book.js` as follows:

```
module.exports = function(Book) {
  Book.buy = function(code, cb) {
    cb(null, 'Processing... ' + code);
  }
```

```
  Book.remoteMethod('buy', {accepts: [{http: function(ctx) {
    // HTTP request object as provided by Express.js
    var request = ctx.req;
    console.log(request.param('code'), request.ip, request.hostname)
    return request.param('code');
  }}],
      returns: {arg: 'response', type: 'string'}
    }
  );
};
```

The request (`ctx.req`) object is the Express.js request. We can call the `request.param()` method (among other Express.js methods, such as `request.ip()` and `request.hostname()`), to extract the code parameter.

The client request is as follows:

```
$ curl http://localhost:3000/api/Books/Buy -X POST -d "code=1"
```

The client response is:

```
{"response":"Processing... 1"}%
```

The server logs are:

```
1 127.0.0.1 localhost
```

■ **Tip** Don't forget to restart the server with `$ slc run` every time you make changes to the source file.

Another place where you can use your Express.js skills is `ch18/loopback/server/server.js`; for example:

```
app.use(middleware());
```

Other Frameworks

The following list introduces some other notable frameworks you might want to use after mastering Express.js (though they do not necessarily depend on Express.js):

- *Hapi* (`http://hapijs.com`): A comprehensive, enterprise-level framework (*Practical Node.js* [Apress, 2014] has a REST API example built with this framework)
- *Total.js* (`http://www.totaljs.com`): A modular web application framework
- *Geddy* (`http://geddyjs.org`): A simple, structured, web framework for Node
- *Compound* (`http://compoundjs.com`): A framework built with the Express + structure + extensions formula in mind (the creator of this framework wrote the foreword to this book)

For more Node.js frameworks, check out `http://nodeframeworks.com`—the hand-picked registry of Node.js frameworks.

Summary

As you've seen from this series of introductions to Sails.js, DerbyJS, and LoopBack, it helps to know Express.js!

This concludes Part 3 of the book, in which you have learned how to solve common problems in Express.js, such as abstracting code, implementing async error handling with domains, securing your app, effortlessly implementing real-time communication between server and client, applying Express.js knowledge in other frameworks, and spanning multiple processes with cluster. Now you're ready for more comprehensive examples than those we've used to demonstrate certain features.

In Part 4, we'll cover four example applications, starting with the Instagram Gallery, which demonstrates a simple server that integrates with a third-party service provider.

PART IV

Tutorials and Examples

CHAPTER 19

Instagram Gallery

If you're reading this book in chronological order, you've made it through the important, but somewhat dry, details of the API reference and have been exposed only to abstract solutions. Now that you've reached Part 4, the excitement begins, because the five chapters in this part are all about coding and examples!

The tutorial in this chapter demonstrates how to use Express.js with an external, third-party service (Storify API). The purpose of this application is to fetch Instagram photos from Storify and display them in a gallery. In addition to Express.js, we'll use the following three modules:

- `superagent` (`https://www.npmjs.org/package/superagent`)
- `consolidate` (`https://www.npmjs.org/package/consolidate`)
- `handlebars` (`https://www.npmjs.org/package/handlebars`)

I chose these modules because they are somewhat popular in Node.js development circles, so you are highly likely to encounter or use them in the future.

Note The full source code for this example is available at `https://github.com/azat-co/sfy-gallery`.

Storify (`http://storify.com`) runs on Node.js (`http://nodejs.org`) and Express.js (`http://expressjs.com`). Therefore, why not use these technologies to write an application that demonstrates how to build apps that rely on third-party APIs and HTTP requests?

Starting the Instagram Gallery

The Instagram Gallery app will fetch a story object and display its title, description, and a gallery of the elements/ images, like the example shown in Figure 19-1.

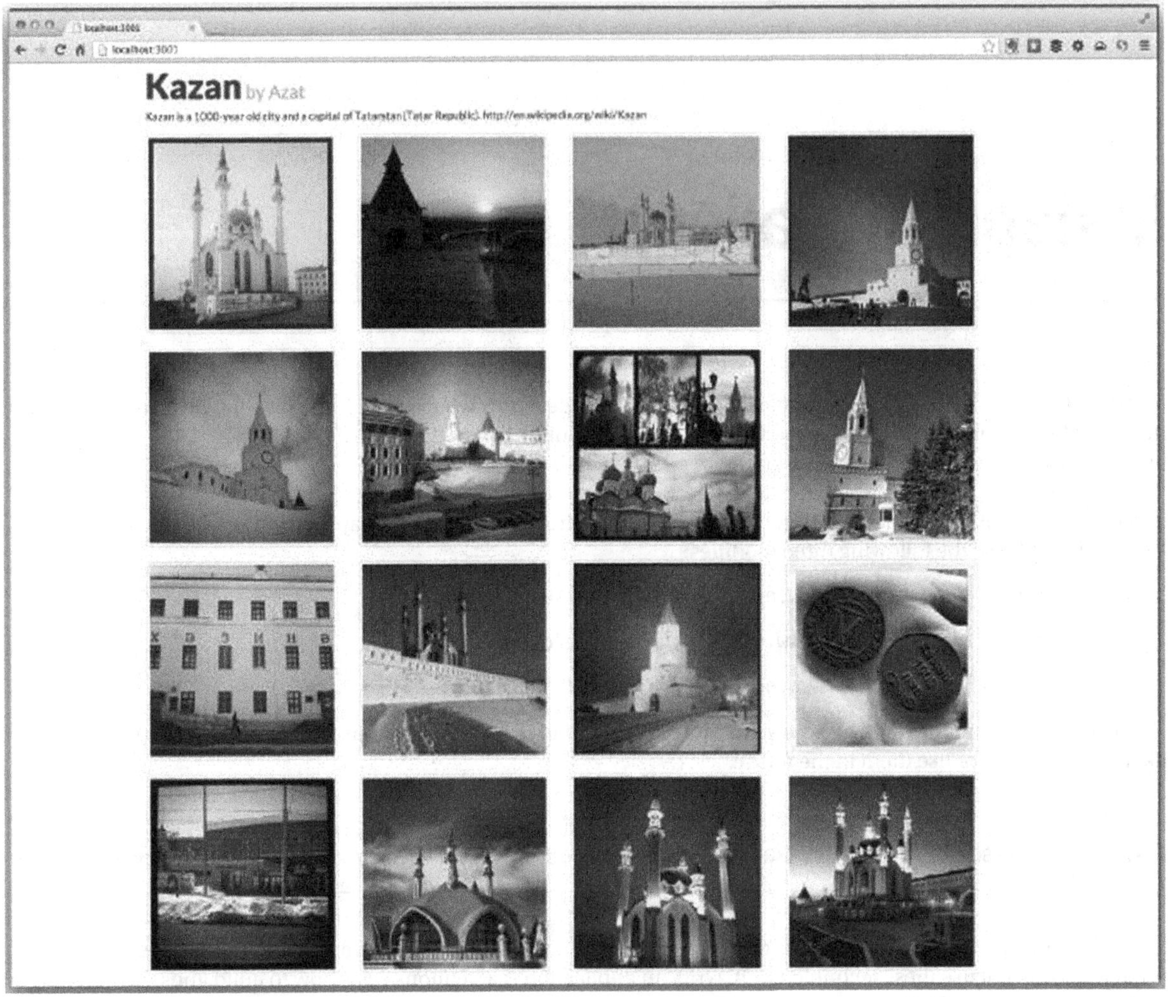

Figure 19-1. Instagram Gallery

■ **Note** In case you're wondering what Kazan is, it's the 1000-year-old capital of Tatar Republic (Tatarstan).

The app's file structure looks like this:

```
- index.js
- package.json
- views/index.html
- css/bootstrap-responsive.min.css
- css/flatly-bootstrap.min.css
```

The CSS files are from the Bootstrap library (`http://getbootstrap.com`) and the Flatly theme (`http://bootswatch.com/flatly`). The `index.js` file is our main Node.js file with the most of the logic, and `index.html` is the Handlebars template. The app uses plain CSS from two files in the `css` folder.

Our dependencies include

- `express` v4.8.1 for the Express.js framework
- `superagent` v0.18.2 for making HTTP(S) requests
- `consolidate` v0.10.0 for using Handlebars with Express.js
- `handlebars` v2.0.0-beta.1 for using the Handlebars template engine

The content of the `package.json` file is as follows:

```
{
  "name": "sfy-gallery",
  "version": "0.2.0",
  "description": "Instagram Gallery: Storify API example written in Node.js",
  "main": "index.js",
  "scripts": {
    "test": "echo \"Error: no test specified\" && exit 1"
  },
  "dependencies": {
    "consolidate": "0.10.0",
    "express": "4.8.1",
    "handlebars": "2.0.0-beta.1",
    "superagent": "0.18.2"
  },
  "repository": "https://github.com/storify/sfy-gallery",
  "author": "Azat Mardan",
  "license": "BSD"
}
```

Let's go ahead and install the modules with

```
$ npm install
```

After NPM is done, create `index.js`. At the beginning of the file, we require the following dependencies:

```
var express = require('express');
var superagent = require('superagent');
var consolidate = require('consolidate');

var app = express();
```

Then, we configure the template engine:

```
app.engine('html', consolidate.handlebars);
app.set('view engine', 'html');
app.set('views', __dirname + '/views');
```

Next, we set up a static folder with middleware:

```
app.use(express.static(__dirname + '/public'));
```

If you want to serve any other story, feel free to do so. All you need is the username of the author and the story slug for my gallery of the capital of Tatarstan, Kazan. Leave the following:

```
var user = 'azat_co';
var story_slug = 'kazan';
```

Paste your values as shown next: Storify API key, username, and _token if you have one. As of this writing, the Storify API is public, meaning there is *no need for authentication* (i.e., no need for keys). In case this changes in the future, request an API key at `http://dev.storify.com/request` or follow the official documentation at `http://dev.storify.com`:

```
var api_key = "";
var username = "";
var _token = "";
```

Let's define the home route (/):

```
app.get('/',function(req, res){
```

Now we'll fetch elements from the Storify API for the route's callback, using the `superagent get()` method:

```
superagent.get("http://api.storify.com/v1/stories/"
  + user + "/" + story_slug)
```

The Storify API endpoint is `"http://api.storify.com/v1/stories/" + user + "/" + story_slug`, which in this example is `http://api.storify.com/v1/stories/azat/kazan`. One of the advantages of `superagent` is that we can write chained methods. For example, `query()` sends data in a query string:

```
.query({api_key: api_key,
  username: username,
  _token: _token})
```

The `set()` method specifies the request headers:

```
.set({Accept: 'application/json'})
```

And `end()` takes the callback to execute when the response is received:

```
.end(function(e, storifyResponse){
  if (e) return next(e);
```

To render the template with the story object that is in the HTTP response body's content property, we use the following:

```
      return res.render('index', storifyResponse.body.content);
    })

})

app.listen(3001);
```

The Storify API returns data as JSON. You can look up the format by going to `https://api.storify.com/v1/stories/azat_co/kazan` (assuming the API is still public, which it is as of this writing). You can see the contracted (i.e., doesn't show every nested object) JSON in Figure 19-2.


```
{
  - content: {
        sid: "516d9496b41520c44701a7fd",
        title: "Kazan",
        slug: "kazan",
        status: "published",
        template: null,
        version: 2,
        permalink: "http://storify.com/azat_co/kazan",
        shortlink: "http://sfy.co/jIlj",
        description: "Kazan is a 1000-year old city and a capital of Tatarstan (Tatar Republic).
        http://en.wikipedia.org/wiki/Kazan",
        thumbnail: "http://distilleryimage2.s3.amazonaws.com/6e863d009b8f11e2aea022000a9d0ee7_7.jpg",
      + date: {…},
        private: false,
        not_indexed: false,
        is_spam: false,
        topics: [ ],
        siteposts: [ ],
      + meta: {…},
      + stats: {…},
        modified: false,
        deleted: false,
        canEdit: false,
      + author: {…},
        comments: [ ],
        page: 1,
        per_page: 20,
        totalElements: 45,
      + elements: […]
    },
    code: 200
}
```


Figure 19-2. *Example of a contracted Storify API output for the story entity*

Viewing the Gallery

Now that we have the app that gets the data from Storify and calls the `index` template to render it, let's take a look at the Handlebars template, which is in the `views/index.html` file:

```
<!DOCTYPE html lang="en">
<html>
  <head>
    <link type="text/css"
      href="css/flatly-bootstrap.min.css"
      rel="stylesheet" />
    <link type="text/css"
```

```
      href="css/bootstrap-responsive.min.css"
      rel="stylesheet"/>
  </head>

  <body class="container">
    <div class="row">
```

Now we use `{{title}}` to display the title of the Storify story and `{{author.name}}` to display its author name:

```
  <h1>{{title}}<small> by {{author.name}}</small></h1>
  <p>{{description}}</p>
</div>
<div class="row">
  <ul class="thumbnails">
```

The next line is a built-in `handlebars` construction that iterates over array items. And, with every iteration, we print a new `<li>` tag:

```
      {{#each elements}}
        <li class="span3">
          <a class="thumbnail" href="{{permalink}}"
          target="_blank">
            <img src="{{data.image.src}}"
              title="{{data.image.caption}}" />
          </a>
        </li>
      {{/each}}
      </ul>
    </div>
  </body>

</html>
```

When you start the app with `$ node .`, you'll see the pictures at `http://localhost:3000`. What happens is that, when you go to the page, the local server quickly makes a request to Storify and gets the images' links from Instagram.

Summary

Express.js and `superagent` allow developers to retrieve and manipulate data provided by third-party services, such as Storify, Twitter, and Facebook, in just a few lines of code. The example presented in this chapter is rather straightforward because it doesn't use a database. But, in the next chapter, the Todo App will show you how to utilize MongoDB.

■ **Note** In most cases, service providers (such as Google, Facebook, and Twitter) require authentication (which is not the case with the Storify API as of this writing). To make OAuth 1.0, OAuth 2.0, and OAuth Echo requests, consider oauth (`https://www.npmjs.org/package/oauth`; GitHub: `https://github.com/ciaranj/node-oauth`), everyauth (`https://www.npmjs.org/package/everyauth`; GitHub: `https://github.com/bnoguchi/everyauth`) and/or Passport (website: `http://passportjs.org/`; GitHub: `https://github.com/jaredhanson/passport`).

CHAPTER 20

Todo App

Todo apps are considered good teaching examples because they have many components that you will see in a typical, real-life project. Also, this sort of app is popular when it comes to showcasing browser JavaScript frameworks. Just look at the famous TodoMVC project (`http://todomvc.com`), which has a few dozen Todo apps for the various front-end JavaScript frameworks.

In our Todo app, we'll use MongoDB, Mongoskin, Jade, web forms, Less style sheets, and cross-site request forgery (CSRF) protection. We'll intentionally *not* use Backbone.js or AngularJS, because the goal is to demonstrate how to build *traditional* web sites with the use of forms, redirects, and server-side template rendering. We'll also look at how to plug in CSRF and Less. As a bonus, there will be a few AJAX/XHR calls to RESTful API-ish endpoints, because it's hard to build a modern user interface/experience without such calls. You should know how to use them in this hybrid web site architecture (traditional server-side HTML rendering with some AJAX/XHR calls).

Note All the source code for this Todo app is at `https://github.com/azat-co/todo-express` for your convenience. Readers constantly contribute to the project, so, by the time this book is in your hands, the code in the GitHub will be different from the code in the book, likely with more features and up-to-date libraries.

This project is rather complex, so before you start coding it, here's an overview of how this chapter presents the steps to achieve the end product:

- Overview
- Setup
- App.js
- Routes
- Jade
- Less

Overview

To preview what we are going to achieve in this chapter, let's start with some screenshots of the Todo app showing how the user interface functions. Figure 20-1 shows the Home page, which has a heading, a menu, and some introductory text. The menu consists of three items:

- *Home*: The currently displayed page
- *Todo List*: A list of tasks to do
- *Completed*: A list of completed tasks

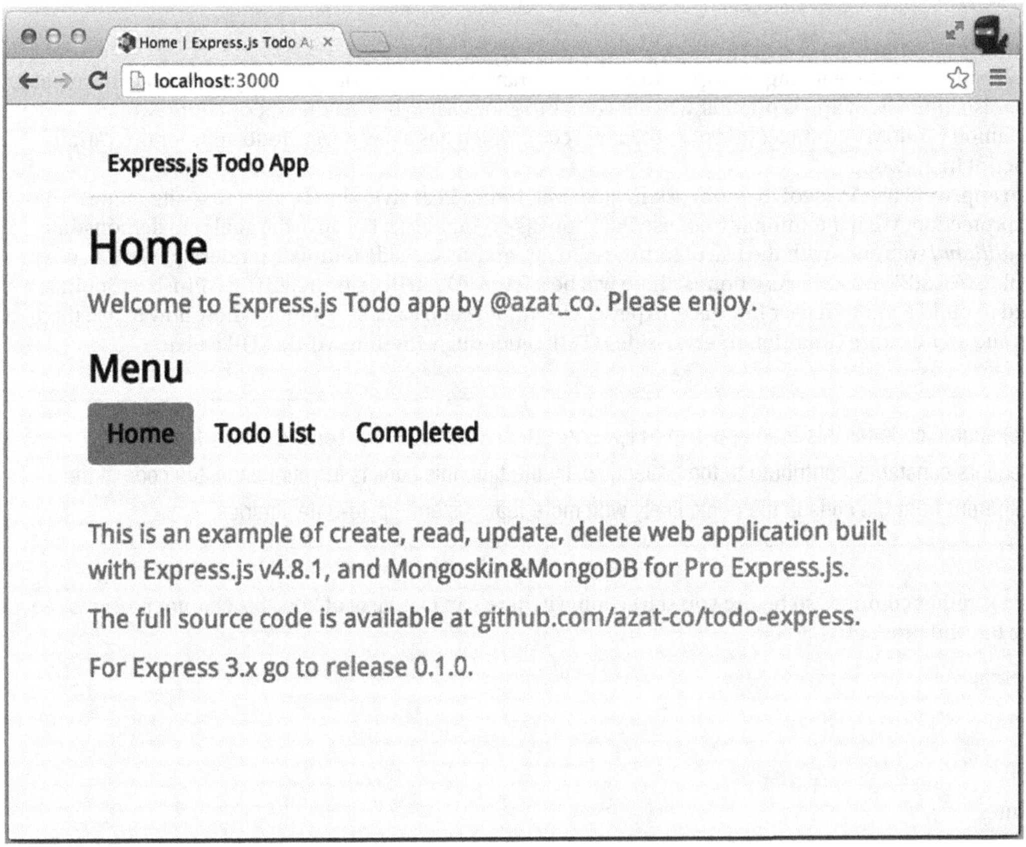

Figure 20-1. *Todo app Home page*

On the Todo List page, there's an empty list, as shown in Figure 20-2. There's also an entry form for the new task and an "add" button.

Figure 20-2. *Empty Todo List page*

Figure 20-3 shows the result of adding four items to the Todo List. Each task has a "done" button to its left and a "delete" button to its right, the functions of which are exactly as you might guess. They mark the task as completed (i.e., move it to the Completed page) and remove the task, respectively.

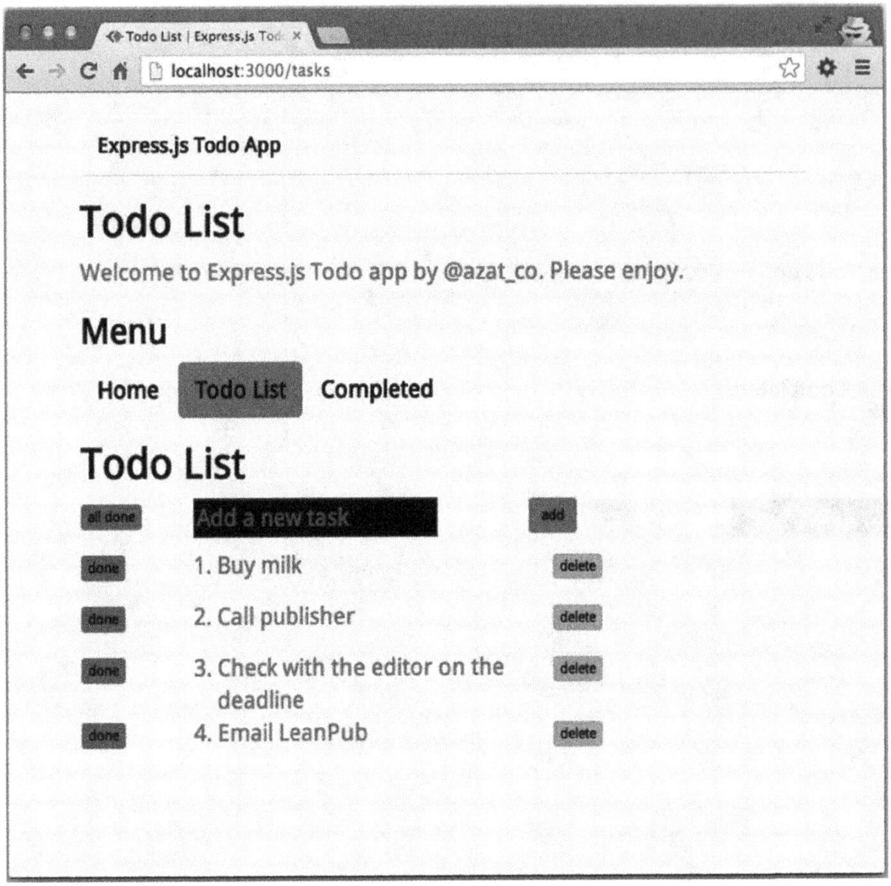

Figure 20-3. *Todo List page with added items*

Figure 20-4 shows the result of clicking the “done” button for the “Buy milk” task. The item has disappeared from the Todo List and the list has been renumbered.

Figure 20-4. *Todo List page with one item marked done*

However, the completed "Buy milk" task has not disappeared from the app altogether. It is now in the Completed list on the Completed page, as shown in Figure 20-5.

Figure 20-5. *Todo app Completed page*

Deletion of an item from the Todo List page after the "delete" button is clicked is the action performed via an AJAX/XHR request. Figure 20-6 shows the purple-highlighted notification message that appears when a task is deleted (in this case, the "Email LeanPub" task). The rest of the logic is implemented via GETs and POSTs (by forms).

Figure 20-6. *Todo List page with removed task*

Setup

We begin the setup of the Todo app by creating a new folder:

```
$ mkdir todo-express
$ cd todo-express
```

As usual, we start by taking care of the dependencies. This command gives us the basic `package.json` file:

```
$ npm init
```

We need to add the following extra dependencies to `package.json`:

- `express` v4.8.1: For Express.js framework
- `body-parser` v1.6.6: For processing payloads
- `cookie-parser` v1.3.2: For processing cookies and for sessions

- express-session v1.7.6: For session support
- csurf v1.5.0: For CSRF security
- errorhandler v1.1.1: For basic error handling
- jade v1.5.0: For Jade template
- less-middleware v1.0.4: For Less support
- method-override v2.1.3: For clients that don't support all HTTP methods
- mongoskin v1.4.4: For MongoDB connections
- morgan v1.2.3: For logging of requests
- serve-favicon v2.1.1: For favicon support

One of the ways to add the preceding list of dependencies is to utilize the --save (-s) option of npm install:

```
$ npm install less-middleware@1.0.4 --save
$ npm install mongoskin@1.4.4 --save
...
```

Another way is to add entries to package.json and run $ npm install:

```
{
  "name": "todo-express",
  "version": "0.2.0",
  "private": true,
  "scripts": {
    "start": "node app.js"
  },
  "dependencies": {
    "body-parser": "1.6.6",
    "cookie-parser": "1.3.2",
    "csurf": "1.5.0",
    "errorhandler": "1.1.1",
    "express": "4.8.1",
    "express-session": "1.7.6",
    "jade": "1.5.0",
    "less-middleware": "1.0.4",
    "method-override": "2.1.3",
    "mongoskin": "1.4.4",
    "morgan": "1.2.3",
    "serve-favicon": "2.1.1"
  }
}
```

Now, install the MongoDB database if you don't have it installed already. The database is not the same as NPM modules mongodb and mongoskin, which are drivers. These libraries allow us to interact with the MongoDB database, but we still need both the driver and the database.

On OS X, you can use brew to install MongoDB (or upgrade to v2.6.3):

```
$ brew update
$ brew install mongodb
$ mongo --version
```

For more flavors of MongoDB installations, check out the official docs[1] and/or *Practical Node.js* (Apress, 2014).

The end version of the app (0.20.0) has the following folder and file structure (`http://github.com/azat-co/todo-express`):

```
/todo-express
  /public
    /bootstrap
      *.less
    /images
    /javascripts
      main.js
      jquery.js
    /stylesheets
      style.css
      main.less
  favicon.ico
  /routes
    tasks.js
    index.js
  /views
    tasks_completed.jade
    layout.jade
    index.jade
    tasks.jade
  app.js
  readme.md
  package.json
```

The `*.less` in the `bootstrap` folder means there are a bunch of Bootstrap (the CSS framework, `http://getbootstrap.com/`) source files. They're available at GitHub.[2]

App.js

This section presents a breakdown of the Express.js-generated `app.js` file with the addition of routes, database, session, Less, and `app.param()` middleware.

First, we import dependencies with the Node.js global `require()` function:

```
var express = require('express');
```

---

[1]`http://docs.mongodb.org/manual/tutorial/install-mongodb-on-os-x/`
[2]`https://github.com/twbs/bootstrap/tree/master/less`

Similarly, we get access to our own modules, which are the app's routes:

```
var routes = require('./routes');
var tasks = require('./routes/tasks');
```

We need the core `http` and `path` modules as well:

```
var http = require('http');
var path = require('path');
```

Mongoskin is a better alternative to the native MongoDB driver because it provides additional features and methods:

```
var mongoskin = require('mongoskin');
```

One line is all we need to get the database connection object. The first parameter follows the standard URI convention of `protocol://username:password@host:port/database`:

```
var db = mongoskin.db('mongodb://localhost:27017/todo?auto_reconnect', {safe:true});
```

We set up the app itself:

```
var app = express();
```

Now, we import the middleware dependencies from NPM modules:

```
var favicon = require('serve-favicon'),
  logger = require('morgan'),
  bodyParser = require('body-parser'),
  methodOverride = require('method-override'),
  cookieParser = require('cookie-parser'),
  session = require('express-session'),
  csrf = require('csurf'),
  errorHandler = require('errorhandler');
```

In this middleware, we *export* the database object to all middleware functions. By doing so, we'll be able to perform database operations in the routes modules:

```
app.use(function(req, res, next) {
  req.db = {};
```

We simply store the `tasks` collection in every request:

```
  req.db.tasks = db.collection('tasks');
  next();
})
```

This line allows us to access `appname` from within every Jade template:

```
app.locals.appname = 'Express.js Todo App'
```

We set the server port, either to the environment variable or, if that's undefined, to 3000:

```
app.set('port', process.env.PORT || 3000);
```

These statements tell Express.js where templates live and what file extension to prepend in case the extension is omitted during the render calls:

```
app.set('views', __dirname + '/views');
app.set('view engine', 'jade');
```

The following displays the Express.js favicon (the graphic in the URL address bar of browsers):

```
app.use(favicon(path.join('public','favicon.ico')));
```

The out-of-the-box logger will print requests in the terminal window:

```
app.use(logger('dev'));
```

The bodyParser() middleware is needed to painlessly access incoming data:

```
app.use(bodyParser.json());
app.use(bodyParser.urlencoded({extended: true}));
```

The methodOverride() middleware is a workaround for HTTP methods that involve headers. It's not essential for this example, but we'll leave it here:

```
app.use(methodOverride());
```

To use CSRF, we need cookieParser() and session(). The following, weird-looking strings are secrets. You want them to be random and to come from environment variables (process.env), not hard-coded.

```
app.use(cookieParser('CEAF3FA4-F385-49AA-8FE4-54766A9874F1'));
app.use(session({
  secret: '59B93087-78BC-4EB9-993A-A61FC844F6C9',
  resave: true,
  saveUninitialized: true
}));
```

The express-session options are covered in Chapter 3, but, as shown in the preceding code, v1.7.6 (which we use here) has a resave option, which saves unmodified sessions if set to true, and a saveUninitialized option, which saves a new, but unmodified session, if set to true. The default value for both options is true. The recommended values are false for resave and true for saveUninitialized.

If you don't specify values for these options, then you'll get warnings, because these options' defaults will likely change in the future. So, it's good to explicitly set the options. Alternatively, to suppress these warnings, you can use the environment variable:

```
$ NO_DEPRECATION=express-session node app
```

Next, we apply the csrf() middleware itself. The order is important: csrf() must be preceded by cookieParser() and session().

```
app.use(csrf());
```

To process Less style sheets into CSS ones, we utilize less-middleware in this manner:

```
app.use(require('less-middleware')(path.join(__dirname, 'public')));
```

The other static files are also in the public folder:

```
app.use(express.static(path.join(__dirname, 'public')));
```

Remember CSRF? The main trick here is to use req.csrfToken(), which is created by the middleware that we previously applied in app.js. This is how we expose the CSRF token to templates:

```
app.use(function(req, res, next) {
  res.locals._csrf = req.csrfToken();
  return next();
})
```

When there's a request that matches route/RegExp with :task_id in it, this block is executed:

```
app.param('task_id', function(req, res, next, taskId) {
```

The value of task ID is in taskId, and we query the database to find that object:

```
req.db.tasks.findById(taskId, function(error, task){
```

It's tremendously important to check for errors and empty results:

```
if (error) return next(error);
if (!task) return next(new Error('Task is not found.'));
```

If there's data, we store it in the request and proceed to the next middleware:

```
    req.task = task;
    return next();
  });
});
```

Now it's time to define our routes. We start with the Home page:

```
app.get('/', routes.index);
```

Next is the Todo List page:

```
app.get('/tasks', tasks.list);
```

The following route will mark all tasks in the Todo List as completed if the user clicks the "all done" button. In a REST API, the HTTP method would be PUT, but, because we are building classical web apps with forms, we have to use POST:

```
app.post('/tasks', tasks.markAllCompleted)
```

The same URL for adding new tasks is used to mark all tasks completed, but, in the previous method (markAllCompleted()), you'll see how we handle flow control:

```
app.post('/tasks', tasks.add);
```

To mark a single task completed, we use the aforementioned :task_id string in our URL pattern (in a REST API, this would be a PUT request):

```
app.post('/tasks/:task_id', tasks.markCompleted);
```

Unlike with the previous POST route, we utilize Express.js param middleware with a :task_id token:

```
app.del('/tasks/:task_id', tasks.del);
```

For our Completed page, we define this route:

```
app.get('/tasks/completed', tasks.completed);
```

In case of malicious attacks or mistyped URLs, catching all requests with * is a user-friendly activity. Keep in mind that, if we had a match previously, Node.js won't come to execute this block.

```
app.all('*', function(req, res){
  res.status(404).send();
})
```

It's possible to configure different behavior based on environments:

```
if ('development' == app.get('env')) {
    app.use(errorHandler());
}
```

Finally, we spin up our application with the good old http method:

```
http.createServer(app).listen(app.get('port'),
  function(){
    console.log('Express server listening on port '
      + app.get('port'));
  }
);
```

The full content of the app.js file follows (the code in the GitHub repo https://github.com/azat-co/todo-express is evolving from community contributions, so it will be an enhanced version of this code):

```
var express = require('express');
var routes = require('./routes');
var tasks = require('./routes/tasks');
var http = require('http');
var path = require('path');
var mongoskin = require('mongoskin');
var db = mongoskin.db('mongodb://localhost:27017/todo?auto_reconnect', {safe:true});
var app = express();

var favicon = require('serve-favicon'),
  logger = require('morgan'),
  bodyParser = require('body-parser'),
  methodOverride = require('method-override'),
  cookieParser = require('cookie-parser'),
  session = require('express-session'),
  csrf = require('csurf'),
  errorHandler = require('errorhandler');

app.use(function(req, res, next) {
  req.db = {};
  req.db.tasks = db.collection('tasks');
  next();
})
app.locals.appname = 'Express.js Todo App'

app.set('port', process.env.PORT || 3000);
app.set('views', __dirname + '/views');
app.set('view engine', 'jade');
app.use(favicon(path.join('public','favicon.ico')));
app.use(logger('dev'));
app.use(bodyParser.json());
app.use(bodyParser.urlencoded({extended: true}));
app.use(methodOverride());
app.use(cookieParser('CEAF3FA4-F385-49AA-8FE4-54766A9874F1'));
app.use(session({
  secret: '59B93087-78BC-4EB9-993A-A61FC844F6C9',
  resave: true,
  saveUninitialized: true
}));
app.use(csrf());

app.use(require('less-middleware')(path.join(__dirname, 'public')));
app.use(express.static(path.join(__dirname, 'public')));
app.use(function(req, res, next) {
  res.locals._csrf = req.csrfToken();
  return next();
})
```

```
app.param('task_id', function(req, res, next, taskId) {
  req.db.tasks.findById(taskId, function(error, task){
    if (error) return next(error);
    if (!task) return next(new Error('Task is not found.'));
    req.task = task;
    return next();
  });
});

app.get('/', routes.index);
app.get('/tasks', tasks.list);
app.post('/tasks', tasks.markAllCompleted)
app.post('/tasks', tasks.add);
app.post('/tasks/:task_id', tasks.markCompleted);
app.delete('/tasks/:task_id', tasks.del);
app.get('/tasks/completed', tasks.completed);

app.all('*', function(req, res){
  res.status(404).send();
})
// development only
if ('development' == app.get('env')) {
  app.use(errorHandler());
}
http.createServer(app).listen(app.get('port'), function(){
  console.log('Express server listening on port ' + app.get('port'));
});
```

Routes

There are only two files in the routes folder. One of them, routes/index.js, serves the home page (e.g., http://localhost:3000/) and is straightforward:

```
exports.index = function(req, res){
  res.render('index', { title: 'Home' });
};
```

The remaining logic that deals with tasks has been placed in todo-express/routes/tasks.js. Let's break down that file a bit further.

We start by exporting a list() request handler that gives us a list of incomplete tasks:

```
exports.list = function(req, res, next){
```

To do so, we perform a database search with a completed=false query:

```
  req.db.tasks.find({
    completed: false
  }).toArray(function(error, tasks){
```

In the callback, we need to check for any errors:

```
if (error) return next(error);
```

Because we use toArray(), we can send the data directly to the template:

```
    res.render('tasks', {
      title: 'Todo List',
      tasks: tasks || []
    });
  });
};
```

Adding a new task requires us to check for the name parameter:

```
exports.add = function(req, res, next){
  if (!req.body || !req.body.name)
    return next(new Error('No data provided.'));
```

Thanks to our middleware, we already have a database collection in the req object and the default value for the task is incomplete (completed: false):

```
req.db.tasks.save({
  name: req.body.name,
  completed: false
}, function(error, task){
```

Again, it's important to check for errors and propagate them with the Express.js next() function:

```
if (error) return next(error);
if (!task) return next(new Error('Failed to save.'));
```

Logging is optional. However, it's useful for learning and debugging:

```
console.info('Added %s with id=%s', task.name, task._id);
```

Lastly, we redirect back to the Todo List page when the saving operation has finished successfully:

```
    res.redirect('/tasks');
  })
};
```

This method marks all incomplete tasks as complete:

```
exports.markAllCompleted = function(req, res, next) {
```

Because we had to reuse the POST route, and because it's a good illustration of flow control, we check for the all_done parameter to determine whether this request comes from the "all done" button or the "add" button:

```
if (!req.body.all_done
  || req.body.all_done !== 'true')
  return next();
```

If the execution has come this far, we perform a database query with the `multi: true` option (update many documents). This query will assign the `completed` property to `true` on all unfinished tasks (`completed: false`) with the `$set` directive.

```
req.db.tasks.update({
  completed: false
}, {$set: {
  completed: true
}}, {multi: true}, function(error, count){
```

Next, we perform significant error handling, logging, and redirection back to Todo List page:

```
    if (error) return next(error);
    console.info('Marked %s task(s) completed.', count);
    res.redirect('/tasks');
  })
};
```

The Completed route is similar to the Todo List route, except for the `completed` flag value, which is `true` in this case:

```
exports.completed = function(req, res, next) {
  req.db.tasks.find({
    completed: true
  }).toArray(function(error, tasks) {
    res.render('tasks_completed', {
      title: 'Completed',
      tasks: tasks || []
    });
  });
};
```

This is the route that takes care of marking a single task as done. We use `updateById`, but we could accomplish the same thing with a plain `update()` method from the Mongoskin/MongoDB API.

On the `$set` line, instead of the `req.body.completed` value, we use the expression `completed: req.body.completed === 'true'`. It is needed because the incoming value of `req.body.completed` is a string and not a boolean.

```
exports.markCompleted = function(req, res, next) {
  if (!req.body.completed)
    return next(new Error('Param is missing.'));
  req.db.tasks.updateById(req.task._id, {
    $set: {completed: req.body.completed === 'true'}},
    function(error, count) {
```

Once more, we perform error and results checks: (`update()` and `updateById()` don't return an object, but, instead, return the count of the affected documents):

```
      if (error) return next(error);
      if (count !==1)
        return next(new Error('Something went wrong.'));
      console.info('Marked task %s with id=%s completed.',
```

```
        req.task.name,
        req.task._id);
      res.redirect('/tasks');
    }
  )
}
```

Delete is the single route called by an AJAX request. However, there's nothing special about its implementation. The only difference is that we don't redirect, but send status 200 back.

Alternatively the remove() method can be used instead of removeById().

```
exports.del = function(req, res, next) {
  req.db.tasks.removeById(req.task._id, function(error, count) {
    if (error) return next(error);
    if (count !==1) return next(new Error('Something went wrong.'));
    console.info('Deleted task %s with id=%s completed.',
      req.task.name,
      req.task._id);
    res.status(204).send();
  });
}
```

For your convenience, here's the full content of the todo-express/routes/tasks.js file:

```
exports.list = function(req, res, next){
  req.db.tasks.find({completed: false}).toArray(function(error, tasks){
    if (error) return next(error);
    res.render('tasks', {
      title: 'Todo List',
      tasks: tasks || []
    });
  });
};

exports.add = function(req, res, next){
  if (!req.body || !req.body.name) return next(new Error('No data provided.'));
  req.db.tasks.save({
    name: req.body.name,
    completed: false
  }, function(error, task){
    if (error) return next(error);
    if (!task) return next(new Error('Failed to save.'));
    console.info('Added %s with id=%s', task.name, task._id);
    res.redirect('/tasks');
  })
};

exports.markAllCompleted = function(req, res, next) {
  if (!req.body.all_done || req.body.all_done !== 'true') return next();
  req.db.tasks.update({
    completed: false
```

```
  }, {$set: {
    completed: true
  }}, {multi: true}, function(error, count){
    if (error) return next(error);
    console.info('Marked %s task(s) completed.', count);
    res.redirect('/tasks');
  })
};

exports.completed = function(req, res, next) {
  req.db.tasks.find({completed: true}).toArray(function(error, tasks) {
    res.render('tasks_completed', {
      title: 'Completed',
      tasks: tasks || []
    });
  });
};

exports.markCompleted = function(req, res, next) {
  if (!req.body.completed) return next(new Error('Param is missing.'));
  req.db.tasks.updateById(req.task._id, {$set: {completed: req.body.completed === 'true'}},
function(error, count) {
    if (error) return next(error);
    if (count !==1) return next(new Error('Something went wrong.'));
    console.info('Marked task %s with id=%s completed.', req.task.name, req.task._id);
    res.redirect('/tasks');
  })
};

exports.del = function(req, res, next) {
  req.db.tasks.removeById(req.task._id, function(error, count) {
    if (error) return next(error);
    if (count !==1) return next(new Error('Something went wrong.'));
    console.info('Deleted task %s with id=%s completed.', req.task.name, req.task._id);
    res.status(204).send();
  });
};
```

So far we've implemented the main server file `app.js` and its routes that perform different database operations. Now we can proceed to the templates.

Jade

In the Todo app, we use four templates:

- `layout.jade`: The skeleton of HTML pages that is used on all pages
- `index.jade`: Home page
- `tasks.jade`: Todo List page
- `tasks_completed.jade`: Completed page

Let's go through each file, starting with `layout.jade`. It starts with `doctype`, `html`, and head types:

```
doctype html
html
  head
```

We should set the appname variable:

```
title= title + ' | ' + appname
```

Next, we include `*.css` files and Express.js will serve their contents from Less files:

```
link(rel="stylesheet", href="/stylesheets/style.css")
link(rel="stylesheet", href="/bootstrap/bootstrap.css")
link(rel="stylesheet", href="/stylesheets/main.css")
```

The body with Bootstrap structure consists of the `.container` and `.navbar` classes. To read more about these and other classes, go to `http://getbootstrap.com/css/`.

```
body
  .container
    .navbar.navbar-default
      .container
        .navbar-header
          a.navbar-brand(href='/')= appname
    .alert.alert-dismissable
    h1= title
    p Welcome to Express.js Todo app by 
      a(href='http://twitter.com/azat_co') @azat_co
      |. Please enjoy.
```

This is the place where other jade templates (like `tasks.jade`) will be imported:

```
block content
```

The last lines include front-end JavaScript files:

```
script(src='/javascripts/jquery.js', type="text/javascript")
script(src='/javascripts/main.js', type="text/javascript")
```

The following is the full `layout.jade` file:

```
doctype html
html
  head
    title= title + ' | ' + appname
    link(rel="stylesheet", href="/stylesheets/style.css")
    link(rel="stylesheet", href="/bootstrap/bootstrap.css")
    link(rel="stylesheet", href="/stylesheets/main.css")
```

```
  body
    .container
      .navbar.navbar-default
        .container
          .navbar-header
            a.navbar-brand(href='/')= appname
      .alert.alert-dismissable
      h1= title
      p Welcome to Express.js Todo app by 
        a(href='http://twitter.com/azat_co') @azat_co
        |. Please enjoy.
      block content
  script(src='/javascripts/jquery.js', type="text/javascript")
  script(src='/javascripts/main.js', type="text/javascript")
```

The `index.jade` file is our Home page and is quite vanilla. Its most interesting component is the `nav-pills` menu, which is a Bootstrap class for tabbed navigation. The rest of the file is just static hypertext:

```
extends layout

block content
  .menu
    h2 Menu
    ul.nav.nav-pills
      li.active
        a(href="/tasks") Home
      li
        a(href="/tasks") Todo List
      li
        a(href="/tasks") Completed
  .home
    p This is an example of create, read, update, delete web application built with Express.js
v4.8.1, and Mongoskin&MongoDB for 
      a(href="http://proexpressjs.com") Pro Express.js
      |.
    p The full source code is available at 
      a(href='http://github.com/azat-co/todo-express') github.com/azat-co/todo-express
      |.
    p For Express 3.x go to 
      a(href="https://github.com/azat-co/todo-express/releases/tag/v0.1.0") release 0.1.0
      |.
```

Next is `tasks.jade`, which uses `extends layout`:

```
extends layout

block content
```

Next is our main page of specific content:

```
.menu
  h2 Menu
  ul.nav.nav-pills
    li
      a(href='/') Home
    li.active
      a(href='/tasks') Todo List
    li
      a(href="/tasks/completed") Completed
h1= title
```

The div with the list class will hold the Todo List:

```
  .list
    .item.add-task
```

The form to mark all items as done has a CSRF token (locals._csrf) in a hidden field and uses the POST method pointed to /tasks:

```
div.action
  form(action='/tasks', method='post')
    input(type='hidden', value='true', name='all_done')
    input(type='hidden', value=locals._csrf, name='_csrf')
    input(type='submit', class='btn btn-success btn-xs', value='all done')
```

A similar CSRF-enabled form is used for new task creation:

```
form(action='/tasks', method='post')
  input(type='hidden', value=locals._csrf, name='_csrf')
  div.name
    input(type='text', name='name', placeholder='Add a new task')
  div.delete
   input.btn.btn-primary.btn-sm(type='submit', value='add')
```

When we start the app for the first time (or clean the database), there are no tasks:

```
if (tasks.length === 0)
      | No tasks.
```

Jade supports iterations with the each command:

```
each task, index in tasks
 .item
   div.action
```

This form submits data to its individual task route:

```
form(action='/tasks/#{task._id}', method='post')
  input(type='hidden', value=task._id.toString(), name='id')
  input(type='hidden', value='true', name='completed')
  input(type='hidden', value=locals._csrf, name='_csrf')
  input(type='submit', class='btn btn-success btn-xs task-done', value='done')
```

The index variable is used to display order in the list of tasks:

```
div.num
  span=index+1
    |. 
div.name
  span.name=task.name
  //- no support for DELETE method in forms
  //- http://amundsen.com/examples/put-delete-forms/
  //- so do XHR request instead from public/javascripts/main.js
```

The "delete" button doesn't have anything fancy attached to it, because events are attached to these buttons from the main.js front-end JavaScript file:

```
        div.delete
          a(class='btn btn-danger btn-xs task-delete', data-task-id=task._id.toString(),
data-csrf=locals._csrf) delete
```

The full source code of tasks.jade is provided here:

```
extends layout

block content

  .menu
    h2 Menu
    ul.nav.nav-pills
      li
        a(href='/') Home
      li.active
        a(href='/tasks') Todo List
      li
        a(href="/tasks/completed") Completed
  h1= title

  .list
    .item.add-task
      div.action
        form(action='/tasks', method='post')
          input(type='hidden', value='true', name='all_done')
          input(type='hidden', value=locals._csrf, name='_csrf')
          input(type='submit', class='btn btn-success btn-xs', value='all done')
      form(action='/tasks', method='post')
        input(type='hidden', value=locals._csrf, name='_csrf')
```

```
        div.name
          input(type='text', name='name', placeholder='Add a new task')
        div.delete
          input.btn.btn-primary.btn-sm(type='submit', value='add')
    if (tasks.length === 0)
      | No tasks.
    each task, index in tasks
      .item
        div.action
          form(action='/tasks/#{task._id}', method='post')
            input(type='hidden', value=task._id.toString(), name='id')
            input(type='hidden', value='true', name='completed')
            input(type='hidden', value=locals._csrf, name='_csrf')
            input(type='submit', class='btn btn-success btn-xs task-done', value='done')
        div.num
          span=index+1
            |. 
        div.name
          span.name=task.name
          //- no support for DELETE method in forms
          //- http://amundsen.com/examples/put-delete-forms/
          //- so do XHR request instead from public/javascripts/main.js
        div.delete
          a(class='btn btn-danger btn-xs task-delete', data-task-id=task._id.toString(),
data-csrf=locals._csrf) delete
```

Last but not least, comes `tasks_completed.jade`, which is just a stripped-down version of the `tasks.jade` file:

```
extends layout

block content

  .menu
    h2 Menu
    ul.nav.nav-pills
      li
        a(href='/') Home
      li
        a(href='/tasks') Todo List
      li.active
        a(href="/tasks/completed") Completed

  h1= title

  .list
    if (tasks.length === 0)
      | No tasks.
    each task, index in tasks
      .item
        div.num
          span=index+1
```

```
        |. 
    div.name.completed-task
      span.name=task.name
```

Finally, we can customize the look of the app with Less.

Less

As previously mentioned, after applying proper middleware in `app.js` files, we can put `*.less` files anywhere under the `public` folder. Express.js works by accepting a request for some `.css` file and then attempting to match the corresponding file by name. Therefore, we include `*.css` files in our jade templates.

Here is the content of the `todo-express/public/stylesheets/main.less` file:

```
* {
  font-size:20px;
}
.item {
  height: 44px;
  width: 100%;
  clear: both;
  .name {
    width: 300px;
  }
  .action {
    width: 100px;
  }
  .delete {
    width: 100px
  }
  div {
    float:left;
  }
}
.home {
  margin-top: 40px;
}
.name.completed-task {
  text-decoration: line-through;
}
```

To run the application, start MongoDB with `$ mongo`, and, in a new terminal window, execute `$ node app` and go to `http://localhost:3000/`—you should see something similar to the page shown earlier in Figure 20-1. In your terminal window, you should see something like this:

```
Express server listening on port 3000
GET / 200 30.448 ms - 1408
GET /stylesheets/style.css 304 7.196 ms - -
GET /javascripts/jquery.js 304 17.677 ms - -
GET /javascripts/main.js 304 27.151 ms - -
GET /stylesheets/main.css 200 453.584 ms - 226
GET /bootstrap/bootstrap.css 200 458.293 ms - 98336
```

Summary

You've learned how to use MongoDB, Jade, and Less. This Todo app is considered *traditional*, because it doesn't rely on any front-end framework and it renders HTML on the server. This was done intentionally to show how easy it is to use Express.js for such tasks. In modern-day development, people often leverage some sort of REST API server architecture with a front-end client built with Backbone.js, AngularJS, Ember.js, or something comparable (see `http://todomvc.com`).

In the Chapter 22 example, we dive deep into the details of how to write such servers. The Chapter 22 application HackHall uses the MEBN (MongoDB, Express.js, Backbone.js, and Node.js) stack. But, before we cover HackHall, we'll spend more time on REST APIs and testing in Chapter 21, which has the REST API example.

CHAPTER 21

REST API

In this tutorial, we'll build a RESTful API. In addition to Express.js, we'll use MongoDB via the Mongoskin library. We'll also use Mocha and SuperAgent to write functional tests.

This tutorial walks you through writing tests using the Mocha and SuperAgent libraries, and then shows you how to use the tests in a test-driven development manner to build a Node.js free-JSON REST API server, utilizing the Express.js framework and Mongoskin library for MongoDB.

Note The full source code for both the test and app files is at `https://github.com/azat-co/rest-api-express` for your convenience. If you want to skip the tutorial and just run the code, you can do so with:

```
$ git clone https://github.com/azat-co/rest-api-express.git
$ cd rest-api-express
$ npm install
$ node express.js
```

In a new terminal window, enter:

```
$ ./node_modules/mocha/bin/mocha express.test.js
```

The source code might be an enhanced version of the code in this chapter because of the ongoing contributions from readers. I encourage you to submit your own pull request!

In this REST API server, we'll perform create, update, remove, and delete (CRUD) operations and harness the Express.js middleware[1] concept with `app.param()` and `app.use()` methods. The chapter is organized into these topics:

- *RESTful API basics*: A primer on RESTful APIs
- *Test coverage*: We'll use the test-driven development (TDD) approach and write tests first
- *Server dependencies*: We'll install the required modules
- *Server implementation*: We'll write the code for the Express.js app

[1]http://expressjs.com/api.html#middleware

■ **Note** In this chapter, our REST API and test examples use a semicolon-less style. Semicolons in JavaScript are absolutely optional, except in two cases: 1) in the for loop, and 2) before expressions/statements that start with a parenthesis (e.g., immediately invoked function expression, or IIFE). Using this style gives you an alternative perspective. Typing fewer semicolons improves speed, and it looks better and is more consistent, because developers tend to miss semicolons from time to time (perfectly running code allows for such sloppiness). Also, some programmers find semicolon-less code more readable.

RESTful API Basics

RESTful APIs became popular because of the demand to have each transaction in a distributed system include sufficient information about the state of the client. In a sense, this standard is stateless, because no information about the clients' states is stored on the server, making it possible for each request to be served by a different system.

Distinct characteristics of a RESTful API (i.e., if an API is RESTful, it usually follows these principles) are as follows:

- It has better scalability support because different components can be deployed independently to different servers.
- It replaces the Simple Object Access Protocol (SOAP) because of the simpler verb and noun structure in REST.
- It uses HTTP methods, such as GET, POST, DELETE, PUT, OPTIONS, and so forth.
- It supports formats other than JSON (although JSON is the most popular). Unlike SOAP, which is a protocol, the REST methodology is flexible in the choice of formats. For example, alternative formats might be Extensible Markup Language (XML) or comma-separated values (CSV) formats.

Table 21-1 outlines an example of a simple CRUD REST API for message collection.

Table 21-1. *Example of the CRUD REST API Structure*

Method	URL	Meaning
GET	`/messages.json`	Return list of messages in JSON format.
PUT	`/messages.json`	Update/replace all messages and return status/error in JSON.
POST	`/messages.json`	Create new message and return its ID in JSON format.
GET	`/messages/{id}.json`	Return message with ID `{id}` in JSON format.
PUT	`/messages/{id}.json`	Update/replace message with ID that equals the value of `{id}`; if `{id}` message doesn't exist, create it.
DELETE	`/messages/{id}.json`	Delete message with ID `{id}`, and return status/error in JSON format.

REST is not a protocol; it's an architecture, in the sense that it's more flexible than a protocol, such as SOAP. Therefore, REST API URLs could look like `/messages/list.html` or `/messages/list.xml`, if we wanted to support these formats.

PUT and DELETE are *idempotent* methods, which means that, if the server receives two or more similar requests, the end result is the same. POST is not idempotent and might affect the state and cause side effects (e.g., creation of multiple duplicate records).GET is *nullipotent*, which means it's safe to call it multiple times, because the results won't change.

■ **Note** You can find more information on REST at Wikipedia (`http://en.wikipedia.org/wiki/Representational_state_transfer`) and in Stefan Tilkov's InfoQ article "A Brief Introduction to REST" (`www.infoq.com/articles/rest-introduction`).

As mentioned in the chapter introduction, in our REST API server, we'll perform CRUD operations and harness the Express.js middleware concept with the `app.param()` and `app.use()` methods. So, our app should be able to process the following commands using the JSON format (`collectionName` is the name of the collection, typically a plural noun, e.g., messages, comments, users, etc.):

- *POST* `/collections/{collectionName}`: Request to create an object; the app responds with the newly created object ID.
- *GET* `/collections/{collectionName}/{id}`: Request with the ID value in the URL; the app retrieves an object with that ID.
- *GET* `/collections/{collectionName}/`: Request to retrieve any items from the collection (`items`); in our example, we'll have the following query options: up to 10 items and sorted by ID.
- *PUT* `/collections/{collectionName}/{id}`: Request with ID to update an object.
- *DELETE* `/collections/{collectionName}/{id}`: Request with ID to remove an object.

Therefore, this server can handle *any* number of collections, not just a single collection, with just six endpoints (e.g., `messages`, as illustrated in Table 21-1).

Test Coverage

Before we do anything else, let's write functional tests that make HTTP requests to our soon-to-be-created REST API server. If you know how to use Mocha, or just want to jump straight to the Express.js app implementation, feel free to do so. You can use CURL terminal commands for testing too.

Assuming that we already have Node.js, NPM, and MongoDB installed, let's create a *new* folder (or if you wrote the tests, use that folder):

```
$ mkdir rest-api-express
$ cd rest-api-express
```

We'll use the Mocha, Expect.js (`https://github.com/Automattic/expect.js`), and SuperAgent (`http://visionmedia.github.io/superagent/`) libraries. To install them, run these commands from the project folder:

```
$ npm install -g mocha@1.18.2 --save-dev
$ npm install expect.js@0.3.1 --save-dev
$ npm install superagent@0.17.0 --save-dev
```

■ **Tip** You can install Mocha globally because it's a command-line tool, but installing Mocha locally will enable you to use different versions of Mocha at the same time—one for each project. To run tests with local Mocha, simply point to `./node_modules/mocha/bin/mocha`. You can copy this into a Makefile, as outlined in Chapter 22, or into `"scripts": {"test": "..."}` of `package.json`. Local Mocha is also required for the configurations of continuous integration (CI).

Now let's create an `express.test.js` file, which will have six test suites in the same folder:

- Creating a new object
- Retrieving an object by its ID
- Retrieving the whole collection
- Updating an object by its ID
- Checking an updated object by its ID
- Removing an object by its ID

HTTP requests are a breeze with SuperAgent's chained functions, which we'll put inside of each test suite. So, we start with dependencies:

```
var superagent = require('superagent')
var expect = require('expect.js')
```

Next, we write our first test case wrapped in the test case (`describe` and its callback). The idea is simple. We make an HTTP request to a local instance of the server. When we send the request, we pass some data and, of course, the URL path, which changes from test case to test case. The main action happens in the request (made by SuperAgent) callback. There, we put multiple assertions, which are the bread and butter of TDD. To be strictly correct, this test suite uses behavior-driven development (BDD) language, but this difference is not essential for our project.

```
describe('express rest api server', function(){
  var id

  it('posts an object', function(done){
    superagent.post('http://localhost:3000/collections/test')
      .send({ name: 'John'
        , email: 'john@rpjs.co'
      })
      .end(function(e,res){
        // console.log(res.body)
        expect(e).to.eql(null)
        expect(res.body.length).to.eql(1)
        expect(res.body[0]._id.length).to.eql(24)
        id = res.body[0]._id
        done()
      })
  })
```

As you may have noticed, we're checking for the following:

- The error object should be null (`eql(null)`).
- The response body array should have one item (`to.eql(1)`).
- The first response body item should have the `_id` property, which is 24 characters long (i.e., a hex string representation of the standard MongoDB `ObjectId` type).

To finish, we save the newly created object's ID in the `id` global variable so that we can use it later for retrievals, updates, and deletions. Speaking of object retrievals, we test them in the next test case. Notice that the `superagent` method has changed to `get()` and the URL path contains the object ID. You can "uncomment" `console.log` to inspect the full HTTP response body:

```
it('retrieves an object', function(done){
  superagent.get('http://localhost:3000/collections/test/'+id)
    .end(function(e, res){
      // console.log(res.body)
      expect(e).to.eql(null)
      expect(typeof res.body).to.eql('object')
      expect(res.body._id.length).to.eql(24)
      expect(res.body._id).to.eql(id)
      done()
    })
})
```

The `done()` callback allows us to test asynchronous code. Without it, the Mocha test case ends abruptly, long before the slow server has time to respond.

The next test case's assertion is a bit more interesting, because we use the `map()` function on the response results to return an array of IDs. In this array, we find our ID (saved in `id` variable) with the `contain()` method, which is a more elegant alternative to native `indexOf()`. It works because the results, which are limited to ten records, come sorted by IDs, and because our object was created just moments ago.

```
it('retrieves a collection', function(done){
  superagent.get('http://localhost:3000/collections/test')
    .end(function(e, res){
      // console.log(res.body)
      expect(e).to.eql(null)
      expect(res.body.length).to.be.above(0)
      expect(res.body.map(function (item){return item._id})).to.contain(id)
      done()
    })
})
```

When it comes time to update our object, we actually need to send some data. We do this by passing an object to SuperAgent's function. Then, we assert that the operation was completed with (`msg=success`):

```
it('updates an object', function(done){
    superagent.put('http://localhost:3000/collections/test/'+id)
      .send({name: 'Peter'
        , email: 'peter@yahoo.com'})
      .end(function(e, res){
        // console.log(res.body)
        expect(e).to.eql(null)
```

```
        expect(typeof res.body).to.eql('object')
        expect(res.body.msg).to.eql('success')
        done()
      })
  })
```

The last two test cases, which assert retrieval of the updated object and its deletion, use methods similar to those we've used before. Here is the full source code for the `rest-api-express/express.test.js` file:

```
var superagent = require('superagent')
var expect = require('expect.js')

describe('express rest api server', function(){
  var id

  it('posts an object', function(done){
    superagent.post('http://localhost:3000/collections/test')
      .send({ name: 'John'
        , email: 'john@rpjs.co'
      })
      .end(function(e,res){
        // console.log(res.body)
        expect(e).to.eql(null)
        expect(res.body.length).to.eql(1)
        expect(res.body[0]._id.length).to.eql(24)
        id = res.body[0]._id
        done()
      })
  })

  it('retrieves an object', function(done){
    superagent.get('http://localhost:3000/collections/test/'+id)
      .end(function(e, res){
        // console.log(res.body)
        expect(e).to.eql(null)
        expect(typeof res.body).to.eql('object')
        expect(res.body._id.length).to.eql(24)
        expect(res.body._id).to.eql(id)
        done()
      })
  })

  it('retrieves a collection', function(done){
    superagent.get('http://localhost:3000/collections/test')
      .end(function(e, res){
        // console.log(res.body)
        expect(e).to.eql(null)
        expect(res.body.length).to.be.above(0)
        expect(res.body.map(function (item){return item._id})).to.contain(id)
        done()
      })
  })
```

```
  it('updates an object', function(done){
    superagent.put('http://localhost:3000/collections/test/'+id)
      .send({name: 'Peter'
        , email: 'peter@yahoo.com'})
      .end(function(e, res){
        // console.log(res.body)
        expect(e).to.eql(null)
        expect(typeof res.body).to.eql('object')
        expect(res.body.msg).to.eql('success')
        done()
      })
  })

  it('checks an updated object', function(done){
    superagent.get('http://localhost:3000/collections/test/'+id)
      .end(function(e, res){
        // console.log(res.body)
        expect(e).to.eql(null)
        expect(typeof res.body).to.eql('object')
        expect(res.body._id.length).to.eql(24)
        expect(res.body._id).to.eql(id)
        expect(res.body.name).to.eql('Peter')
        done()
      })
  })

  it('removes an object', function(done){
    superagent.del('http://localhost:3000/collections/test/'+id)
      .end(function(e, res){
        // console.log(res.body)
        expect(e).to.eql(null)
        expect(typeof res.body).to.eql('object')
        expect(res.body.msg).to.eql('success')
        done()
      })
  })
})
```

To run the tests, we can use the `$ mocha express.test.js` command. For now, the tests should fail, because we have yet to implement the server!

For those of you who require multiple versions of Mocha, another alternative, which is better, is to run your tests using local Mocha binaries:

```
$ ./node_modules/mocha/bin/mocha express.test.js
```

This, of course, assumes that you have installed Mocha locally into `node_modules`.

■ **Note** By default, Mocha doesn't use any reporters, and the result output is lackluster. To receive more explanatory logs, supply the `-R <name>` option (e.g., `$ mocha test -R spec` or `$ mocha test -R list`).

Dependencies

As in the previous tutorial (Chapter 20), we'll utilize Mongoskin, a MongoDB library, which is a better alternative to the good old, plain, native MongoDB driver for Node.js.[2] In addition, Mongoskin is more lightweight than Mongoose and is schema-less. For more insight, please check out `https://github.com/kissjs/node-mongoskin#comparation`.

Express.js is a wrapper for core Node.js HTTP module objects (`http://nodejs.org/api/http.html`). The Express.js framework is built on top of Connect middleware (`https://github.com/senchalabs/connect`) and provides tons of convenience. Some people compare the framework to Ruby's Sinatra because it's non-opinionated and configurable.

If you created a `rest-api-express` folder in the previous section, simply run these commands to install modules for the application:

```
$ npm install express@4.8.1 --save
$ npm install mongoskin@1.4.1 --save
```

The final `package.json` file might look like this:

```
{
  "name": "rest-api-express",
  "version": "0.0.4",
  "description": "",
  "main": "express.js",
  "scripts": {
    "start": "node express.js",
    "test": "mocha express.test.js"
  },
  "repository": {
    "type": "git",
    "url": "https://github.com/azat-co/rest-api-express.git"
  },
  "author": "Azat Mardan",
  "license": "BSD-2-Clause",
  "bugs": {
    "url": "https://github.com/azat-co/rest-api-express/issues"
  },
  "dependencies": {
    "body-parser": "1.9.2",
    "express": "4.10.1",
    "mongoskin": "1.4.4",
    "morgan": "1.5.0"  },
  "devDependencies": {
    "expect.js": "0.3.1",
    "mocha": "2.0.1",
    "superagent": "0.20.0"  }
}
```

[2] `https://github.com/mongodb/node-mongodb-native`

Server Implementation

To implement the server, we first need to define our dependencies:

```
var express = require('express'),
  mongoskin = require('mongoskin'),
  bodyParser = require('body-parser')
  logger = require('morgan')
```

After version 3.x, Express.js streamlines the instantiation of its app instance so that this line gives us a server object:

```
var app = express()
```

To extract parameters from the body of the requests, we'll use `body-parser` middleware. (How to use middleware was covered in Chapter 4.) These are the statements for JSON and URL-encoded functions:

```
app.use(bodyParser.json())
app.use(bodyParser.urlencoded({extended: true}))
```

The morgan (`logger`) middleware allows us to see incoming requests:

```
app.use(logger('dev'))
```

Middleware (in this[3] and other forms[4]) is a powerful and convenient pattern in Express.js and Connect to organize and reuse code.

As with the `bodyParser()` method, which saves us from writing extra code (for parsing a body object of an HTTP request), Mongoskin makes it possible to connect to the MongoDB database in one effortless line of code, compared to the native MongoDB driver's code:

```
var db = mongoskin.db('@localhost:27017/test', {safe:true});
```

■ **Note** If you wish to connect to a remote database, such as MongoHQ (`https://www.mongohq.com/home`), substitute the string with your username, password, host, and port values. Here is the format of the URI string:

```
mongodb://[username:password@] host1[:port1][,host2[:port2],... [,hostN[:portN]]] [/[database]
[?options]]
```

The `app.param()` method is another Express.js middleware. It basically says "do something every time there is this value in the URL pattern of the request handler." In our case, we select a particular collection when a request pattern contains a string `collectionName` prefixed with a colon (you'll see it later in the routes):

```
app.param('collectionName', function(req, res, next, collectionName){
  req.collection = db.collection(collectionName)
  return next()
})
```

[3]http://expressjs.com/api.html#app.use
[4]http://expressjs.com/api.html#middleware

Merely to be user-friendly, let's include a root route with a message:

```
app.get('/', function(req, res, next) {
  res.send('please select a collection, e.g., /collections/messages')
})
```

Now the real work begins. Here is how we retrieve a list of items that is sorted by `_id (sort: {'_id':-1})` and that has a limit of ten (`limit: 10`):

```
app.get('/collections/:collectionName', function(req, res, next) {
  req.collection.find({},{
    limit: 10, sort: {'_id': -1}
  }).toArray(function(e, results){
    if (e) return next(e)
    res.send(results)
  })
})
```

Have you noticed a `:collectionName` string in the URL pattern parameter? This, and the previous `app.param()` middleware, are what give us the `req.collection` object that points to a specified collection in our database.

The object-creating endpoint is slightly easier to grasp, because we just pass the whole payload to the MongoDB method (a.k.a. free-JSON REST API):

```
app.post('/collections/:collectionName', function(req, res, next) {
  req.collection.insert(req.body, {}, function(e, results){
    if (e) return next(e)
    res.send(results)
  })
})
```

Single-object-retrieval functions (e.g., `findById()`) are faster than `find()`, but they use a different interface. They return an object directly instead of a cursor—please be aware! The ID is coming from the `:id` part of the URL path with `req.params.id` Express.js magic:

```
app.get('/collections/:collectionName/:id', function(req, res, next) {
  req.collection.findById(req.params.id, function(e, result){
    if (e) return next(e)
    res.send(result)
  })
})
```

The PUT request handler gets more interesting, because `updateById()` (as `update()`) doesn't return the augmented object; instead, it returns a count of affected objects.

Also, `{$set: req.body}` is a special MongoDB operator (operators tend to start with a dollar sign) that sets values. In this case, we update *any* body data sent to us. This is called the free-JSON API approach. It's great for prototyping, but in most systems, you need to perform validation (you can use the `express-validator` middleware, covered in Chapter 15).

The second {safe: true, multi: false} parameter is an object with options that tell MongoDB to wait for the execution before running the callback function and to process only one (the first) item:

```
app.put('/collections/:collectionName/:id', function(req, res, next) {
  req.collection.updateById(req.params.id,
    {$set: req.body},
    {safe: true, multi: false},
    function(e, result){
        if (e) return next(e)
        res.send((result === 1) ? {msg: 'success'} : {msg: 'error'})
    }
  )
})
```

Finally, the following is the DELETE method, which utilizes Mongoskin's removeById() method and outputs a custom JSON message ({msg: success}) in the event of success:

```
app.delete('/collections/:collectionName/:id', function(req, res, next) {
  req.collection.removeById(req.params.id, function(e, result){
    if (e) return next(e)
    res.send((result === 1)?{msg: 'success'} : {msg: 'error'})
  })
})
```

■ **Note** The app.delete() method is an alias for the now-deprecated (but still used in older projects) app.del().

The last line, that actually starts the server on port 3000 in this case, is:

```
app.listen(3000, function(){
  console.log('Express server listening on port 3000')
})
```

Just in case something is not working well, here is the full code of the rest-api-express/express.js file:

```
var express = require('express'),
  mongoskin = require('mongoskin'),
  bodyParser = require('body-parser'),
  logger = require('morgan')

var app = express()
app.use(bodyParser())
app.use(logger('dev'))

var db = mongoskin.db('mongodb://@localhost:27017/test', {safe:true})

app.param('collectionName', function(req, res, next, collectionName){
  req.collection = db.collection(collectionName)
  return next()
})
```

```
app.get('/', function(req, res, next) {
  res.send('please select a collection, e.g., /collections/messages')
})

app.get('/collections/:collectionName', function(req, res, next) {
  req.collection.find({} ,{limit: 10, sort: {'_id': -1}}).toArray(function(e, results){
    if (e) return next(e)
    res.send(results)
  })
})

app.post('/collections/:collectionName', function(req, res, next) {
  req.collection.insert(req.body, {}, function(e, results){
    if (e) return next(e)
    res.send(results)
  })
})

app.get('/collections/:collectionName/:id', function(req, res, next) {
  req.collection.findById(req.params.id, function(e, result){
    if (e) return next(e)
    res.send(result)
  })
})

app.put('/collections/:collectionName/:id', function(req, res, next) {
  req.collection.updateById(req.params.id, {$set: req.body}, {safe: true, multi: false},
  function(e, result){
    if (e) return next(e)
    res.send((result === 1) ? {msg:'success'} : {msg: 'error'})
  })
})

app.delete('/collections/:collectionName/:id', function(req, res, next) {
  req.collection.removeById(req.params.id, function(e, result){
    if (e) return next(e)
    res.send((result === 1)?{msg: 'success'} : {msg: 'error'})
  })
})

app.listen(3000, function(){
  console.log('Express server listening on port 3000')
})
```

Exit your editor and run this command in your terminal:

```
$ node express.js
```

And in a different window (without closing the first one—let the server run), enter either:

```
$ mocha express.test.js
```

Or

```
$ ./node_modules/mocha/bin/mocha express.test.js
```

Or

```
$ npm test
```

The terminal output from Mocha should look like this:

```
......
  6 passing (57ms)
```

In the server terminal window, you should see something like this:

```
Express server listening on port 3000
POST /collections/test 200 35.242 ms - 73
GET /collections/test/54724135101acb1334635994 200 4.254 ms - 71
GET /collections/test 200 5.181 ms - 108
PUT /collections/test/54724135101acb1334635994 200 4.037 ms - 17
GET /collections/test/54724135101acb1334635994 200 1.638 ms - 75
DELETE /collections/test/54724135101acb1334635994 200 1.382 ms - 17
```

If you really don't like Mocha and/or BDD, you can always use CURL. For example, here's how to make a POST request:

```
$ curl -d "name=peter&email=peter337@rpjs.co" http://localhost:3000/collections/proexpressjs-readers
$ curl http://localhost:3000/collections/proexpressjs-readers
```

In this case, the output was:

```
[{"name":"peter","email":"peter337@rpjs.co","_id":"541714c23f5b557785700d4c"}]%
...
[{"_id":"541714c23f5b557785700d4c","name":"peter","email":"peter337@rpjs.co"}]%
```

GET requests also work in the browser. For example, you can go to `http://localhost:3000/collections/proexpressjs-readers` to get the list of items in the collection.

In this tutorial, our tests are longer than the app code itself, so abandoning test-driven development might be tempting, but believe me, *the good habits of TDD will save you hours of work* during any serious development project when the complexity of the application you are working on is high.

Summary

The Express.js and Mongoskin libraries are great resources when you need to build a simple REST API server in a few lines of code. Later, if you need to expand the libraries, they also provide a way to configure and organize your code. NoSQL databases like MongoDB are good at handling free-REST APIs, which means that you don't have to define schemas and that you can throw any data at it and it'll be saved.

In the next chapter, we'll combine the REST API approach with a front-end framework, Backbone.js, that will fetch the data from the server, compile it, and render HTML in the browser (unlike the Todo app from Chapter 20, which handles templates on the server).

CHAPTER 22

HackHall

The HackHall app is a true MVC application. It has the REST API server with a front-end client that is written in Backbone.js and Underscore. For the purpose of this chapter, we'll illustrate how to use Express.js with MongoDB via Mongoose ORM/ODM (object-relational mapping/object-document mapping) for the back-end REST API server. In addition, the project utilizes OAuth directly and via Passport, sessions, and Mocha for TDD. It's hosted on Heroku and is in active development (see the nearby Note).

Note The HackHall source code used in this chapter is available in the public GitHub repository (`https://github.com/azat-co/hackhall`) under the v3.1.0 release (`https://github.com/azat-co/hackhall/releases/tag/v3.1.0`, `https://github.com/azat-co/hackhall/tree/v3.1.0`, and `https://github.com/azat-co/hackhall/archive/v3.1.0.zip`). Future versions might differ from this chapter's example and could have more features.

This chapter is structured as follows:

- What is HackHall?
- Running HackHall
- Structure
- Package.json
- Express.js app
- Routes
- Mongoose models
- Mocha tests

What Is HackHall?

HackHall is an open source project for online communities. Its implementation at `http://hackhall.com` is a curated social network/membership community and collaboration tool for hackers, hipsters, designers, entrepreneurs, and pirates (just kidding). The HackHall community is akin to a combination of Reddit, Hacker News, and Facebook Groups with curation. You can apply to become a member at `http://hackhall.com`.

The HackHall project is in its early stages, roughly beta. We plan to extend the code base in the future and bring in more people to share skills, wisdom, and passion for programming. You can watch a quick demo video of HackHall.com at `http://youtu.be/N1UILNqeW4k`.

In this chapter, we'll cover the v3.1.0 release, which has the following features:

- OAuth 1.0 with the oauth module (https://www.npmjs.org/package/oauth) and AngelList API (https://angel.co/api)
- E-mail and password authentication
- Password hashing
- Mongoose models and schemas
- Express.js structure with routes in modules
- JSON REST API
- Express.js error handling
- Front-end client Backbone.js app (for more info on Backbone.js, download, or read online, my *Rapid Prototyping with JS* tutorials, at http://rapidprototypingwithjs.com/)
- Environment variables with Foreman's .env
- TDD tests with Mocha
- Basic Makefile setup
- SendGrid e-mail notifications
- GitHub login

Running HackHall

To get the source code for HackHall, you can navigate to the hackhall folder or clone it from GitHub:

```
$ git clone https://github.com/azat-co/hackhall.git
$ git checkout v3.1.0
$ npm install
```

If you plan to test an AngelList, or GitHub integrations (optional), then you should sign up for their API keys as a developer. After you do so, you need to pass the values via environment variables to the app. HackHall is using a Heroku and Foreman (http://ddollar.github.io/foreman) setup approach (the .env file) for these sensitive API keys. The Foreman gem is a command-line tool that manages Procfile-based applications. The Heroku toolbelt includes it. To store keys in environment variables, simply add an .env file like this (replace the values following = with your own values):

```
ANGELLIST_CLIENT_ID=254C0335-5F9A-4607-87C0
ANGELLIST_CLIENT_SECRET=99F5C1AC-C5F7-44E6-81A1-8DF4FC42B8D9
GITHUB_CLIENT_ID=9F5C1AC-C5F7-44E6
GITHUB_CLIENT_SECRET=9F5C1AC-C5F7-44E69F5C1AC-C5F7-44E6
GITHUB_CLIENT_ID_LOCAL=9F5C1AC-C5F7-44E1
GITHUB_CLIENT_SECRET_LOCAL=9F5C1AC-C5F7-44E69F5C1AC-C5F7-44E6
...
```

Note that there are no spaces before or after the equal sign (=).

After you have the .env file and values, use foreman with nodemon:

```
$ foreman run nodemon server
```

If you are confused about foreman or prefer not to install it, then you can create a shell file with your environment variables and use it to launch the server.

After you create an AngelList app and register it, you can obtain the AngelList API keys at https://angel.co/api. Similarly, for GitHub, you'll need to register as a developer to be able to create an app and get API keys. SendGrid works via the Heroku add-on, so you obtain the username and password from the Heroku web interface.

The following is how my .env looks for v3.1.0 (with the keys replaced with placeholders), in which I have two sets of GitHub keys, one for the local app and one for the production (hackhall.com) app, because the callback URL for each of them is different. The callback URL is set on GitHub when you register the apps.

```
ANGELLIST_CLIENT_ID=AAAAAAAAAAAAAA
ANGELLIST_CLIENT_SECRET=AAAAAAAAAAAAAA
GITHUB_CLIENT_ID=AAAAAAAAAAAAAA
GITHUB_CLIENT_SECRET=AAAAAAAAAAAAAA
GITHUB_CLIENT_ID_LOCAL=AAAAAAAAAAAAAA
GITHUB_CLIENT_SECRET_LOCAL=AAAAAAAAAAAAAA
SENDGRID_USERNAME=AAAAAAAAAAAAAA@heroku.com
SENDGRID_PASSWORD=AAAAAAAAAAAAAA
COOKIE_SECRET=AAAAAAAAAAAAAA
SESSION_SECRET=AAAAAAAAAAAAAA
ANGELLIST_CLIENT_ID_LOCAL=AAAAAAAAAAAAAA
ANGELLIST_CLIENT_SECRET_LOCAL= AAAAAAAAAAAAAA
EMAIL=AAAAAAAAAAAAAA
```

Cookie and session secrets are used to encrypt the cookie (browser) and session (store) data.

Putting sensitive information into the environment variables allowed me to make the *entire* HackHall source code available to the public. I also have one more variable that I set in the Heroku web interface for this app (you can sync .env to/from the cloud with the Heroku config [https://devcenter.heroku.com/articles/config-vars] or use the web interface). This variable is NODE_ENV=production. I use it when I need to determine the GitHub app to use (local vs. the main live one).

Download and install MongoDB, if you don't have it already. The databases and third-party libraries are outside the scope of this book. However, you can find enough materials online (see, e.g., http://webapplog.com) and in the previously referenced *Rapid Prototyping with JS*. Before you launch the application, I recommend running the seed-script.js file or seed.js file to populate your database with information, as described next.

To seed the database hackhall with a default admin user by running the seed-script.js MongoDB script, enter

```
$ mongo localhost:27017/hackhall seed-script.js
```

Feel free to modify seed-script.js to your liking (be aware that doing so erases all previous data!). For example, use your bcryptjs hashed password (skip to the seed.js instructions for automated hashing of seed data). You'll see an example of hashing later.

First, we clean the database:

```
db.dropDatabase();
```

Then, we define an object with user information:

```
var seedUser ={
  firstName: 'Azat',
  lastName: 'Mardan',
  displayName: 'Azat Mardan',
  password: 'hashed password',
  email: '1@1.com',
  role: 'admin',
  approved: true,
  admin: true
};
```

Finally, save the object to the database using the MongoDB shell method:

```
db.users.save(seedUser);
```

Whereas `seed-script.js` is a MongoDB shell script, `seed.js` is a mini Node.js application to seed the database. You can run the Node.js database-seeding program with:

```
$ node seed.js
```

The `seed.js` program is more comprehensive (it has password hashing!) than the MongoDB shell script `seed-script.js`. We begin by importing the modules:

```
var bcrypt = require('bcryptjs');
var async = require('async');
var mongo =  require ('mongodb');
var objectId = mongo.ObjectID;
```

Similar to in `seed-script.js`, we define the user objects, only this time the passwords are plain/unhashed:

```
seedUsers = [{...},{...}];
```

The `seedUsers` array object might look like this (add your own user objects!):

```
{
  firstName:   "test",
  lastName:    "Account",
  displayName: "test Account",
  password:    "hashend password",
  email:       "1@1.com",
  role:        "user",
  admin: false,
  _id: objectId("503cf4730e9f580200000003"),
  photoUrl: "https://s3.amazonaws.com/photos.angel.co/users/68026-medium_jpg?1344297998",
  headline: "Test user 1",
  approved: true
}
```

This is the asynchronous function that will hash our plain passwords:

```
var hashPassword = function (user, callback) {
```

The bcryptjs module stores salts inside of the hashed passwords, so there's no need to store salts separately; 10 is the hashing complexity (the higher the better):

```
  bcrypt.hash(user.password, 10, function(error, hash) {
    if (error) throw error;
    user.password = hash;
    callback(null, user);
  });
};
```

Here, we define variables that we'll use later:

```
var db;
var invites;
var users;
var posts;
```

We connect to MongoDB with the native driver:

```
var dbUrl = process.env.MONGOHQ_URL || 'mongodb://@127.0.0.1:27017/hackhall';
mongo.Db.connect(dbUrl, function(error, client){
  if (error) throw error;
    else {
      db=client;
```

Next, we assign collections to objects and clean all the users, just in case:

```
      invites = new mongo.Collection(db, "invites");
      users = new mongo.Collection(db, "users");
      posts = new mongo.Collection(db, "posts");
      invites.remove(function(){});
      users.remove(function(){});
```

You can uncomment this line if you want this script to remove the posts as well:

```
      // posts.remove();
      invites.insert({code:'smrules'}, function(){});
```

Insert a dummy post (feel free to be creative here):

```
      posts.insert({
        title:'test',
        text:'testbody',
        author: {
         name:seedUsers[0].displayName,
         id:seedUsers[0]._id
         }
      }, function(){});
```

We use an asynchronous function, because hashing might be slow (that's a good thing, because slower hashes are harder to hack with brute force):

```
    async.map(seedUsers, hashPassword, function(error, result){
      console.log(result);
      seedUsers = result;
      users.insert(seedUsers, function(){});
      db.close();
    });
  }
});
```

To start the MongoDB server, open a new terminal window and run:

```
$ mongod
```

After MongoDB is running on localhost with default port 27017, go back to the project folder and run `foreman` (this command reads from Procfile):

```
$ foreman start
```

Or, you can use nodemon (`http://nodemon.io`; GitHub: `https://github.com/remy/nodemon`) with a more explicit `foreman` command:

```
$ foreman run nodemon server
```

If you open your browser to `http://localhost:3000`, you should see a login screen similar to that shown in Figure 22-1 (for v3.1.0).

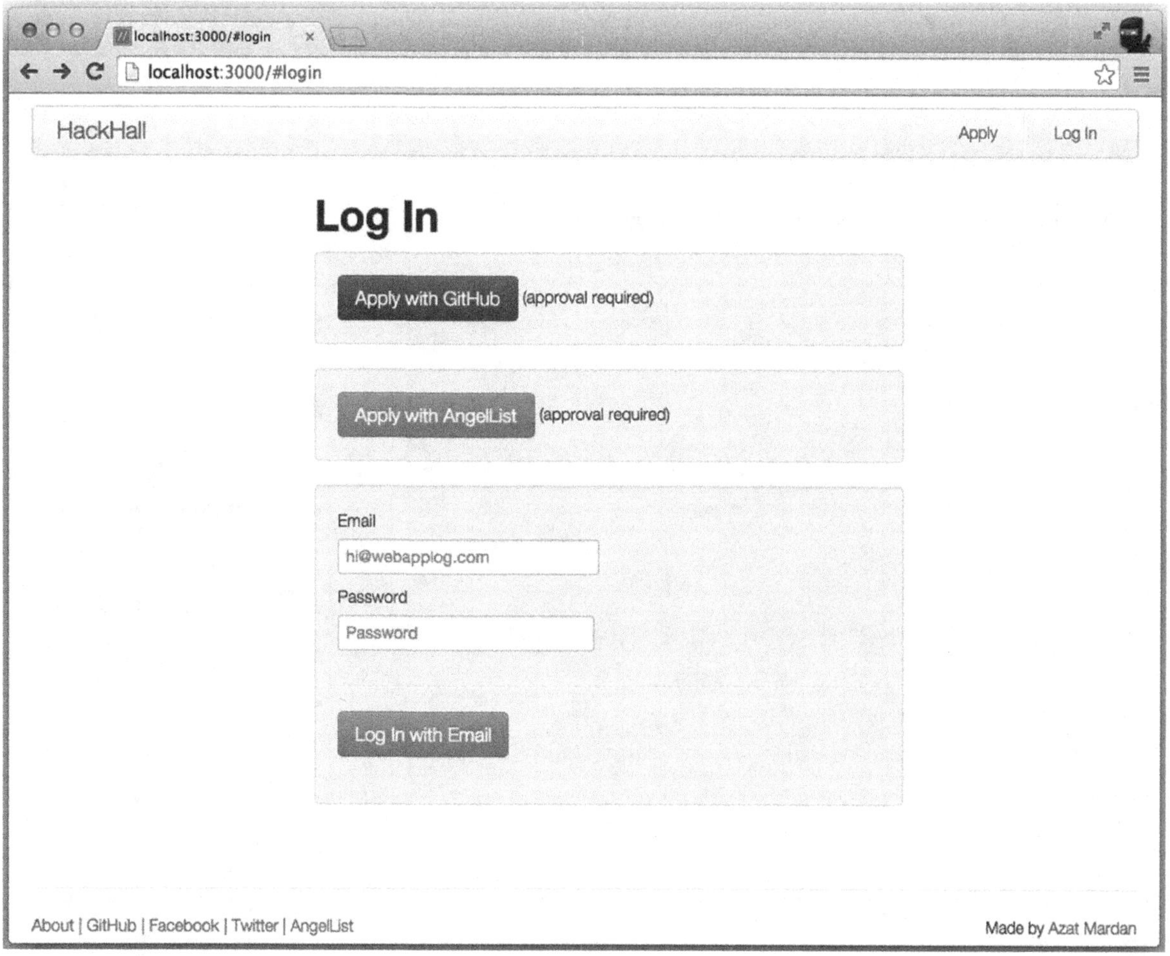

Figure 22-1. *HackHall v3.1.0 login page running locally*

Enter your username and password (the ones from your `seed.js` or `seed-script.js` file) to gain access. Use the unhashed (i.e., plain) version of the password.

After successful authentication, users are redirected to the Posts page, as shown Figure 22-2 (your data, such as post names, will be different; the "test" post is a byproduct of running Mocha tests).

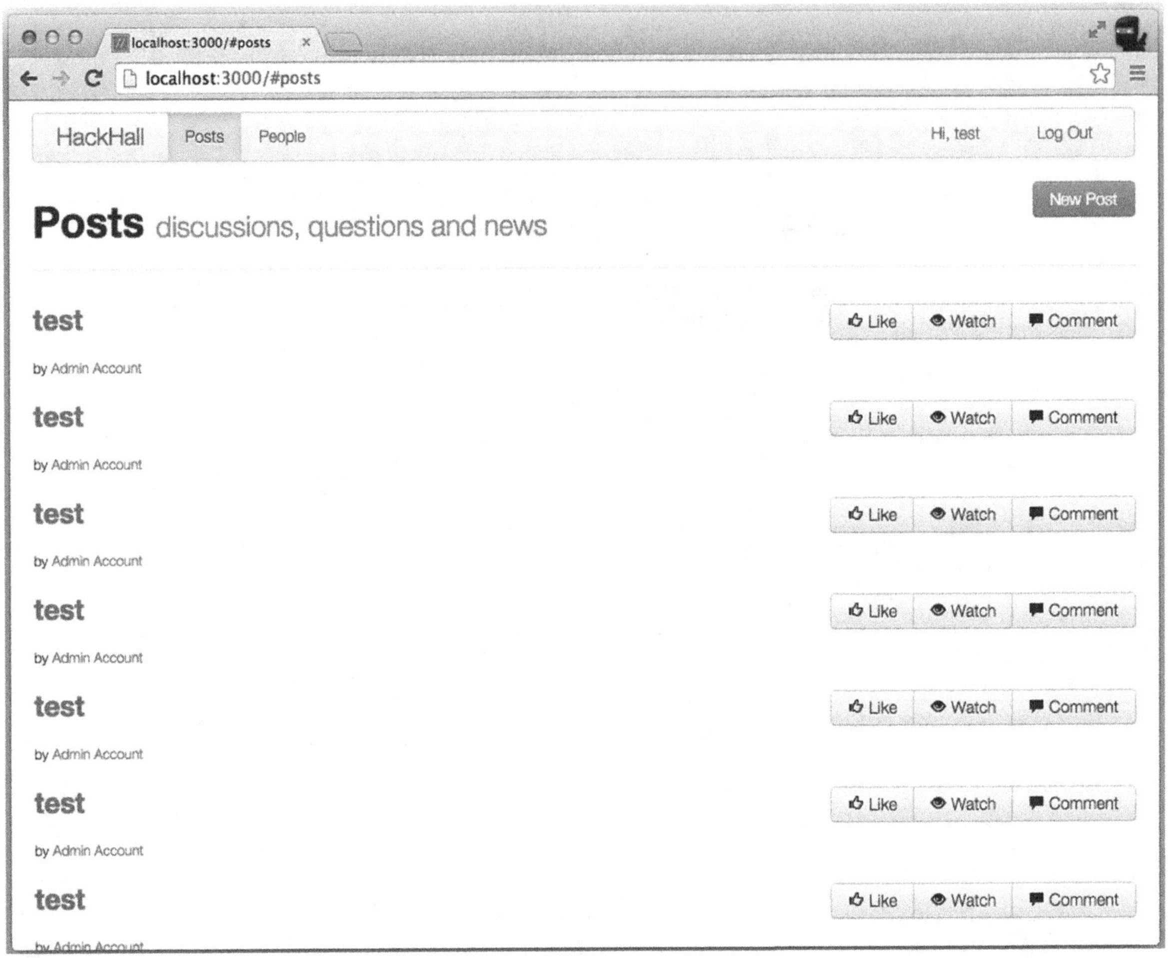

Figure 22-2. *HackHall Posts page*

If you click a "Like" button for a post, the "You like the post now!" message should be displayed and the Like counter should increase on that post, as shown in Figure 22-3. The same thing happens for the Watch buttons. Authors can edit and remove their own posts. Admins can edit and remove any posts. There are People and Profile pages, which you will see later in the chapter.

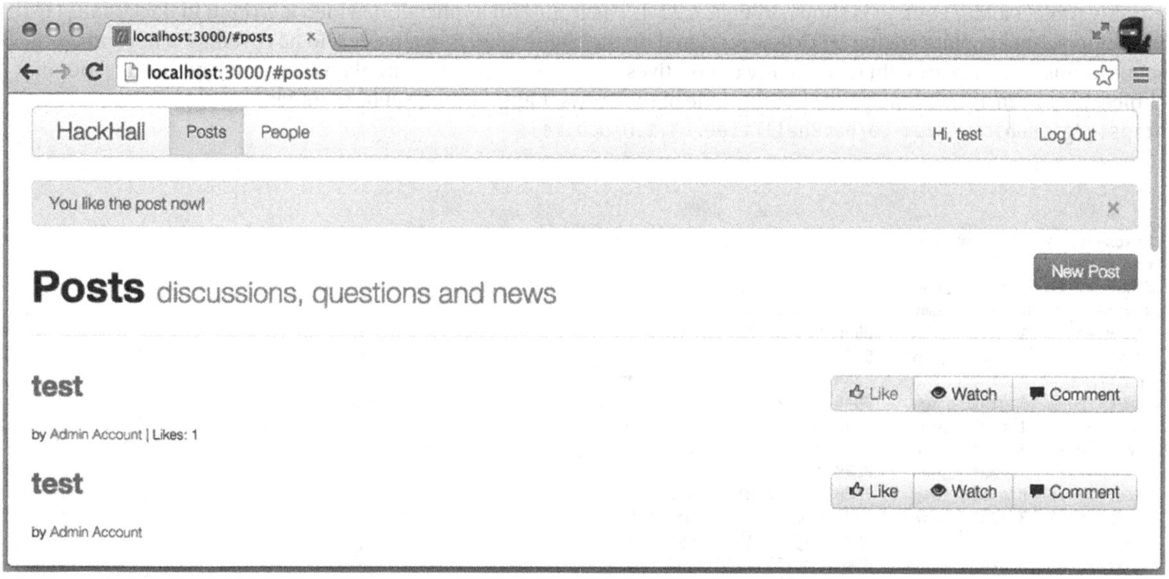

Figure 22-3. *HackHall Posts page with a liked post*

So, now you've seen how HackHall v3.1.0 might look right out of the box on your local machine. The following sections will walk you through some of the concepts and patterns that were used when implementing this application. This chapter is less detailed than previous chapters, because I'm assuming that you're already familiar with the topics covered in those chapters; repeating all the details would take too much space and would likely bore you.

Structure

Here is the structure of HackHall and a brief description of what each of the folders and files contains:

- `/api`: App-shared routes
- `/models`: Mongoose models
- `/public`: Backbone app, static files, such as front-end JavaScript, CSS, and HTML
- `/routes`: REST API routes
- `/tests`: Mocha tests
- `/lib`: Internal (in-house) libraries
- `.gitignore`: List of files that `git` should ignore
- `Makefile`: Makefile to run tests
- `Procfile`: Cedar stack file needed for Heroku deployment
- `package.json`: NPM dependencies and HackHall metadata
- `readme.md`: Description of project
- `server.js`: Main HackHall server file
- `.env`: Secret values that you don't want to share or leak to others

My project folder content is shown in Figure 22-4. The front-end application, which is written in Backbone.js with the Underscore template engine (HTML is rendered on the client side), is extensive and its coverage is beyond the scope of this book, because there are many alternatives to Backbone.js (with Angular.js being one of the most popular choices). You can always look up the source code of the browser app from the `public` folder: `https://github.com/azat-co/hackhall/tree/v3.1.0/public`.

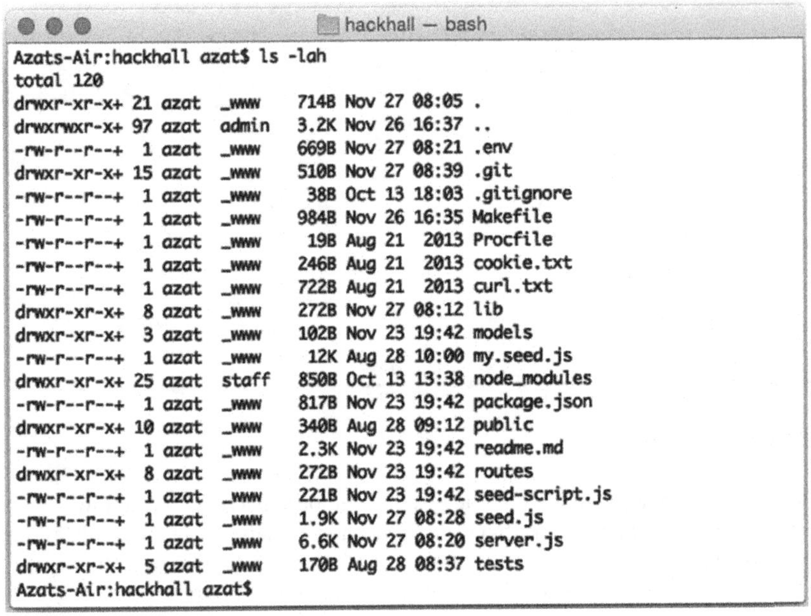

hackhall — bash
Azats-Air:hackhall azat$ ls -lah
total 120
drwxr-xr-x+ 21 azat _www 714B Nov 27 08:05 .
drwxrwxr-x+ 97 azat admin 3.2K Nov 26 16:37 ..
-rw-r--r--+ 1 azat _www 669B Nov 27 08:21 .env
drwxr-xr-x+ 15 azat _www 510B Nov 27 08:39 .git
-rw-r--r--+ 1 azat _www 38B Oct 13 18:03 .gitignore
-rw-r--r--+ 1 azat _www 984B Nov 26 16:35 Makefile
-rw-r--r--+ 1 azat _www 19B Aug 21 2013 Procfile
-rw-r--r--+ 1 azat _www 246B Aug 21 2013 cookie.txt
-rw-r--r--+ 1 azat _www 722B Aug 21 2013 curl.txt
drwxr-xr-x+ 8 azat _www 272B Nov 27 08:12 lib
drwxr-xr-x+ 3 azat _www 102B Nov 23 19:42 models
-rw-r--r--+ 1 azat _www 12K Aug 28 10:00 my.seed.js
drwxr-xr-x+ 25 azat staff 850B Oct 13 13:38 node_modules
-rw-r--r--+ 1 azat _www 817B Nov 23 19:42 package.json
drwxr-xr-x+ 10 azat _www 340B Aug 28 09:12 public
-rw-r--r--+ 1 azat _www 2.3K Nov 23 19:42 readme.md
drwxr-xr-x+ 8 azat _www 272B Nov 23 19:42 routes
-rw-r--r--+ 1 azat _www 221B Nov 23 19:42 seed-script.js
-rw-r--r--+ 1 azat _www 1.9K Nov 27 08:28 seed.js
-rw-r--r--+ 1 azat _www 6.6K Nov 27 08:20 server.js
drwxr-xr-x+ 5 azat _www 170B Aug 28 08:37 tests
Azats-Air:hackhall azat$

Figure 22-4. *Content of the HackHall base folder*

Package.json

As always, let's start with the `package.json` file and dependencies. The "new" libraries that we haven't used previously in this book are `passport` (OAuth integration), `sendgrid` (e-mail notifications), `mongoose` (MondoDB ORM/ODM), and `bcryptjs` (password hashing). Everything else should be familiar to you. We'll be using Express.js middleware modules and utilities (async, mocha).

This is what `package.json` looks like (use newer versions at your own discretion):

```
{
  "name": "hackhall",
  "version": "3.1.0",
  "private": true,
  "main": "server",
  "scripts": {
    "start": "node server",
    "test": "make test"
  },
  "dependencies": {
    "async": "0.9.0",
    "bcryptjs": "2.0.2",
    "body-parser": "1.6.6",
```

```
    "cookie-parser": "1.3.2",
    "csurf": "1.5.0",
    "errorhandler": "1.1.1",
    "express": "4.8.1",
    "express-session": "1.7.6",
    "method-override": "2.1.3",
    "mongodb": "1.4.9",
    "mongoose": "3.8.15",
    "mongoose-findorcreate": "0.1.2",
    "mongoskin": "1.4.4",
    "morgan": "1.2.3",
    "oauth": "0.9.12",
    "passport": "0.2.0",
    "passport-github": "0.1.5",
    "sendgrid": "1.2.0",
    "serve-favicon": "2.1.1"
  },
```

The devDependencies category is for modules that you don't need in production:

```
  "devDependencies": {
    "mocha": "1.21.4",
    "superagent": "0.18.2"
  },
  "engines": {
    "node": "0.10.x"
  }
}
```

Express.js App

Let's jump straight to the server.js file and take a look at how it's implemented. First, we declare dependencies:

```
var express = require('express'),
  routes = require('./routes'),
  http = require('http'),
  util = require('util'),
  path = require('path'),
  oauth = require('oauth'),
  querystring = require('querystring');
```

Next, we do the same for the Express.js middleware modules (no need for a separate var, except to show the difference in purpose of the modules):

```
var favicon = require('serve-favicon'),
  logger = require('morgan'),
  bodyParser = require('body-parser'),
  methodOverride = require('method-override'),
  cookieParser = require('cookie-parser'),
  session = require('express-session'),
  csrf = require('csurf');
```

Next, we have an internal e-mail library that uses SendGrid via a Heroku add-on:

```
var hs = require(path.join(__dirname, 'lib', 'hackhall-sendgrid'));
```

The log messages with different font colors are nice to have, but are, of course, optional. We accomplish this coloring with escape sequences in `lib/colors.js`:

```
var c = require(path.join(__dirname, 'lib', 'colors'));
require(path.join(__dirname, 'lib', 'env-vars'));
```

Passport (`http://passportjs.org`, `https://www.npmjs.org/package/passport`, `https://github.com/jaredhanson/passport`) is for GitHub OAuth. Using `passport` is a higher-level approach of implementing OAuth than using `oauth`:

```
var GitHubStrategy = require('passport-github').Strategy,
  passport = require('passport');
```

Then, we initialize the app and configure middleware. The `process.env.PORT` environment variable is populated by Heroku, and in the case of a local setup, falls back on `3000`. The rest of the configuration should be familiar to you from Chapter 4.

```
app.set('port', process.env.PORT || 3000  );
app.use(favicon(path.join(__dirname,'public','favicon.ico')));
app.use(logger('dev'));
app.use(bodyParser.json());
app.use(bodyParser.urlencoded({extended: true}));
app.use(methodOverride());
```

The values passed to `cookieParser` and session middleware are needed for authentication. Obviously, these secrets are supposed to be private:

```
app.use(cookieParser(process.env.COOKIE_SECRET));
app.use(session({
  secret: process.env.SESSION_SECRET,
  key: 'sid',
  cookie: {
    secret: true,
    expires: false
  },
  resave: true,
  saveUninitialized: true
}));
```

This is how we serve our front-end client Backbone.js app and other static files, such as CSS:

```
app.use(express.static(__dirname + '/public'));
```

Error handling is broken down into three functions, with `clientErrorHandler()` dedicated to AJAX/XHR requests from the Backbone.js app (responds with JSON). Right now, we only declare the functions. We'll apply them with `app.use()` later.

The first method, logErrors(), checks if err is a string and, if it is, creates an Error object. Then, the execution goes to the next error handler.

```
function logErrors(err, req, res, next) {
  if (typeof err === 'string')
    err = new Error (err);
  console.error('logErrors', err.toString());
  next(err);
}
```

As previously mentioned, clientErrorHandler is dedicated to AJAX/XHR requests from the Backbone.js app (responds with JSON) by checking req.xhr, and it will send a JSON message back or go to the next handler:

```
function clientErrorHandler(err, req, res, next) {
  if (req.xhr) {
    console.error('clientErrors response');
    res.status(500).json({ error: err.toString()});
  } else {
    next(err);
  }
}
```

The last error handler, errorHandler(), will assume that the request is not AJAX/XHR (otherwise clientErrorHandler() would have caught it, but this order will be defined later with app.use()), and will send a string back:

```
function errorHandler(err, req, res, next) {
  console.error('lastErrors response');
  res.status(500).send(err.toString());
}
```

Recall that we determine process.env.PORT and fall back on local setup value 3000 using ||. We do a similar thing with a MongoDB connection string. We pull the Heroku add-on URI string from the environment variable or fall back to local settings:

```
var dbUrl = process.env.MONGOHQ_URL
  || 'mongodb://@127.0.0.1:27017/hackhall';
var mongoose = require('mongoose');
```

Now, we create a connection:

```
var connection = mongoose.createConnection(dbUrl);
connection.on('error', console.error.bind(console,
  'connection error:'));
```

Sometimes it's a good idea to log the connection open event:

```
connection.once('open', function () {
  console.info('Connected to database')
});
```

The Mongoose models live in the `models` folder:

```
var models = require('./models');
```

This middleware will provide access to two collections within our route methods:

```
function db (req, res, next) {
  req.db = {
    User: connection.model('User', models.User, 'users'),
    Post: connection.model('Post', models.Post, 'posts')
  };
  return next();
}
```

The lines below are just new names for the imported `routes/main.js` file authorization functions:

```
var checkUser = routes.main.checkUser;
var checkAdmin = routes.main.checkAdmin;
var checkApplicant = routes.main.checkApplicant;
```

We then move onto the AngelList OAuth routes for AngelList login. This is a standard, three-legged OAuth 1.0 strategy where we initiate the auth (`/auth/angellist`), redirect users to the service provider (AngelList), and then wait for the user to come back from the service provider (`/auth/angellist`):

```
app.get('/auth/angellist', routes.auth.angelList);
app.get('/auth/angellist/callback',
  routes.auth.angelListCallback,
  routes.auth.angelListLogin,
  db,
  routes.users.findOrAddUser);
```

■ **Tip** For more information on OAuth and Node.js OAuth examples, take a look at my book *Introduction to OAuth with Node.js* (2014), available at `https://gumroad.com/l/oauthnode`.

The next few lines of code deal with Passport and GitHub login logic. Implementing OAuth using Passport requires less manual effort than using the OAuth module.

Let's skip to the main application routes, starting with `app.get('/api/profile')`. The `api/profile` is used by the Backbone.js app, and it returns a user session, if the user is logged in. The request travels via `checkUser` and `db`, with the former authorizing and the latter populating the database info.

```
// MAIN
app.get('/api/profile', checkUser, db, routes.main.profile);
app.delete('/api/profile', checkUser, db, routes.main.delProfile);
app.post('/api/login', db, routes.main.login);
app.post('/api/logout', routes.main.logout);
```

The Posts and Users collections routes are for manipulating with posts and users:

```
// POSTS
app.get('/api/posts', checkUser, db, routes.posts.getPosts);
app.post('/api/posts', checkUser, db, routes.posts.add);
app.get('/api/posts/:id', checkUser, db, routes.posts.getPost);
app.put('/api/posts/:id', checkUser, db, routes.posts.updatePost);
app.delete('/api/posts/:id', checkUser, db, routes.posts.del);

// USERS
app.get('/api/users', checkUser, db, routes.users.getUsers);
app.get('/api/users/:id', checkUser, db,routes.users.getUser);
app.post('/api/users', checkAdmin, db, routes.users.add);
app.put('/api/users/:id', checkAdmin, db, routes.users.update);
app.delete('/api/users/:id', checkAdmin, db, routes.users.del);
```

These routes are for new members that haven't been approved yet (i.e., they've submitted an application):

```
//APPLICATION
app.post('/api/application', checkAdmin, db, routes.application.add);
app.put('/api/application', checkApplicant, db, routes.application.update);
app.get('/api/application', checkApplicant, db, routes.application.get);
```

The following is the catch-all-else route:

```
app.get('*', function(req, res){
  res.status(404).send();
});
```

We apply the error handlers in the order in which we want them to be called:

```
app.use(logErrors);
app.use(clientErrorHandler);
app.use(errorHandler);
```

The `require.main === module` is a clever trick to determine if this file is being executed as a stand-alone or as an imported module:

```
http.createServer(app);
if (require.main === module) {
  app.listen(app.get('port'), function(){
```

We show the blue log message:

```
    console.info(c.blue + 'Express server listening on port '
      + app.get('port') + c.reset);
  });
}
else {
  console.info(c.blue + 'Running app as a module' + c.reset)
  exports.app = app;
}
```

To save space, I won't list the full source code for `hackhall/server.js`, but you can view it at `https://github.com/azat-co/hackhall/blob/v3.1.0/server.js`.

Routes

The HackHall routes reside in the hackhall/routes folder and are grouped into several modules:

- hackhall/routes/index.js: Bridge between server.js and other routes in the folder
- hackhall/routes/auth.js: Routes that handle the OAuth "dance" with the AngelList API
- hackhall/routes/main.js: Login, logout, and other routes
- hackhall/routes/users.js: Routes related to users' REST API
- hackhall/routes/application.js: Routes that handle submission of an application to become a user
- hackhall/routes/posts.js: Routes related to posts' REST API

index.js

Let's peek into hackhall/routes/index.js, where we've included other modules:

```
exports.posts = require('./posts');
exports.main = require('./main');
exports.users = require('./users');
exports.application = require('./application');
exports.auth = require('./auth');
```

auth.js

In this module, we handle the OAuth dance with the AngelList API. To do so, we rely on the https library:

```
var https = require('https');
```

The AngelList API client ID and client secret are obtained at https://angel.co/api and stored in environment variables. I added two applications: one for local development and the other for production, as shown in Figure 22-5. The app picks one of them, based on the environment:

```
if (process.env.NODE_ENV === 'production') {
  var angelListClientId = process.env.ANGELLIST_CLIENT_ID;
  var angelListClientSecret = process.env.ANGELLIST_CLIENT_SECRET;
} else {
  var angelListClientId = process.env.ANGELLIST_CLIENT_ID_LOCAL;
  var angelListClientSecret = process.env.ANGELLIST_CLIENT_SECRET_LOCAL;
}
```

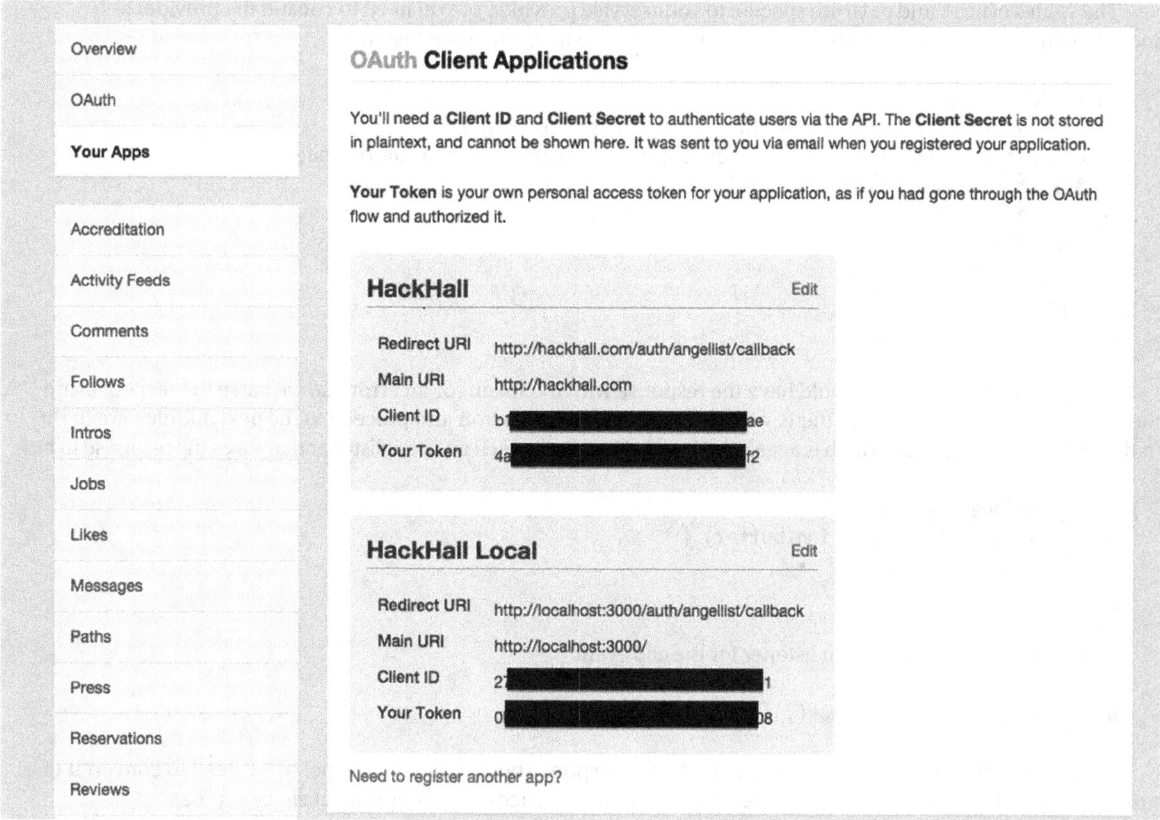

Figure 22-5. *My AngelList apps*

The `exports.angelList()` method will redirect users to the `https://angel.co/api` web site for authentication. This method is invoked when we navigate to `/auth/angellist`. The request's structure is described in the documentation at `https://angel.co/api/oauth/faq`.

```
exports.angelList = function(req, res) {
  res.redirect('https://angel.co/api/oauth/authorize?client_id=' + angelListClientId +
'&scope=email&response_type=code');
}
```

After users allow our app to access their information, AngelList sends them back to this route to allow us to make a new (HTTPS) request to retrieve the token:

```
exports.angelListCallback = function(req, res, next) {
  var token;
  var buf = '';
  var data;
  var angelReq = https.request({
```

The values of host and path are specific to your service provider, so you need to consult the provider's documentation when you implement OAuth. These are the values for AngelList API:

```
host: 'angel.co',
path: '/api/oauth/token?client_id=' + angelListClientId +
  '&client_secret=' + angelListClientSecret + '&code=' + req.query.code +
  '&grant_type=authorization_code',
port: 443,
method: 'POST',
headers: {
  'content-length': 0
}
```

At this point, the callback should have the response with the token (or an error), so we parse the response and check for the access_token. If it's there, we save the token in the session and proceed to the next middleware in the /auth/angellist/callback, which is angelListLogin. First, let's attach an event listener that saves the response in buf:

```
}, function(angelRes) {
  angelRes.on('data', function(buffer) {
    buf += buffer;
  });
```

Then, we attach another event listener for the end event:

```
  angelRes.on('end', function() {
```

The buf object at this moment should have the full response body in a Buffer type, so we need to convert it to a string type and parse. The data should have only two properties, access_token and token_type ('bearer'):

```
    try {
      data = JSON.parse(buf.toString('utf-8'));
    } catch (e) {
      if (e) return next(e);
    }
```

Let's check for the access_token to be 100% sure:

```
    if (!data || !data.access_token) return  next(new Error('No data from AngelList'));
    token = data.access_token;
```

Now, we can save token in a session and call the next middleware:

```
    req.session.angelListAccessToken = token;
    if (token) {
      next();
    }
    else {
      next(new Error('No token from AngelList'));
    }
  });
});
```

The rest of the request code finishes the request and deals with an error event:

```
  angelReq.end();
  angelReq.on('error', function(e) {
    console.error(e);
    next(e);
  });
}
```

So, the user has been granted access to our AngelList app and we have the token (angelListCallback). Now, we can get the user profile information by directly calling the AngelList API with the token from the previous middleware (angelListLogin). The order of the middleware functions is dictated by the route /auth/angellist/callback, so we begin angelListLogin with the HTTPS request:

```
exports.angelListLogin = function(req, res, next) {
  var token = req.session.angelListAccessToken;
  httpsRequest = https.request({
    host: 'api.angel.co',
```

Again, the exact URL is different for each service:

```
    path: '/1/me?access_token=' + token,
    port: 443,
    method: 'GET'
  },
  function(httpsResponse) {
    var userBuffer = '';
    httpsResponse.on('data', function(buffer) {
      userBuffer += buffer;
    });
```

The next event listener will parse the buffer-type object into the normal JavaScript/Node.js object:

```
    httpsResponse.on('end', function(){
      try {
        data = JSON.parse(userBuffer.toString('utf-8'));
      } catch (e) {
        if (e) return next(e);
      }
```

At this point in the execution, the system should have data fields filled with the user information (/1/me?access_token=... endpoint). You can see an example of such response data in Figure 22-6.

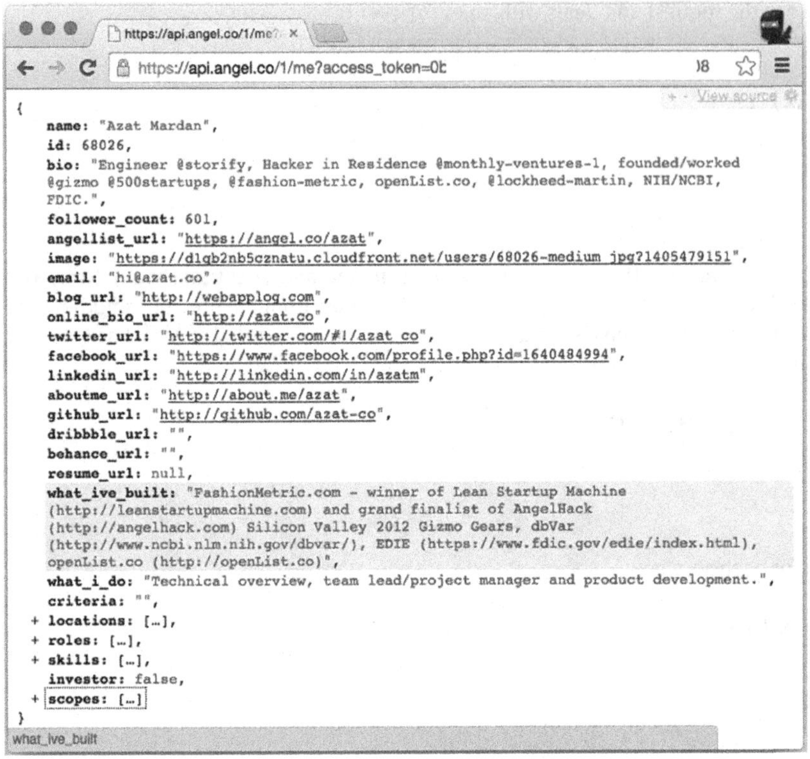

Figure 22-6. *Example of the AngelList user info response*

We still have to check whether the object is empty or not and, if it's not empty, we save the user data on the request object:

```
        if (data) {
          req.angelProfile = data;
          next();
        } else
          next(new Error('No data from AngelList'));
        });
      }
    );
    httpsRequest.end();
    httpsRequest.on('error', function(e) {
      console.error(e);
    });
};
```

The full source code for the `hackhall/routes/auth.js` file at the time of this writing is at `https://github.com/azat-co/hackhall/blob/v3.1.0/routes/auth.js` (which is subject to change as the HackHall version evolves).

main.js

The hackhall/routes/main.js file is also interesting, because it has these methods:

- checkAdmin()
- checkUser()
- checkApplicant()
- login()
- logout()
- profile()
- delProfile()

The checkAdmin() function performs authentication for admin privileges. If the session object doesn't carry the proper flag, we call the Express.js next() function with an error object:

```
exports.checkAdmin = function(request, response, next) {
  if (request.session
    && request.session.auth
    && request.session.userId
    && request.session.admin) {
    console.info('Access ADMIN: ' + request.session.userId);
    return next();
  } else {
    next('User is not an administrator.');
  }
};
```

Similarly, we can check for only the approved user without checking for admin rights:

```
exports.checkUser = function(req, res, next) {
  if (req.session && req.session.auth && req.session.userId
    && (req.session.user.approved || req.session.admin)) {
    console.info('Access USER: ' + req.session.userId);
    return next();
  } else {
    next('User is not logged in.');
  }
};
```

If an application is just an unapproved user object, we can also check for that:

```
exports.checkApplicant = function(req, res, next) {
  if (req.session && req.session.auth && req.session.userId
    && (!req.session.user.approved || req.session.admin)) {
    console.info('Access USER: ' + req.session.userId);
    return next();
  } else {
    next('User is not logged in.');
  }
};
```

In the login function, we search for e-mail. Because we don't store the plain password in the database—we store only its encrypted hash—we need to compare the password hashes using bcryptjs. Upon a successful match, we store the user object in the session, set the auth flag to true (req.session.auth = true), and proceed. Otherwise, the request fails:

```
var bcrypt = require('bcryptjs');
exports.login = function(req, res, next) {
  console.log('Logging in USER with email:', req.body.email)
  req.db.User.findOne({
      email: req.body.email
    },null, {
      safe: true
    }, function(err, user) {
      if (err) return next(err);
      if (user) {
```

We use the asynchronous bcryptjs method compare(), which returns true, if the plain password matches the saved hashed password:

```
        bcrypt.compare(req.body.password, user.password, function(err, match) {
          if (match) {
```

So, all is good: the system assigns session flags and saves user info in the session. These values will be used on all auth-required (protected) routes to identify the user:

```
            req.session.auth = true;
            req.session.userId = user._id.toHexString();
            req.session.user = user;
```

There's a separate boolean for admins:

```
            if (user.admin) {
              req.session.admin = true;
            }
            console.info('Login USER: ' + req.session.userId);
```

The JSON {msg: 'Authorized'} object is an arbitrary convention that you can customize, but you must keep it the same on the server and the client (to check the server response):

```
            res.status(200).json({
              msg: 'Authorized'
            });
          } else {
            next(new Error('Wrong password'));
          }
        });
      } else {
        next(new Error('User is not found.'));
      }
    });
};
```

The logging-out process removes any session information:

```
exports.logout = function(req, res) {
  console.info('Logout USER: ' + req.session.userId);
  req.session.destroy(function(error) {
    if (!error) {
      res.send({
        msg: 'Logged out'
      });
    }
  });
};
```

This route is used for the Profile page, as well as by Backbone.js for user authentication:

```
exports.profile = function(req, res, next) {
```

We don't want to expose all the user fields, so we whitelist only the fields that we want to get:

```
  var fields = 'firstName lastName displayName' +
    ' headline photoUrl admin approved banned' +
    ' role angelUrl twitterUrl facebookUrl linkedinUrl githubUrl';
```

This is a custom method created via Mongoose functionality for the reason that it has quite extensive logic and is called more than once:

```
  req.db.User.findProfileById(req.session.userId, fields, function(err, obj) {
    if (err) next(err);
    res.status(200).json(obj);
  });
};
```

It's important to allow users to delete their profiles. We utilize the `findByIdAndRemove()` method and remove the session with `destroy()`:

```
exports.delProfile = function(req, res, next) {
  console.log('del profile');
  console.log(req.session.userId);
  req.db.User.findByIdAndRemove(req.session.user._id, {},
    function(err, obj) {
      if (err) next(err);
      req.session.destroy(function(error) {
        if (err) {
          next(err)
        }
      });
      res.status(200).json(obj);
    }
  );
};
```

The full source code of the `hackhall/routes/main.js` file is available at `https://github.com/azat-co/hackhall/blob/v3.1.0/routes/main.js`.

users.js

The routes/users.js file is responsible for the RESTful activities related to User collections. We have these methods:

- getUsers()
- getUser()
- add()
- update()
- del()
- findOrAddUser()

First, we define some variables:

```
var path = require('path'),
  hs = require(path.join(__dirname, '..', 'lib', 'hackhall-sendgrid'));

var objectId = require('mongodb').ObjectID;

var safeFields = 'firstName lastName displayName headline photoUrl admin approved banned role
angelUrl twitterUrl facebookUrl linkedinUrl githubUrl';
```

Then, we define the method getUsers(), which retrieves a list of users where each item has only the properties from the safeFields string:

```
exports.getUsers = function(req, res, next) {
  if (req.session.auth && req.session.userId) {
    req.db.User.find({}, safeFields, function(err, list) {
      if (err) return next(err);
      res.status(200).json(list);
    });
  } else {
    return next('User is not recognized.')
  }
}
```

The getUser() method is used on the user profile page. For administrators (the current user, not the user we fetch), we add an extra field, email, and invoke the custom static method findProfileById():

```
exports.getUser = function(req, res, next) {
  var fields = safeFields;
  if (req.session.admin) {
    fields = fields + ' email';
  }
  req.db.User.findProfileById(req.params.id, fields, function(err, data){
    if (err) return next(err);
    res.status(200).json(data);
  })
}
```

To see the `getUser()` method in action, you can navigate to a user profile page, as shown in Figure 22-7. Admins can manage users' accounts on the Profile page. So, if you're an admin, you'll see an extra Role drop-down that sets the role for this user.

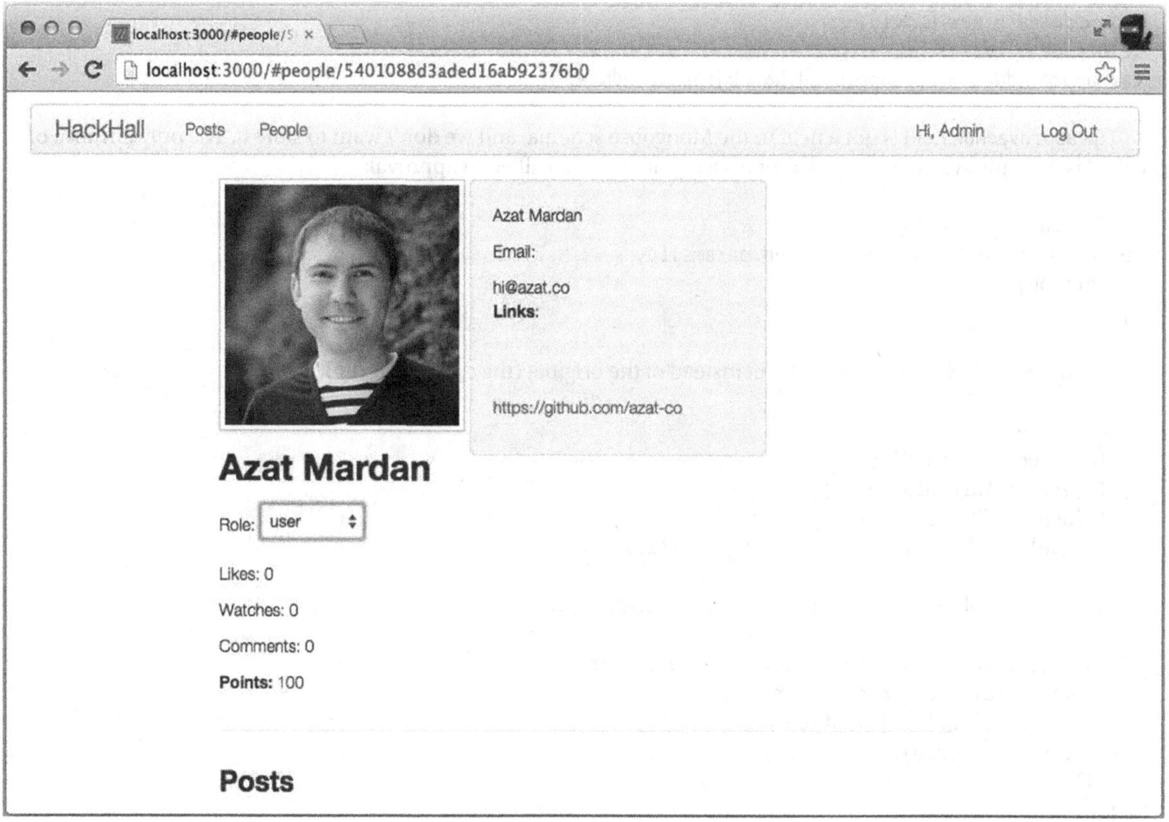

***Figure 22-7.** HackHall Profile page when logged in as admin*

The `add()` method is straightforward:

```
exports.add = function(req, res, next) {
  var user = new req.db.User(req.body);
  user.save(function(err) {
    if (err) next(err);
    res.json(user);
  });
};
```

The update() method is also used for the approval of new users (approvedNow == true). In case of success, we send an e-mail using the internal method notifyApproved() from the lib/hackhall-sendgrid.js file:

```
exports.update = function(req, res, next) {
var obj = req.body;
  obj.updated = new Date();
  delete obj._id;
  var approvedNow = obj.approved && obj.approvedNow;
```

The approvedNow field is not a field in the Mongoose schema, and we don't want to store it. The only purpose of the field is to let the system know whether it's a regular update call or an approval:

```
  delete obj.approvedNow;
  req.db.User.findByIdAndUpdate(req.params.id, {
    $set: obj
  }, {
```

This option will give us the new object instead of the original (the default is true):

```
    new: true
  }, function(err, user) {
    if (err) return next(err);
    if (approvedNow && user.approved) {
      console.log('Approved... sending notification!');
```

So, the approval went successfully and we can send an e-mail:

```
      hs.notifyApproved(user, function(error, user){
        if (error) return next(error);
        console.log('Notification was sent.');
        res.status(200).json(user);
      })
    } else {
```

If it was a regular update, and not an approval, then we just send back the user object:

```
      res.status(200).json(user);
    }
  });
};
```

Figure 22-8 shows how approval looks in the user interface, when you're logged in with admin rights. There is a drop-down menu that admins can use to approve, delete, or ban applicants.

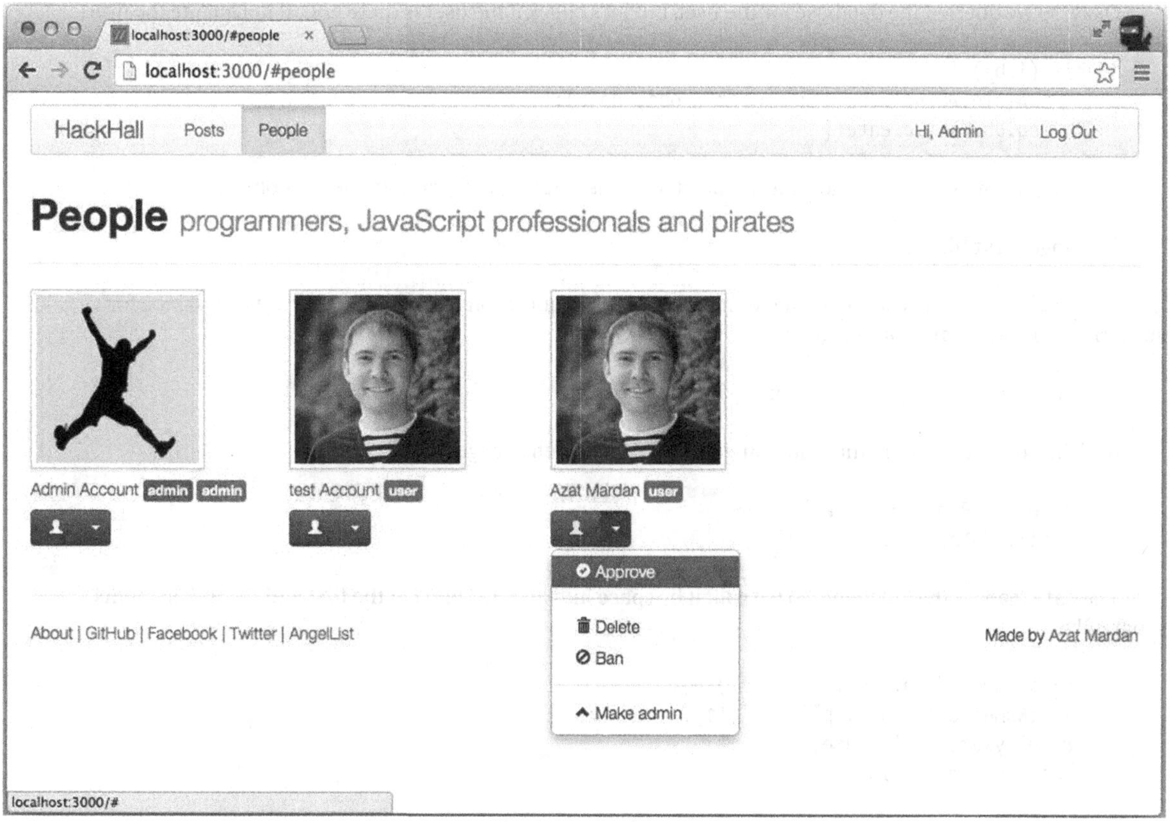

Figure 22-8. *HackHall People page with admin rights (logged in as admin)*

To delete a user, we call `findByIdAndRemove()`:

```
exports.del = function(req, res, next) {
  req.db.User.findByIdAndRemove(req.params.id, function(err, obj) {
    if (err) next(err);
    res.status(200).json(obj);
  });
};
```

Lastly, the `findOrAddUser()` method is employed when a user logs in with AngelList. You can use `findOrCreate` supplied by the plug-in (and that's what is used in the GitHub OAuth flow), but for the sake of learning, it's good to know how to implement the same functionality on your own. It will also reinforce your asynchronous way of thinking and your understanding of how to refactor code when you compare `findOrCreate` with this function:

```
exports.findOrAddUser = function(req, res, next) {
  var data = req.angelProfile;
  req.db.User.findOne({
    angelListId: data.id
  }, function(err, obj) {
    console.log('angelList Login findOrAddUser');
    if (err) return next(err);
```

Okay, so we queried the database for the user, but let's check if the user is there and, if not, create the user:

```
if (!obj) {
  console.warn('Creating a user', obj, data);
  req.db.User.create({
```

We map/normalize all the fields that we need from the AngelList response to the user object.

```
angelListId: data.id,
```

This token is what we can use to make subsequent API requests on behalf of the user without asking for authorization and permissions each time:

```
angelToken: req.session.angelListAccessToken,
```

And, just in case, we store the whole AngelList object as well in `angelListProfile`:

```
angelListProfile: data,
email: data.email,
```

The `data.name` is the full name, so we split it by space into an array and get the first and second elements separately:

```
firstName: data.name.split(' ')[0],
lastName: data.name.split(' ')[1],
displayName: data.name,
headline: data.bio,
```

The image is just a URL to the file, not a binary field:

```
    photoUrl: data.image,
    angelUrl: data.angellist_url,
    twitterUrl: data.twitter_url,
    facebookUrl: data.facebook_url,
    linkedinUrl: data.linkedin_url,
    githubUrl: data.github_url
  }, function(err, obj) {
    if (err) return next(err);
console.log('User was created', obj);
```

Okay, so the user document has been successfully created. But the system must log in the user right away, so we set the `session` flag to `true`:

```
req.session.auth = true;
```

We need to save the newly created user ID in the session so that we can use it on other requests from this client:

```
req.session.userId = obj._id;
req.session.user = obj;
```

The admin needs to be promoted by another admin. The default database value for new users is taken care of by the Mongoose schema (with the default of `false`). However, the session value needs to be set here, so we authenticate as a regular user by default:

```
      req.session.admin = false;
      res.redirect('/#application');
      }
    );
  } else {
```

When the user document is in the database, we just log in the user and redirect either to posts or their membership application:

```
        req.session.auth = true;
        req.session.userId = obj._id;
        req.session.user = obj;
        req.session.admin = obj.admin;
        if (obj.approved) {
          res.redirect('/#posts');
        } else {
          res.redirect('/#application');
        }
      }
    })
  }
```

The full source code for the `hackhall/routes/users.js` file is available at `https://github.com/azat-co/hackhall/blob/v3.1.0/routes/users.js`.

`users.js` provides functionality to the REST API routes of the People page that allows a user to visit other users' profiles, as shown in Figure 22-9. In that screenshot, the first Azat's profile is from seeding the database. The second Azat's profile is from my logging in with GitHub.

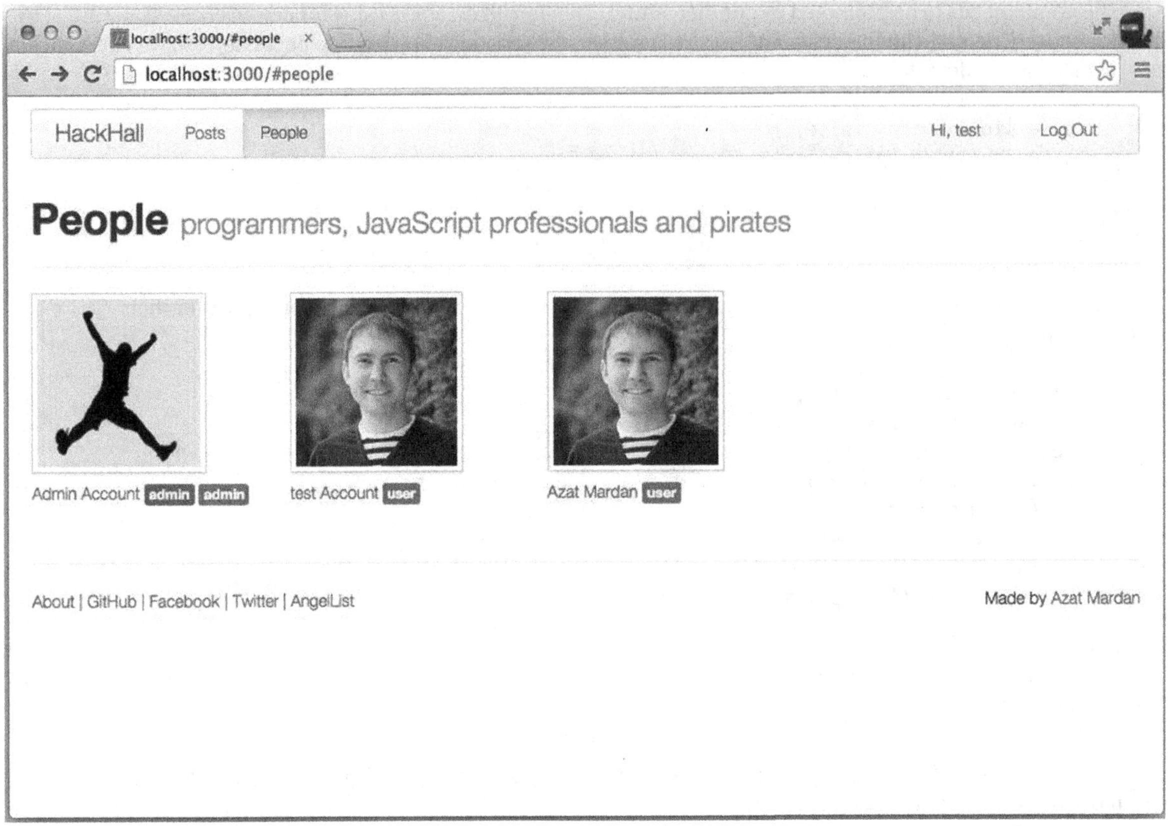

Figure 22-9. *HackHall People page*

application.js

The `hackhall/routes/application.js` file ("application" in the sense of applying, not as in app!) deals with new users applying to join the HackHall community. They need to be approved to ensure that only real and serious members join HackHall.com. In your local version, you might want to suppress the e-mail notifications regarding submitting and approving of an application.

Merely to add a user object (with `approved=false` by default) to the database (e-mail membership application), we use this method:

```
exports.add = function(req, res, next) {
  req.db.User.create({
    firstName: req.body.firstName,
    lastName: req.body.lastName,
    displayName: req.body.displayName,
    headline: req.body.headline,
    photoUrl: req.body.photoUrl,
    password: req.body.password,
    email: req.body.email,
    angelList: {
      blah: 'blah'
    },
```

```
    angelUrl: req.body.angelUrl,
    twitterUrl: req.body.twitterUrl,
    facebookUrl: req.body.facebookUrl,
    linkedinUrl: req.body.linkedinUrl,
    githubUrl: req.body.githubUrl
  }, function(err, obj) {
    if (err) return next(err);
    if (!obj) return next('Cannot create.')
    res.status(200).json(obj);
  })
};
```

We let the users update information in their applications with this method:

```
exports.update = function(req, res, next) {
  var data = req.body;
```

The `_id` needs to be removed first, because we don't want to change it:

```
  delete data._id;
```

In the `findByIdAndUpdate()` method, we employ the user ID from the session, not the one from the body, because it cannot be trusted:

```
  req.db.User.findByIdAndUpdate(req.session.user._id, {
    $set: data
  }, function(err, obj) {
    if (err) return next(err);
    if (!obj) return next('Cannot save.')
```

It's probably okay to send the whole thing back (`obj`), because it's this user's info anyway:

```
    res.status(200).json(obj);
  });
};
```

Select a particular object with the `get()` function:

```
exports.get = function(req, res, next) {
  req.db.User.findById(req.session.user._id,
```

Limit the field that we get back:

```
    'firstName lastName photoUrl headline displayName'
      + 'angelUrl facebookUrl twitterUrl linkedinUrl'
      + 'githubUrl', {}, function(err, obj) {
      if (err) return next(err);
      if (!obj) return next('cannot find');
      res.status(200).json(obj);
    })
};
```

The following is the full source code of the hackhall/routes/applications.js file:

```
exports.add = function(req, res, next) {
  req.db.User.create({
    firstName: req.body.firstName,
    lastName: req.body.lastName,
    displayName: req.body.displayName,
    headline: req.body.headline,
    photoUrl: req.body.photoUrl,
    password: req.body.password,
    email: req.body.email,
    angelList: {
      blah: 'blah'
    },
    angelUrl: req.body.angelUrl,
    twitterUrl: req.body.twitterUrl,
    facebookUrl: req.body.facebookUrl,
    linkedinUrl: req.body.linkedinUrl,
    githubUrl: req.body.githubUrl
  }, function(err, obj) {
    if (err) return next(err);
    if (!obj) return next('Cannot create.')
    res.status(200).json(obj);
  })
};

exports.update = function(req, res, next) {
  var data = req.body;
  delete data._id;
  req.db.User.findByIdAndUpdate(req.session.user._id, {
    $set: data
  }, function(err, obj) {
    if (err) return next(err);
    if (!obj) return next('Cannot save.')
    res.status(200).json(obj);
  });
};

exports.get = function(req, res, next) {
  req.db.User.findById(req.session.user._id,
    'firstName lastName photoUrl headline displayName angelUrl facebookUrl twitterUrl linkedinUrl
     githubUrl', {}, function(err, obj) {
      if (err) return next(err);
      if (!obj) return next('cannot find');
      res.status(200).json(obj);
    })
};
```

Figure 22-10 shows how the membership application page looks at this point.

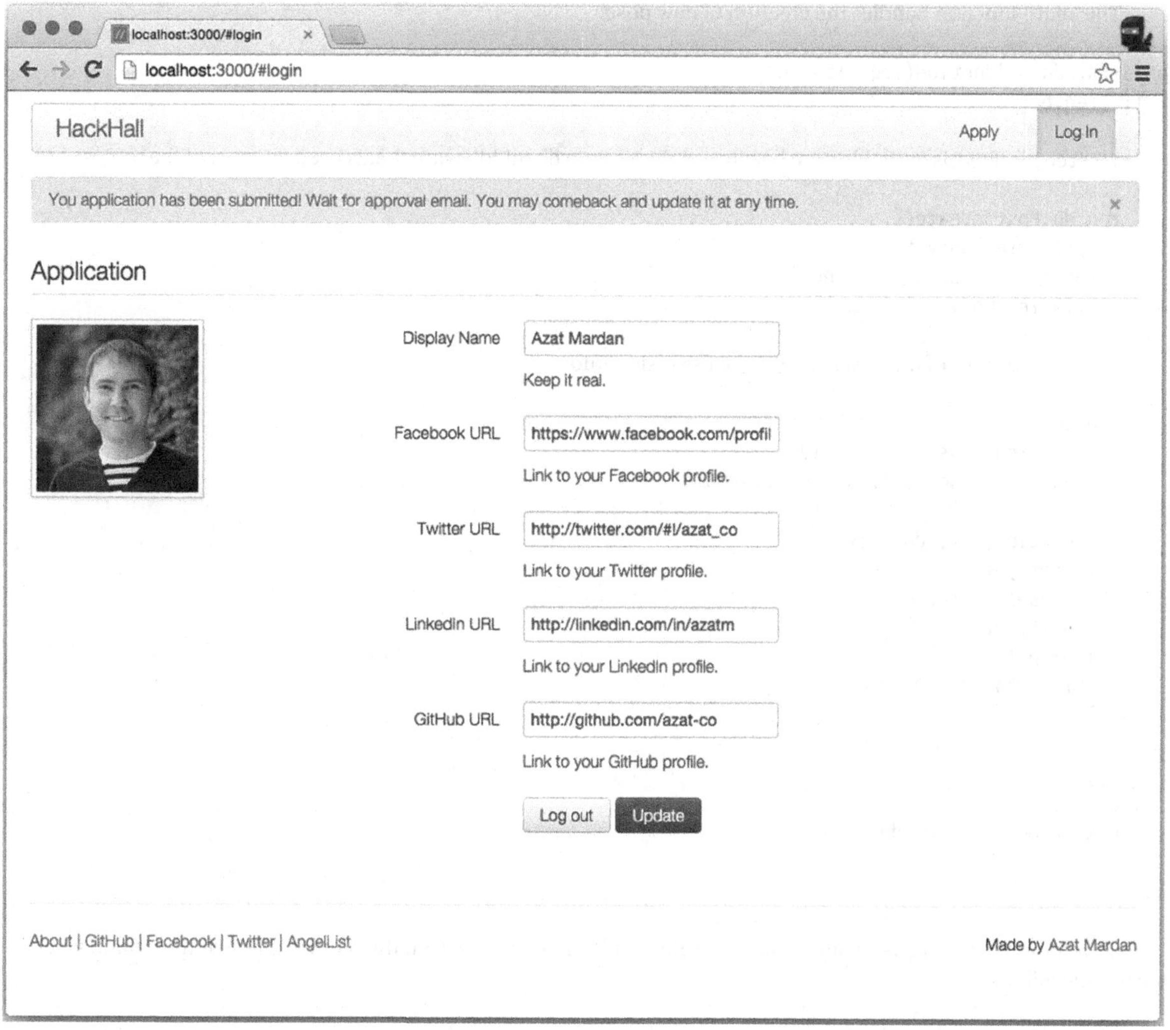

***Figure 22-10.** HackHall membership application page*

posts.js

The last routes module that we need to dissect is `hackhall/routes/posts.js`. It takes care of adding, editing, and removing posts, as well as commenting, watching, and liking.

We use the object ID for conversion from HEX strings to proper objects:

```
objectId = require('mongodb').ObjectID;
```

The default values for the pagination of posts are as follows:

```
var LIMIT = 10;
var SKIP = 0;
```

The add() function handles the creation of new posts:

```
exports.add = function(req, res, next) {
  if (req.body) {
```

The req.db.Post is available here because of the custom db middleware that is used on most of the routes:

```
    req.db.Post.create({
      title: req.body.title,
      text: req.body.text || null,
      url: req.body.url || null,
```

We set the author of the post from the user's session info:

```
      author: {
        id: req.session.user._id,
        name: req.session.user.displayName
      }
    }, function(err, docs) {
      if (err) {
        console.error(err);
        next(err);
      } else {
        res.status(200).json(docs);
      }

    });
  } else {
    next(new Error('No data'));
  }
};
```

To retrieve the list of posts using either the values of limit and skip from the request query or the default values, we use the following:

```
exports.getPosts = function(req, res, next) {
  var limit = req.query.limit || LIMIT;
  var skip = req.query.skip || SKIP;
  req.db.Post.find({}, null, {
    limit: limit,
    skip: skip,
```

We sort the results by their ID, which typically lists the results in chronological order (for more precise results, we could have used the created field here):

```
    sort: {
      '_id': -1
    }
  }, function(err, obj) {
```

At this point, we check to see if there are any posts in the obj, and then, we perform a loop to add some helper flags such as admin, own, like, and watch:

```
if (!obj) return next('There are not posts.');
var posts = [];
docs.forEach(function(doc, i, list) {
```

The doc object is a Mongoose document object that has a lot of magic, so it's best to convert the data to a normal object:

```
var item = doc.toObject();
```

Now, we can check whether or not the user has admin rights, and if the user has them, then we set item.admin to true, but on the property of the new object item. This is redundant, as the client app has the admin flag elsewhere, but it's convenient to have this info on each post for representation purposes, because admins can edit and remove any post:

```
if (req.session.user.admin) {
  item.admin = true;
} else {
  item.admin = false;
}
```

The next line checks whether or not the user is the author of this particular post:

```
if (doc.author.id == req.session.userId) {
  item.own = true;
} else {
  item.own = false;
}
```

This line checks whether or not this user liked this post:

```
if (doc.likes && doc.likes.indexOf(req.session.user._id) > -1) {
  item.like = true;
 } else {
  item.like = false;
 }
```

This line checks whether or not this user watches this post:

```
  if (doc.watches && doc.watches.indexOf(req.session.user._id) > -1) {
    item.watch = true;
    } else {
      item.watch = false;
    }
    posts.push(item);
  });
```

Here's where we form the response body:

```
    var body = {};
    body.limit = limit;
    body.skip = skip;
    body.posts = posts;
```

To include the total number of documents (posts) for pagination, we need this quick query:

```
    req.db.Post.count({}, function(err, total) {
      if (err) return next(err);
      body.total = total;
      res.status(200).json(body);
    });
  });
};
```

For the individual post page, we need the getPost() method. We can pass the properties that we want, not as a string, as in users.js, but as an object as well:

```
exports.getPost = function(req, res, next) {
  if (req.params.id) {
    req.db.Post.findById(req.params.id, {
```

This is another way to limit fields that we want to be returned from the database:

```
      title: true,
      text: true,
      url: true,
      author: true,
      comments: true,
      watches: true,
      likes: true
    }, function(err, obj) {
      if (err) return next(err);
      if (!obj) {
        next('Nothing is found.');
      } else {
        res.status(200).json(obj);
      }
    });
  } else {
    next('No post id');
  }
};
```

The del() function removes specific posts from the database. The findById() and remove() methods from Mongoose are used in this snippet. However, the same thing can be accomplished with just remove().

```
exports.del = function(req, res, next) {
  req.db.Post.findById(req.params.id, function(err, obj) {
    if (err) return next(err);
```

The following is just a sanity check to confirm that the client is either an admin or the author of the post that we are about to delete:

```
    if (req.session.admin || req.session.userId === obj.author.id) {
      obj.remove();
      res.status(200).json(obj);
    } else {
      next('User is not authorized to delete post.');
    }
  })
};
```

To like the post, we update the post item by prepending the post.likes array with the ID of the user:

```
function likePost(req, res, next) {
  req.db.Post.findByIdAndUpdate(req.body._id, {
```

This is a neat MongoDB operand to add values to arrays:

```
    $push: {
      likes: req.session.userId
    }
  }, {}, function(err, obj) {
    if (err) {
      next(err);
    } else {
      res.status(200).json(obj);
    }
  });
};
```

Likewise, when a user performs the watch action, the system adds a new ID to the post.watches array:

```
function watchPost(req, res, next) {
  req.db.Post.findByIdAndUpdate(req.body._id, {
    $push: {
      watches: req.session.userId
    }
  }, {}, function(err, obj) {
    if (err) next(err);
    else {
      res.status(200).json(obj);
    }
  });
};
```

The updatePost() method is what calls like or watch functions, based on the action flag sent with the request (req.body.action):

```
exports.updatePost = function(req, res, next) {
  var anyAction = false;
  if (req.body._id && req.params.id) {
```

This logic is for adding a like:

```
    if (req.body && req.body.action == 'like') {
      anyAction = true;
      likePost(req, res);
```

The next condition is for adding a watch:

```
    } else if (req.body && req.body.action == 'watch') {
      anyAction = true;
      watchPost(req, res);
```

This one is for adding a comment to the post:

```
    } else if (req.body && req.body.action == 'comment'
      && req.body.comment && req.params.id) {
      anyAction = true;
      req.db.Post.findByIdAndUpdate(req.params.id, {
        $push: {
          comments: {
            author: {
              id: req.session.userId,
              name: req.session.user.displayName
            },
            text: req.body.comment
          }
        }
      }, {
        safe: true,
        new: true
      }, function(err, obj) {
        if (err) throw err;
        res.status(200).json(obj);
      });
```

Lastly, when none of the previous conditions of action are met, updatePost() processes the changes to the post itself (title, text, etc.) made by the author or admin (req.body.author.id == req.session.user._id || req.session.user.admin):

```
    } else if (req.session.auth && req.session.userId && req.body
      && req.body.action != 'comment' &&
      req.body.action != 'watch' && req.body != 'like' &&
      req.params.id && (req.body.author.id == req.session.user._id
      || req.session.user.admin)) {
      req.db.Post.findById(req.params.id, function(err, doc) {
```

In this context, the doc object is a Mongoose document object, so we assign the new values to its properties and invoke save(), which triggers the pre-save hook defined in the model (covered in the next section, "Mongoose Models"):

```
        if (err) next(err);
        doc.title = req.body.title;
        doc.text = req.body.text || null;
        doc.url = req.body.url || null;
        doc.save(function(e, d) {
          if (e) return next(e);
```

It's a rule to send back the updated object:

```
          res.status(200).json(d);
        });
      })
    } else {
      if (!anyAction) next('Something went wrong.');
    }

  } else {
    next('No post ID.');
  }
};
```

The full source code for the hackhall/routes/posts.js file is available at https://github.com/azat-co/hackhall/blob/v3.1.0/routes/posts.js.

This concludes coding the routes for the New Post page (see Figure 22-11), where users can create a post (e.g., a question).

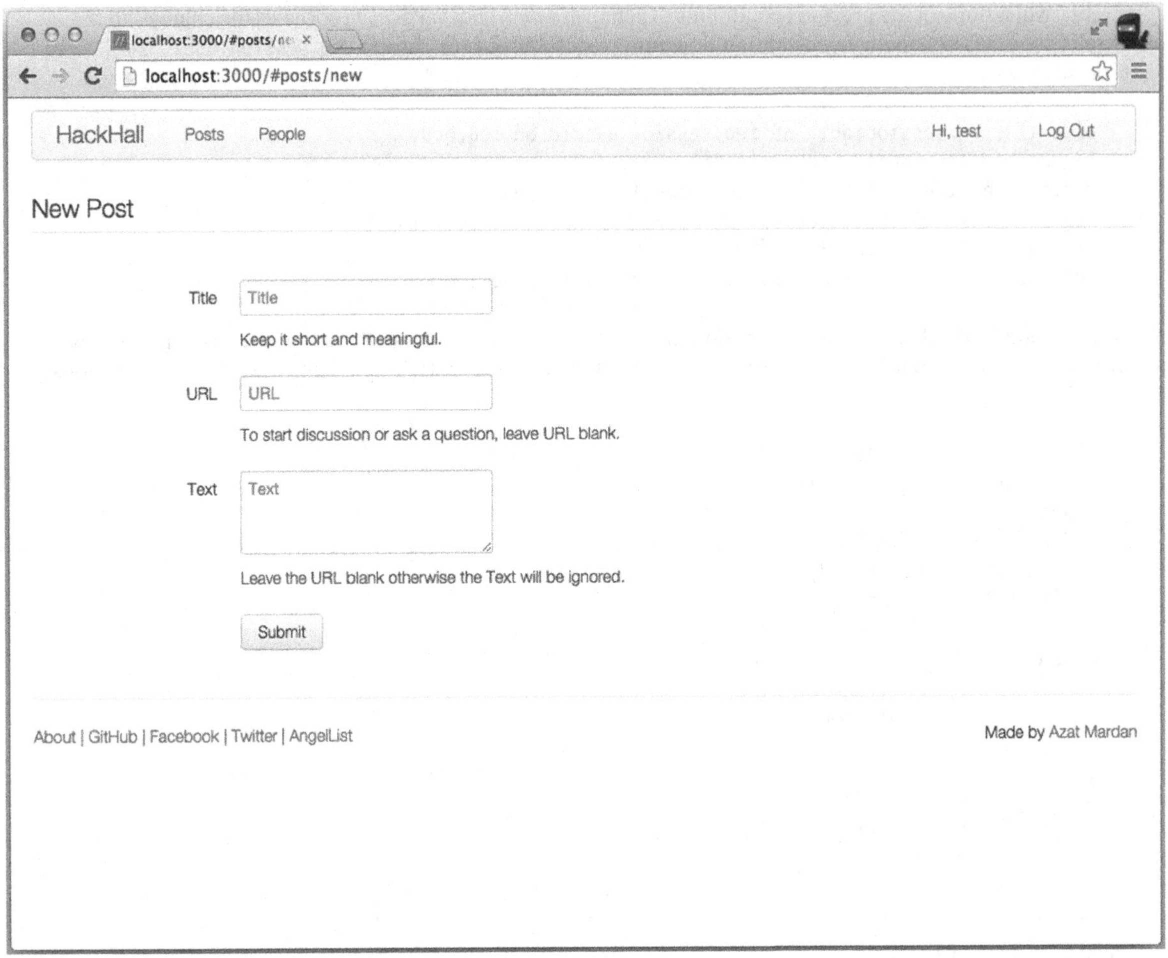

Figure 22-11. *HackHall New Post page*

We're done with the routes files! Do you remember that HackHall is a true MVC application? Next, we'll cover the models.

Mongoose Models

Ideally, in a big application, we would break down each model into a separate file. Right now, in the HackHall app, we have them all in `hackhall/models/index.js`.

As always, our dependencies look better at the top:

```
var mongoose = require('mongoose');
```

This reference will be used for Mongoose data types:

```
var Schema = mongoose.Schema;
```

This array will be used as an enumerated type:

```
var roles = 'user staff mentor investor founder'.split(' ');
```

The Post model represents a post with its likes, comments, and watches. Each property in the schema sets a certain behavior for the property. For example, `required` means that this property is required, and `type` is the Mongoose/BSON data type.

■ **Tip** For more information on Mongoose, please consult its official documentation (`https://gumroad.com/l/mongoose`), *Practical Node.js* (Apress, 2014), and a new online course.

We define `Schema` with the `new` operand:

```
var Post = new Schema ({
```

Then, we have a `title` field that is required (`type` of `String`) and that is automatically trimmed of whitespace at the beginning and end:

```
  title: {
    required: true,
    type: String,
    trim: true,
```

The RegExp says "a word, a space, or any of the characters `,.!?`" and be between 1 and 100 characters in length":

```
    match: /^([\w ,.!?]{1,100})$/
  },
```

Then, we define `url` with the maximum of 1000 characters (that should be enough for long URLs, right?) and turn trimming on:

```
  url: {
    type: String,
    trim: true,
    max: 1000
  },
```

We define similar field properties for `text`:

```
  text: {
    type: String,
    trim: true,
    max: 2000
  },
```

comments is an array of comments for this post. Each comment object has a text and author. The author id is a reference to the User model:

```
comments: [{
  text: {
    type: String,
    trim: true,
    max:2000
  },
  author: {
    id: {
      type: Schema.Types.ObjectId,
      ref: 'User'
    },
    name: String
  }
}],
```

The post can be watched or liked by a user. These features are implemented by having arrays watches and likes with user IDs:

```
watches: [{
  type: Schema.Types.ObjectId,
  ref: 'User'
}],
likes: [{
  type: Schema.Types.ObjectId,
  ref: 'User'
}],
```

Next, we enter the author information and make each field in the nested object a required field:

```
author: {
  id: {
    type: Schema.Types.ObjectId,
    ref: 'User',
    required: true
  },
  name: {
    type: String,
    required: true
  }
},
```

Lastly, we add the time and date fields. It's good to have timestamps of events, such as when this post was created and when it was updated the last time. For this, we use `Date.now` as the default field. The `updated` property will be set by the pre save hook, or it can be set manually on each `save()`. (The pre save hook code is provided after this schema code.):

```
  created: {
    type: Date,
    default: Date.now,
    required: true
  },
  updated:  {
    type: Date,
    default: Date.now,
    required: true
  }
});
```

Going back to the `updated` field, to ensure that we don't have to set the timestamp manually each time we update (`save()`) the post, we utilize a pre save hook that checks if the field has been modified (has a new value). If it has not been modified, then we set it with a new date and time. This hook works only when you call `save()`; not when you use `update()` or a similar method. The callback has an asynch `next()` function, as you might see in Express.js middleware:

```
Post.pre('save', function (next) {
  if (!this.isModified('updated')) this.updated = new Date;
  next();
})
```

The `User` model can also serve as an application object (when `approved=false`). Let's define the schema as this:

```
var User = new Schema({
  angelListId: String,
```

The `Mixed` type allows us to store anything:

```
  angelListProfile: Schema.Types.Mixed,
  angelToken: String,
    firstName: {
    type: String,
    required: true,
    trim: true
  },
  lastName: {
    type: String,
    required: true,
    trim: true
  },
  displayName: {
    type: String,
    required: true,
    trim: true
  },
```

```
  password: String,
  email: {
    type: String,
    required: true,
    trim: true
  },
```

Roles are enum, because the value can be only one of the values from the roles array ([user, staff, mentor, investor, founder]):

```
  role: {
    type: String,
    enum: roles,
    required: true,
    default: roles[0]
  },
```

Here are some of the required boolean flags:

```
  approved: {
    type: Boolean,
    default: false
  },
  banned: {
    type: Boolean,
    default: false
  },
  admin: {
    type: Boolean,
    default: false
  },
```

Now a short bio statement:

```
  headline: String,
```

We won't store the photo binary, only the URL to it:

```
  photoUrl: String,
```

The angelList is a loose type that will have the AngelList profile:

```
  angelList: Schema.Types.Mixed,
```

It's good to keep logs to track when this document was created and when it was updated the last time (we set the time manually in the update() method of users.js):

```
  created: {
    type: Date,
    default: Date.now
  },
```

```
  updated: {
    type: Date,
    default: Date.now
  },
```

We need some social media URLs:

```
  angelUrl: String,
  twitterUrl: String,
  facebookUrl: String,
  linkedinUrl: String,
  githubUrl: String,
```

We reference the IDs of posts that this user authored, liked, watched, and commented on as arrays of objects (they will be ObjectIDs):

```
  posts: {
    own: [Schema.Types.Mixed],
    likes: [Schema.Types.Mixed],
    watches: [Schema.Types.Mixed],
    comments: [Schema.Types.Mixed]
  }
});
```

For convenience, we apply the findOrCreate plug-in (https://www.npmjs.org/package/mongoose-findorcreate):

```
User.plugin(findOrCreate);
```

Mongoose plug-ins act like mini modules. This allows you to add extra functionality to your models. Another way to add extra functionality is to write your own custom method. Such a method can be static (attached to the entire category of entities) or an instance (attached to the specific model).

In routes, you've seen findProfileById() twice: once in main.js and once in users.js. To avoid duplication, the code was abstracted as a Mongoose static method of the User schema. It retrieves information, such as comments, likes, etc., which is why we have multiple nested Mongoose calls.

The findProfileById() method might look a bit complicated initially, but there is nothing difficult here—just a few nested database calls so that we can have full user information. This info includes, not only the username, e-mail address, and so forth, but all the posts, likes, watches, and comments made by the user. This information is used for gamification purposes on the Profile page to convert the number of comments, likes, and watches into points. But let's start with the first basic query and limit the fields that we request (to avoid leaking passwords and e-mail addresses):

```
User.statics.findProfileById = function(id, fields, callback) {
  var User = this;
  var Post = User.model('Post');

  return User.findById(id, fields, function(err, obj) {
    if (err) return callback(err);
    if (!obj) return callback(new Error('User is not found'));
```

After a user is found, we find the user's posts by using the _id and displayName. The fields option is set to null so we can pass other arguments, and the results are sorted by the creation date. In the callback we check for errors and exit (callback(err)) if there is an error.

```
Post.find({
  author: {
    id: obj._id,
    name: obj.displayName
  }
}, null, {
  sort: {
    'created': -1
  }
}, function(err, list) {
```

It's vital to handle errors on each nested callback:

```
  if (err) return callback(err);
  obj.posts.own = list || [];
```

Now that we have saved the list of this user's posts into obj.posts.own, the next query finds all the posts this user liked:

```
  Post.find({
    likes: obj._id
  }, null, {
```

The chronological order is ensured by created:

```
    sort: {
      'created': -1
    }
  }, function(err, list) {
    if (err) return callback(err);
```

In case, this user didn't like any of the posts, yet we account for that with an empty array:

```
    obj.posts.likes = list || [];
```

This query gets the posts that this user watches:

```
    Post.find({
      watches: obj._id
    }, null, {
      sort: {
        'created': -1
      }
    }, function(err, list) {
```

The err and list objects from the previous context are masked by this closure's err and list, but we don't really care. This style allows for variable name reuse:

```
        if (err) return callback(err);
        obj.posts.watches = list || [];
```

The last query finds posts where this user left comments:

```
        Post.find({
          'comments.author.id': obj._id
        }, null, {
          sort: {
            'created': -1
          }
        }, function(err, list) {
          if (err) return callback(err);
          obj.posts.comments = [];
```

After we get the list of posts in which this user left comments, there might be some posts where this particular user left more than one comment. For this reason, we need to go through that list of posts, and through each comment, and compare the author's ID with the user ID. If they match, then we include that comment into the list:

```
          list.forEach(function(post, key, arr) {
            post.comments.forEach(function(comment, key, arr) {
              if (comment.author.id.toString() == obj._id.toString())
                obj.posts.comments.push(comment);
            });
          });
```

Finally, we invoke the callback with proper data and null errors:

```
          callback(null, obj);
        });
      });
    });
  });
 });
}
```

Lastly, we export the schema objects so they can be compiled into models in another file:

```
exports.Post = Post;
exports.User = User;
```

The full source code for hackhall/models/index.js is available at https://github.com/azat-co/hackhall/blob/v3.1.0/models/index.js.

Mocha Tests

One of the benefits of using REST API server architecture is that each route, and the application as a whole, become very testable. The assurance of the passed tests is a wonderful supplement during development—the so-called test-driven development approach introduced in Chapter 21.

The HackHall tests live in the `tests` folder and consist of:

- `hackhall/tests/application.js`: Functional tests for unapproved users' information
- `hackhall/tests/posts.js`: Functional tests for posts
- `hackhall/tests/users.js`: Functional tests for users

To run tests, we utilize a Makefile. I like to have various targets in a Makefile, because it gives me more flexibility. Here are the tasks in this example:

- `test`: Run all tests from the `tests` folder
- `test-w`: Rerun tests each time there is a file change
- `users`: Run the `tests/users.js` tests for user-related routes
- `posts`: Run the `tests/posts.js` tests for posts-related routes
- `application`: Run the `tests/application.js` tests for application-related routes

This is how the Makefile might look, starting with options for Mocha:

```
REPORTER = list
MOCHA_OPTS = --ui tdd
```

Then we define a task `test`:

```
test:
	clear
	echo Seeding **********************
	node seed.js
	echo Starting test *********************
	foreman run ./node_modules/mocha/bin/mocha \
	--reporter $(REPORTER) \
	$(MOCHA_OPTS) \
	tests/*.js
	echo Ending test
```

Similarly, we define other targets:

```
test-w:
	./node_modules/mocha/bin/mocha \
	--reporter $(REPORTER) \
	--growl \
	--watch \
	$(MOCHA_OPTS) \
	tests/*.js
```

```
users:
	clear
	echo Starting test *********************
	foreman run ./node_modules/mocha/bin/mocha \
	--reporter $(REPORTER) \
	$(MOCHA_OPTS) \
	tests/users.js
	echo Ending test

posts:
	clear
	echo Starting test *********************
	foreman run ./node_modules/mocha/bin/mocha \
	--reporter $(REPORTER) \
	$(MOCHA_OPTS) \
	tests/posts.js
	echo Ending test

application:
	clear
	echo Starting test *********************
	foreman run ./node_modules/mocha/bin/mocha \
	--reporter $(REPORTER) \
	$(MOCHA_OPTS) \
	tests/application.js
	echo Ending test

.PHONY: test test-w users posts application
```

Therefore, we can start tests with the `$ make` or `$ make test` command (to run the Makefile in the example, you have to have the `foreman` tool and `.env` variables).

All 36 tests should pass (as of this writing in HackHall v3.1.0), as shown in Figure 22-12.

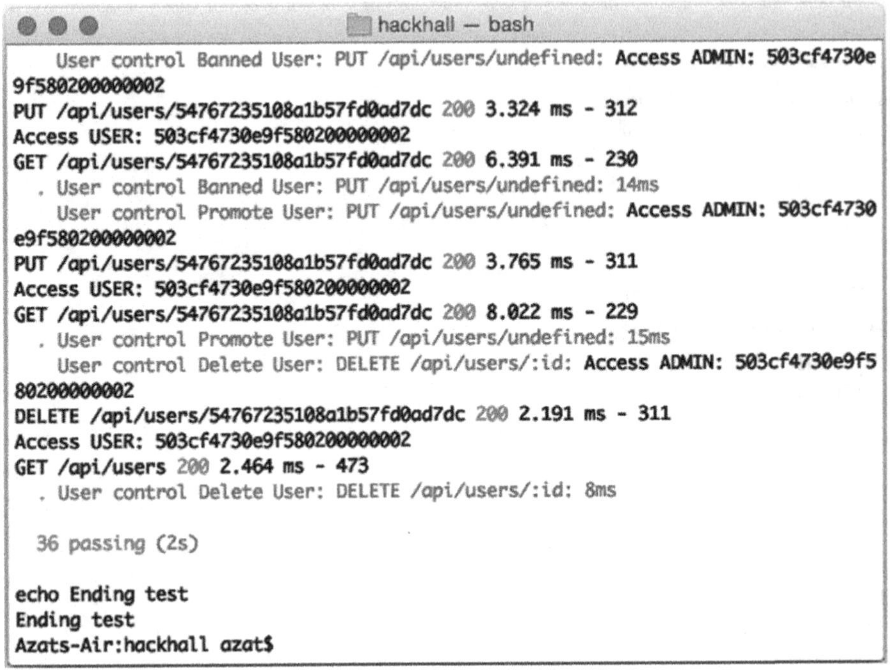

Figure 22-12. *Results of running all Mocha tests*

Tests use a library called superagent (https://npmjs.org/package/superagent; GitHub: https://github.com/visionmedia/superagent). The tests are similar in concept to those for the REST API in Chapter 21. We log in, then make a few requests, while checking for their correct response.

For example, this is the beginning of hackhall/tests/application.js in which we have a dummy user object with a hashed password (bcrypt.hashSync()):

```
var bcrypt = require('bcryptjs');

var user3 = {
  firstName: 'Dummy',
  lastName: 'Application',
  displayName: 'Dummy Application',
  password: bcrypt.hashSync('3', 10),
  email: '3@3.com',
  headline: 'Dummy Application',
  photoUrl: '/img/user.png',
  angelList: {blah:'blah'},
  angelUrl: 'http://angel.co.com/someuser',
  twitterUrl: 'http://twitter.com/someuser',
  facebookUrl: 'http://facebook.com/someuser',
  linkedinUrl: 'http://linkedin.com/someuser',
  githubUrl: 'http://github.com/someuser'
}
```

```
var app = require ('../server').app,
  assert = require('assert'),
  request = require('superagent');
```

We start the server:

```
app.listen(app.get('port'), function(){
  console.log('Express server listening on port ' + app.get('port'));
});
```

The next line will store the client object so that we can log in and make authorized requests as that user:

```
var user1 = request.agent();
var port = 'http://localhost:'+app.get('port');
var userId;
```

We use the admin user that was created by `seed.js`:

```
var adminUser = {
  email: 'admin-test@test.com',
  password: 'admin-test'
};
```

Next, we create a test suite:

```
suite('APPLICATION API', function (){
```

This is a test suite preparation (empty at the moment):

```
  suiteSetup(function(done){
    done();
  });
```

The following is the first test case definition with the POST call to `/api/login`:

```
  test('log in as admin', function(done){
    user1.post(port+'/api/login').send(adminUser).end(function(res){
        assert.equal(res.status,200);
      done();
    });
  });
```

Let's check that we can get protected resource `/api/profile`:

```
  test('get profile for admin',function(done){
    user1.get(port+'/api/profile').end(function(res){
        assert.equal(res.status,200);
      done();
    });
  });
  test('submit application for user 3@3.com', function(done){
```

Here, we create a new application for membership using user3 data and a hashed password:

```
    user1.post(port+'/api/application').send(user3).end(function(res){
      assert.equal(res.status,200);
      userId = res.body._id;
      done();
    });
  });
```

Then, we log out user1 and check that we've logged out:

```
  test('logout admin',function(done){
    user1.post(port+'/api/logout').end(function(res){
        assert.equal(res.status,200);
      done();
    });
  });
  test('get profile again after logging out',function(done){
    user1.get(port+'/api/profile').end(function(res){
        assert.equal(res.status,500);
      done();
    });
  });
```

Now, we try to log in as user3 by using a plain password, as though it was entered on the web page (system will hash it to compare with the hashed password):

```
  test('log in as user3 - unapproved', function(done){
    user1.post(port+'/api/login').send({email:'3@3.com', password:'3'}).end(function(res){
        assert.equal(res.status, 200);
      done();
    });
  });

...
```

Assuming you got the general idea from this test case, there's no need to list all the mundane test cases. Of course, you can get the full content for `hackhall/tests/application.js`, `hackhall/tests/posts.js`, and `hackhall/tests/users.js` at `https://github.com/azat-co/hackhall/tree/v3.1.0/tests`.

■ **Caution** Do not store plain passwords/keys in the database. Any serious production app should, at least, salt the passwords[1] before storing them. Use `bcryptjs` instead!

---

[1]https://crackstation.net/hashing-security.htm

By now, you should be able to run the application and tests locally (either by copying from the book or downloading the code). If you get the API keys, you should be able to log in with AngelList and GitHub, as well as send/receive e-mails with SendGrid. At the bare minimum, you should be able to log in locally using the e-mail and password that you specified in your database seeding script.

Summary

Now you know all the tips and tricks used in building HackHall, which includes important, real production application components, such as REST API architecture, OAuth, Mongoose and its models, MVC structure of Express.js apps, access to environment variables, and so on.

As mentioned in this chapter, HackHall is still in active development, so the code will continue to evolve. Make sure you follow the repository on GitHub. You can visit the live HackHall.com app and join the community by applying for membership! And, of course, you can make a contribution by submitting a pull request.

This chapter concludes our journey into Express.js and related web development topics. The task of covering an evolving framework is a difficult one, akin to shooting at a moving target, so my goal in this chapter was to get you the most up-to-date information and, most importantly, to show you some of the more fundamental aspects, such as code organization. I also put a lot of energy into explaining and repeating examples of the middleware pattern. If you are under the pressure of a deadline, or simply prefer just-in-time learning (learn when you need it vs. learn for the future), then you will find plenty of code to copy and paste into your own project. I know that building your own project is more fun than borrowing another abstract application from a tutorial.

I hope you have enjoyed the examples and the book! I want to hear from you via Twitter (`@azat_co`) and e-mail (`hi@azat.co`). The appendices that follow will serve as a reference. And don't forget to claim your two-page print-ready Express.js 4 cheat sheet (the link to download it is in Appendix C).

Summary

APPENDIX A

Related Reading and Resources

This short appendix provides several of the most useful Node.js resources for further learning:

Other Node.js frameworks

Node.js books

JavaScript classics

Other Node.js Frameworks

The Express.js framework is, no doubt, the most mature, popular, robust, tested, and used project for Node.js web services. As of this writing, Express.js is also the NPM repository with the highest number of stars from the NPM community, as shown in Figure A-1. There are plenty of real production apps that rely on Express.js 2.x and 3.x, including Storify[1] (acquired by LiveFyre[2]), DocuSign,[3] the new MySpace,[4] LearnBoost,[5] Geeklist,[6] Klout,[7] Prismatic,[8] Segment.io,[9] and more.[10]

[1]http://storify.com
[2]http://web.livefyre.com
[3]https://www.docusign.com
[4]https://myspace.com
[5]https://www.learnboost.com
[6]https://geekli.st/home
[7]https://klout.com/home
[8]http://getprismatic.com/home
[9]https://segment.com
[10]http://expressjs.com/applications.html

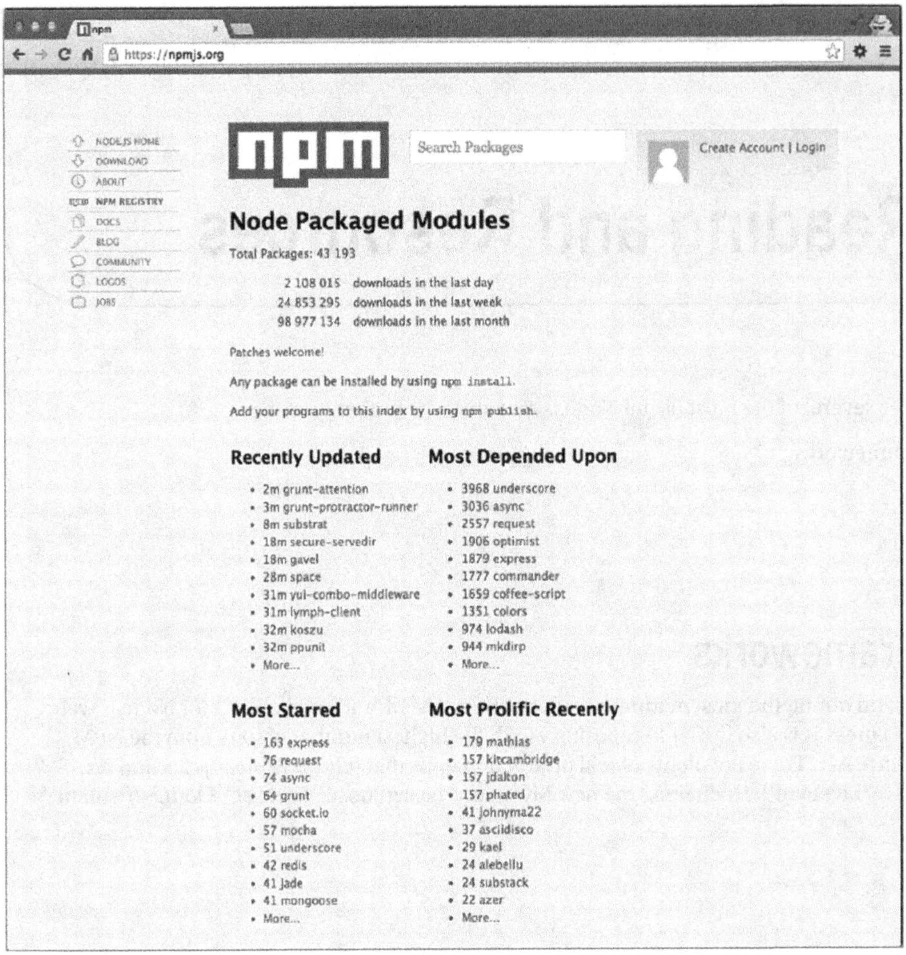

***Figure A-1.** Express.js is the most starred NPM repository*

Nevertheless, there are plenty of alternative Node.js frameworks to Express.js. To help developers navigate the numerous options, I've created an analog to the TodoMVC collection (`http://todomvc.com`): Node Frameworks (`http://nodeframework.com`), the MVC frameworks page of which is shown in Figure A-2. By the way, some of the more comprehensive frameworks depend on Express.js (e.g., SailsJS[11]), so it's great that you are getting to know Express.js!

[11]`https://github.com/balderdashy/sails/blob/v0.9.0/package.json#L32`

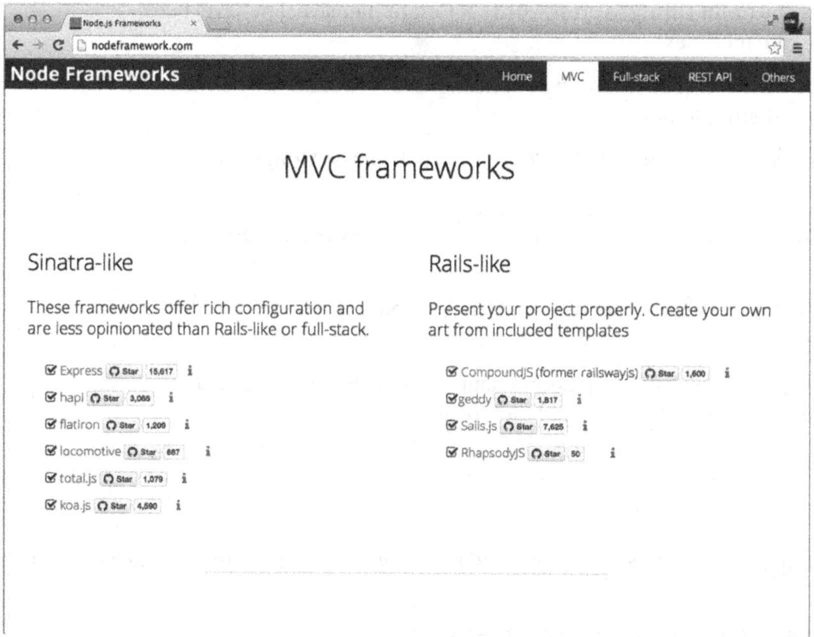

Figure A-2. *Node Frameworks provides a list of Node.js frameworks and their stats*

Node.js Books

For more core Node.js overview and/or information about other components of the Node.js stack, such as databases and WebSockets, please consider these resources:

- *Practical Node.js*: *Building Real-World Scalable Web Apps*, by Azat Mardan (Apress, 2014): A Step-by-step guide to learning how to build scalable, real-world, web applications, taking you from installing Express.js to writing full-stack web applications.
- *Rapid Prototyping with JS*: *Agile JavaScript Development*[12] (Azat Mardan, 2013): A Beginner-to-intermediate book on Node.js, MongoDB, and Backbone.js.
- *JavaScript and Node FUNdamentals*: *A Collection of Essential Basics*[13] (Azat Mardan, 2014): A Short read on simple, but important concepts of browser JS and Node.
- *Introduction to OAuth with Node.js*: *Twitter API OAuth 1.0, OAuth 2.0, OAuth Echo, Everyauth and OAuth2.0 Server Examples*[14] (Azat Mardan, 2014): A mini book about different OAuth scenarios.

[12] http://rpjs.co
[13] https://leanpub.com/jsfun
[14] https://gumroad.com/l/oauthnode

- *Pro Node.js for Developers*, by Colin J. Ihrig (Apress, 2013): A Comprehensive, low-level book on Node.js sans any non-core modules.
- *Node.js in Action*, by Mike Cantelon et al. (Manning Publications, 2013): A Book by a variety of authors about Express.js and other topics.
- *Learning Node*, by Shelley Powers (O'Reilly Media, 2012): Covers Express, MongoDB, Mongoose, and Socket.IO.
- *Node Cookbook*, by David Mark Clements (Packt Publishing, 2012): Covers databases and WebSockets.
- *Node: Up and Running*, by Tom Hughes-Croucher and Mike Watson (O'Reilly Media, 2012): A brief overview of Node.js.
- *Smashing Node.js: JavaScript Everywhere*, by Guillermo Rauch (Wiley, 2012): Covers Express.js, Jade, and Stylus, from the creator of Mongoose ORM for MongoDB.

JavaScript Classics

For a deeper understanding of JavaScript, the most misunderstood and most popular programming language, be sure to read these proven classics:

- *Eloquent JavaScript, Second Edition*, by Marijn Haverbeke (No Starch Press, 2014): Programming fundamentals in JavaScript coding.
- *JavaScript: The Good Parts*, by Douglas Crockford (O'Reilly Media, 2008): Deals with the tricky parts of the JavaScript language.

Courses

If you liked this book, then check out Azat's Node.js courses: Node Program (`http://nodeprogram.com`) and Mongoose Course (`http://mongoosecourse.com`).

APPENDIX B

Migrating Express.js 3.x to 4.x: Middleware, Route, and Other Changes

Express.js 4 (`http://expressjs.com`) is the latest (as of May 2014), major version of the most popular, mature, and robust Node.js framework for web apps, services, and APIs. There are some breaking changes in the transition from 3.x to 4.x, so this appendix serves as a brief migration guide, with coverage of the following:

- Introducing unbundled middleware in Express.js 4
- Removing deprecated methods from Express.js 4 apps
- Other Express.js 4 changes
- Exploring the new Express.js 4 route instance and how to chain it
- Further Express.js 4 migration reading links

Even if you have no intention of working with version 3, this guide might be useful to you, because it sheds light on the rationale for making the changes from Express 3 to 4, and the philosophy behind those changes.

Introducing Unbundled Middleware in Express.js 4

Let's start with the biggest change that will break most of your Express.js 3.x projects. This is also the most discussed (and long awaited?) Express.js news on the Internet. Yes, it's unbundled middleware.

Personally, I'm not sure whether it's good news or bad news, because I kind of liked not having to declare extra dependencies. However, I can see the arguments in favor of unbundling as well, including benefits, such as keeping the Express.js module small, upgrading middleware packages independently, and so forth.

So, what is unbundled middleware? Remember the magic middleware that we were able to use, simply by typing `app.use(express.middlwarename())`? Well, they were coming from the `Connect` library, but now they are no longer part of Express.js. It was customary to write, for example, `app.use(express.cookieParser())` in Express.js 3.x. Those modules are essential for pretty much any web application. They were part of the `Connect` library, but Express.js 4.x doesn't have `Connect` as a dependency. This means that, if we want to use middleware (and we sure do!), we'll need to include middleware explicitly, like this:

```
$ npm install body-parse@1.0.2 --save
```

Then, in the Express.js main configuration file (e.g., `app.js`), we use the included module like this:

```
var bodyParser = require('body-parse')
// ... other dependencies
app.use(bodyParser())
// ... some other Express.js app configuration
```

Table B-1 describes the unbundled middleware that developers will have to replace: all except static. That's right, static was left out (for convenience?). The table lists the Express.js 3.x middleware names and their NPM module counterparts for Express.js 4.x usage.

Table B-1. *Middleware comparison*

Express.js 3.x	Express.js 4.x	GitHub Link
express.bodyParser	body-parser	https://github.com/expressjs/body-parser
express.compress	compression	https://github.com/expressjs/compression
express.timeout	connect-timeout	https://github.com/expressjs/timeout
express.cookieParser	cookie-parser	https://github.com/expressjs/cookie-parser
express.cookieSession	cookie-session	https://github.com/expressjs/cookie-session
express.csrf	csurf	https://github.com/expressjs/csurf
express.error-handler	errorhandler	https://github.com/expressjs/errorhandler
express.session	express-session	https://github.com/expressjs/session
express.method-override	method-override	https://github.com/expressjs/method-override
express.logger	morgan	https://github.com/expressjs/morgan
express.response-time	response-time	https://github.com/expressjs/response-time
express.favicon	serve-favicon	https://github.com/expressjs/serve-favicon
express.directory	serve-index	https://github.com/expressjs/serve-index
express.static	serve-static	https://github.com/expressjs/serve-static
express.vhost	vhost	https://github.com/expressjs/vhost

To make matters a bit more complicated, the Express.js/Connect team is dropping support for the modules shown in Table B-2 and recommending that you use the alternatives:

Table B-2. *Dropped modules and their alternatives*

Dropped Module	Alternatives
cookieParser	cookies and keygrip
limit	raw-body
multipart	connect-multiparty and connect-busboy
query	qs
staticCache	st and connect-static

Many of these unbundled Express.js/Connect modules are in need of maintainers[1]; this is your opportunity to make a dent in the Node.js universe!

Removing Deprecated Methods from Express.js 4 Apps

This section discusses those methods that are deprecated and how to replace them.

app.configure()

Most people have probably never used `app.configure()`, a nice, but nonessential, method intended primarily for setting up environments. If you have used it, just replace `app.configure('name', function(){...})` with `if (process.env.NODE_ENV === 'name') {...}`. For example, this old Express.js 3 production configuration

```
app.configure('production', function() {
  app.set('port', 80)
})
```

becomes the following in Express.js 4.x:

```
if (process.env.NODE_ENV === 'production') {
  app.set('port', 80)
}
```

app.router

One of the good changes in Express.js 4 is that it has eliminated the need to write `app.router`! So now, basically, the order of middleware and routes is the only thing that counts, whereas in Express.js 3x developers were able to augment the order of execution by placing `app.router` somewhere in the middle.

If you have any middleware that is supposed to be ordered after the routes, move it *after the route,* in just the order you want them.

For example, error handling middleware that is executed after routes in the Express.js 3.x configuration:

```
app.use(express.cookieParser())
app.use(app.router)
app.use(express.errorHandler())
app.get('/', routes.index)
app.post('/signup', routes.signup)
```

migrates into this code in Express.js 4.x:

```
var cookieParse = require('cookie-parser')
var errorHandler = require('errorhandler')
...
app.use(cookieParser())
app.get('/', routes.index)
app.post('/signup', routes.signup)
app.use(errorHandler())
```

---

[1] https://github.com/senchalabs/connect#middleware

In other words, `app.use()` and routes with verbs, such as `app.get()`, `app.post()`, `app.put()`, and `app.del()`, became equal counterparts.

res.on('header')

The `res.on('header')` event was removed from Connect 3.

res.charset

In Express.js 4.x, use `res.type()` or `res.set('content-type')` instead of `res.charset` in Express.js 3.x.

res.headerSent

In Express.js 4.x, use `res.headersSent` instead of `res.headerSent`.

req.accepted()

In Express.js 4.x, use `req.accepts()` instead of `req.accepted()`.

`req.accepts` in Express.js 4.x is powered by the module `accepts` (`https://github.com/expressjs/accepts`), which the GitHub documentation indicates was extracted from Koa (`http://koajs.com`) for general use.

Other Express.js 4 Changes

This section covers some other Express.js 4 changes.

app.use()

Amazingly, `app.use()` now accepts URL parameters. This is another step toward making `app.use()` and verb route methods equal and less confusing. The parameter is in the `req.params` object.

For example, if we need to get an ID from the URL, in Express.js 4.x middleware we can write

```
app.use('/posts/:slug', function(req, res, next) {
  req.db.findPostBySlug(req.params.slug, function(post){
  ...
  })
})
```

res.location()

In Express.js 4, `res.location()` no longer resolves relative URLs.

app.route()

See the upcoming section "Exploring the New Express.js 4 Route Instance and How to Chain It" for details about the role of `app.route()` in Express.js 4.

json spaces

In Express.js 4, `json spaces` is off by default in development.

req.params

`req.params` is an object, not an array.

res.locals

`res.locals` is an object now.

req.is

`req.is` in Express.js 4.x has been replaced by the module `type-is` (`https://github.com/expressjs/type-is`), which was also extracted from Koa.js (`http://koajs.com`) for general use, per the GitHub documentation.

Express.js Command-Line Generator

For the command-line generator, use

```
$ sudo npm install -g express-generator
```

instead of the plain old `$ sudo npm install -g express`.

Exploring the New Express.js 4 Route Instance and How to Chain It

The `app.route()` method gives us the new Express.js 4 route instance. Before we explore it, let's take a look at the router itself.

The `Router` class has been supercharged in Express.js 4.x. In Express.js 3.x, the app instance used router, but now we can create many route instances and use them for specific paths by attaching particular middleware and other logic. This can be used to reorganize code.

Here's a basic example of how developers can use `Router` in Express.js 4.x. Let's say we have reviews for two categories: books and games. The review's logic is similar to and packaged as a router:

```
var express = require('express')
var app = express()
var router = express.Router()

router.use(function(req, res, next) {
  //process each request
});

router.get('/', function(req, res, next) {
  // get the home page for that entity
  next();
});
```

```
router.get('/reviews', function(req, res, next) {
  // Get the reviews for that entity
  next();
});

app.use('/books', router);
app.use('/games', router);

app.listen(3000);
```

`app.route()` or `router.route()` returns *the new Express.js 4.x route instance,* which we can chain like this:

```
router.route('/post/:slug')
  .all(function(req, res, next) {
    // Runs each time
    // We can fetch the post by id from the database
  })
  .get(function(req, res, next) {
    //Render post
  })
  .put(function(req, res, next) {
    //Update post
  })
  .post(function(req, res, next) {
    //Create new comment
  })
  .del(function(req, res, next) {
    //Remove post
  })
```

In Express.js 3.x, without the route chain, we would have to type the same path again and again (increasing the risk of typos):

```
router.all('/post/:slug', function(req, res, next) {
  // runs each time
  // we can fetch the post by ID from the database
})
router.get('/post/:slug', function(req, res, next) {
  //render post
})
router.put('/post/:slug', function(req, res, next) {
  //update post
})
router.post('/post/:slug', function(req, res, next) {
  //create new comment
})
router.delete('/post/:slug', function(req, res, next) {
  //remove post
})
```

The same route instance can also have its own middleware, param, and HTTP verb methods (as illustrated above).

Further Express.js 4 Migration Reading Links

So, overall, the Express.js 4.x changes are not very dramatic, and the migration can be a relatively painless process. But, before you hit `$ git checkout -b express4` to create a new Git branch of `express4` for your migration from 3.x to 4.x, consider carefully whether you really need to migrate! I know of many successful production applications that haven't updated their main framework versions. At Storify, we used to run Express.js 2.x when 3.x was available, and it was not a big deal. As another example, from the Ruby world, I'm aware of many apps and developers still working with Ruby on Rails 2.x, even though Ruby on Rails 4.x is available.

In case you decide to go with Express.js 4, don't rely just on this brief overview. Take a look at these additional resources to help make the transition from Express.js 3.x to 4.x easier:

- The official migration guide[2]
- New features in Express.js 4.x[3]
- Express.js 4.x documentation[4]

Express.js 4, Node.js and MongoDB REST API Tutorial[5]

[2]https://github.com/strongloop/express/wiki/Migrating-from-3.x-to-4.x
[3]https://github.com/strongloop/express/wiki/New-features-in-4.x
[4]http://expressjs.com/4x/api.html
[5]http://webapplog.com/express-js-4-node-js-and-mongodb-rest-api-tutorial/

Further Express.js 4 Migration Reading Links

APPENDIX C

Express.js 4 Cheat Sheet

Pro Express.js is an extensive book with many examples to teach you about middleware, patterns, and configurations. Therefore, when you start working on your own project, you will find it useful to have a quick reference of the most important functions and commands—a cheat sheet. I've created my own Express.js 4 cheat sheet, shown in Figure C-1, and I am giving it as a gift to *Pro Express.js* readers. You can download an awesome, print-ready PDF of this cheat sheet for free (regular price is $4.99) at `https://gum.co/NQiQ/AC30238A-5C5C`. This link is for readers of Pro Express.js *only*, so please don't share it with anyone.

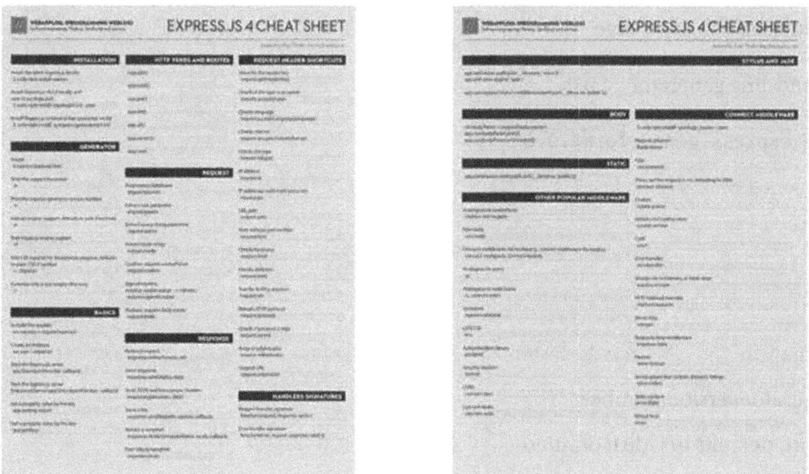

***Figure C-1.** Express.js 4 Cheat Sheet*

The information from the cheat sheet is available in this appendix and online at `https://github.com/azat-co/cheatsheets/blob/master/express4/index.md`. The cheat sheet has the following sections:

- Installation
- Generator
- Basics
- HTTP Verbs and Routes
- Request
- Request Header Shortcuts

- Response
- Handlers Signatures
- Stylus and Jade
- Body
- Static
- Connect Middleware
- Other Popular Middleware

The cheat sheet is good for Express 4.10.4 as of this writing.

Installation

- Install the latest Express.js locally:

  ```
  $ sudo npm install express:
  ```

- Install Express.js v4.2.0 locally and save to `package.json`

  ```
  $ sudo npm install express@4.2.0 --save
  ```

- Install Express.js command-line generator v4.0.0

  ```
  $ sudo npm install -g express-generator@4.0.0
  ```

Generator

Usage: `$ express [options] [dir]`

Options:

- `-h`: Print the usage information
- `-V`: Print the express-generator version number
- `-e`: Add ejs engine support, defaults to jade if omitted
- `-H`: Add hogan.js engine support
- `-c <library>`: Add CSS support for (less|stylus|compass), defaults to plain CSS if omitted
- `-f`: Generate into a non-empty directory

Basics

- Include the module:

  ```
  var express = require('express')
  ```

- Create an instance:

  ```
  var app = express()
  ```

- Start the Express.js server:

  `app.listen(portNumber, callback)`

- Start the Express.js server:

  `http.createServer(app).listen(portNumber, callback)`

- Set a property value by the key:

  `app.set(key, value)`

- Get a property value by the key:

  `app.get(key)`

HTTP Verbs and Routes

- `app.get(urlPattern, requestHandler[, requestHandler2, ...])`
- `app.post(urlPattern, requestHandler[, requestHandler2, ...])`
- `app.put(urlPattern, requestHandler[, requestHandler2, ...])`
- `app.delete(urlPattern, requestHandler[, requestHandler2, ...])`
- `app.all(urlPattern, requestHandler[, requestHandler2, ...])`
- `app.param([name,] callback)`:
- `app.use([urlPattern,] requestHandler[, requestHandler2, ...])`

Request

- `request.params`: Parameters middleware
- `request.param`: Extract one parameter
- `request.query`: Extract query string parameter
- `request.route`: Return route string
- `request.cookies`: Cookies, requires `cookie-parser`
- `request.signedCookies`: Signed cookies, requires `cookie-parser`
- `request.body`: Payload, requires `body-parser`

Request Header Shortcuts

- `request.get(headerKey)`: Value for the header key
- `request.accepts(type)`: Checks if the type is accepted
- `request.acceptsLanguage(language)`: Checks language
- `request.acceptsCharset(charset)`: Checks charset

- `request.is(type)`: Checks the type
- `request.ip`: IP address
- `request.ips`: IP addresses (with trust-proxy on)
- `request.path`: URL path
- `request.host`: Host without port number
- `request.fresh`: Checks freshness
- `request.stale`: Checks staleness
- `request.xhr`: True for AJAX-y requests
- `request.protocol`: Returns HTTP protocol
- `request.secure`: Checks if protocol is `https`
- `request.subdomains`: Array of subdomains
- `request.originalUrl`: Original URL

Response

- `response.redirect(status, url)`: Redirect request
- `response.send(status, data)`: Send response
- `response.json(status, data)`: Send JSON and force proper headers
- `response.sendfile(path, options, callback)`: Send a file
- `response.render(templateName, locals, callback)`: Render a template
- `response.locals`: Pass data to template

Handlers Signatures

- `function(request, response, next) {}`: Request handler signature
- `function(error, request, response, next) {}`: Error handler signature

Stylus and Jade

```
app.set('views', path.join(__dirname, 'views'))
app.set('view engine', 'jade')
app.use(require('stylus').middleware(path.join(__dirname, 'public')))
```

Body

```
var bodyParser = require('body-parser')
app.use(bodyParser.json())
app.use(bodyParser.urlencoded())
```

Static

```
app.use(express.static(path.join(__dirname, 'public')))
```

Connect Middleware

```
$ sudo npm install <package_name> --save
```

- body-parser: Request payload
- compression: Gzip
- connect-timeout: Times out the request in ms, defaulting to 5000
- cookie-parser: Cookies
- cookie-session: Session via Cookies store
- csurf: CSRF
- errorhandler: Error handler
- express-session: Session via in-memory or other store
- method-override: HTTP method override
- morgan: Server logs
- response-time: Response time middleware
- serve-favicon: Favicon
- serve-index: Serves pages that contain directory listings
- serve-static: Static content
- vhost: Virtual Host

Other Popular Middleware

- cookies and keygrip: Analogous to cookieParser
- raw-body: Raw body
- connect-multiparty, connect-busboy: Connect middleware for multiparty, connect middleware for busboy
- qs: Analogous to query
- st, connect-static Analogous to staticCache
- express-validator: Validation
- less: Less CSS
- passport: Authentication library
- helmet: Security headers
- connect-cors: CORS
- connect-redis: Connect Redis

APPENDIX D

ExpressWorks

ExpressWorks is an automated workshop that walks you through the building of Express.js servers, processing of GET, POST, and PUT requests, and extraction of query string, payload, and URL parameters. ExpressWorks provides you with tasks and hints. You write the solutions to these tasks. Then, after you write a solution as an Express.js app, ExpressWorks verifies your solution to the problem.

ExpressWorks is based on workshopper[1] and inspired by stream-adventure[2] by @substack[3] and @maxogden.[4] This appendix consists of the following brief introduction to ExpressWorks:

- Installation
- Usage
- Resetting
- Tasks

Installation

The recommended global installation for ExpressWorks v0.0.23 is as follows:

```
$ npm install -g expressworks@0.0.23
$ expressworks
```

If you encounter errors, try

```
$ sudo npm install -g expressworks@0.0.23
```

Another approach (for advanced developers) is to use the local installation. To do so, run and install the following locally:

```
$ mkdir node_modules
$ npm install expressworks@0.0.23
$ cd node_modules/expressworks$ node expressworks
```

[1]https://github.com/rvagg/workshopper
[2]https://github.com/substack/stream-adventure
[3]https://twitter.com/substack
[4]https://twitter.com/maxogden

Usage

After you have completed the installation, ExpressWorks understands these commands:

- `$ expressworks`: Show a menu to interactively select a workshop.
- `$ expressworks list`: Show a newline-separated list of all the workshops.
- `$ expressworks select NAME`: Select a workshop.
- `$ expressworks current`: Show the currently selected workshop.
- `$ expressworks run program.js`: Run your program against the selected input.
- `$ expressworks verify program.js`: Verify your program against the expected output.

Resetting

If you want to reset the list of completed tasks, as shown in Figure D-1, empty the `~/.config/expressworks/completed.json` file.

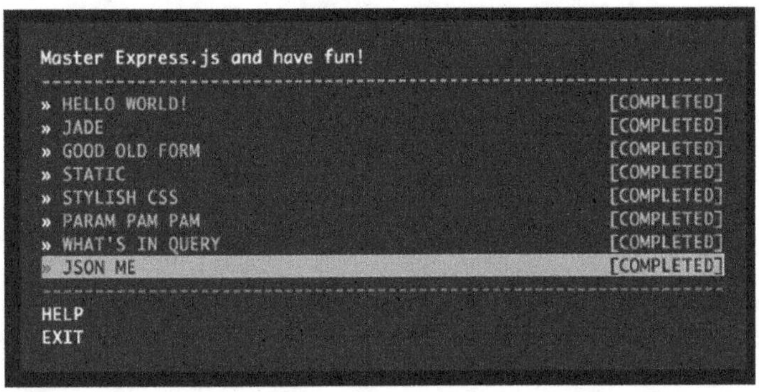

Figure D-1. *Completed tasks*

Tasks

This section describes some of the tasks you'll come across.

Hello World

Create an Express.js app that runs on `localhost:3000`, and outputs "Hello World!" when somebody goes to root `'/home'`.

ExpressWorks provides you with `process.argv[2]`, which is the port number.

Jade

Create an Express.js app with a home page (`/home`) rendered by a Jade template engine that shows the current date (`toDateString`).

Good Old Form

Write a route ('/form') that processes an HTML form input (<form><input name="str"/></form>) and prints the str value backward.

Static

Apply static middleware to the server index.html file without any routes. The index.html file is provided and usable via the process.argv[3] value of the path to it. However, you can use your own file with this content:

```
<html>
  <head>
    <link rel="stylesheet" type="text/css" href="/main.css"/>
  </head>
  <body>
    <p>I am red!</p>
  </body>
</html>
```

Stylish CSS

Style your HTML from the previous example with some Stylus middleware. The path to the main.styl file is provided in process.argv[3], or you can create your own file/folder from these:

```
p
color red
```

The index.html file is as follows:

```
<html>
  <head>
    <title>expressworks</title>
    <link rel="stylesheet" type="text/css" href="/main.css"/>
  </head>
  <body>
    <p>I am red!</p>
  </body>
</html>
```

Param Pam Pam

Create an Express.js server that processes PUT /message/:id requests (e.g., PUT /message/526aa677a8ceb64569c9d4fb).

The response of this request returns id SHA1 hashed with a date:

```
require('crypto')
  .createHash('sha1')
  .update(new Date().toDateString().toString() + id)
  .digest('hex')
```

What's in a Query

Write a route that extracts data from a query string in the GET `/search` URL route (e.g., `?results=recent&include_tabs=true`) and then transforms and outputs it back to the user in JSON format.

JSON Me

Write a server that reads a file (file name is passed in `process.argv[3]`), then parses it to JSON, and outputs the content to the user with `res.json(object)`.

Summary

ExpressWorks is a command-line tool that will help you to get acquainted with some of the basics of Express.js. If you have enjoyed this learning approach, check out the similar workshops/tools that are available to you at no cost at `http://nodeschool.io`.

Index

I

J

K

L

M

N

O

P

Q

R

S

T

U, V, W, X, Y, Z